Building A Great Railroad

A History of the
Atlantic Coast Line Railroad Company

By Glenn Hoffman, Ph.D.

Edited by Richard E. Bussard,
CSX CORPORATE COMMUNICATIONS AND PUBLIC AFFAIRS

Acknowledgements

This book is dedicated to
W. Thomas Rice,
last chairman and president of the Alantic Coast Line Railroad,
whose vision and determination added to the success of
Building a Great Railroad.

The editor and publisher of this book would like to recognize the important contributions of those listed below, as well as of the many others whose identities are unknown. Without the help of so many, publication of this history of the Atlantic Coast Line Railroad would not have been possible.

Leonard Anderson, retired treasurer, Atlantic Coast Line Railroad and Seaboard Coast Line Industries.

Patricia Aftoora, corporate secretary, CSX Transportation

Gary Riccio, president, and **Larry Goolsby**, secretary-treasurer, Atlantic Coast Line and Seaboard Air Line Railroads Historical Society

Frank Funk, president, and **Susan Platt**, executive director, Wilmington Railroad Museum, Wilmington, North Carolina.

Susan Carter, curator, Henry B. Plant Museum, Tampa, Florida.

Peggy C. Organes, Freelance Creative Services, Jacksonville, Florida.

Sarah Gravitt, CSX Corporation, Richmond, Virginia - cover design.

Building A Great Railroad
A History of the Atlantic Coast Line Railroad
by Glenn Hoffman, Ph.D.
edited by Richard E. Bussard
Copyright © 1998 CSX Corporation
All Rights Reserved.

Library of Congress Catalog Card Number: 98-73348

$\mathcal{P}$reface

Like the history of America, the history of the Atlantic Coast Line Railroad, one of America's great railroads, is filled with exciting events, colorful characters, high finance and complex politics.

Spanning the 133 years from 1834 to 1967, the history that follows chronicals the enormous number of acquisitions, mergers and consolidations that linked at least 125 small separate roads into a giant system that would provide efficient interstate rail service through entire regions of the country.

As the ACL grew during its illustrious early history, there were periods of great growth and achievement, as well as periods of misfortune and disappointment. These events are well described by author Dr. Glenn H. Hoffman (now deceased), a professor of history at the University of Florida, who was retained by the company in the mid-1960s to record this history.

A number of officers, as well as some employees, of Atlantic Coast Line contributed much time and effort to this project by providing research, personal accounts and other data to Dr. Hoffman, which became part of this history. Acknowledgement is given to CSX Transportation, the Wilmington (N.C.) Railroad Museum, the Atlantic Coast Line Railroad and Seaboard Air Line Railroad Historical Society and many individuals for the photographs used in this book.

As a scholar and historian, Dr. Hoffman was meticulous in his documentation of the facts of this book. Unfortunately, during the years between completion of the manuscript and publication of this book, Dr. Hoffman's hundreds of footnotes disappeared and regretfully, could not be included.

— Editor

About the editor

A veteran Florida journalist, Richard E. Bussard spent 30 years as an editor and writer in the newspaper profession, before joining Seaboard Coast Line Railroad. His career included 20 years as city editor, and then managing editor, of the *Jacksonville Journal,* as well as stints with the *Columbus (Ohio) Citizen* and the *Leesburg (Florida) Commercial*. Under his leadership, the *Jacksonville Journal* won numerous state and national awards for public service, in-depth reporting and spot news reporting, including a Pulitzer Prize for news photography. In 1981, Bussard founded a weekly newspaper, *The Beaches Sun-Times*, in Jacksonville Beach, Florida.

Bringing his expertise to SCL in 1982, Mr. Bussard started the *Family Lines News*, a company newspaper for the newly combined Seaboard Coast Line and Louisville & Nashville railroads. Over the next 15 years, the newspaper changed names several times, reflecting company changes from consolidation as Seaboard System Railroad (*Seaboard System News*) to the addition of the Chessie System Railroad forming CSX Transportation (*CSX News*). Through it all one thing remained constant, employees of the railroad were kept informed of exciting company activities by Dick Bussard and his staff.

Recently, Dick turned his talents to editing the historical manuscript of the Atlantic Coast Line Railroad, which sat waiting for publication for 25 years. The result is a book that is both accurate and enjoyable.

— Publisher

Table of Contents

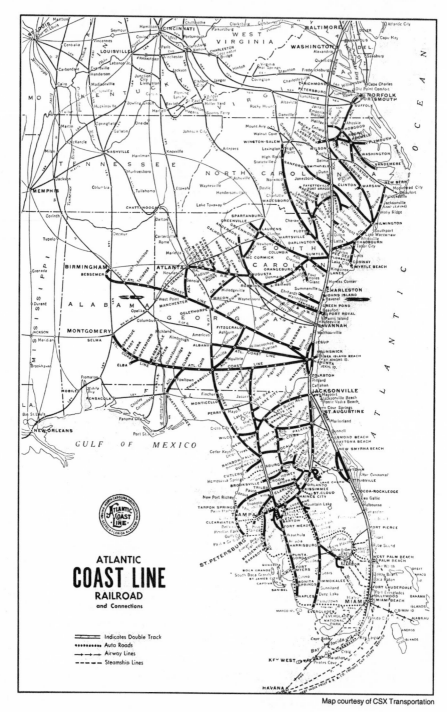

No. 1: *The Atlantic Coast Line Railroad, as it was configured in 1952.*

Chapter I

Birth of the Atlantic Coast Line Railroad

A Meeting with Destiny

The story of the Atlantic Coast Line Railroad Company actually began when the Wilmington & Weldon Railroad was incorporated on January 3, 1834, even though the events leading up to the eventual creation of the Coast Line did not occur until 1867. In that year, the president of the Wilmington & Weldon Railroad Company, Robert R. Bridgers, made several trips from his home in Tarboro, North Carolina, to Baltimore, Maryland, in an effort to sell $749,000 of bonds on behalf of his railroad. He had already spent more than $1 million trying to rebuild the Wilmington & Weldon following the Civil War; but, he needed more capital and was having difficulty raising more money.

It is of historical interest to note that Robert Bridgers had served in the Congress of the Confederate States during the Civil War, from 1862-65. He was elected president of the Wilmington & Weldon in 1865.

After two attempts to sell bonds in New York had proved unsuccessful —northern investors still took a dim view of southern securities — Bridgers took his quest to European money markets. He had no better luck overseas. Finally, he tried Baltimore, then considered the gateway to the South, and he met with more success. In the course of his negotiations with Baltimore bankers, Bridgers came in contact with two prosperous merchants who had recently founded a bank, the Safe Depository Company. The new bankers, Benjamin F. Newcomer and William T. Walters, agreed to purchase and arrange the sale of $580,000 in bonds.

The deal went much farther than financial arrangements for floating a bond issue. Walters and Newcomer were Baltimore business leaders who wanted to see their city expand its "Southern Gateway" traditions; and they were interested in railroads that would funnel traffic into Baltimore. Thus their willingness to underwrite the Wilmington & Weldon bond issue. Newcomer was already involved in railroading as a director of the Northern Central Railway Company since 1861. The Northern Central, with its southern terminus at Baltimore, was a subsidiary of the Pennsylvania Railroad.

At the end of the Civil War, agents of the Pennsylvania had bought the rights to an old, unused Maryland rail charter for a Baltimore and Potomac railroad. In August 1866, construction began on the railroad, and in February 1867, Congress approved a "branch line" into the District of Columbia.

With studies under way for a tunnel through Baltimore, the Pennsylvania was about to establish through service to Washington, D.C. Just across the Potomac, a newly chartered company, the Alexandria & Fredericksburg Railroad, was planning a line to the northern terminus of the Richmond, Fredericksburg & Potomac. Unbroken rail service between Baltimore and Richmond seemed certain.

Small wonder, then, that Walters and Newcomer shared Robert Bridgers' optimism about the future of the Wilmington & Weldon and, for that matter, other railroads south of Richmond. They entered into an alliance with Bridgers that lasted until Bridgers' death in 1888. The essence of the agreement was that Walters and Newcomer would provide Bridgers with the financial backing necessary to improve the Wilmington & Weldon and for securing the necessary through connections. For his part, Bridgers would assist them in gaining control of his railroad, plus other lines that might be valuable in building a trunk line.

In the Beginning . . .

The Wilmington & Weldon Railroad, which would become the parent of the Atlantic Coast Line Railroad, had been incorporated as the Wilmington & Raleigh Railroad Company. Constructed between 1834 and 1840, the railroad, however, ran from Wilmington to Weldon rather than to Raleigh, whose citizens had refused to support the project.

Service began over the line on March 9, 1840, with a grand celebration that included speeches and a barbecue for 550 who turned out for the festivities, which included a 161-gun salute for the railroad's 161 miles. This was the longest trackage owned by any one railroad in the world at that time.

With rail connections to cities in the North, and its own line of steamships to Charleston, South Carolina, the Wilmington & Raleigh was awarded a contract to carry United States mail. The mail contract was important to the prestige of the railroad as well as assuring dependable revenue for the company. The route was promoted as the Great Southern Mail Line.

The Wilmington & Raleigh was originally built with flat iron rails secured to wooden sills, but this type of track was expensive to maintain, so replacement with heavier iron rails began in 1848. Though it struggled in its early years, by 1851 the company had grown into an efficient and financially-sound railroad. In 1851, it installed its first telegraph line. On February 14, 1855, by special act of the North Carolina Legislature, the name of the railroad was changed to the Wilmington & Weldon Railroad Company to more accurately reflect its service territory. On August 1, 1860, the Wilmington & Weldon completed a branch line from Rocky Mount, North Carolina, to Tarboro (home of Robert R. Bridgers).

When the Civil War broke out in 1861, the Wilmington & Weldon was a center of activity and played a major role in the movement of troops and supplies for the South. As the war progressed, the railroad was heavily damaged by Confederate and Union troops. When the war ended in April 1865, work began immediately to repair the damage to track and bridges. Service resumed on August 27, 1865, with only four locomotives and 15 freight cars. There was no passenger service.

Bridgers' Vision

The railroad's new president, Robert Bridgers, raised $900,000 to make repairs. When service was first restored, train speeds were limited to 10 miles per hour; but as improvements continued, train speeds gradually increased and in less than a year speeds averaged about 18 miles an hour. Two years after the war ended, the Wilmington & Weldon was back in good operating condition. That's when Bridgers, whose vision saw the line as a major link between the North and cities in the South, began his push to improve and expand his railroad.

Bridgers saw the future expansion of his railroad in through freight. For more than a year he had been pushing for special rates on goods shipped to New York and other Northern cities, arguing that lower rates would result in enormous increases in volume of through freight business. He was proved right almost immediately.

In the fall of 1867, he reported to investors:

"We now have through-freighting arrangements between Boston, New York, Philadelphia, Baltimore, Portsmouth, Va., and Wilmington, N.C., with extension of these lines to all places on the Wilmington & Manchester Railroad, to Cheraw and all places on that road, to Charleston and all places on the Northeastern Railroad, to Augusta and Atlanta, Ga., and to all the principal places on the South Carolina . . .

"The subject of our passenger and freight connections with other roads brings prominently to view the importance of looking to new routes that are multiplying around us — I may mention the route now under contract from Baltimore to the Potomac, near Acquia Creek, that will be a very important adjunct. Another road has been chartered to run from Alexandria to or near Fredericksburg, Virginia, that will be equally as a feeder to our Southern coast line."

From his description, it was clear that President Bridgers regarded "our Southern coast line" as comprising the Richmond-to-Charleston rail route, and he predicted the prosperity of the Wilmington & Weldon with improvement of connections between and beyond these points. There were five railroads forming the route southward from Richmond: the Richmond & Petersburg, the Petersburg, the Wilmington & Weldon, the Wilmington & Manchester, and the Northeastern of South Carolina.

While he was pleased with the physical and financial health of the Wilmington & Weldon, Bridgers was far from satisfied. His railroad could greatly increase its business if an unbroken north-south route could be established. Physical connections had recently been completed at Richmond and at Petersburg, but a gap still remained at Wilmington, where passengers and freight had to be ferried across the Cape Fear River.

Efforts to build a bridge and a connecting line had been stalled by a lack of money. The Wilmington Railway Bridge company, chartered on June 23, 1866, was organized and jointly owned by three railroad companies — the Wilmington & Weldon, the

Wilmington & Manchester, and the Wilmington, Charlotte & Rutherford (later the Seaboard Air Line). Construction started in 1867, but the bridge and road would not be ready until November 1, 1869. The insolvency of the Wilmington & Manchester, however, was a serious impediment to the bridge project, and to through connections.

The Wilmington & Manchester had been incorporated in South Carolina on December 18, 1846, and by a supplementary act on January 9, 1847. Work had started in 1849 and had been completed in 1853. The 170 miles of five-foot gauge track ran from Eagle Island, on the west bank of the Cape Fear River across from Wilmington, to Kingsville (Denmark), South Carolina.

Built to the Kingsville junction with the Charleston & Hamburg Railroad, the new line was expected to receive considerable traffic from cities such as Augusta and Columbia bound for the port of Wilmington. For that reason, the Charleston & Hamburg did not cooperate in the venture. Counting on expanded business created by the new line, the Wilmington & Manchester was sold at foreclosure in 1857 and reorganized. The Wilmington & Weldon Railroad held 1,060.5 shares, and the State of South Carolina held 2,000 shares in the reorganized Wilmington & Manchester, showing the orientation of the line.

The new company fared no better. It suffered losses of equipment and track during the Civil War and its recovery after the war was incomplete. When it reopened in 1867, the Wilmington & Manchester carried little freight, leaving it in heavy debt.

The fortunes of the Wilmington & Weldon were bound inextricably to the Wilmington & Manchester. Robert Bridgers saw an alliance with a revitalized Wilmington & Manchester as essential to his company. His board of directors authorized Bridgers to enter into such covenants and agreements that were in the best interest of both companies. A year later, the stockholders authorized the officers of the company to arrange with the owners of the Wilmington & Manchester for consolidation of management and joint operation of the two railroads.

A Plan Unfolds

They also authorized the sale of their company's stock in Wilmington & Manchester. The shares were purchased by a group headed by William T. Walters and B.F. Newcomer. This was one step in a well-organized plan to obtain financial control of both the Wilmington & Weldon and the Wilmington & Manchester — a plan that had developed out of President Bridgers' bond-selling trip to Baltimore.

Financial interrelationships facilitated the takeover. Both railroad companies owned significant amounts of each other's stock, and the State of North Carolina owned large blocks of stock in both companies.

With Bridgers' help, his associates in Baltimore could buy stock held by the two railroad companies, from the state of North Carolina, and from private investors, all as one financial operation. Walters began to buy privately held shares in both companies in December 1867. By the following November, he and a Baltimore associate, Thomas Kensett, held the largest individual blocks of Wilmington & Weldon stock. Since the Wilmington & Weldon was in good condition, it was enough at that time to acquire a majority of its stock. The Wilmington & Manchester required more drastic action — buying enough stock for interim control, then securing enough of its bonds to foreclose and reorganize.

Syndicating Finances

To secure the necessary capital, Walters and Newcomer formed a syndicate. At a meeting held at Barnum's Hotel in Baltimore on September 14, 1868, a syndicate agreement was signed, and 38 subscribers pledged a total of $1.2 million for the express purpose of acquiring full control of the Wilmington & Manchester. This endeavor was entitled *The Southern Railway Project*. W. T. Walters and Company subscribed to the largest amount, $115,000.

Other prominent Baltimore investors were Enoch Pratt, Samuel M. Shoemaker, George Small, Thomas C. Jenkins, Joseph W. Jenkins, and of course, Benjamin Newcomer. J. Edgar Thomson, president of the Pennsylvania Railroad Company, Thomas A. Scott, vice president and later successor to Thomson as president of the Pennsylvania, and J. Donald Cameron, later United States Senator from Pennsylvania, were other important members of the group. D. Willis James bought a block of $200,000 in subscriptions for himself and seven other residents of New York City.

The Pennsylvania Railroad's Tom Scott, a man of vision, very likely had played an important role in preparations for the Southern Railway Project. Since the Pennsylvania would soon have direct physical connections to Washington and Richmond, Scott and Thomson were eager to secure access to the lines south of Richmond. Formation of a syndicate to acquire some of these roads suited their interests well.

The agreement for the Southern Railway Project provided only for acquiring the Wilmington & Manchester. The $1.2 million was subscribed and the trustees (Walters, Newcomer and James) were appointed for that purpose. The Wilmington & Manchester acquisition, however, served to give syndicate members common interest also in the Wilmington & Weldon, as well as in other connecting railroads. Indeed, later developments indicate that far-reaching plans were discussed on September 14, 1868, for an all-encompassing system of southern railroads in which the two Wilmington roads were only the first components.

Gaining Control

With such a liberal injection of capital and with help from Robert Bridgers, Walters and Newcomer accelerated their efforts to obtain more stock in both Wilmington railroad companies. Bridgers had arranged for his company to sell its 1,060.5 shares of Wilmington & Manchester stock for $5 a share. Months of negotiating and expensive lobbying finally brought results when, on March 31, 1869, the North Carolina State Board of Education reached agreement to sell 4,000 shares of Wilmington & Weldon stock to Walters for $37 a share, and 2,000 shares of Wilmington & Manchester to the trustees of the Southern Railway Project at $5 a share. Legislation authorizing the sales was passed on April 12 and the shares were transferred on April 19.

With these large blocks of stock and many odd-lot purchases, Walters, Newcomer and James held a majority of the outstanding capital stock of the Wilmington & Manchester by the summer of 1869. Having spent a total of only $36,836.19 for 7,261.5 shares, they took control of the board, and elected Bridgers president of the company. Shortly afterwards, the Wilmington & Manchester company sold its 2,050 shares of Wilmington & Weldon stock to Walters and Newcomer.

Control of the Wilmington & Weldon was thus gained simultaneously with the advancement of the Southern Railway Project. On May 29, 1869, Walters sold more than 2,700 shares of Wilmington & Weldon stock to other members of the syndicate, retaining some 2,700 for himself. Acquisition of stock continued, and by 1872, Walters held 5,340 shares, Newcomer, 2,109, and members of the syndicate, a total of about two-thirds of the outstanding 14,526 shares. Walters, Newcomer and Shoemaker replaced three North Carolinians on the board in 1869, and the following year, J. Donald Cameron was made a director and Newcomer was elected vice president. The Wilmington & Weldon was sufficiently in hand.

The Wilmington & Manchester posed a more difficult problem. Strong opposition to the sale of the company resulted in complicated court proceedings that included a series of injunctions to block the sales. Perseverance, not to mention the purchase of many bonds from bond holders, finally paid off. On January 5, 1870, the road was sold by a referee of the courts in the City of Wilmington to William T. Walters, trustee for, and on behalf of the project's subscribers. That portion of the railroad in North Carolina sold for $275,000, while the portion in South Carolina went for $250,000. In addition to charters from both North Carolina and South Carolina, the railroad received authorization from South Carolina to build a branch from the Wilmington & Manchester to the City of Augusta, Georgia.

Controlling Still More

With authority granted in the charters from North and South Carolina, the members of the purchasing syndicate proceeded to organize themselves into the Wilmington,

Columbia & Augusta Railroad Company. It was nearly the exact group of original subscribers who met again at Barnum's Hotel in Baltimore on April 26, 1870, to approve bylaws and elect officers. Robert Bridgers was elected president, and seven of the authorized 10 seats on the board were filled, all by familiar names: J. Donald Cameron, William T. Walters, B.F. Newcomer, Samuel M. Shoemaker, Thomas Kensett, William H. Graham and D. Willis James.

Gaining control of the old Wilmington & Manchester had proved to be more expensive than anticipated. The entire original subscription had gone into the purchase. Now an estimated $1 million more was needed for new rails and equipment and for constructing a line to Columbia. The immediate need for so much additional capital was met with a second subscription in the financial organization plan. Included in the first mortgage debt of $3,200,00 were the following: $1,300,000 to pay off the 7% first bonds; $600,000 as profit to the original subscribers; $50,000 to Bridgers by contract, and $50,000 to trustees for their service. In addition, $1,200,000 in bonds were sold at 80%, netting $960,000.

As a result, the Wilmington, Columbia & Augusta Railroad was top-heavy in funded debt. Northern capital was difficult to obtain by southern railroads. Walters, Newcomer and Bridgers may have been enthusiastic about the future of their railroad, but most of their associates apparently insisted on face-value paper bearing high interest. On one point all seemed to agree: with good management and improved connections, the WC&A would be worth more than it had cost.

Developing the WC&A

There were obvious advantages in the fact that the Wilmington, Columbia & Augusta was wholly owned and controlled by the syndicate. Policy-making for their new railroad would be free from the dissident voices of local shareholders. The staggering size of the funded debt perhaps reflected a naively optimistic desire for guaranteed yield on the investment, but it posed no problem in corporate control. The bondholders were also the stockholders. Closely held, the WC&A would presumably be the nuclear corporation in a combination of railroads along the Atlantic coast.

The beginnings of the WC&A were most auspicious. Installments on the second subscription were paid regularly, and new locomotives and rolling stock were purchased. Traffic volumes were doing well. By September of 1871, the WC&A had 162 miles of track in sound condition and equipment that included 18 locomotives, 14 passenger cars and 236 freight cars.

Also encouraging was the opening of friendly connections for the railroad. During the first months of operation, the WC&A held a majority block of shares in a useful connecting railroad — the Cheraw & Darlington. From a junction with the WC&A at Florence, this little road ran 40 miles in a northerly direction to Cheraw, S.C., where it connected with other railroads then being constructed. The syndicate trustees had taken advantage of an opportunity to buy 4,013 shares of Cheraw & Darlington stock (probably from a bank in Charleston). For the bargain price of $40,130, the Cheraw & Darlington became a permanent part of the system.

The Cheraw & Darlington had been chartered in 1847 as a line to connect Cheraw, a regional trade center, with the Northeastern Railroad at Florence, and thus with the port of Charleston.

The Wilmington, Columbia and Augusta Railroad's greatest need was for an extension to Columbia. President Bridgers regarded this as imperative from the start. The WC&A charter in South Carolina specifically authorized the company to build to Columbia from any point on its line, but Bridgers thought that time and money might be saved by the purchase or lease of an existing line. The obvious choice was the South Carolina Railroad, formerly the Charleston & Hamburg, which ran directly to Columbia from Wateree Junction, at that time the terminus of the WC&A. In July 1870, Bridgers and Walters, with the help of J.D. Cameron and S.M. Shoemaker, set out to lease that portion of the South Carolina Railroad. Negotiations continued for months, apparently with every expectation of success.

At a meeting held in Barnum's Hotel in Baltimore on January 4, 1871, WC&A stockholders authorized abandoning construction that already had started on the road to Columbia, and instead voted to secure, by purchase or agreement, other lines that already existed. Agreement could not be reached and the officers of the South Carolina portion of the railroad apparently even blocked the purchase of right of way for a line paralleling their company's tracks.

Bridgers and his associates finally decided to build a new road in the fall of 1871. They dismantled and abandoned the several miles of line between Sumter and Kingsville, using the materials in construction of a 42-mile road along a more direct route from Sumter to Columbia. The project was pushed hard, for there was new incentive. The Walters syndicate now had control of the Charlotte, Columbia & Augusta Railroad, which meant that a friendly line was available between Columbia and Augusta. The Columbia extension was placed in service at the beginning of 1872. With access to important inland trade centers, the WC&A enjoyed a sharp increase in business — about 60 percent in the first eight months.

Tightening the Wilmington & Weldon

Important changes also were taking place on the Wilmington & Weldon. Walters, Newcomer and Shoemaker went to Wilmington for a board meeting on January 6, 1870. During this meeting, and a meeting that followed on March 25, many new policies were adopted. Some of the homey practices of locally owned railroads were replaced with more impersonal, business-like policies. For one thing, the names of stockholders along with the number of shares they owned would no longer be published in the annual report. Salaries and responsibilities of the company's officers were fixed, and firmer employment practices were adopted. One resolution stipulated that "No information of any character be furnished by any of the officers or employees of this company from any of its books for publication without the authority of the board."

The trustees in Baltimore found that far too many stockholders, dignitaries and business patrons had passes to ride free on the Wilmington & Weldon. The board canceled all existing passes, and only the president could issue passes in the future. Passes were limited to officers and employees of the company, "except in cases where the interest of the company manifestly requires that this rule be remitted."

President Bridgers in later years would enjoy telling the story about a farmer near Goldsboro who requested a pass. Bridgers responded with a polite but firm letter of refusal. The farmer would not take "no" for an answer. He folded the president's letter so that only the graciously worded last paragraph and the president's signature were visible and the farmer traveled free for months before the ruse was discovered.

A Winning Combination

Of greater importance were measures taken to integrate management and operations of the WC&A and the Wilmington & Weldon. Appointed to serve under President Bridgers as officers of both companies were: W. Thomson, as secretary and treasurer; G.L. Dudley, as auditor; and Augustus Pope, general ticket and freight agent. On January 1, 1871, all the central officers of the WC&A, including those not serving the Wilmington & Weldon, were moved into the Wilmington & Weldon office building. The transportation, roadway and machinery departments of the two companies remained separate, but all under one head, Superintendent William Mac Ray of the WC&A.

The next stage of consolidating the two companies was the most important one of all. In the spring of 1872, Benjamin Newcomer worked out a plan for leasing the Wilmington & Weldon to the WC&A. On May 24, the directors of both companies met in Baltimore and agreed to the basic terms of the lease. On November 20, 1872, a special meeting of stockholders of both companies was held in the president's office in Wilmington and both groups voted unanimously to approve the lease.

If there was opposition from local people, it had been effectively overcome. The terms of the lease were appealing to Wilmington & Weldon stockholders. In return for assuming all Wilmington & Weldon assets for 99 years, the WC&A guaranteed to pay interest on the bonded indebtedness of the Wilmington & Weldon, to refrain from encumbering the company with new debts, and to pay the Wilmington & Weldon stockholders guaranteed dividends of 5% in December 1872; 6% in 1873, and 7% in semiannual installments thereafter.

Walters and Newcomer expected the lease to be advantageous to their group. For one thing, it placed the Wilmington & Weldon under the control of the closely held WC&A, eliminating dissent from local stockholders. For another, it promised financial benefits for the syndicate. Future increases in business would very likely produce profits beyond the dividends guaranteed to Wilmington & Weldon stockholders. The surplus Wilmington & Weldon profits would help pay the interest on WC&A bonds, and perhaps even dividends on WC&A stock.

The two Wilmington roads were now effectively combined under control of the Walters group. The arrangements made good sense as the nucleus of a railroad system. The roads to the south of Wilmington were five-foot gauge; the roads to the north were standard gauge. The WC&A gave access to both the Charleston coastal routes and to the important inland trade centers such as Columbia, Augusta and Atlanta. The Wilmington & Weldon was a standard-gauge outlet to the Pennsylvania Railroad and the cities of the northeast. The termini of the two roads had been joined by completion of the Wilmington Railway Bridge Project in 1869.

At some point during this period an ingenious invention partially bridged the break in gauge. A gravity pit was constructed for changing the trucks on cars used regularly in through trains. The cars were moved over the hole one by one, the trucks of one gauge dropped free and the trucks of the new gauge were inserted, and the train proceeded on its way — with new motive power, of course.

A Wilmington-centered rail system included a safety factor. At a time when it was not certain that an all-rail route to the North could compete successfully with coastal shipping, the port of Wilmington afforded a water outlet for traffic from both directions. As President Bridgers put it, "How far an all-rail line can compete for the far-off southern business, with rival lines running to the coast and thence by sea to the northern trade centers, remains a problem to be solved. If this experiment should not succeed we can fall back on the port of Wilmington and command a full share of the business. The true interest of the line requires both the all-rail line and the port of Wilmington."

So Begins a Rail System

The combination of the Wilmington & Weldon and the WC&A clearly was a logical beginning for building a rail system along the Atlantic coast.

A gentleman from Georgia descended from the first-class WC&A passenger coach in Wilmington one day in mid-January 1871. The gentleman was Augustus Pope, lately of Atlanta, where he had served as general freight agent of the Western & Atlantic Railway of Georgia. President Bridgers had been in Georgia looking over the Western & Atlantic in connection with a plan to lease that railroad, and had made Pope's acquaintance. Departing from his usual policy of promoting within the ranks of his own companies,

Bridgers appointed Pope to the position of general passenger and freight agent for the Wilmington roads. An experienced traffic man, Augustus Pope was hired to promote business, especially through traffic, and he swung into his new duties with an abundance of energy and resourcefulness. Among his many contributions to the system, Pope selected and promoted the name "Atlantic Coast Line."

A handbill dated March 1, 1871, advertised: "The Great Atlantic Coast Line for the movement of freight and passengers via Wilmington & Weldon and Wilmington, Columbia & Augusta Rail Roads and their various connections North & South."

Pope had moved fast, but the name had been chosen carefully and especially for its appeal to pleasure, and to invalid travelers to the South. The new designation drew from earlier titles and uses. In the 1850's a travel agency in Baltimore had promoted the Washington to Charleston (via Weldon and Wilmington) route as "The Great Southern Mail Line." Bridgers had referred to "our Southern coast line" in his report to Wilmington & Weldon stockholders in 1867.

However, the traveling public and railroad men typically spoke of the "Weldon route" in those days, as distinguished from the "Danville route." With approval from President Bridgers and the gentlemen in Baltimore, Pope's name for the route was incorporated in a suitably designed trademark and was used for passenger and freight traffic promotion. It was not long before the public, railroad men, newspapers and commercial journals were speaking of "The Atlantic Coast Line" and the "Coast Line roads."

The name at first merely designated the freight and passenger routes formed by the two Wilmington roads and their cooperative connections. It soon took on a broader meaning. As W.T. Walters' syndicate got control of connecting railroads — a process already under way when Augustus Pope arrived in Wilmington — the trunk of the sizable railway system took shape under the name, **The Atlantic Coast Line**.

Wilmington & Weldon,
and
Wilmington, Columbia & Augusta
RAIL ROADS.
Office Gen'l Freight and Ticket Agent,
Wilmington, N. C., March 1, 1871.

The Great Atlantic Coast Line

FOR THE MOVEMENT OF

FREIGHT AND PASSENGERS,

—VIA—

Wilmington & Weldon

AND

WILMINGTON, COLUMBIA & AUGUSTA RAIL ROADS
And their various connections North & South.

These lines offer for the transportation of Passengers First Class Day Coaches on all Day Lines; Good Sleeping Cars on all Night Trains.

Double Daily Schedule, on quick time, making sure and close connections at either terminus, and giving to NORTH BOUND PASSENGERS THE SAME TRAINS FROM RICHMOND OR BALTIMORE, AS BY ANY OTHER ROUTE, and likewise to SOUTHERN BOUND PASSENGERS EQUALLY QUICK TRANSIT and by the same trains from AUGUSTA, MACON, MONTGOMERY and ATLANTA as by any other route.

Through Tickets procurable at all main Stations to all points North, South and West.

Special inducements offered to EMIGRANTS AND SETTLERS locating along the line of each road.

Freight Tariffs—at prorated competing rates—made between all Northern and Southern cities.

Rates guaranteed. Loss, damages and overcharges promptly settled.

Freights moved in car load quantities, NORTH or SOUTH and WEST from Wilmington without transfer.

All enquiries concerning Freight and Passenger business promptly answered, and every possible facility of tariff and transportation offered.

A. POPE,
General Freight and Ticket Agent

Atlantic Coast Line annual report

*No. 2: This poster, published on March 1, 1871, introduced the name
Atlantic Coast Line Railroad.*

The Southern Railway Security Company

The Dream — E Pluribus Unum

While the two Wilmington companies — the Wilmington, Columbia & Augusta and the Wilmington & Weldon — were being united, financial operations were in progress that would deeply affect development of the Atlantic Coast Line. In the course of their meeting on April 26, 1870, the new owners of the WC&A did far more than provide an organization for that company. Before the group left Barnum's Hotel that day, W. T. Walters, B. F. Newcomer and Tom Scott won general agreement for a plan to buy enough small southern railroads to form a railway system for the whole region. The modest "Southern Railway Project" expanded quickly into a major undertaking in railroad finance. It was not many months before the Walters-Scott syndicate controlled over 2,000 miles of southern railroads, through a corporation entitled The Southern Railway Security Company.

Such ambitious expansion in the objectives of the syndicate required much new capital. This was raised in two ways: (1) by further investment by members of the group, and (2) by admitting a "major partner" into the syndicate. The "partner" was the Pennsylvania Railroad Company. The Pennsylvania assuredly had the resources for a full-scale invasion of the South. The company's yearly gross earnings from the lines owned and controlled east of Pittsburgh alone were running in the neighborhood of $20 million — roughly 35 times the revenue of the Wilmington & Weldon, for example. The Pennsylvania officials also had a good incentive for investing in southern railroads. They were building a line to Washington, D. C., in direct competition with the Baltimore & Ohio; and John Garrett, the B&O president, was making moves that threatened to shut the Pennsylvania out of southern connections.

Here was reason enough for Tom Scott to launch a campaign to dominate those southern railroads which would feed traffic through Washington and Baltimore. In addition, Scott apparently shared Walters' and Newcomer's conviction that southern railroads would be profitable when properly organized and provided with direct connections to the North. Scott sold the plan to the directors of the Pennsylvania, as a means of protecting the company's investment in the Washington line. Since the project coincided with Scott's own ventures in the West (first with the Union Pacific and then the Texas & Pacific), he probably also envisioned a line that would swing westward through Virginia and Tennessee, linking his roads into a nation-spanning empire. The syndicate members probably agreed, in their April 1870 meeting, to explore the possibilities for obtaining a charter and organizing themselves into a company; but time was too precious to spend on this additional consideration. Tom Scott and his agents, along with Walters, Newcomer and other members of the syndicate, became prodigiously active in the affairs of southern railroads in the spring and summer of 1870.

Forming a Holding Company

In early 1871, Scott, Walters and Newcomer began organizing the Baltimore syndicate into an incorporated company. Scott's political influence in Pennsylvania was such that procuring a charter was a relatively simple matter. The Pennsylvania Legislature passed "An Act to Incorporate the Overland Contract Company," ratified March 22, 1871. This charter granted the powers and privileges accorded in that of the Pennsylvania Company, which had been obtained, nearly a year before, by the Pennsylvania Railroad Company for organizing their western holdings. The new corporation was empowered to own and operate all types of railroad and railroad-related properties, and to hold securities of other companies.

The newly established Southern Railway Security Company met in Philadelphia on April 5, 1871, and elected a board of directors, with George Cass as president and Benjamin F. Newcomer as treasurer. They also made formal location of the company's office in New York City and adopted the name of the company. A stockholders meeting in New York a month later authorized issuing capital stock up to $10 million, although little more than half that amount was ever utilized by the company. Judging from a later financial statement, the initial capitalization was $4,945,250 — 98,905 shares paid in at par value of $50 per share. Of this total, a considerable portion represented equities already held by the syndicate in the Wilmington, Columbia & Augusta and the Wilmington & Weldon Railroads. These were turned over to the Southern Railway Security Company, presumably valued according to their market price in April and May of 1871; and the members of the syndicate were issued shares in the Security Company, according to their respective contributions to the syndicate to date. Of the 3,000 shares of WC&A stock outstanding, 2,938 were turned over to the Security Company — indicating nearly one hundred percent participation by original subscribers to the Southern Railway Project. The Security Company also received 8,491 shares of Wilmington & Weldon stock. Even at par, these would represent only about $1,100,000, and they were probably credited at a somewhat lesser value in the initial capitalization of the Security Company. In other words, something like $4,000,000 in additional funds and securities were paid into the Southern Railway Security Company during the early months of its existence.

Some of this new capital came from subscriptions by individual members of the syndicate, including important new members like Daniel James of Liverpool, England. The Pennsylvania Railroad Company, however, was unquestionably the major source of additional capital and the largest single stockholder in the new holding company. It probably subscribed to at least $1,000,000 of the initial stock issue, and subsequently acquired a larger interest. The Richmond & Danville purchase alone cost about $600,000; and this was but one of several instances in which the Pennsylvania bought stocks which ended up in the Security Company portfolio. Between 1871 and the Fall of 1873, the Pennsylvania Railroad Company contributed about $2,600,000 in stock purchases and loans to the Southern Railway Security Company. Thus, with formation of the Southern Railway Security Company, the syndicate's center of gravity shifted perceptibly from Baltimore to Philadelphia.

Once organized, the Southern Railway Security Company acquired railroad properties with startling speed. This was partly because the project had been underway for some time, but the corporate entity gave added unity and focus to the project. As President Cass stated,

> "The object and purpose of this organization is to secure the control of such Southern Rail Roads as may be essential to the formation of through-lines between New York, Philadelphia, Baltimore, Washington City, and the principal cities of the South, by ownership of the capital stock of said companies, by leases, and by contract relations . . . Local managements, working in accord with the more enlarged sphere of operations of this Company, will bring these roads and others in the Southern states into harmonious action . . ."

Sewing Up the South

Robert R. Bridgers must have been impressed by the events he had set in motion with his bond-selling trips to Baltimore. His vision of a through route along the Atlantic coast was beginning to materialize, but as only one facet of a much grander scheme. Walters and Newcomer still concentrated on their project for a Richmond-to-Charleston line, while cooperating fully with Scott's efforts to get railroads in other areas of the South. The Atlantic Coast Line was one of three basic trunk lines formed under the Southern Railway Security Company. For a time it seemed to contemporary observers that the Pennsylvania Railroad Company had set out to acquire all the railway real estate in the South.

With the help of his friend Simon Cameron in the Senate, Tom Scott obtained permission from Congress, on June 21, 1870, to extend a branch line via the Long Bridge across the Potomac, to connect with existing or future railroads in Virginia. At the same time, he was casting about for a solution for a "future railroad" in Virginia. In spite of determined opposition by B & O agents and local railroad men, in March of 1871, the Virginia Legislature passed a bill chartering the Washington & Richmond Railroad. The Pennsylvania group decided, instead, to use the Alexandria & Fredericksburg, which had not yet constructed its road.

By the fall of 1871, the Pennsylvania Railroad Company and friends held a controlling interest in the Alexandria & Fredericksburg. Tom Scott and W. T. Walters were among the directors elected. It was rumored that they also had acquired the Richmond, Fredericksburg & Potomac. They had probably tried, because the Alexandria & Fredericksburg was an essential link between Washington and Richmond. If the effort was made, it fell short of majority ownership. The RF&P, however, maintained a friendly attitude toward the Pennsylvania's interests. Construction of the Alexandria & Fredericksburg began at once, and arrangements were now complete for unbroken rail connections between Washington and Richmond.

The first major target south of Richmond was the Richmond & Danville, a valuable railroad with its main line between Richmond and Greensboro. Tom Scott began an energetic campaign to secure this company in the summer of 1870. An intricate sequence of negotiations in Richmond was aimed at acquiring the large interest held by the State of Virginia. The Virginia Legislature approved sale this stock to the Richmond & Danville in July 1870, and Tom Scott made arrangements with the company to pay the state and take possession of this controlling block of shares. The deal was essentially completed in the early months of 1871, although the 24,000 shares of Richmond & Danville stock were not officially transferred until August 31, 1871.

Concurrently with the Richmond & Danville negotiations, Walters, Scott, J. D. Cameron and some other members of the Baltimore group (including a new adherent, Henry B. Plant, president of the Southern Express Company) formed a special syndicate to lease the Western & Atlantic Railroad, which ran from Atlanta to Chattanooga. Robert Bridgers evaluated the property, and the lease was signed in the fall of 1870. They thereby rescued a railroad from an exceedingly corrupt state administration in Georgia and secured an important connection for other lines which their holding company would control.

Linking Atlanta

Among the "principal cities of the South," Atlanta ranked high. The Security Company centered much of its attention on the Richmond-to-Atlanta route. Control of the Richmond & Danville was only the beginning. The holding company supported the Richmond & Danville in its construction of a new 265-mile road from Charlotte to Atlanta — the Atlanta & Richmond Air-Line. The Richmond & Danville had started the Air-Line in 1869, but most of the road was built between 1871-73. The Security Company financial statement of May 1, 187. (about the time the Air-Line was completed) listed among its assets $3,428,795.01 in advances made by the Richmond & Danville Railroad Company for constructing and equipping the Air-Line.

Part of the North Carolina Railroad ran from Greensboro to Charlotte, so it served as the middle segment of the Richmond & Danville's (and the Security Company's) trunk line to Atlanta, This route later formed the basis, and inspired the name, of the Piedmont Air Line — predecessor of the modern Southern Railway Company. The other half ran eastward from Greensboro to Goldsboro, where it connected with the Wilmington & Weldon, thus providing a link between the Richmond-to-Atlanta and the Coast Line routes.

Before the end of 1871, the Security Company held enough stock in the Charlotte, Columbia & Augusta to claim control. Addition of the 195-mile road gave the Richmond & Danville a line from Charlotte, North Carolina, to Augusta, Georgia. It also provided the lower Coast Line roads with access to Augusta, once the WC&A extension to Columbia was completed.

Westward Ho

Meanwhile, Tom Scott was making progress on a line west of the mountains. In November of 1871, he arrived at an agreement with Richard T. Wilson, president of the East Tennessee, Virginia & Georgia Railroad, and brought his road into the system. The Pennsylvania soon transferred a block of 10,000 shares in the East Tennessee to the Southern Railway Security Company, and R. T. Wilson became a director of the holding company. The Pennsylvania had no direct connection to the East Tennessee's northern end at Bristol, but at its southern "Y"end, the Western & Atlantic (already under lease to an associated syndicate) provided connections at Chattanooga and at Dalton, Georgia. Then, in March of 1872, the Security Company negotiated a lease of the Memphis & Charleston, whose 290-mile road (not yet completed all the way into Chattanooga) ran westward to Memphis. Here was Tom Scott's potential access to the Southwest.

The Original Thirteen

The Southern Railway Security Company's roster of controlled railroads was quite impressive by the summer of 1872. In addition to the acquisitions described thus far, two Coast Line roads — the Richmond & Petersburg and the Northeastern — were also in the fold, under circumstances to be related shortly. The holding company and its leaders held, at this point, a system of 13 southern railroads with a combined mileage of 2,131 miles. In two short years, the Southern Railway Security Company had put together the basis for a railroad system for the southern states. One main line paralleled the Atlantic coast; another route followed along the fall line to Atlanta, giving access to the cotton kingdom and the port cities on the Gulf of Mexico, and still another line reached toward the Southwest and transcontinental connections.

A project of such dimensions naturally aroused opposition. One person who took a very dim view of the Southern Railway Security Company was William Mahone, once described as "the poker-playing railroad Bismarck of Virginia." Mahone wanted Virginia railroads to be run by, and for, Virginians. He also wanted to keep his road, the Atlantic, Mississippi & Ohio from being suffocated by either the Baltimore & Ohio or the Pennsylvania Railroad. He became alarmed at the sale of the state's shares in the Richmond & Danville in July 1870, and was soon circulating pamphlets exposing the "Bucktail Swindle," as he termed the affair. He tried to block the Walters group's purchase of the state-owned Richmond & Petersburg stock in March of 1871. The citizens of Norfolk were informed by Mahone that the Pennsylvania's control of the Richmond lines would divert traffic from his railroad and consequently their port. They held huge mass meetings of protest. This fiery champion of local interests went so far as to propose to his arch-rival John Garrett, president of the Baltimore & Ohio, and to John Y. Robinson, president of the Baltimore Steam Packet Company, that they join forces to frustrate the designs of the Pennsylvania Railroad Company. On March 18, 1872, Mahone wrote to a friend, "Scott's great scheme of southern subjugation will break down, mark my word for it. We have nothing to fear from his infernal designs, if we will only stand firm in Virginia and do our duty to the Commonwealth."

The opinions of William Mahone and many other Southerners notwithstanding, Tom Scott and the Southern Railway Security Company were a beneficent force for southern railroads. Some of the improvements were obvious; others harder to measure. Quality of management of roads under the holding company was generally raised. Roads that had fought or ignored each other now cooperated to their mutual benefit. New physical connections improved quality of service on the roads in the system and enormously increased their potential rate of traffic. On July 2, 1872, the first trains ran over the Baltimore & Potomac into Washington. A short time later they crossed the Potomac and went southward on the Alexandria & Fredericksburg for an uninterrupted journey to Richmond. *The Commercial and Financial Chronicle* commented on the significance of the Alexandria & Fredericksburg line:

> The completion of this road is expected to reduce the running time between Philadelphia and Richmond from 15 hours to 12. The road extends from Alexandria to Quantico Creek, 23 miles, and joins the Richmond, Fredericksburg & Potomac extension . . . This Road is due to the energy and perseverance of the Southern Railway Company, the efforts and sagacity of which are just beginning to be appreciated.

The Southern Railway Security Company certainly made positive contributions to the nascent Atlantic Coast Line. The two Wilmington roads benefited immediately from improved connections. President Bridgers informed Wilmington & Weldon stockholders in November 1871: "It is a matter of congratulation to the company that for the first time in its history the field is open for freight and travel, both to the North and South, without subordination to the interest of rival lines." Of even greater significance, some of the connecting railroads over which the Security Company gained control became integral parts of the Atlantic Coast Line. The Northeastern and the Richmond & Petersburg were secured permanently; the Petersburg only temporarily.

Bringing in the Northeastern

The Northeastern Railroad Company of South Carolina was incorporated December 16, 1851, by special act of the South Carolina Legislature. It had been initiated largely in Charleston, as a move to keep the Wilmington & Manchester Railroad from drawing too much regional trade to the port of Wilmington. Construction was begun on the five-foot gauge line in 1853, and the entire 102 miles of road between Charleston and Florence, South Carolina, were open to service on October 5, 1857.

Local public interest in the company was reflected in its stock distribution — of 17,587 shares, the city of Charleston held 8,000, banks of the city 1,600, the state of South Carolina 4,000, and individuals only 3,987.

The road ran through sparsely-settled, pine-woods territory. Aside from modest local traffic in naval stores, it was dependent upon exchange of traffic at Florence with the Wilmington & Manchester and the Cheraw & Darlington roads. It was just beginning to do a profitable business (receipts for 1859 were 110% greater than in 1858) at the outbreak of the Civil War.

The Northeastern participated in an interesting facet of the Confederate war effort. In 1864, when David C. Ebaugh had completed the shell of his torpedo boat, *David*, he towed it to the Northeastern dock. There, it was hoisted onto a flat car and taken to the company's shops, where Master of Machinery John Chalk helped fit it with a small steam engine that had run the shop's machinery. *David* was an operational failure, but only, its builder maintained, because the Navy men attached the torpedo frame improperly.

Even before the destructive last months of the War, the Northeastern's roadway and equipment were badly deteriorated. Superintendent Solomons managed to save most of the rolling stock by moving it to Florence when Sherman's forces approached Charleston from the south. The company's depot and offices in Charleston, however, were destroyed along with most of its bridges, including the large one across the Santee River. Considering the general poverty of the area, reconstruction of the road was remarkably successful. The Santee Bridge was finished, and service over the entire line resumed, on March 20, 1866. By February of 1867, most of the $214,175 spent for restoration had been paid out of operating income and sales of salvaged iron and other materials. Northeastern President A.F. Ravenel recognized that improvements in business for his road would have to come from increases in through traffic; and he expressed impatience at the slowness of the rebuilding of the Wilmington & Manchester to the north and especially of the Savannah & Charleston to the south.

The Northeastern Railroad Company was garnered from the midst of the wholesale financial pillaging of South Carolina properties during Governor Robert K. Scott's Reconstruction Era administration. A Republican railroad ring under "Honest John" Patterson was raiding the Greenville & Columbia and the Blue Ridge lines. Patterson had been associated with Simon Cameron's political machine in Pennsylvania, so the Walters syndicate had a useful source of information and influence. Morris K. Jesup was elected to the Northeastern board on April 6, 1870, apparently on the strength of a large stock purchase he made independently. Within a few months, the members of the syndicate held a majority of the company's stock. The Southern Railway Security Company ended up with 9,129 shares at an average cost of $10.50 per share.

Capture of the Northeastern made its Florence-to-Charleston road a permanent segment of the Atlantic Coast Line. For many years, until transport of commodities from Florida developed, the Northeastern's main significance to the system was for through-passenger business. Scheduling and operation of passenger trains were correlated immediately with the WC&A. President Ravenel observed, in April 1871, "From Charleston northward . . . a double daily service (Sundays excepted) has been established by the main roads forming the Atlantic Coast Line." A year later he reported, "The completion of the road from Fredericksburg to Washington, and to the Tunnel at Baltimore, both now in active progress, will relieve the Atlantic Coast Line of the present transfers and delays at those points and should render it an attractive route to the Passenger."

Joining North and South

The next acquisition — the Richmond & Petersburg — was at the other end of the route. This short road was strategically located. It ran from where it connected with the Richmond, Fredericksburg & Potomac Railroad, to Petersburg, Virginia, where it joined the Petersburg Railroad and intersected William Mahone's Atlantic, Mississippi & Ohio. The Richmond & Petersburg would be the Coast Line's access to northern connections. Financial control of this company was imperative.

The Richmond & Petersburg Railroad Company had been incorporated by an act of the Virginia Legislature dated March 14, 1836, and organized in the same year. Construction of its 22-mile line from Richmond to the bank of the Appomattox River, across from Petersburg, had begun in 1836, delayed by the panic of 1837, and finally completed on September 17, 1838.

The company's charter contained some rather striking provisions. For one thing, the Richmond & Petersburg could build its bridges so that they could serve for travel by horseback or carriage, and for passage of live stock; and tolls could be charged for such use. On another point, maximum charge for passengers was set at eight cents per mile. The exception was passengers who traveled no more than 10 miles could be charged 50 cents extra for stopping and starting the train.

The first tracks on the Richmond & Petersburg were constructed of wooden stringers with a light flat bar-rail fastened to the top of them. These were replaced by a heavier flat rail in 1843 and regular heavy iron rails in 1853. The most expensive single item in the construction of the Richmond & Petersburg was the bridge which carried the tracks across the James River from Manchester into Richmond. At the other end of the line the tracks halted at Pocohantas, on the north bank of the Appomattox River, and a wagon bridge was used to transfer freight and passengers across into Petersburg.

During the Civil War the road served as the main artery into Richmond, the capital of the Confederacy. When Lee's troops withdrew from Richmond on April 3, 1865, they burned the bridge over the James River and the depot at Richmond. The company resumed partial service in the summer of 1865, and began construction immediately on a new bridge at Richmond. The bridge measured 2,862 feet between abutments, and cost $118,245. It was ready for use on May 25, 1866. With special authorization from the Virginia Legislature, the Richmond & Petersburg established physical connection with the Petersburg Railroad by means of a bridge across the Appomattox River, which was opened for service on August 20, 1867. Under good management, the Richmond &

Petersburg recovered quickly; its gross earnings in 1869 were $160,945 — the highest in its history.

Robert Bridgers and other syndicate representatives descended on Richmond in January 1871, for an intensive campaign of legislative persuasion. They found themselves in a contest of several weeks duration against William Mahone, who desired the R&P as a connection for his own road. On March 28, 1871, the Virginia Legislature passed a bill authorizing the sale of the state's holdings in the Richmond & Petersburg to H. K. Ellyson of Richmond, who was acting as agent for the Walters syndicate. Two days later the *Shenandoah Democrat* contributed an interesting interpretation of the transaction, probably more expressive of local sentiment than fact:

> The Richmond & Petersburg Railroad case has been finally disposed of by the Legislature. It seems that there were two purchasers for the state's interest — General Mahone and a Mr. Walters, of Baltimore — the former offering $200 per share for it, and the latter $150. Contrary to all precedent, and the law regulating public auctions, the lowest bidder got the stock. The loss to the state is $200,000.

The 5,471 shares purchased from the state were transferred to the Southern Railway Security Company, which held a total of 6,871 shares by March of 1872. The syndicate moved slowly in taking over the Richmond & Petersburg. Voting rights were scaled so that their large blocks of stock did not command a clear voting majority. B. F. Newcomer attended stockholders meetings in July and November of 1871, but the only syndicate representative placed on the board was H. K. Ellyson — Thomas H. Wynne was re-elected president. The Security Company allowed the annual meeting of 1872 to fail for lack of a quorum, so the officers remained the same. The gentlemen from Baltimore evidently felt that the R&P was well managed, and they may have wished to avoid the appearance of complete seizure of the company. Besides, there was really no point in making personnel or policy changes for the Richmond & Petersburg Company until its line joined that of other Coast Line companies; and the Security Company did not have control of the connecting road to the south, the Petersburg.

Yankee Go Home

In the case of the Petersburg Railroad Company, local interests were holding firm against the "outside capitalist." At the time that the Baltimore group became interested in the Petersburg, the State of Virginia had no interest in the company. The City of Petersburg held nearly 5,000 shares, and the balance of the 13,232 shares of the company's stock were held, for the most part, by residents of Petersburg. An implacable foe of the syndicate, William Mahone, had many friends and much influence in Petersburg. One of the directors of the Petersburg Railroad was also on the board of Mahone's road, the Atlantic, Mississippi & Ohio. The Security Company's capital was not welcome here. The City of Petersburg did sell its interest in the Petersburg Railroad, but to a group of local men headed by Reuben Ragland.

Chartered in 1830 and in service on October 1, 1833, the Petersburg was the oldest of Coast Line railroads. Its first track was constructed with iron straps measuring ½" by 2" placed on yellow pine rails 5" x 9", secured onto white oak sills, 12" in diameter. Its 61-mile line from Petersburg, Virginia, to Weldon, North Carolina, made it one of the earliest of the true railroad operations in the United States. The company was a combination of public and private enterprise, with the State of Virginia Board of Public Works subscribing to $160,000 in stock, the City of Petersburg, $43,600, and individuals, $196,400. The state increased its holding in the company by first buying $150,000 in the company's bonds and then, in 1844, converting the bonds to stock. In 1849, the state transferred its interest in the railroad company to the town of Petersburg to be applied to the construction of another railroad. The city later sold some of its shares to individuals. An interesting capitalization resulted. The stock totaled 13,232 shares; of these in 1868, the City of Petersburg owned 3,235 shares of preferred stock (with voting- rights) and 1,520 shares of common stock, and private stockholders held the rest. Voting rights were scaled, with one vote for each share up to 10, and one vote for each five shares over 10.

The Petersburg line did not actually cross the Roanoke River and enter Weldon until 1843, when a bridge was completed to keep the Portsmouth & Roanoke, a new road under hostile management, from monopolizing business at Weldon. When this bridge was destroyed by fire on March 25, 1857, a friendlier Portsmouth & Roanoke management agreed to let the Petersburg use its bridge and its tracks between Garysburg and Weldon — an arrangement which lasted until November 1, 1872, when the Petersburg completed another bridge of its own.

The Petersburg had a rather stormy early history. One of the earliest roads to receive a contract for carrying U. S. mail, it experienced numerous operating difficulties due to unreasonable conditions imposed in the contract. Political interference, small stockholder intransigence, and questionable management contributed to a rather checkered financial record. The track was finally re-laid in 1850 with heavy iron rails, and the company enjoyed a relatively prosperous decade prior to the Civil War.

During the War, the Petersburg served as part of the vital north-south communication line for the Confederacy. Beginning in May 1864, it was subjected to repeated attacks by the Union forces, and in December of that year, over half the road's total length was destroyed. The Federal Government returned the road to management of the company after Lee's surrender. The task of reconstruction was immense and it was poorly handled. Moreover, as other railroads were restored or constructed, the Petersburg's local traffic potential decreased. A logical solution for the Petersburg was to function as part of a through route. A promising beginning was made in August 1867. Physical connection with the Richmond & Petersburg was made, and the Petersburg immediately signed an agreement with the R&P and the RF&P, which provided for joint ownership of through passenger trains to be run the length of these three connected railroads.

Reuben Ragland and his board took control of the Petersburg in March of 1872. The plans of Walters, Newcomer and Bridgers had received a serious setback and, as subsequent developments were to demonstrate, something in the nature of a catastrophe had struck the Petersburg Railroad Company. Within three months, the company was well on its way to bankruptcy. Ragland achieved an impressive financial coup by claiming that dividend payments were in arrears for dozens of years on his 4,490 shares of preferred stock. With supporting opinions from three attorneys, he got stockholder approval (he held nearly half the voting shares) of his contention that 3% annual dividends should have been paid on the preferred shares out of gross receipts, and in addition that the preferred stock should have received dividends equal to that paid on the common stock out of net profits. Ragland became wealthier by $249,350, and the Petersburg went that much farther into debt. In the same June 12 meeting, the stockholders set the president's salary at $12,000 (the norm for presidents of the largest southern roads was about $5,000) and elected Reuben Ragland to the post. A year later, Ragland consented (graciously we hope) that his salary be reduced to $8,000 per annum.

The financial drain on the Petersburg was serious enough, but the new management brought additional problems. Under Ragland's leadership, the road encountered hostility in every direction. Ragland described the Petersburg's predicament in 1872:

"Since the end of the war in 1865, powerful combinations, railroad giants, have been struggling for control of, and supremacy over, the commerce of the South. On the 20th March, 1872, the present Board found that our connections at both ends had passed into the hands of parties who might elect to be friends of adversaries. . . that our Road was lying like the trunk of a tree sawed off just above the roots and just below the branches. . . The Board prefered to have and own a road of their own, wholly free from outside domination and control."

To the Rescue

The sentiment for local control may have been admirable, but it proved expensive for the Petersburg. Ragland tried to get an agreement with the Walters roads for through freight and failed. Since one of the obstacles to such an agreement was ostensibly the limitations on rate setting in the Petersburg charter, Ragland applied to the Legislature for charter amendment. The Virginia Senate refused to ratify the change. Desperate for a means of increasing freight traffic, the Petersburg made overtures to William Mahone, hoping to use his line to City Point on the James River for steamship connections. Mahone responded with unacceptable demands. The officials of the RF&P continued their refusal to route through freight over the Petersburg at the high rates that the road was required to charge. Shorn of through freight connections, and limited to light local traffic, the road was in a bad way. It seemed doubtful in the early months of 1873, whether the company could stay solvent long enough for Reuben Ragland to realize more personal gains. The Petersburg, however, was an essential link in the Atlantic Coast Line, so Ragland held an excellent position for bargaining with the Walters syndicate. The solution came in good time.

On May 26 and 27, the boards of the Petersburg and the Richmond & Petersburg Railroads approved a contract agreement which merged their transportation and traffic departments into the Richmond and Weldon Route. The Southern Railway Security Company had obviously bid high for Ragland's cooperation. They agreed to give Ragland the presidencies of both their roads, the Richmond & Petersburg and the Richmond & Weldon Route. The executive committee of the Route, moreover, would be composed of two members of the Petersburg board, one member of the R&P board, and one nominee of the Southern Railway Security Company. Ragland thus secured an equal voice in control of the new route, and also increased his salary income substantially. The Security Company apparently arranged for additional financial assistance for Ragland, including a commitment that $500,000 in Petersburg second mortgage bonds would be offered through "bankers in Baltimore."

Everyone A Winner

The Atlantic Coast Line was now intact from Richmond to Charleston. The Security Company had paid dearly to get Ragland's railroad integrated into their system, but the returns from through freight traffic were expected to justify the sacrifices. With direct physical connections to the big northern cities almost completed, the Atlantic Coast Line seemed at the point of paying for a strenuous five-year campaign of building.

Robert Bridgers was enthusiastic as he watched his dream take shape. In November of 1872, he reported Wilmington & Weldon net profits of a record $230,833, observing:

"This is the best exhibit the Company has ever made, and can be relied on for continuance in the future as it has resulted from permanent causes.

"The extension of the Wilmington, Columbia & Augusta Rail Road from Sumter to Columbia, and the purchase of the Charlotte, Columbia & Augusta Rail Road by the Southern Railway Security Company, has given full Southern connections which were never had before. These new connections have given quite an increase of business, and this will in the future be much larger, as there has not been sufficient time for its development."

President Bridgers gained an advantage from the Security Company's control of the Charlotte, Columbia & Augusta. He signed a traffic contract with that company, on May 29, 1873, which practically gave the WC&A an extension to Augusta. Correlated schedules, rate divisions, and car interchange at Columbia were provided for, plus the right of the CC&A to share depot facilities and the services of shipping clerks at Augusta. Still more, the WC&A gained the right to run its own trains intact over the Charlotte, Columbia & Augusta road at times when the latter railroad could not handle all the business. The Northeastern was a direct party to the contract, and the entire Coast Line benefited from the direct entry to Augusta.

Expenses for the WC&A were higher, and receipts lower, than had been anticipated during these first years, so Walters and Newcomer drew on Security Company resources to ease the financial pressure, They sold the WC&A's 4,513 shares of Cheraw & Darlington stock to the holding company in the fall of 1871, for $10 per share. In addition, the Security Company later accepted WC&A notes for $42,455 to enable the railroad company to meet interest payments on its bonds. The WC&A balance sheet was thus kept respectable until all the improvements in connections would bring prosperity. A contract between the Security Company and the Southern Express Company was improving income from that business, and another contract with the Pennsylvânia Railroad promised to increase freight and passenger business for all the roads south of Richmond. The Atlantic Coast Line was indebted in many ways to the Southern Railway Security Company.

As the year 1873 began, the future looked rosy for the Southern Railway Security Company and all the parties associated with it. Much of the confusion of Reconstruction was subsiding in the South, and if economic revival was rather slow, it was definitely underway. Though dividends had been disappointing, most of the lines were showing solid increases in revenues. The annual meeting of the Southern Railway Security Company was held in New York City on June 3. James Roosevelt was elected president. The other members of the board were William T. Walters and Benjamin F. Newcomer of Baltimore; Thomas A. Scott of Philadelphia; J. Donald Cameron of Harrisburg; also Morris K. Jesup, H.B. Plant, R.T. Wilson, C.W. Cass and D. Willis James, all of New York.

Unified and Uniform

The stockholders were informed of a master plan (already adopted by the board) for bringing "under one direct control, each division of our three grand trunk lines." William O. Hughart, who had been hired to manage the leased Memphis & Charleston, was now appointed general manager of the Security Company, and given the task of coordinating the operations of all the roads. Financial management was to be simplified by changing the fiscal years of many of the subsidiary companies so that all would end on September 30. Moreover, all auditing and accounting departments would be reorganized under central control, using standardized forms and procedures. One Bureau of Supplies would achieve substantial savings by procuring uniform rolling stock, rail, and other materials for all the lines. The region served was to be organized into territorial divisions, within which common freight and passenger agencies would eliminate destructive competition, unstable rate situations, and expensive duplication of efforts. A Bureau of Information and Immigration was envisaged to promote settlement in the areas served, a policy which presumably "would tend to commend the Southern Railway Security Company to the people of the South."

The import of such plans was clear. The Southern Railway Security Company was aiming at a unified railroad system for the South. Although purely conjectural, it seems likely that eventual merger of the subsidiary companies was planned. Accomplishment of Newcomer's and Hughart's plan would achieve a degree of integration, in practice, to which formal corporate merger could contribute little. All that was needed was enough time and money.

On July 1, 1873, the Baltimore tunnel was ready for use, which meant that trains from the South could roll into the new Union Depot and from there northward on the Northern Central. A month or so later, a more modest tunnel operation brought the tracks of the Philadelphia, Wilmington & Baltimore into the Union Depot, giving the Pennsylvania a straight-line Baltimore-to-New York run. It had taken longer than anticipated, but this completed all the improvements in connections which had occasioned the Pennsylvania Railroad's invasion of the South.

The Dream is Over

Then came the great panic of 1873. The "Black Friday" stock market crash of September 19 was triggered by news of the failure of Jay Cooke and Company; the ensuing financial crisis deepened into a serious and stubborn depression. For all practical purposes, the Southern Railway Security Company disintegrated in the dreary closing months of 1873.

The panic caught Tom Scott badly over-extended in his western projects and nearly destroyed him financially. When his creditors relented and gave him another lease on life, he concentrated on salvaging his position in the Texas & Pacific. He had no time or resources to devote to the Southern Railway Security Company. Three years later he would comment on his personal investment in the holding company: "I am sorry to say I have over $400,000 [in stock] today that I would like to sell at 10 cents on the dollar." The directors of the Pennsylvania refused to back any of Scott's commitments outside their own system, and the expenditures in the South came under particular criticism. In the fall of 1873, the Pennsylvania wrote off its investment in the Southern Railway Security Company and withdrew from the combination.

The stockholders of the Southern Railway Security Company held a special meeting in New York City on November 21, 1873. Drastic measures were necessary. Little income would be forthcoming from the depression-ridden subsidiary companies, and the holding company could not maintain its expenditures for lease rentals and interest on nearly $3 million in debts. With the Pennsylvania Railroad Company pulling back, the rest of the stockholders had no alternative. They agreed that the Security Company should terminate leases and contracts that required outlay, and that it should sell enough properties to retire its debts. These decisions ended the active life of the company. James Roosevelt resigned the presidency and William Hughart was elected to fill the office in a caretaker role. Henry Walters continued as treasurer.

On December 16, Henry Walters went to Richmond for meetings of the Richmond & Petersburg board and stockholders. The Richmond & Weldon Route contract with the Petersburg was terminated by mutual consent, very likely because the Security Company could not continue its financial commitments to Reuben Ragland. A short time later the Security Company arranged to surrender its lease of the Memphis & Charleston, officially returning the road to its owners as of April 30, 1874.

Stocks in several companies were sold or transferred until two of the three trunk lines were lost to the Security Company. The 24,000 shares of Richmond & Danville stock, and an interest of nearly $4 million in the Atlanta & Richmond Air-Line (the latter for a reported $1,825,000), were transferred to the Pennsylvania Railroad Company. The Richmond & Danville retained its lease of the North Carolina Railroad and, with help from the Pennsylvania, managed to keep its system together through the depression years. Similarly, Richard L. Wilson got control of his East Tennessee, Virginia & Georgia Railroad back from the Security Company; and after the Memphis & Charleston lease was canceled, he also became president of that company. The East Tennessee later built a fair-sized system from these beginnings.

In the absence of records, the details of the transactions by which the Security Company disposed of most of its properties are not known. In some instances the formal sales contracts probably had the practical effect of canceling Security Company notes held by the Pennsylvania, by Richard Wilson and his backers, and by the Baltimore group. It is also possible that Wilson, the Pennsylvania, and other stockholders received some of their original properties back by simply surrendering their stock in the Security Company. Some of the securities sold, such as stocks and bonds of the Mobile & Montgomery Railroad Company and 4,000 shares in the Western Railroad of Alabama, may have been used to settle outsiders' claims against the holding company.

The Southern Railway Security Company was left with its holdings in Coast Line roads, with one exception. The 8,491 shares of Wilmington & Weldon stock (the most marketable equities in the Security Company's portfolio) were transferred to the persons who had originally deposited them with the company. Then Walters and Newcomer, who held 5,340 and 2,109 shares respectively, sold most of their Wilmington & Weldon stock during December of 1873 — much of it to their associates. W. T. Walters, for example, sold 1,500 shares to James Roosevelt, 600 shares to D. W. James, and 400 shares to W. E. Dodge. Coupled with the resignations of Roosevelt as president of the Security Company, and of James as a director in the WC&A, these transactions indicate that the New York group insisted on withdrawing from the combination and realizing whatever they could from their investment. Their shares in the Security Company were apparently bought by Walters and Newcomer with Wilmington & Weldon stock.

By the spring of 1874, the Southern Railway Security Company had lost most of its properties and many of its stockholders. It still, however, retained controlling interests in the Richmond & Petersburg, the Northeastern, the Cheraw & Darlington, the Charlotte, Columbia & Augusta, and the Wilmington, Columbia & Augusta. The Wilmington & Weldon was also still firmly held, both through its lease to the WC&A and the large numbers of shares in friendly hands. With economic recovery, the holding company might yet serve as the organizing vehicle for the Atlantic Coast Line.

The panic of 1873 had abruptly halted the first phase of railroad consolidation in the South. Under Tom Scott's leadership the Southern Railway Security Company had aimed for a complete railway system for the southern states — aimed, of course, toward the Northeast — and it had failed. The approaches to consolidation that were ultimately successful were quite different. The three great railroads of the Southeast — the Seaboard Air Line, the Southern Railway, and the Atlantic Coast Line Railroad — would grow separately through expansion and merger of operating companies. Of the three, the Atlantic Coast Line would be the last to consolidate into one large corporation. It is just possible that the sobering experience with Tom Scott's empire building contributed to the careful policies followed by W. T. Walters and his associates after 1873.

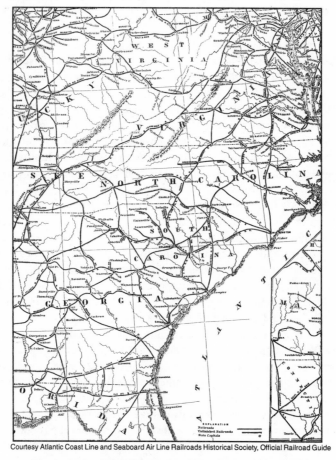

Courtesy Atlantic Coast Line and Seaboard Air Line Railroads Historical Society, Official Railroad Guide

No. 3: *Railroads along the Southeastern Coast in 1870,*
including those that would make up the Atlantic Coast Line.

Chapter III

Growing Pains — Atlantic Coast Line 1873-1878

Survival of the Fittest

The depression of the 1870's was a dismal period for the economy of the South, and for the Coast Line railroads and its Baltimore investors. The Walters syndicate, however, persevered.

From the vantage point of late 1873, it was by no means certain that a long depression was in the offing or that the Southern Railway Security Company could not survive. It was the formal organization for the abbreviated syndicate, and it still held railroad securities of potentially high value and yield. Walters, Newcomer, and many of their associates determined to hold onto the Coast Line railroads, and they apparently expected the Security Company to serve their purposes.

Altered circumstances called for some changes in organization and policies. One of the earliest was canceling the Richmond & Weldon Route contract between the Richmond & Petersburg and the Petersburg railroads, in December of 1873. At the same time, Reuben Ragland resigned as president, and new officers were elected for the Richmond & Petersburg. T. R. Scott was made president; and W. T. Walters and R. R. Bridgers replaced two local members of the board, giving the Walters group a three-to-two majority for the first time. The Richmond & Petersburg was henceforward a closely controlled Coast Line company.

Well situated and admirably managed, the Richmond & Petersburg showed increased profits, even in years when other lines were struggling to make ends meet. In fact, freight tonnage remained fairly constant and income from through passengers increased, so that the R&P actually showed record revenues and profits in 1875. The company withdrew most of a new bond issue from the market in 1876, and used current income to retire maturing mortgage bonds. Improved connections to the North offset the depression for this little railroad.

The Petersburg, once more unattached to the Coast Line, entered on an extremely chaotic period. Workers went on strike for back pay. Cars were attached on foreign roads for non-payment of bills. Inept stockholder cliques ousted incumbent officers for mismanagement. Coast Line companies declined to route freight over the road because of refusals to honor agreements. Bondholders brought foreclosure suits for failure to meet interest payments. Such were the problems that beset Reuben Ragland and his successors. A measure of order was restored in May of 1877, when the company was placed under a receiver.

Another, more important reorganization move brought the Charlotte, Columbia & Augusta into closer alliance with the Wilmington roads. John B. Palmer, president of the

CC&A, was elected president of the Wilmington, Columbia & Augusta Railroad Company at a board meeting held in Baltimore on March 17, 1874. Robert Bridgers stepped down to vice president, and continued as general manager. Placing Palmer officially at the head of the Wilmington railroads reflected three salient facts about the CC&A: first, a majority of its stock was still held by the Security Company; second, it was a longer railroad (195 miles) than either of the Wilmington roads; and third, it was regarded as a vital connection to the interior for the Wilmington-centered Atlantic Coast Line.

Walters and Newcomer obviously intended to hold the Charlotte, Columbia & Augusta as an integral part of their railroad system. The Wilmington, Columbia & Augusta remained, however, the key company during these years of financial struggle. Wholly owned by the Security Company, and the lessee of Wilmington & Weldon, the WC&A was the heart of their railroad holdings. Walters, Newcomer and Bridgers did everything they could to keep it solvent.

A Serious Situation

Keeping the WC&A financially sound posed quite a challenge. President Bridgers and the board had invested heavily in repairs and new equipment for the WC&A and the Wilmington & Weldon. Both roads were in fine operating condition and prepared for heavy traffic increases when the depression hit. Expenditures were cut immediately, but the fiscal damage had been done. The Wilmington, Columbia & Augusta Railroad Company entered the depression with a burden of more $540,000 in annual interest and rental payments:

Interest on $3,200,000 WC&A first mortgage bonds @ 7% $224,000
Interest on $600,000 WC&A convertible income bonds @ 7% 42,000
Rental dividends on $1,456,200 Wilmington & Weldon stock @ 7% 101,934
Interest on $1,619,100 Wilmington & Weldon bonds @ 6%/7% 106,850
Interest on $934,257 WC&A floating debt @ 7% 65,398
Total annual payments $540,182

The weakness in this situation centered more on the WC&A than on the Wilmington & Weldon. Through most of the depression years the Wilmington & Weldon earned enough to cover interest on its bonds and 7% annual dividends to its stockholders. Of course, some of the WC&A's floating debt had been incurred for improvements on the Wilmington & Weldon; and had the latter company been on its own, it probably would have passed some semiannual dividends in order to meet these costs. The Wilmington & Weldon lease paid the WC&A a profit of $71,642 in 1874, but this dwindled and then vanished in succeeding years. The decline in gross earnings for both companies was serious:

	Wilmington & Weldon	Wilmington, Columbia & Augusta
1873	$739,577	$722,124
1874	711,409	661,462

1875	661,295	593,597
1876	604,698	532,311
1877	548,462	518,225

Not only was the WC&A's drop in gross earnings sharper, but its operating expenses stayed higher than the Wilmington & Weldon. During the depression years the Wilmington & Weldon's operating ratio averaged only 59%, while the WC&A's operating ratio averaged 73%. For continued solvency the WC&A obviously depended heavily on the Wilmington & Weldon lease.

United We Stand

Newcomer and Bridgers hoped to draw further strength from the Wilmington & Weldon. They proposed, in November of 1875, that the accounts of the two Wilmington companies be consolidated, which would both reduce costs and relieve the WC&A of some financial pressure. This proposal was blocked by determined opposition on the part of local Wilmington & Weldon stockholders and the counsel for both companies, W. A. Wright.

By the autumn of 1875 the situation was desperate. Business was not improving, and the financial condition of the WC&A was so bad that the president's report was "not ready" in time for the annual stockholders' meeting. J. B. Palmer declined his re-election to the presidency, possibly because of a policy disagreement. He was given the vice-presidency and a seat on the board, and Robert Bridgers once more became president. The sad state of affairs was thoroughly aired at a special board meeting ten days later, on November 27. The WC&A showed a deficit of nearly $100,000 for the year. Obviously, something had to be done.

The board decided to ask the bondholders for permission to fund the next three coupons on the first mortgage bonds until 1886. President Bridgers pointed out that expenses could be cut by filling in several trestle sites and by using the Wilmington & Weldon depot for both railroads. He also recommended moving the WC&A's shops to Florence, where their use and expense could be shared with the Northeastern. These proposals were all approved when permission for funding the bond coupons was granted. In the summer and fall of 1876, Bridgers bought additional land, and built a larger depot, new warehouses, and a permanent wharf for the use of both railroads at Wilmington. The trestles on the WC&A line which had been so expensive to maintain were replaced by grade fills. The fine new shops at Florence, placed on a 40-acre tract along with houses for employees, enabled the WC&A and the Northeastern to abandon their separate installations at Eagle Island and Charleston.

These improvements doubtless resulted in substantial operating thrift in the years which followed. Unfortunately they cost over $150,000, much of which was charged against the Wilmington companies in the fiscal year ending September 30, 1876, which was not a good year. Net operating revenues for both companies combined were at a new low of $355,610. Even with the reprieve from interest on its bonds, the WC&A had failed to gain ground. Unless business improved dramatically, the key company in the combination evidently could not continue. Gross earnings simply were too low for the WC&A to sustain such a heavy burden of debt.

Holding Company In Trouble

The grim prospects in Wilmington and elsewhere prompted an important decision by the Walters syndicate. On October 10, shortly after the close of the railroad companies' fiscal year, the stockholders of the Southern Railway Security Company held a special meeting "to take into consideration the financial condition of the Company, and to take such action in regard to the same as may seem best for the interests of the stockholders." The financial condition of the holding company surely was not good. The WC&A, in which it held nearly exclusive ownership, was not paying interest on its bonds or on its notes with the Security Company. The CC&A was not doing much better. The Northeastern and the Richmond & Petersburg were in sound condition, but not prosperous enough to pay dividends. The only dividend-paying corporation under its control was the Wilmington & Weldon, but the Security Company no longer held any Wilmington & Weldon stock. The meeting apparently resulted in the decision to liquidate the remaining holdings and dissolve the company.

On December 9 1876, the *Commercial and Financial Chronicle* published a notice that W. T. Walters, in accordance with a resolution of the stockholders in the Southern Railway Security Company, would receive at his office, No. 68 Exchange Place, Baltimore, Maryland, bids on the following properties:

6,871	shares of Richmond & Petersburg stock
2,952	shares of stock and $600,000 convertible income bonds of the Wilmington, Columbia & Augusta
9,129	shares of Northeastern (of South Carolina) stock
4,513	shares of Cheraw & Darlington stock
13,024	shares of Charlotte, Columbia & Augusta stock
10	shares of South Carolina Central stock
$11,000	Wilmington, Columbia & Augusta first mortgage bonds and certain real estate in Atlanta, Georgia.

If any of the Security Company's major properties were actually sold before the bid deadline of December 30, none went to outsiders. It is possible in view of the depressed market value of the securities, that no acceptable bids were tendered. Judging from later events, Walters and Newcomer had no intention of losing any of the controlling blocks in Coast Line companies. The decision to dissolve the company had been taken, and the formalities observed; but the books of the Southern Railway Security Company were not closed just yet.

With the WC&A defaulting on interest payments and business remaining slack, the control of the railroad company began to pass to the bondholders, many of whom also still had a claim on the WC&A stock in the Security Company portfolio. Enoch Pratt, one of the trustees of the first mortgage, was present at a meeting of the WC&A board on April 2, 1877. After agreeing that resumption of interest payments due June 1 would be impossible, the group decided that "the true interests of the bondholders will be best promoted by continuing the work now in progress of filling trestles, and by furnishing 1,500 tons of steel rails for the Wilmington, Columbia & Augusta Road, and a like amount for the Wilmington & Weldon Road." Pratt, Brown, and Walters agreed to lend the money for the steel rails, providing that interest on this floating debt be paid from the net receipts of the roads before any interest were paid on the bonds. At the same meeting, Bridgers was authorized to equip passenger trains used for the double daily service on the two Wilmington roads with Westinghouse brakes, at an estimated cost of $12,000.

The WC&A might have presented a sick looking balance sheet, but, no doubt at Bridgers' urging, Walters and his Baltimore associates were willing to continue to invest money in order to improve its efficiency and, thereby, its ability to compete. If they had to forgo interest on their bonds, well, the WC&A was still their railroad. However, the Wilmington & Weldon received the same benefits from their continued investments, and it was no longer returning a profit on the lease. It must have been rather galling to the Baltimore investors that all the minority stockholders in the Wilmington & Weldon were happily accepting their 7% dividends and bearing none of the financial burdens in maintaining the WC&A and operations for both roads. On the other hand, local stockholders in the Wilmington & Weldon suspected that profits from their road were being siphoned off to help pay interest to WC&A bondholders. Four lean years in succession were bound to provoke resentments.

Divided We Fall

The reports for the fiscal year ending September 30, 1877, forced a showdown. At the regular November meetings, the Baltimore group digested the unpalatable fact that net earnings of the two Wilmington roads had shrunk still further — to a combined total of only $295,986. Since the WC&A's yearly obligations for both companies were now close to $550,000, the combination of the two roads obviously could not be continued without some changes.

Walters, Newcomer and Bridgers decided to make one last effort to maintain the corporate ties between the Wilmington & Weldon and the Wilmington, Columbia & Augusta. All the existing financial arrangements for their Coast Line railroad combination were at stake here. The issue was broached when, on January 12, 1878, the directors of WC&A addressed a letter to the Wilmington & Weldon stockholders. They pointed out that the WC&A was in no position to meet payment of dividends on Wilmington & Weldon stock due January 15. They proposed that the Wilmington & Weldon stockholders agree to a bond issue of $150,000 against their road, proceeds from the sale of which would be turned over to the WC&A as partial payment for all the improvements which the lesser company had made on the larger. In the meantime, the WC&A board called an early meeting of its bondholders to see if arrangements could be made to meet the dividend payment within the 90-day grace period. The implication was clear enough — the local stockholders of Wilmington & Weldon could not expect continued dividends unless they would allow their property to bear part of the burden which the WC&A bondholders were now bearing. The letter expressed the hope that these arrangements could be made, because, "in view of the close relations of the two Companies, and the great advantages to both in the way of economy. . . of being under one administration, it is exceedingly desirable to continue the present relations."

Initial steps went smoothly enough. The bond issue was approved the very next day by the Wilmington & Weldon board, and the certificates were soon ready for sale. Then the situation deteriorated rapidly. A number of Wilmington & Weldon stockholders met at the Produce Exchange in Wilmington on the afternoon of January 30. Donald McRae read a statement listing his objections to the proposals emanating from Baltimore. His position was approved by those present, and he was chosen to head a committee of five "to take such action as may seem most advisable in the interest of the stockholders resident in Wilmington." The committee soon published a circular protesting against the $150,000 bond issue as being in violation of the terms of the lease.

The revolt by local Wilmington & Weldon stockholders had been building for some time. They resented their railroad being controlled and directed from Baltimore, and many of them, as shippers and merchants, objected to the prevailing low through rates and disparately high local rates. This sentiment had been expressed at the annual meeting on November 2, 1877, when W. A. Wright moved:

> "That the chairman appoint a committee of five Stockholders who reside in the State of North Carolina, to examine the condition of the Road and its equipment; and to compare the rates, both for freight and passage, at present in force with those of former years, when the management of the affairs of the Company was entirely in the hands of citizens of this state."

The fact was, the Walters' group no longer had incontestable control of the Wilmington & Weldon. W. T. Walters himself had been selling Wilmington & Weldon stock. Since December of 1873, when he had held 5,340 shares, Walters had continued to sell, until he held only 702 shares in January, 1876. He and Newcomer together held 1,002 shares, more than any single local stockholder, but many of the shares once held by the syndicate were no longer in cooperative hands. Some of their closest associates were probably questioning the wisdom of continuing the existing arrangement.

Faced with angry opposition from local Wilmington & Weldon stockholders, and discouraged by the financial prospects of the WC&A, Walters and Newcomer decided to fall back and regroup. The WC&A board agreed to let the Wilmington & Weldon dividend go unpaid, and thereby to forfeit the lease. Since the WC&A on its own could not maintain its funded debt, the Walters group decided, as bondholders, to foreclose and reorganize that company. The Wilmington & Weldon Railroad Company was returned to the management of its own board on April 15, 1878. On the same date, the WC&A was placed under the receivership of Robert R. Bridgers, by the United States Circuit Court for the Eastern District of North Carolina. Symptomatic of the feeling in North Carolina, were the comments by the *Raleigh News* on the lease termination and the WC&A receivership:

> Matters of very great import are here involved, and large interest of some of our citizens, in Wilmington especially, are hereby put in jeopardy. That there has been scheming and management to "freeze out" the local and small stockholders in both the Wilmington & Weldon and the WC&A Roads, there can scarcely be a doubt. That there are combinations to own and control all the railroad property in North Carolina by keen manipulators outside of the State has been patent for some time. That the enterprising and public spirited businessmen of Wilmington have been duped and driven to the wall, is too certain for further suppression of indignation.

The Wilmington Morning Star, on April 10, 1878, printed these remarks and then pointed out the respects in which the *Raleigh News* was in error. For example, there were no local stockholders in the WC&A, and therefore none were being duped or frozen out by the receivership. However, the Wilmington editor did say of the Wilmington & Weldon that "the prevailing opinion among its stockholders is that their stock will now yield them quite as large a dividend as it did under the lease.'"

Demise of the Holding Company

Final dissolution of the Southern Railway Security Company accompanied the foreclosure of the WC&A. Having lost control of both Wilmington railroads, the holding company no longer served a useful purpose. Moreover, the value of all its WC&A securities (except $11,000 in first mortgage bonds) had been erased. The controlling blocks of shares in the Richmond & Petersburg, the Northeastern, and the Cheraw & Darlington were retained by W. T. Walters and his associates. The 13,024 shares of Charlotte, Columbia & Augusta stock, however, were sold to the Pennsylvania Railroad Company, which soon deposited them to the Richmond & Danville.

It must have been difficult for Walters and Newcomer to surrender this important component of the Coast Line. They may simply have been unable to mobilize enough capital to settle all the obligations of the Security Company. It is also possible that the Pennsylvania Railroad Company held some of the final claims against the holding company and insisted upon the WC&A stock for the Richmond & Danville. It was with considerable satisfaction, according to his son's testimony, that Benjamin Newcomer "drew the check that paid the last dollar of the company's indebtedness." The books of the Southern Railway Security Company were closed.

Thus ended the first railroad syndicate formed by Walters and Newcomer. The failure was due largely to the economic depression, but they and Bridgers had erred in overestimating the potential of the WC&A. Even in prosperous times, with all its improved connections and its control of the Wilmington & Weldon, the WC&A probably would not have been as profitable as its financial plan demanded. A better solution would have to be found.

Augustus Pope Promotes the Railroad

In spite of all the financial tribulations, the railroads improved their operations during the depression years. Through physical improvements and development of long-haul traffic patterns, the Atlantic Coast Line began to take on the semblance, if only vaguely, of a modern railroad system.

Many of the changes centered in Augustus Pope's efforts as general freight and ticket agent. From almost the moment of his arrival in 1871, Pope had begun advertising the Atlantic Coast Line as the "fastest and most pleasant means of reaching Florida" and such less remote winter resorts as Savannah and Charleston.

Competition from steamship lines posed a real challenge to his salesmanship, as did the crude equipment and uneven condition of the railroads. One lady's description of her trip from Washington, D. C., to Green Cove Springs, Florida, in February of 1872, gives caustic testimony:

"The trip to Florida from Washington or New York may be made wholly by sea or by rail, or by mixture of both. Steamer lines are the cheap modes of conveyance to Florida. The Empire Line charge $20 for a cabin passage from New York to Savannah, and $10 additional will take the passenger to Jacksonville. For $27.75, the traveler can come by the Baltimore line to Jacksonville, with option of rail or steamer at Savannah. This trip is made in 62 hours to Savannah and a few more hours to Jacksonville.

"The entire trip from Washington to Jacksonville may be made by rail in 2½ days, but the expense will be greater, say $36 to $38, with a very lively addition of expenses if you stop at any of the hotels *en route*, and a certain addition of $5 or $6 dollars per day for meals, and still more for sleeping cars. When a traveler compares these exorbitant rates with the scant comforts he receives in return, he will be apt to conclude that to hang a certain number of railroad presidents would not at all diminish the number of honest people in the world. I fear that traffic in horses, whether of iron or ordinary flesh, has the like demoralizing effect.

"I shall pass on to things actually seen and suffered. . . I had partly in my mind the discomforts a traveler experiences the moment he enters the cars at Richmond bound south. As there are two trains which thus depart, it will avert some misapprehension to say I refer specially to both. True, I did not go on the Danville train, but on that which was going via Petersburg and Weldon; but I had a trial of the Danville cars last November, and I can testify that they were as cold and wretchedly uncomfortable as those I encountered the other day. It was an unusually cold spell of weather all the way to Charleston. I left Richmond at 2:30 p.m., and reached Charleston the same hour next day. The distance is 457 miles; for which you pay $18.50, exclusive of the sleeping-car charges. This time is not bad, considering that the track is bad; but the charge, in view of the accommodations furnished, is unquestionably exorbitant.

"There are four different roads between these two points, and you have, of course, as many coupons to be manipulated by as many conductors. You change cars four times, I think, but not your fate. It is the same story in each — a cold flooring to the car and shivering feet for 24 long hours, and windows which let in a draft on your defenseless head if you dare to go to sleep; and a stove fire which, by its frequent changes of temperature compares well with our American climate . . . We held no indignation meeting that weary night from Weldon to Wilmington; we simply alternated between frequent cat-naps and journeys to the stove, mingled with prayers for the morrow and the end of our route. How happy would I have been but for that occasion only to be a railroad president, with a skin as thick as those functionaries possess."

The traveler is somewhat confused on particulars. She had been on five different railroads, but had probably changed cars only three times at Weldon, Wilmington, and Florence. There was normally no change at Petersburg, for the R&P and the Petersburg ran the same train straight through to Weldon. If this indignant traveler had completed the trip to Florida by rail (she got off at Charleston and took a steamer to Jacksonville), she would have been treated to a jouncing transfer ride over cobblestone streets, and a ferryboat ride across the Ashley River at Charleston, a rough trip on the worn iron rails of the Charleston and Savannah, another omnibus transfer in Savannah, and a tediously round-about trip through Dupont, Georgia, and Live Oak, Florida, before finally reaching Jacksonville. Much remained to be done before direct connections and comfortable accommodations could be offered to travelers between New York City and Florida.

Even making allowances for possible overstatement for literary effect, some contemporary advertising claims were perhaps a bit exaggerated. A schedule published in June of 1872, described the Great Atlantic Coast Line as "a route unsurpassed in all its essentials of speed, safety, and certain connections. . . In the line of comfort this route is now unexcelled. Its equipment is perfect." The patron was further assured, "The 9:00 a.m., 1:00 p.m., and 9:30 p.m. trains leaving New York offer excellent connections through, without break of rest."

Properly interpreted this meant that the extra-fare passenger bound for Charleston could take a parlor car from New York to Baltimore on the 1:00 p.m. train; transfer to a sleeper or another parlor car at Baltimore; catch a nap on the Potomac steamer out of Washington after 11:20 p.m.; board another parlor car at about 4:00 a.m. at Fredericksburg; change cars at Weldon; finally board a Pullman sleeping car at Wilmington at 5:45 p.m., and descend at Charleston at about 6 o'clock the next morning. Some of these car changes were caused by breaks in connections; others, by the nature of the equipment. The Pullman sleeping cars on the Coast Line roads were of the early, fixed-berth type, so that passengers changed to Pullman parlor cars or coaches for daytime portions of a journey.

Passenger Service Improves

In all fairness many improvements in connections had been accomplished by June of 1872, and others followed in rapid succession. The WC&A line to Columbia, South Carolina had just been finished, and the passenger could now remain on one coach from Wilmington to Augusta. The new roads into Washington, D. C., were all completed a few months later, affording an unbroken train ride from the nation's capital southward through Richmond. When the tunnels in Baltimore were ready, in the summer of 1873, it became physically possible (using the truck-changing pit at Wilmington) to pull a car from New York City to Charleston or Augusta. As a general practice, however, this had to wait for several years until the nature of traffic, equipment, and cooperation between railroad companies would make it feasible.

Having the Charlotte, Columbia & Augusta as part of the Coast line helped enormously in promoting through traffic. Its line into Augusta enabled Pope to advertise connections to Atlanta and New Orleans. In fact, the Columbia and Augusta route was as important for Coast Line passenger business in the 1870's as was the line to Charleston. One reason was the growth of Aiken, South Carolina, as a popular winter resort. A special set of through connections was arranged so that the Florida-bound tourist could swing inland to Aiken, spend some time at B. P. Chatfield's Highland Park Hotel, and then proceed via Augusta and Savannah to Florida.

Niceties of service were added to induce travelers to choose the Coast Line rather than a steamship or a competing railroad route. Baggage could be checked through from New York to a destination in the south as early as 1872. A schedule folder dated September 1, 1875, contained the following:

SPECIAL NOTICE

Attentive Stewardesses accompany all
trains of the ATLANTIC COAST LINE ROADS,
to see that the LADIES and CHILDREN are made comfortable.

It became easier to sell an all-rail route to Charleston, Savannah and Florida as the equipment and roadways were improved. Passenger trains were equipped with the Westinghouse automatic air brake on the Northeastern in 1873, and on the Richmond & Petersburg and the two Wilmington roads in 1877. Between 1876 and 1878 the Coast Line roads began regularly to install 56 lb. steel rails as the old iron needed replacing. Such improvements not only increased the safety and comfort of passenger trains;

together with elimination of transfer-points they permitted faster schedules. The reductions in scheduled times between major points were marked:

	1872	1875	1876	1880
New York City to Augusta	44:30 hrs.	41:20 hrs.	39:00 hrs.	35:36 hrs.
Richmond to Augusta	29:00 hrs.	26:50 hrs.	25:35 hrs.	21:24 hrs.
New York City to Charleston	44:00 hrs.	39:10 hrs.	36:15 hrs.	33:00 hrs
Richmond to Charleston	25:30 hrs.	25:00 hrs.	22:50 hrs.	18:45 hrs.

An important link in the route to Florida was completed late in 1877, when the Ashley River Railroad Company opened its bridge and connecting line, eliminating the gap at Charleston between the Northeastern and the Savannah & Charleston. The scheduled time between New York City and Jacksonville, Florida, was cut from 65 hours in 1876 to 57 hours in 1880. The practice of wintering in Florida gained momentum even during the depression of the 1870's, and Jacksonville, St. Augustine, and Palatka vied for the tourist trade.

An Advertising Office Opens

Augustus Pope had considerable assistance in informing the public of the advantages of using the Coast Line. A ticket agency for the Atlantic Coast Line had opened in New York City with an address in June of 1872 at 263 Broadway, which by September of 1875 was changed to its permanent location at 229 Broadway. W. J. Walker was general agent, J. H. White was southern passenger agent, and H. P. Clark served for several years as freight agent, in this office. Ticket offices were also opened in Boston, Philadelphia, Baltimore, and Washington, to promote throughbusiness on the line. It was Jonah H. White of the New York office who published, in 1876, an attractive little booklet entitled *Guide to and through Florida, the Land of Flowers*. Described in glowing terms were the climate and geography of the state, as well as tourist attractions and economic opportunities at towns reached by railroads and the St. Johns River.

All this expansion of sales activity was sound practice, necessitated by the competitive situation; but it coincided, unfortunately, with the lean depression years. A committee of local Wilmington & Weldon directors (one of whom was Donald McRae) suggested in 1879 that the costs of conducting and promoting through business be investigated to see whether they were justified by income from this source. The next year, an auditing committee reported the expense of passenger soliciting agents as "inordinately high" — about 10 per cent of gross revenues from through passenger business. In view of the fact that Wilmington & Weldon receipts on reduced rates from through passengers held up somewhat better than local passenger revenues during the depression period, the promotional expenditures were probably justified.

Pope Turns Attention to Freight

Augustus Pope faced an even stiffer challenge in developing the Atlantic Coast Line into a suitable route for freight business. Robert Bridgers' vision of large volumes of through freight moving from points on the WC&A in unbroken rail connections to the cities of the northeast was far from being realized in the 1870's. The break in gauge at Wilmington, the failure to gain control of the Petersburg, awkward rate restrictions placed on both the Richmond & Petersburg and the Petersburg by the State of Virginia, and inadequate or non-existent provisions for car interchange with distant roads were some of the obstacles to southern through freight. Moreover, the southern coastal states were simply not exchanging large volumes of goods with northern commercial centers — at least not goods in which the time factor was important enough for a coastal rail route to supersede coastwise shipping. Southern products such as cotton, typically moved by rail from the interior to ports like Charleston and Savannah, and then by steamship to New York, Boston or foreign ports. The Wilmington roads were at a disadvantage even for this type of freight business, as the entrance to the Wilmington harbor at that time could accommodate only shallow draft vessels.

The optimum solution for through freight required an outlet to the north that would utilize the full length of the two Wilmington roads, avoid routing north of Weldon on the Petersburg, and permit tariffs that would be competitive with the steamship lines. The Seaboard & Roanoke line from Weldon to Norfolk (more accurately Portsmouth and Pinners Point) provided this outlet. Once established, the major route for Coast Line through freight for more than a decade was Columbia or Augusta (via Florence, Wilmington, and Weldon) to Portsmouth. In Pope's words, "A large proportion of the cotton of the Weldon Road was controlled by Norfolk merchants and marketed at that city. The cotton movement from the line of the WC&A, the Charlotte, Columbia & Augusta and beyond, and especially Macon, Athens, and Atlanta, in which the Coast Line was participating, moved, as a rule, through Norfolk to New York and New England." Car interchange and tariff division contracts with the Seaboard & Roanoke kept this arrangement intact for many years. The Wilmington & Weldon benefited particularly from this routing of heavy staples. Shipments from Augusta and Atlanta that otherwise would have gone to Charleston or have been transferred to ships at Wilmington were reloaded from WC&A cars and hauled the full length of the Wilmington & Weldon, and on to Norfolk.

A Fledgling Produce Business

Two items of major importance for Atlantic Coast Line freight revenues in later years — truck crops and Florida citrus — had their modest beginnings in this period. With local cotton production very low, and the naval stores and other forest products business declining, new products were needed as sources for local-freight revenues.

Pope set out to encourage vegetable production by farmers from Weldon to Charleston, distributing information on techniques of cultivation, packing, shipping, and marketing. He also offered them daily service via an all-rail route or via Norfolk shipping to Baltimore, Philadelphia and New York.

One of the most interesting problems Pope wrestled with was providing refrigerated facilities for transporting strawberries. After an unsuccessful experiment with heavy ice chests carried in express cars, he hit upon the happy solution of using enclosed baggage trucks. Six of these, equipped with ice chambers at the top, were built in the Wilmington & Weldon shops. Iced and loaded with crates of strawberries, they were rolled onto flat cars which took them via the Wilmington & Weldon, and the Seaboard & Roanoke, to Norfolk. There, they went by steamer to New York City. This 1870's version of "piggyback" service was begun in response to a request from one small grower at Rocky Point, North Carolina, but it stimulated and served a growing industry until refrigerator cars and economical rail service were available.

During the years that Augustus Pope was freight agent, the only important outlet for the Florida orange crop was down the St. Johns River by steamboat to Jacksonville. From there, coastwise shipping provided the best access to the northeast. In the late 1870's, Pope began a campaign to get some of this business, sending soliciting agents to contact Florida shippers and freight clerks on the riverboats. Though the rail connections from Jacksonville to Charleston were still fairly primitive, many shippers, with Coast Line shipping receipts and bills of lading in hand, began to use the rail route in order to get their oranges delivered to New York a day or so earlier.

Through Traffic Succeeding

By and large, these efforts to promote traffic via improved rail connections were successful. Through freight and passenger business held up better during the depression, both in volume and revenues, than did the local business. For example, in the year ending September 30, 1875, the Wilmington & Weldon carried 139,235 bales of cotton; 70,660 of these were received from other railroads, and 118,416 were delivered to connecting roads at Weldon. During the same year, 60% of the general merchandise tonnage came from Portsmouth and Richmond for delivery to stations on or beyond the line. The same relative importance of through business can be seen in a comparison of passenger revenues for two depression years following the peak year ending September 30, 1873:

	1873	1874	1877
Wilmington & Weldon and WC&A			
combined receipts from local passengers	$241,852	$183,169	$122,847
combined receipts from through passengers	$188,866	$176,453	$151,996

Augustus Pope's policies as chief traffic agent for the Atlantic Coast Line reflected a basic change in orientation for the Wilmington roads under the Walters syndicate. Then, they had been primarily local railroads, serving Wilmington and the region tributary to its port. Now, they were the nucleus of an extensive system of rail connections, engaging actively in competition for through business.

The management was moved by considerations of achieving an efficient and profitable railroad operation, and these considerations were often in conflict with the interests of local businessmen. Citizens of Wilmington, who felt they had a proprietary claim on these railroads, found it difficult to understand why it might cost as much to send a small shipment of general merchandise 75 miles to Goldsboro, as it cost an Augusta merchant to ship a carload of cotton 516 miles to Norfolk. They resented Pope as an outsider, and they repeatedly objected to his rate policies.

From the standpoint of railroad men, it made good sense to improve connections and to set through rates for passenger and freight business low enough to meet the competition. Every additional increment of revenue from this source meant that much more income derived from a given investment in roadway and equipment. Hence, the fiercer the competition, the greater tended to be the disparity between through rates and local rates.

Cooperation Among Competitors

Numerous attempts were made during this period, in the south as in other parts of the nation, to reduce the destructiveness of competition through agreements among railroad companies. The Coast Line roads participated in two fairly successful organizations of southern railroads, These were the Green Line and the Southern Railway & Steamship Association.

The Green Line Transportation Company had begun in 1868 with an agreement signed by representatives of five railroad companies, including the Louisville & Nashville and the Western & Atlantic. The Green Line had the primary purposes of controlling rates and providing a system of car exchange for freight moved from Chicago, Louisville, Nashville, and Cincinnati to southern ports, especially Charleston, Savannah, and Brunswick. It was probably no coincidence that soon after Augustus Pope came to Wilmington from the Western & Atlantic, the WC&A and the CC&A were both listed as members of the Green Line. Since the organization focused on through-freight connections to southern ports from the 5-foot gauge Louisville & Nashville Railroad, the Wilmington & Weldon did not join. For that matter, the WC&A drew relatively little business from this source. The Green Line did serve however to point to future directions in through-freight business. Long-haul rates jointly set by cooperating railroads would aid in promoting traffic, and a system of car exchange would make it possible for shipments to move without reloading between points as widely separated as Louisville and Savannah.

The Southern Railway & Steamship Association, often called the "Southern Pool," was a much larger, and more ambitious, project for regulating traffic competition. The Wilmington & Weldon was one of 20 railroad companies participating in founding the Association in October of 1875. By 1879, the membership included 40 railroad companies and 29 steamship lines.

Coast Line officials were particularly interested in the initial objectives of the organization: to apportion business and stabilize rates between trade centers in the South and the cities of the Northeast. The depression and the disintegration of the Southern Railway Security Company's system were pushing the lines into a competitive scramble for the meager business available. Some of the fiercest rate wars actually occurred after the establishment of the Association. In order to force non-member lines to stop rate-cutting, the Commissioners of the Association ordered drastic reductions in rates, in February and March of 1876. Compare the old and successive new rates between New York and Atlanta (in cents per 100 pounds on the numbered classes):

Class:	1	2	3	4	5	6
Old rate	170	140	110	90	80	60
February rate	60	60	55	50	45	40
March rate	25	25	25	20	20	20

The offending companies could not hold out against this kind of cooperative action. Within a few days after the second reduction, the conflict ended, and rates were restored to about 85% of the old level.

Early in 1879, Augustus Pope distributed a small booklet advertising the Atlantic Coast Line Freight Route. Included was an index of freight items marked according to the "Classification adopted by Convention of the Southern Railway and Steamship Association, held in Atlanta, Georgia, November 26th to 28th, 1878, for the use of all Lines from Eastern and Western points to all points South, with the revisions to date by the Rate Committee, taking effect April lst, 1879. . . " There were number classifications "1" through "6", and letter classifications "A" through "H", plus a much-used "S"(special) category, which included cotton.

The Association was soon afterwards rendered more effective by provisions for an auditing agent to check the accounts of member companies and a deputy commissioner to supervise all through business to New York, Baltimore, and Providence. With the troublesome cotton traffic settled by a pooling agreement, and a standard classification of freight items adopted, the Southern Railway & Steamship Association began to stabilize long-haul freight business in the southeast.

Finances and the Future

From 1879 on, rates were generally maintained at profitable levels. This effective Southern Pool would contribute substantially to the healthy growth of the Atlantic Coast Line during the 1880's.

The immediate prospects for Coast Line traffic, however, were very grim. Volume and revenues in all categories of business reached low ebb for the two Wilmington roads in 1878 and 1879. For one example, the WC&A carried only 64,942 bales of cotton in 1878-79, as compared to 122,885 bales carried back in 1874-75. The drop was in volume received at Columbia, down from 79,184 bales in 1874-75 to only 12,965 bales in 1878-79. Most other traffic categories showed a similar decline in through-business received at Columbia, and for the same major reason — the Charlotte, Columbia & Augusta was no longer part of the Atlantic Coast Line. The CC&A was being integrated with the Richmond & Danville, and much of the passenger and freight business that Augustus Pope had developed for his Augusta-Columbia-Wilmington-Weldon route now went via Columbia, Charlotte, and Greensboro to Richmond.

The financial reverses suffered by the Walters syndicate in 1878 had directly and immediately affected the Wilmington roads. Loss of the CC&A disrupted a major traffic pattern, and it profoundly altered the evolution of the Atlantic Coast Line. The system was forcibly oriented more toward the Charleston route, and its future prosperity linked more firmly to the development of Florida.

Regrouping and Recovery 1878-1884

Starting Over

The Walters syndicate held on through the depression years of the 1870s, and weathered a crisis point in 1878, when the Wilmington, Columbia & Augusta forfeited its lease of the Wilmington & Weldon and went into receivership, and even when the Southern Railway Security Company was finally dissolved. At the very time when the fortunes of the Walters group seemed to reach their lowest ebb, they were making new and ultimately successful arrangements for financial control of Atlantic Coast Line roads.

They held their interests in the Wilmington & Weldon, while they made plans for reorganizing the WC&A. They also managed to hold onto their stock interests in the Northeastern, the Cheraw & Darlington, and the Richmond & Petersburg. By the beginning of 1880, they would again have the situation well in hand. Waldo Newcomer, writing years later of his father's career, described this recovery of fortunes:

> "Still undismayed, Mr. Newcomer and Mr. Walters formed another syndicate, offering the opportunity of participation to all those who had been with them thus far. Again the debris was taken in hand, and by close personal attention and hard work they were enabled in 1882 — fourteen years after the formation of the first syndicate — to commence the regular payment of dividends."

Walters and Newcomer had two immediate objectives in forming a new syndicate: first, to salvage as many as possible of the Security Company's holdings; and second, to provide a unifying organization that would replace the holding company and the WC&A. The new syndicate, with Walters, Newcomer, and Henry Plant as trustees, did manage to purchase the Security Company holdings in Coast Line railroads, with the notable exception of the Charlotte, Columbia & Augusta. Invitations to subscribe to the new syndicate were evidently extended to all stockholders in the expired holding company. Since the books of the Southern Railway Security Company were closed without any assets to be distributed, only those who subscribed to this new purchasing syndicate continued as owners of their former properties.

This new syndicate held a relatively modest portfolio of securities in four railroad companies: 6,871 shares of Richmond & Petersburg stock, 9,129 shares of Northeastern, 4,513 shares of Cheraw & Darlington; and after the foreclosure sale and reorganization of the WC&A, its $11,000 in first mortgage bonds were transformed into a meager 33 shares of stock and $5,500 in bonds in that company, which were also added to the new syndicate's holdings. Though limited, this package of securities served to unify those associated with W. T. Walters in their campaign for financial control of a system of southern railroads.

Reshuffling the Deck

The roads in which the syndicate held stock were related only as segments of a Wilmington-centered system; so the members of the syndicate protected their interests by maintaining or increasing their individual holdings of Wilmington & Weldon and WC&A stocks. Though there were no important new adherents to the group, Walters and Newcomer received increased support from, notably, H. B. Plant, S. M. Shoemaker, Thomas Jenkins and sons, and Morris K. Jesup.

The new syndicate provided a continuity of financial cooperation during foreclosure and receivership of the WC&A. Since the first Walters syndicate had formed for purchasing and holding the WC&A, the decision of the bondholders to foreclose on that company, the subsequent demise of the Southern Railway Security Company, and the formation of the new syndicate were related moves in a general financial regrouping in 1878-79.

The Wilmington, Columbia & Augusta Railroad remained in receivership from April 15, 1878, until January 2, 1880. Its management, under Robert Bridgers as receiver, remained the same; and its situation improved along with the gradual return of prosperity to the region. Relieved of the financial drains it had suffered under the holding company, the road's operational health was enhanced considerably under the receivership.

The WC&A bondholders proceeded with deliberations for reorganization. They met in Baltimore on December 9, 1876, and signed an agreement not to sell any of their bonds, all of which were deposited with the Safe Deposit & Trust Company. Of the original $3.2 million in first mortgage bonds, $3,152,500 was represented in this agreement. B. F. Newcomer, Thomas C. Jenkins, John S. Gilman, J. A. Tompkins and Frank A. Clark were appointed a committee to cooperate with the mortgage trustees, George S. Brown and Enoch Pratt, in purchasing the WC&A, and in preparing a reorganization plan. The foreclosure sale took place in Wilmington on October 1, 1879. The property had been evaluated by the court at 20% of its total indebtedness, so the official price was $860,500. A sum of $20,000 was paid immediately in cash, and the remainder of the price was met by delivering to the court $4,197,402.94 in the bonds, coupons and certificates of indebtedness of the old company. The properties and rights of the old Wilmington, Columbia & Augusta Railroad Company were formally transferred to a new company of the same name on January 2, 1880. The WC&A bondholders, who originally were also stockholders, had bought their property back at a scaled down valuation.

The "new" owners of the WC&A met in Baltimore on January 21, and adopted a financial organization plan. The new corporation would be capitalized on the basis of 9,600 shares of $100 par stock, and be mortgaged for $1,600,000; $1,000 of new bonds plus 6 shares of stock were distributed for each $2,000 of bonds held in the old company. In practice, this meant that a person with $2,000 in bonds, from full participation in the original organization of the WC&A, surrendered a package of certificates (stock, 7% income bonds, and coupons for unpaid interest) with a face value of about $3,200, for one technically worth $1,600. Lest this seem like a drastic loss, it should be noted that the subscriber's original investment in these securities was only $1,350.

To view this on a broader level, the members of the syndicate, who had bought the WC&A in 1870, had issued to themselves $4,100,000 in securities against a property which was probably worth no more than the $2,160,000 they had paid for its purchase and renovation. Now, after nearly ten years of scant return on their investment, and the outlays for important improvements in their railroad, largely the same group of men reduced their claims and equities to $2,560,000.

In essence, the Walters group went through the formalities of foreclosing and reorganizing the WC&A in order to reduce its funded debt — owed almost entirely to themselves, and to wipe out its floating debt — owed, again, largely to themselves, as stockholders in the Southern Railway Security Company.

The old financial scheme had reflected the high hopes of the Walters group for handsome returns from developing a trunk line. They had expected the WC&A, with its access both to the coastal and interior areas south of Wilmington, to be the prosperous key segment of the trunk; and, with its lease of the Wilmington & Weldon, to be the financial vehicle for rendering the profits from both companies. They had been disappointed on both counts, so the Wilmington, Columbia & Augusta was now recapitalized and mortgaged at a reasonable level.

Renewed Confidence

It is notable that W. T. Walters received only 300 shares of stock in the reorganized company, indicating that he had sold, at some point, about two-thirds of his WC&A bonds. His fortunes and his confidence in the WC&A apparently revived, because he steadily bought new shares until, in 1885, he was the largest stockholder with 1,200 shares. Morris K. Jesup demonstrated his enthusiasm for the WC&A as an investment, by accumulating 1,000 shares within a few months after the reorganization.

On February 11, 1880, the stockholders of the WC&A met and organized their company. Continuity of control is indicated by the list of directors elected: R. R. Bridgers, George S. Brown, B. F. Newcomer, H. B. Short, Enoch Pratt, W. T. Walters, S. Y. Shoemaker, J. D. Cameron, H. B. Plant, and George C. Jenkins. Most of these men (Short and Plant being the exceptions) had participated in the original purchase of the WC&A. They all had been members of the Walters group for some years. At their first meeting, the directors elected Robert Bridgers as president, and W. T. Walters, vice president.

The New Star — The Wilmington & Weldon

Having reorganized the Wilmington, Columbia & Augusta Railroad Company, the Walters group turned most of their attention elsewhere. They no longer used this company as the pivotal corporation in controlling the Atlantic Coast Line system. Walters and Newcomer gradually centered financial and policy control of the Atlantic Coast Line in the Wilmington & Weldon Railroad Company. This move did not begin until 1880. During the months of receivership, foreclosure, and reorganization of the WC&A, Walters and Newcomer took little part in the direction of the Wilmington & Weldon. With business slack, and their financial organization disrupted, there was nothing to be accomplished anyway. Then too, the situation at Wilmington called for a cooling-off period.

When on April 15, 1878, the Wilmington & Weldon Railroad was returned to its own directorship, many of the grounds for dispute between stockholders in Baltimore and these in North Carolina were, at one stroke, removed. The company and its properties were in sound condition. Against assets of $3,446,809, there was a funded debt of $1,619,100 and a floating debt of only $36,713.

As part of a special statement issued by President Bridgers on May 31, the investigating committee of "five stockholders who reside in the State of North Carolina" included their report. It conceded first, that the road and equipment were in better condition than before the lease began, and second, that the rate policies of the Wilmington & Weldon were similar to those followed by other southern railroads. The local stockholders also found, however, that, contrary to widespread opinion, their road was really not doing enough business to pay 7% dividends while investing in needed improvements. In order to continue the policy of replacing iron rails with steel, dividends were reduced to 3% annually, beginning in 1878. Disbelief persisted on this point, however. At the November meeting, a Wilmington stockholder moved that an auditing committee be appointed to check the books; there were no discrepancies uncovered. In response to a strong general sentiment for economy, the board appointed three of its local members in March of 1879 to scrutinize all categories of expenditures, including salaries of top officials, for advisable reductions in costs. The committee had only one recommendation of this nature, when it reported in November: the cost of conducting and promoting through business should be studied to see whether it was justified by the revenues from such business.

Walters and Newcomer kept discreetly in the background during this period. They firmly but quietly supported Bridgers and his policies; while allowing the board members from Wilmington and Tarboro to answer local complaints and allay local suspicions. Happily, no serious attempt was made to end the consolidation of management and facilities between the Wilmington & Weldon and the WC&A. With the WC&A neutralized as a company, it no longer posed the spectre of Baltimore domination. Indeed, with their president, Bridgers, acting as receiver, Wilmington & Weldon stockholders could now regard the WC&A their captive. So the Wilmington & Weldon continued to share its executive department and its offices, depot and wharf at Wilmington, with the WC&A. With local stockholders placated, and a safe proportion of the stock in cooperative hands, Walters and Newcomer were able to keep their individual investments in the company fairly modest until business recovery increased their financial resources.

On the Upswing

The 1879-80 fiscal year was a major turning point for the Atlantic Coast Line railroads, as it was for many other enterprises in the United States. The southeastern region shared in the nationwide business recovery, unmistakably in progress by the closing months of 1879. Not only was the prosperity swing of gratifying breadth and duration, but it also began the shift away from the "one-crop economy" in the South. There was increased production of grains, fruits, and vegetables for shipment to northern markets. Livestock raising became important in many areas, and new mining and manufacturing enterprises appeared. Textile mills, especially, began to locate in the South — several of them in the Florence and Greenville areas of South Carolina. Production of cottonseed oil also grew into an important industry during these years.

The traditional products of the region — cotton, tobacco and forest products — also responded to increased demand in the national market. A succession of good crop years, beginning in 1880, helped considerably. Late in 1882, the *Manufacturer's Record* observed:

> Never before have the agricultural productions of the southern states been so abundant as this year. A cotton crop of from 6,700,000 to 7,000,000 bales seems to be assured. This means probably not less (even allowing for possible lower prices) than fifty million dollars more to the South for its cotton crop than in 1881.

Though there would be temporary interruptions, such as the nationwide panic of 1884, the South was entering upon a period of solid economic growth. The Coast Line railroads were both contributors to and beneficiaries of this growth. With the upturn in business activity, the Coast Line railroads once more became profitable operations. In 1880, the volume of cotton transported from the Columbia area of South Carolina by the WC&A, alone, literally doubled. It, and the Northeastern, also benefited from a lively boom in the forest products business. These roads not only drew increased tonnage from new saw mills along their lines, they also added to their revenues by renting old iron rails to expanding lumbering concerns. Along with this expansion in production and movement of traditional products, shipments of truck crops and Florida oranges began to provide significant freight revenues. Spectacular increases occurred in through business, both freight and passenger. Freight tonnage carried by the Richmond & Petersburg doubled between 1879 and 1883. Through-passenger revenues from the Northeastern, in 1883, were more than twice those in 1879, even though rates had been reduced. Through-passenger revenue nearly doubled on the Wilmington & Weldon during the same years.

The Coast Line railroads all began to show marked improvement in total operating revenues. For illustration, there was a sharp contrast between the reports for the last depression year, ending September 30, 1879, and the year 1881.

Gross Receipts for:	1879	1881
Wilmington & Weldon	$505,957	$750,917
WC&A	$478,310	$640,956
Northeastern	$346,268	$484,760
Richmond & Petersburg	$154,622	$185,905

These welcome changes were soon followed by dividend declarations. The Richmond & Petersburg, which had managed to pay 4% annual dividends since 1878, increased the payment to 5% in 1881. Wilmington & Weldon stockholders once more received a full 6% annual return commencing with the semi-annual dividend of July 1881. A milestone of significance was reached when, in January of 1882, Walters, Newcomer, and their associates received their first dividends as stockholders in the WC&A — an event they were to enjoy semi-annually for the rest of the corporate life of the company. The Northeastern followed suit by declaring one semi-annual dividend for January 1883, and commencing full annual 6% payments in 1884.

New Alliances

Although most of the newfound profits were due to the general economic prosperity, other factors contributed substantially. Walters and Newcomer enhanced the profit potential of their system by entering into alliances with investors in other railroads. They joined the Clyde syndicate which purchased the Richmond & Danville, and they associated themselves with Henry Plant in his development of a railroad system south of Charleston.

In the opening months of 1880, W. P. Clyde, of New York City, organized a syndicate which bought control of the Richmond & Danville from the Pennsylvania Railroad Company. Several of the members of the Clyde syndicate — R. T. Wilson, C. M. McGhee, H. B. Plant, and of course, Walters and Newcomer — had participated in the Southern Railway Security Company. The new group also included John and Daniel Stewart, Thomas M. Logan, and Thomas Branch & Company, all of Richmond, and Thomas Clyde of Philadelphia. The Clyde interests already controlled an important steamship line. Under a charter obtained from the Virginia legislature in March of 1880, the syndicate proceeded to organize the Richmond & West Point Terminal Railway & Warehouse Company, which acquired, in the course of a few months, some 1,200 miles of railway for the Richmond & Danville system. A combination bringing this much strength to the Piedmont Air Line system was better to have as a friend than as an enemy. Since neither Walters nor Newcomer served as an officer in any of the Richmond & Danville companies, their financial commitment to the central objectives of the syndicate was evidently limited. Their membership in the Clyde syndicate seemed to be in the nature of a financial alliance between the Atlantic Coast Line and the Piedmont Air Line.

Cooperative Traffic Management

The Atlantic Coast Line derived some important advantages from the new combination of interests. An immediate effect was renewal of freight exchange at Columbia, South Carolina, to the particular benefit of the WC&A and the Northeastern. Such benefits were soon realized many fold, under a cooperative traffic arrangement entitled "The Associated Railways of Virginia and the Carolinas." On September 11, 1880, the Atlantic Coast Line and the Piedmont Air Line concluded an agreement that strengthened and enlarged the effectiveness of the Southern Pool for their traffic areas. As the *Railway Gazette* observed, "Changes of ownership of the stock of some of the lines. . . having occurred during the past year, settlement of issues became more possible than formerly, and the idea of cooperative traffic management advanced by gentlemen most largely interested found favor."

Augustus Pope, of the Coast Line, and T. M. R. Talbott, of the Richmond & Danville, were the main authors of the agreement. The preamble expressed the aims very clearly:

It is deemed of mutual advantage to both the. . . lines and the Companies constituting them, that both their Passenger and Freight Traffic should be conducted under joint management and in accordance with the principles hereinafter set forth, for the purpose of regulating competition and economizing expenditures, whereby the net revenues of all the Companies parties hereto will, it is believed, be augmented; and,

It is deemed important to so harmonize the interests of the Parties hereto and combine them into one common interest as to be constitute practically an alliance between them for mutual protection. . .

The first clause of the contract placed the traffic management of all the participating railroads under jointly-appointed officials. Appointed later, for both lines, were Augustus Pope as general passenger agent and Solomon Haas (of the Richmond & Danville) as general freight agent. Other clauses provided for:

1. mutual concessions on traffic in which both lines were interested,
2. removal of all independent soliciting agents, and joint payment (pro-rated) of all agents employed,
3. mutual aid and protection in case of attacks from other lines,
4. preferential routing of traffic over the lines party to the agreement,
5. mutual agreement on rates and cooperation with the Southern Railway and Steamship Association in rate agreements,
6. a three-man arbitration board, composed of W. P. Clyde, B. F. Newcomer (or their designated representatives) and "a third person of like fitness," to which all disputes should be appealed, and
7. agreement on equal rates, traffic exchange, and traffic divisions at several specific points, such as Columbia, South Carolina, and Richmond, Virginia.

The agreement became effective September 15, 1880. Sol Haas and Augustus Pope moved into jointly-maintained offices in Richmond, and the two major north-south lines in the region entered upon a decade of cooperative traffic management.

The Seaboard Air Line very shortly became party to the agreement by a separate contract, largely on the basis of its connections with Coast Line roads. A revision of the agreement, made two years later, provided an auditor for the Association, who was given full access to the records of participating companies. The work of the auditor immediately improved enforcement of the agreement. It also reduced friction, by producing accurate accounts of the joint expenses which were pro-rated among the several companies. Augustus Pope resigned, effective August 31, 1882, and his post as general passenger agent for the Association was not filled. Sol Haas served alone, thereafter, as traffic manager for all three lines. His position was confirmed when the organization was renewed for another five years, in a contract negotiated June 23, 1885. The only other basic change at that time was the inclusion of the Seaboard Air Line signatory to the central agreement.

A Secret Contract

The same day (June 23, 1885) as agreement was reached on the main contract by representatives of all three lines, Henry Walters and B. F. Newcomer held a later session with W. P. Clyde and F. W. Huidekoper, in the Atlantic Coast Line office in Baltimore. They signed a secret sub-agreement, the terms of which solidified the benefits of the Association for the Atlantic Coast Line and the Piedmont Air Line. They divided the north-south passenger business as follows: the traffic between eastern cities and Charleston was conceded to the Coast Line; that between eastern cities and western points, reached via Augusta, Macon, and Atlanta, was conceded to the Piedmont Air Line; passenger business to Columbia and Aiken, South Carolina, would be open to both lines, but the lucrative traffic to the health resort town of Aiken would be pooled. The importance to the Atlantic Coast Line of Henry Plant's railroads caused Walters and Newcomer to insist on a qualification— "But nothing herein contained shall be construed as preventing the Atlantic Coast Line from participating in the business of New Orleans, Mobile and such other points in the southwest as it reaches via its Savannah, Florida & Western connection." This secret sub-agreement dealt with particular points of tension between the Coast Line and Piedmont Air Line, and it had no apparent prejudicial effect on the Seaboard's interests. It was probably kept apart from the main contract in order to avoid newspaper comments on a pooling agreement. It did, underline, however, the fact that the Coast Line and Richmond & Danville systems were the major partners in the Associated Railways.

Remaining in force until 1890, although with diminishing effectiveness after passage of the Interstate Commerce Act, this traffic alliance removed much of the competitive pressure on rates for north-south business. Rates tended to be equalized, or "blanketed," in successive zones southward from Richmond, so that commercial centers served by the Coast Line enjoyed rates as low as those reached by the Piedmont Air Line. Another advantage, which doubtless was applauded by stockholders in Wilmington, was reduction of soliciting expenses for through freight and passenger business. The Associated Railways of Virginia and the Carolinas contributed in many ways to the prosperity of the member lines during the important growth period of the 1880's. It proved to be so mutually beneficial, that the railroads maintained the Association seven years after the dissolution of the Clyde syndicate, which had fostered the agreement in the first place.

Clyde Saves the Petersburg

In another, quite different way, the Clyde syndicate rendered invaluable assistance to the Atlantic Coast Line. It rescued the Petersburg Railroad from imminent foreclosure and made it a controlled segment of the Coast Line. During April of 1881, a pool committee representing the Clyde syndicate accumulated all of an issue of $487,500 of Petersburg second mortgage bonds and 7,645 shares of stock, and offered to pay all the back interest on $500,000 of first mortgage bonds.

The bondholders accepted the plan; and, on May 10, 1881, the company emerged from four years of receivership. The alliance between the Richmond & Danville interests and the Coast Line leadership was reflected in the directors elected on March 15, 1882: Fred R. Scott, president of the Richmond & Petersburg, and a loyal representative of the Walters group; W. H. Palmer, T. M. Logan and Joseph Bryan, all members of the Clyde syndicate , the last two very active in Richmond & Danville affairs; R. G. Pegram, past president and receiver of the Petersburg, and representative of the minority, local, stockholders. E. T. D. Myers, for many years superintendent of the Richmond, Fredricksburg & Potomac, was chosen president. Thus the Petersburg immediately became a cooperating member of the Coast Line Railroad combination. President Myers signed the Associated Railways of Virginia and the Carolinas contract in August of 1882. That same year, another contract was signed by which the Coast Line roads obtained new sleeping cars from the Pullman Company.

From the time that the Clyde syndicate had brought together the Walters group and Thomas Branch & Company of Richmond — previously competitors for control of the Petersburg — a solution for saving the Petersburg had been in the offing. Greater volume of business for the Petersburg resulted largely from more favorable connections. Its gross revenues jumped from $206,683 in 1879 to $300,261 in 1881 and to $335,178 in 1883, with the largest increases coming in through-freight receipts. By placing the Petersburg in sound financial condition and under friendly management, the Clyde syndicate had filled an awkward gap in the Coast Line.

Henry Plant's Own System

The financial strength of Walters and Newcomer was augmented during this period by the expanded resources and activities of one of their old associates in the Security

Company — Henry B. Plant. Drawing perhaps from his Southern Express Company, Henry Plant seemed to have an ample supply of investment capital as the depression ended. He subscribed heavily to the new Walters syndicate, bought 500 shares of Wilmington & Weldon stock, and, in 1880, became a director in both Wilmington companies. Between 1879 and 1882, he and Morris Jesup arranged to purchase 3,400 and 4,026, respectively, additional shares in the Northeastern Railroad Company, most of these representing the remaining holdings of the City of Charleston. The Northeastern was now almost completely owned by the Walters group, with Plant and Jesup holding the largest individual interests in the company. Henry Plant also participated in the Clyde syndicate; and, when that combination gave way to a realignment, his position in the Richmond & Danville Railroad Company was strong enough to command a seat on its board in 1884. Plant's stake in both the Richmond & Danville and the Atlantic Coast Line may have been the main financial tie between the two systems and the key to their continuing cooperation. The extent of Henry Plant's participation in financial control of the Coast Line roads was especially significant in view of the fact that he was beginning to put together a new railroad system south of Charleston.

From its very inception, the Plant System was closely linked in operations and financial control with the Atlantic Coast Line. Henry Plant initiated his railroad system on November 9, 1879, by purchasing the Atlantic & Gulf Railroad. The Atlantic & Gulf was available at foreclosure — the culmination of financial problems firmly based on a 237-mile main line that ran from Savannah to almost nowhere. With due apologies to the good people of Bainbridge, Georgia, that city was far short of the railroad's intended, and needed, connections with Pensacola, Mobile, and New Orleans.

The Atlantic & Gulf Railroad Company had been organized in 1856, under authority of a special act of the Georgia legislature. Heavily backed by the state government (with a generous land grant and a large financial investment), the road was to develop the southern portion of Georgia by giving access to both Gulf and Atlantic ports. An earlier company, the Savannah & Albany, had just completed a line from Savannah to Screven. So the first segment of the Atlantic & Gulf was a 28-mile line from Screven to Waycross, Georgia, which opened in July 1859. Construction then reached westward to Thomasville by the spring of 1861. An extension farther west to Bainbridge had to be abandoned because of the war, as did a project for a line swinging southward from Dupont, Georgia, toward Live Oak, Florida. Then, on May 1, 1863, the Atlantic & Gulf acquired the line from Screven to Savannah by absorbing the Savannah, Albany & Gulf Railroad Company (earlier the Savannah & Albany).

The end of hostilities left the Atlantic & Gulf deteriorated, but not destroyed. With borrowed capital the road was quickly restored and the extension to Bainbridge completed. The line providing Florida connections at Live Oak was also constructed and placed in service March 4, 1865. Another good branch, this one running northward from Thomasville, was obtained by absorbing the South Georgia & Florida Railroad Company, in 1869, and by completing its line into Albany by June of the following year. Money, however, was not available for the most essential project — construction of 165 miles of road from Bainbridge to Pollard, Alabama, to connect with existing roads to Pensacola, Mobile, and New Orleans. The Atlantic & Gulf had difficulty in meeting its interest payments, even before the depression began; it was in no condition to weather the lean years that followed. The road was placed in receivership on February 19, 1877.

The SF&W Emerges

Henry Plant's purchase of the Atlantic & Gulf was made possible by support from New York financiers, particularly Morris K. Jesup. It was Jesup who, as surviving trustee for the second mortgage, had sued for foreclosure in 1877. Then over two years later, Plant was permitted to purchase the road for only $300,000, with the property still subject to mortgages amounting to $2,710,000. In return for accepting the claims of the bondholders, Plant received full control of the railroad. He proceeded to organize a new company, the Savannah, Florida & Western Railway Company, with himself as president and major stockholder. Of an initial stock issue of 20,000 of $100-par shares, Plant himself held 19,482 shares. If he could meet interest payments on the bonds, his control would be uncontested. A court order gave the new company possession of the railroad on December 8, 1879; another dismissed the receivers the following May 11. Plant put operation of the railroad in the hands of a General Manager Henry S. Haines, of Savannah. Thus began the Savannah, Florida & Western, destined to be the parent company of a sizable railroad empire.

Organizing the Savannah, Florida & Western under these conditions was a daring gamble for Henry Plant. In order to carry the burden of inherited and new debts, the new company would have to get a shaky railroad operating profitably, in short order. It was a well-calculated gamble. For one thing, business conditions were clearly improving. For another, he had a plan, and the financial resources, for improving the SF&W's rail connections in all directions.

The SF&W needed an improved connection to the north, access to Mobile and New Orleans, and better entry into Florida. The first of these aims would be accomplished by seizing and rebuilding the SF&W's northern connection, the bankrupt and decrepit Savannah & Charleston.

The Savannah & Charleston had been originally organized July 12, 1854, as the Charleston & Savannah. It placed 88.5 miles of main line, from St. Andrews, S.C, to the Savannah River, in service by January 1, 1859. A few months later, a bridge was completed across the Savannah River , as was connection with the Savannah & Albany's line at Central Junction (near Savannah). The Civil War brought disaster to the Charleston & Savannah; Sherman's troops left it with only a right-of-way and a roadbed. The bondholders foreclosed and bought the remains of the property on November 20, 1866, reorganizing it as the Savannah & Charleston.

The new company had difficulty raising capital, and the rebuilding process was painfully slow. It was March of 1870, before the Savannah River was again bridged, and the line restored to Central Junction. As late as 1873-74, the only good thing about a trip on the road was the scenery. The Savannah & Charleston defaulted on interest payments even before the depression began; and it was placed in receivership on April 28, 1874. One important improvement on the line was made during the receivership. A short line bridging the Ashley River and connecting with the Northeastern at Charleston went into operation on January 1, 1878.

At a foreclosure sale held June 7, 1880, Henry Plant purchased the Savannah & Charleston Railroad for $320,000 in cash and securities of the old company. The decree by the Court of Common Pleas of South Carolina made the sale absolute — eliminating all earlier claims on the property. However, Plant was able to get such a decree of sale by virtue of a pool agreement, dated and signed the same day. The agreement was essentially between Plant and the Walters syndicate on the one hand, and the holders of first preferred and second preferred income bonds in the old company on the other. The agreement had some interesting provisions:

1. The new company was to be controlled for one year by a board of directors consisting of H. B. Plant, W. T. Walters, B, F. Newcomer, A. F. Ravenel (president of the Northeastern), W. H. Brawley (representing the 6% 1st preferred bondholders), and William Cutting and C. G. Memminger (representing the 7% 2nd preferred bondholders).

2. The new company would immediately execute a mortgage and issue 7% bonds for reimbursing Plant the $50,000 spent toward the purchase, for repairing and equipping the railroad, and for paying other claims and organizing expenses.

3. All subscribers to the agreement would have the right to buy a proportionate share of the bonds, and to receive 25% of the amount paid in stock of the company.

4. 5,000 shares of $100 par capital stock would be issued, and the shares remaining after the distribution to purchasers of new bonds would be divided among the old bondholders, half among holders of the 1st preferred income bonds and half among holders of 2nd preferred income bonds.

5. Voting rights would remain for five years with holders of new bonds — one vote per $100.

Linked to the Coast Line

The new corporation, named the Charleston & Savannah Railroad Company, was organized thusly, and Henry Plant was elected its president. Significantly, the only persons who bought bonds in the new company and participated in the initial distribution of stock were H. B. Plant (400 shares), W. T. Walters (225), B. F. Newcomer (200), M. K. Jesup (125), and Thomas C. Jenkins. No one outside the Walters group had any voting rights in the Charleston & Savannah Company for five years. There were endless disputes over execution of the original purchase agreement, and it would be more than a decade before the basic stock distribution was accomplished; but Henry Plant and his

Baltimore and New York associates had secured control of the railroad which connected Plant's SF&W with the Coast Line system.

Viewed altogether, Henry Plant's financial moves during 1879 and 1880 exhibited a striking pattern of cooperation with Morris Jesup, W. T. Walters, and Benjamin Newcomer. He and Jesup had joined the new Walters syndicate, which purchased controlling interests in several Coast Line companies, from the defunct Southern Railway Security Company. He and Jesup had begun, in 1879, to acquire large holdings of WC&A and Wilmington & Weldon shares. During the same period, he and Jesup had arranged to acquire over 7,400 shares of Northeastern stock, giving the Walters group nearly exclusive ownership of that company. With support from the Walters group, Plant secured the Charleston & Savannah; and with Jesup's backing, he gained nearly sole ownership of the Savannah, Florida & Western.

The timing and relationship of these moves indicate agreement on a definite plan. Henry Plant was aiding Walters and Newcomer in their efforts to cement the Coast Line roads into an effective trunk line from Richmond to Charleston; and they and Jesup were helping Plant to extend a system of connecting roads below Charleston into Georgia and Florida. Walters and Newcomer retained predominate voice in the roads north of Charleston; Plant assumed control of acquisitions south of Charleston. Continued cooperation was assured, however, by Plant's large interest in the Northeastern, and by Walter's and Newcomer's heavy investments in the Charleston & Savannah. The route to Florida was financially interlocked at Charleston.

The Way to Florida

While capturing the Charleston & Savannah, Plant was also giving considerable attention to improving the SF&W's connections in other directions. By the spring of 1880 he had underway a project for extending the coastal route to Jacksonville, Florida. The road constructed was called the Waycross Short Line, an aptly-named extension of the SF&W which ran 70 miles directly from Waycross to Jacksonville.

The Waycross Short Line was officially constructed by two separate railroad companies chartered in 1880 especially for that purpose. The East Florida Railway Company, organized March 15, 1880, completed its 37 miles of road from the St. Mary's River to Jacksonville on April 30, 1881. The Waycross & Florida Railroad Company, organized March 4, 1880, built approximately 33 miles of lines in Georgia between the St. Mary's River and Waycross. On April 30, 1880, both companies leased their lines to the SF&W; in 1884, both companies were consolidated and became part of the SF&W.

The Savannah, Florida & Western ran its first scheduled train over the Waycross Short Line on May 1, 1881. It was a gala event. Henry Plant and H. L. Haines sent engraved invitations to Florida dignitaries and businessmen:

"Dear Sir: The management takes pleasure in notifying you of the opening of this line through between Charleston, Savannah, and Jacksonville. You are respectfully invited, with the privilege of being accompanied by a lady, to take a trip over the East Florida Railway and its connections between Charleston, Savannah and Jacksonville, at any time that may suit your convenience during the next thirty days. Please present the enclosed pass to conductor."

The Waycross Short Line eliminated the round-about, time-consuming trip through Dupont, Georgia, and Live Oak, Florida, to Jacksonville. It reduced the distance between Savannah and Jacksonville by nearly 100 miles, and the time from 14 to 6½ hours.

Other improvements kept pace. Within two years after he purchased the roads, Plant virtually rebuilt the Charleston & Savannah and the SF&W. The main line tracks were completely relaid with steel rail, and on October 29, 1882, a new iron bridge over the Savannah River was completed. New passenger cars with the latest in appointments provided, for the first time, a safe and comfortable trip southward from Charleston. Good rail service to Florida could now be offered by the Coast Line. By December of 1882, one could board the Atlantic Coast Line's fast mail train number 40 in New York City, and be in Jacksonville in 36½ hours.

Plant Completes His Goal

Access to New Orleans took a bit longer, for Plant waited to benefit from someone else's efforts. About February 1, 1883, the Pensacola & Atlantic Railroad (completed under Louisville & Nashville auspices) began Florida service from Chattahoochee to Pensacola. Plant simultaneously completed an extension of the SF&W from Climax, Georgia, to Chattahoochee. The aim of the old Atlantic & Gulf undertaking was finally accomplished — the SF&W offered connections to New Orleans via Savannah, Waycross, Thomasville, Pensacola, and Mobile. For the Coast Line roads, too, this was hailed as a major accomplishment. The main Charleston route of the Atlantic Coast Line could now compete for through traffic to New Orleans, without encroaching on Richmond & Danville territory. At the time, this was regarded as more important than the direct line to Jacksonville, Florida.

Henry Plant's gamble in talking over the old Atlantic & Gulf was turning out well. His railroad system was profitably launched and expanding. His success meant much to Coast Line roads north of Charleston, for it enormously improved their prospects for through freight and passenger business.

Attention to Accommodations

In order to exploit fully the improved connections to Florida and the Gulf cities, better sleeping car service was essential. The Coast Line roads had already made some progress in this direction. President Bridgers had gone so far as to send Augustus Pope to interview a renowned lung specialist in Boston on the question of through sleeping car service to Jacksonville for his patients. According to Pope, the physician was so critical of the Coast Line's transfer of passengers from sleeping cars to parlor cars at scheduled points, that his opinion contributed to negotiations with the Pullman Company for the new convertible type sleeping cars. Soon after the opening, late in 1877, of the Ashley River connection line at Charleston, the Coast Line had begun to run a Pullman car from New York to Savannah, in cooperation with the Pennsylvania and the Savannah & Charleston railroads.

The through service to Savannah required changing the tracks of sleeping cars from standard to five-foot gauge at Wilmington. This was done by means of an ingenious device — a gravity truck transfer pit. At the approach to the pit, "I" beams were placed under the car, with the beam ends resting on trucks on parallel tracks. Thus suspended, the car was moved over the pit. The trucks of one-gauge dropped free; trucks of the new gauge were inserted; and, coupled to a new train, the car continued to its destination. The reader may entertain some doubts whether the passengers all slept through this process, but at least they did not have to change cars.

On April 24, 1882, a contract was signed with Pullman's Palace Car Company to supply the Coast Line and Plant roads with new sleeping and parlor cars. Not only did this bring fine new equipment to the route; it was also an important unifying force. A subsequent contract, dated October 10, 1882, established an Atlantic Coast Line Sleeping Car Association, with Benjamin Newcomer, President Myers of the Petersburg, and General Manager Haines of the SF&W, as trustees. Another contract with the Pullman Company, dated October 14, provided for the purchase of a 75% interest in these cars by the Car Association.

The several Coast Line companies, the Charleston & Savannah, and the SF&W paid allotted portions of the Car Association's investment. The amount paid by each was assigned by the trustees on the basis of each road's mileage use of the cars. The Wilmington & Weldon, for example, paid $39,600 initially; the WC&A, $48,000. Since Pullman was building cars costing in the neighborhood of $20,000 each, at this time, the initial order was probably for about 14 cars.

The new cars were placed in service in January of 1883, and a few months later President Myers of the Petersburg enthusiastically reported that "a considerable revenue is derived from a source which was formerly one of expense." The Atlantic Coast Line and SF&W passenger agents lost no time in advertising the latest and most elegant in passenger accommodations from New York to Jacksonville and New Orleans. The service was arranged so that a passenger could take one Pullman Palace Car on Atlantic Coast Line from New York to Savannah, and another from Savannah through to New Orleans. The traveler could remain on one car from Washington, all the way to Jacksonville.

Thanks largely to the accomplishments and cooperation of Henry Plant, the Atlantic Coast Line now offered comfortable (and profitable) passenger service to Florida and the Gulf cities.

New Motive Power

The Coast Line roads shared a general deficiency in all categories of rolling stock at the onset of business expansion 1879-1880. The pressure for economizing during the depression had been such that no new locomotives, and very little other equipment, had been added since the early 1870's.

The most marked increase of business, and therefore the most keenly felt shortage equipment, was experienced by the WC&A. For freight business alone, the WC&A added 75 new cars in 1881 and 150 new cars in 1882. The Northeastern added 62 box cars and 40 flat cars in 1881-82, and about as many more in 1883. The Wilmington & Weldon also had to more than double its freight carrying capacity in the three years ending 1883.

Comparable additions had to be made to the supply of motive power. The WC&A, with the greatest needs, began first with the purchase of two Rogers four-driver, 16-inch cylinder, 69,300 pound locomotives at a cost of $9,700 each. These, and three more, were placed in service in by September of 1881. In October 1882, two Rogers 79,200 pound, six-driver, 17-inch cylinder Rogers locomotives were delivered to the WC&A. The following September, three more big Rogers four-driver locomotives were delivered.

The Wilmington & Weldon, which was not caught so short of motive power, waited until 1882 to add two Rogers 16-inch, 69,300 pound locomotives; two similar models were added in 1883 and 1884. The gentler grades of the Wilmington & Weldon road did not require the heavy locomotives used on the WC&A.

The locomotive complement of the Northeastern at the beginning of 1880 consisted of two secured from the Rhode Island locomotive works in the spring of 1873. There were eleven assorted Rogers, Baldwins and Norrises, the most recent of which was dated 1861 and the oldest of which went back as far as 1855. This antiquated collection was beefed up somewhat by the purchase of the old WC&A locomotives. In October of 1882, four new Rogers 16-inch cylinder models were delivered, with a like number of Rogers 17-inch models, the next year.

The Richmond & Petersburg roster of motive power illustrates, rather nicely, the locomotive history of the period, When first purchased, they were given such colorful names as "Westward Ho," "Buffalo," "Tiger," "Reindeer," and "Pocohantas." Numbers were added in 1874 and the names dropped altogether in 1876. The R&P got through the 1870's with a complement of eight locomotives. All of these had been purchased in the post-war period with the exception of the "Mazeppa," which dated as early as 1854, but had been rebuilt in R&P shops in 1870. In 1881 a used McKay and Alden four-driver was purchased and given the number "1," in place of the old Richard Norris "Westward Ho." Locomotive No. 9, a Rogers 75,000 pound four-driver, was placed in service in November 1883. By 1883, all the R&P locomotives had been converted to coal burners, a change that came later on the Coast Line roads farther removed from the coal fields.

The Case for Better Bridges

By 1884 some of the drastic needs for equipment had been met on the Coast Line roads, but it was only a modest beginning. As President Bridgers reported that year to Wilmington & Weldon stockholders, "The motive power and rolling stock of the company are in good condition, but it is to be regretted that there is not a larger supply."

Failure to keep up with the times in one instance proved costly to the Richmond & Petersburg, and embarrassing to the entire Coast Line. President Scott, for several years, resisted attempts of the stockholder's examining committee to persuade him that the wooden bridges on the R&P should be replaced by iron. Surely this statement in President Scott's report, November 1878, deserves a place in the roster of famous last words: "The bridges [all of which are of wood] are strong and safe. Experience proves that the more old-fashioned wooden bridges are much safer than the more graceful iron structures, now so popular; and with proper protection and care they are everlasting." On March 26, 1882, the R&P's long bridge across the James River caught fire and burned completely in less than an hour. Augustus Pope, who happened to be in his office at Richmond, spent a very busy Sunday arranging for omnibus transfer of passengers from south of the river to the Richmond, Fredericksburg & Potomac line north of the Byrd Street Station, which had also burned. He made the passenger transfer trip up Broad Street in Richmond as much like a guided tour of historical sights as possible, and also negotiated new schedule connections with the RF&P and the Pennsylvania in Washington. Passengers were thus adequately provided for, but through freight was halted completely. It took J. R. Kenly, who had just become superintendent of the R&P, two months of furious effort to construct a temporary wooden bridge and restore the connection. The cost of the temporary bridge and in loss of revenues to the R&P, alone, was estimated at $60,000 above insurance coverage. A new iron bridge was finally available for use early in 1884.

Road Construction

In one important respect the Walters' railroads were fairly well prepared for the upsurge in business, which they enjoyed from 1880 to 1884. Their roadways were in good condition, with large portions of their track mileage in steel rails. The R&P had begun to lay steel rails in 1876; the Wilmington roads and the Northeastern, in 1877. By

1884, this process was nearly completed. Although the steel rails used were very light by modern standards — 56 pounds to the yard — they were vastly superior to iron in both wearing quality and rigidity. Rapid replacement with steel rails was stimulated by appealingly low prices. They were considered a bargain in 1876, at around $80.00 a ton; prices eased subsequently and then, in the fall of 1882, plummeted to $40.00 per ton. By December of 1883, steel rails were selling for $35.00 per ton, and some as low as $32.25. The *Manufacturer's Record* observed, "For those contemplating railroad building, the present seems to be a remarkably favorable time." Henry Plant was actively demonstrating his concurrence; and so, with Walter's and Newcomer's support, was Robert Bridgers.

An extensive program for building branch and connecting roads for the Atlantic Coast Line was in progress by 1881. One such project began as early as 1878, when the Cheraw & Darlington agreed to complete construction of 25 miles of line from Cheraw, South Carolina, to Wadesboro, North Carolina, for the Cheraw & Salisbury Railroad Company. The agreement also permitted the Cheraw & Darlington to operate the road upon its completion in 1880.

The Cheraw & Salisbury had an interesting history, one that reads like a study in frustration. It had been chartered originally in 1856, in North Carolina, and in 1857, in South Carolina, as the "Cheraw & Coal Fields Railroad Company." William Godfrey of the Cheraw & Darlington contributed some interesting information: "It was to extend from Cheraw to Cumnock coal mines in Chatham County, North Carolina, this being the only coal mine being worked at that time. . . south of Virginia. No work was done on the road till 1864, when, as a war measure, the construction was commenced in order to bring this coal via Cheraw to Charleston for the Confederate Navy and 'Blockade Runners'. . . For labor to build the road, the large slave owners in the lower part of South Carolina sent all of their men to work in construction for their board. . . As the war ended, before the grading was done, the work was abandoned. . ."

Under a new act of 1868, the property was reorganized in 1869 as the "Cheraw & Salisbury Railroad Company." As seen in Chapter II, the Walters syndicate had bought 4,000 shares of stock in the company, and purchased from it large blocks of shares in the Northeastern and Cheraw & Darlington companies. For lack of funds and endless debates over the gauge to be used, nothing beyond some grading of the right-of-way was accomplished until 1878. The road would finally, in 1892, be bought at foreclosure by the Cheraw & Darlington.

More typical of the new phase of construction, the Central Railroad of South Carolina was organized, in 1881, to construct a line from Lanes Station on the Northeastern to Sumter on the WC&A line. This cut-across road gave the Northeastern access to some of the traffic from Columbia, and other points in the interior of the state, that normally had been going by other lines to Charleston. Since the WC&A was also involved in this traffic, the corporate solution settled upon was a joint lease of the Central

Railroad of South Carolina by the Northeastern and the WC&A. The new road was delivered to the leasees on April 1, 1882, and service commenced on that date. About the same time construction began on a Wilmington & Weldon feeder line, called the "Scotland Neck branch," which ran from Halifax, just below Weldon, to the little town of Scotland Neck, eventually reached as far as Pamlico Sound. The Scotland Neck branch was opened for service on October 1, 1882. Now that the component roads had been fitted together into a trunk line, the construction of branch roads that gave access to new sources of local business, made good sense.

Low Rates — No Roads

In the course of 1883, Robert Bridgers formulated plans for a much more ambitious construction project — the trunk line, itself, would be shortened. This would be done by constructing a line southward from Wilson, North Carolina, on the Wilmington & Weldon, through Fayetteville and into South Carolina, to join the WC&A line just north of Florence.

Unfortunately for these plans, the latest session of the South Carolina legislature had created a state railroad commission with the power to regulate rates. In September of 1883, the South Carolina Railroad Commission completed and placed in effect a standard tariff of maximum rates on passenger and freight traffic. In spite of eloquent and repeated protests from railroad officials (Robert Bridgers included), local rates were reduced to about the level of prevailing through rates. The WC&A and the Northeastern suffered sharp reductions in revenues from local business. During the ensuing year, the Northeastern carried 5,107 more local passengers for $7,110 less revenue from this source. President Revenel explained:

"This is obviously due to the lower rates of transportation for our local travel, prescribed to us by the Railroad Act, and the erroneous assumption that its reduced rates would be more than compensated for by the greater amount of travel they would create. The above figures are a practical refutation of that idea. It is well understood that in all populous sections, 'low fares make travel,' but in those with a sparse populations, with limited means, the rule does not apply with equal force."

The gentlemen from Baltimore were especially bitter about this encroachment on their property rights. Investment in further construction surely would not be justified if low rate levels could be dictated by state governments. President Bridgers continued to press for the construction project and the differences were aired openly during the annual stockholders meeting in November of 1883. The resolution which finally carried spoke volumes:

"Whereas: In view of the evils which have grown out of the legislation of some of the southern states, whereby stockholders have been practically deprived of the management of their own railroads, and of the dangerous agitation of the same subject in North Carolina:

Resolved: that all consideration of the subject of constructing a branch road from the Wilmington & Weldon road in the direction of Florence be for the present postponed."

This move may have been intended to influence state legislators in North Carolina, but it also smacked largely of "cutting off one's own nose..." Robert Bridgers thought so, and did not trouble to disguise his opinion. He observed impatiently in his report to the WC&A stockholders the following year, "The hope has been indulged that branch feeding roads contributing to the value of this property would be built; but with the law creating a Commission, capitalists seem to fear further investments." Acceptance of state regulatory legislation came hard, but Robert Bridgers would have only a few months to wait before starting his Wilson-to-Florence cut-off. The policy of constructing branch roads was soon resumed.

President Bridgers' frustration over postponement of his "cut-off" project was doubtless softened by satisfaction over another event. On November 16, 1883, just two days before the unhappy Wilmington & Weldon stockholders meeting, the nations' railroads went on "standard time." Bridgers had been one of the leading advocates of standardizing time within zones, serving for many years as president of the Southern Time Convention.

The Triumvirate

Beginning in 1880, Newcomer and Walters took an increasingly active part in managing the Wilmington & Weldon Company. They were soon using it as the corporate vehicle for correlating financial and operating policies for all the Coast Line companies.

The Wilmington & Weldon had a tradition of directors' participation in the management of the company — to a degree that most modern corporate executives would find insufferable — and the gentlemen from Baltimore took full advantage of this tradition. From 1880 on, they were members of every important committee designated by the Board of Directors. In 1880, they and Bridgers served as a committee to arrange a bond issue renewal; in 1881 Newcomer and Walters were designated a committee to arrange a new stock issue. By 1883, they and Bridgers were a permanent executive committee empowered to act in the name of the Board of Directors. These same three men were also the dominant directors in other Coast Line companies; so the policies adopted for the Wilmington & Weldon were readily implemented from Richmond to Charleston. In a very real sense they were providing a rudimentary central management for the Atlantic Coast Line. W. T. Walters was in effect serving as president, Benjamin Newcomer, as secretary-treasurer, and Robert Bridgers, as general manager of the entire system.

In keeping with this trend, was Bridgers' appointment of J. F. Divine as superintendent of all the Coast Line roads south of Weldon. Captain Divine had joined the Wilmington & Weldon in 1866 as master of machinery. He had been superintendent of the W&W since 1872, and of the WC&A since 1877. This was an important step toward merging the operating departments of the several railroads.

Walters and Newcomer achieved firm control of the Wilmington & Weldon during this period. They started buying small lots of its stock in 1880, but their decisive move came the following year. At the stockholders meeting in November 1881, they won approval for a large new stock issue. Ostensibly they took advantage of good market prices in the company's stock to finance construction of the Scotland Neck branch, to pay for Pullman cars, and to redeem some recently-issued 7% gold bonds. The Baltimore brokerage firm of J. Harmaus Fisher & Son bought 2,000 shares, all of which ended eventually in the hands of W. T. Walters and his associates. Their bank, the Safe Deposit & Trust Company, received 4,301 shares to hold against $391,000 surrendered bonds. By the spring of 1884, the Walters group had secured over two-thirds of a total of 20,824 shares in Wilmington & Weldon stock. It was probably no coincidence that the same months saw the Clyde syndicate dissolving, and thousands of Richmond & Danville shares changing hands at premium prices. Profitable sales of Richmond & Danville stock may have provided some of the financial resources that Newcomer and Walters brought to bear on the Wilmington & Weldon. In any case, the Walters group now held a majority interest in the Wilmington & Weldon. The corporation began its career as a holding company.

The Future Unfolds

In the spring of 1884, the Wilmington & Weldon Railroad Company purchased 4,600 shares of Petersburg stock. This was a quiet transaction which accompanied the general dissolution of the Clyde syndicate. The Walters group finally had uncontested control of the "maverick" segment of the Atlantic Coast Line. Fred Scott, Benjamin Newcomer, and (portending the future) W. T. Walters' son, Henry, invaded Petersburg in December of 1884 with proxies for a solid majority of the 13,242 shares outstanding. They elected W. T. Walters, B. F. Newcomer, R. R. Bridgers, F. R. Scott and D. W. Lassiter (the only local man) as directors; and they continued E. T. D. Myers in the presidency. It is noteworthy that President Myers received a salary of $2,000 — quite a reduction from the handsome income which Reuben Ragland had extracted from the company 10 years earlier. Thus ended some fifteen years of struggle over the Petersburg. An unbroken rail line from Richmond to Charleston was finally secured.

Walters, Newcomer, and Bridgers had gone far, by 1884, toward realizing the plan formulated back in 1867. They had secured financial control of the necessary component railroads and had established the Atlantic Coast Line as a through route. With Plant's expansion into Florida, the Line was acquiring a potential beyond their original expectations. It still remained, however, to consolidate the Atlantic Coast Line into an efficient railroad system.

No. 4: *Henry Walters grew up with the Atlantic Coast Line and its predecessors,
assuming leadership from his father, William T. Walters, in 1884,
and remaining active until his death on November 30, 1931.*

Chapter V

Forging A Railroad System — 1884-1898

Henry Walters at the Helm

The years 1884 and 1885 can be regarded as a major watershed in the history of the Atlantic Coast Line. This was true for a number of reasons, but none more important than an action taken by the Wilmington & Weldon Board at a meeting held in Baltimore on June 13, 1884:

> In view of the important position occupied and held by this Company as part of the Atlantic Coast Line, Mr. Newcomer recommended that this Board should authorize its Executive Committee to unite with the other roads constituting the Line in selecting some suitable and well-qualified gentleman for the position of General Manager of the Line, Whereupon it was Resolved that Mr. Henry Walters be nominated as the choice of this Board for the above position, and that any action taken by the Executive Committee looking to his selection for the place and the amount of compensation to be pro-rated among the roads will be fully approved by this Board.

Not surprisingly, the other companies concurred in the decision reached by the Wilmington & Weldon Board, and Henry Walters became General Manager of the Coast Line. Henry Walters, 36 years of age and better known at this point in his life by his nickname "Harry," was the only son of William T. Walters. Young Harry had been carefully groomed for his position as railroad leader and bearer of the Walters name. As a youngster, he had attended Loyola College in Baltimore, and had spent four years, from 1861 to 1865, in Paris with his father, who as an outspoken sympathizer with the Southern cause was virtually a refugee from Baltimore. Harry received his B. A. degree from Georgetown University in 1869 and a B. S. from Lawrence Scientific School, Harvard University, in 1873. His first railroad experience was with the engineering corps assigned to the construction of the Valley Railroad in Virginia in the mid-1870's. He subsequently served for several years in the operating superintendent's office of the Pittsburgh & Connellsville Railroad. Since both these roads were subsidiaries of the Baltimore & Ohio, a firm not noted for its cordial relationships with the Newcomer and Walters group, he apparently secured these positions on his own qualifications and held them on his own merit.

By the time Henry Walters moved into the office building in Wilmington in the summer of 1884, he was a person of considerable dimensions — an educated gentleman in the best Baltimore tradition and a well-trained, practical railroad man. A quiet reserved person, his strength lay in his ability to subject a situation to penetrating analysis and then to state his position with disconcerting directness and economy of words. He restricted his confidence to those whom he knew well and respected. His own no-nonsense manner of tending to business commanded first-rate performances from those who worked with him. All his personal strengths were amplified manyfold by the weighty fact that his father headed the group of controlling stockholders in the Coast Line companies. It is difficult to imagine a more ideal choice of leadership for meshing the several Coast Line roads into an efficient railroad system.

It did not take the new General Manager long to get started on his task. He arrived well-versed in Coast Line affairs. He had personally held stock in the two Wilmington companies since the early '70s, and he had served as a director of the Wilmington & Weldon since June 20, 1882. In the fall of 1883, he had spent several weeks in Wilmington getting acquainted with the operations of the companies centered there. He had struck up a warm friendship with Edwin B. Borden, a Wilmington & Weldon director and businessman from Goldsboro, who gave him good advice on ways to improve the transportation department. In his travels to other points on the Line, he had been particularly impressed with John R. Kenly's work as Superintendent of the Richmond & Petersburg. Thus prepared, he was in a position to take hold immediately.

As the first General Manager of the Line, Henry Walters' task was to integrate all facets of the operation of the eight different railroad companies. The job was largely accomplished within a year and a half. In the process he introduced two especially revolutionary changes: first, he extended the authority of a common executive staff to the two northern-most roads — the Petersburg and the Richmond & Petersburg; second, he organized a transportation department to serve all of the component roads as if they constituted one railroad.

Much progress had already been made toward integrating the operations of the roads south of Weldon, before Henry Walters took command. The Wilmington & Weldon and the WC&A had been run practically as one railroad since 1870, with Robert Bridgers as President of these two companies. Bridgers had been General Manager of the Northeastern, the Central of South Carolina, the Cheraw & Darlington, and the Cheraw & Salisbury Railroads. J.F. Divine had served as Superintendent of all these roads. Now, the Petersburg and the R & P were also placed under the central office in Wilmington. By 1886, all Atlantic Coast Line Railroads were managed by the following Executive Department:

H. Walters,	General Manager
J. F. Divine,	General Superintendent
Sol Haas,	Traffic Manager
T. M. Emerson,	General Freight and Passenger Agent
W. A. Riach,	General Auditor
J. R. Kenly,	Superintendent of Transportation
B. R. Dunn,	Engineer of Roadway

Henry Walters was not responsible for all of these appointments. Captain Divine was inherited from the period of Bridgers' active direction, and his responsibilities as General Superintendent of the Coast Line were now reduced to construction and maintenance of roadway, equipment, and all fixed installations. The position of Superintendent of Transportation was newly created, and Walters chose John Kenly for this key post. Sol Haas was serving nominally as Traffic Manager under the Associated Railways of Virginia and the Carolinas arrangement, which had been in effect with the

Richmond & Danville and the Seaboard Air Line since 1880. Thomas M. Emerson, however, was Henry Walters' personal choice as head of the Freight and Passenger department for the Atlantic Coast Line.

Besides contributing greater unity and efficiency, the centralized management also reduced costs. These savings reached farther than just the general Executive Department. By the time that Henry Walters undertook to organize this end of the Line, his father's group had secured control of the Richmond, Fredericksburg & Potomac. A plan was developed for the R&P, the Petersburg, and the RF&P which eliminated duplication of officials and workers — from the presidencies down to shop foremen and yard forces. By 1886, salary and wage expenditures for these three small railroads were reduced from $54,273 to $34,417, a yearly savings of nearly $20,000. Moreover, this was accomplished without placing the RF&P under the Executive Department. Though controlled by the Walters group, the RF&P was not to be completely absorbed into the Coast Line system south of Richmond.

One continuing obstacle to integrated operations was the separate existence of the several railroad companies, with their differing regulations and internal structures. The two Wilmington companies had been integrated since the Walters group had taken control of them. Most of the other companies however, had independent traditions, with differing lines of management responsibility and widely divergent sets of operating regulations. These differences were troublesome enough in dealing with the Northeastern and the Cheraw & Darlington; but they were especially difficult in the northernmost roads, the Petersburg and the Richmond & Petersburg. After wrestling with this confused set of relationships for three years, Henry Walters convinced his father and Benjamin Newcomer that some basic changes should be made. The solution they adopted was the formation of the "Atlantic Coast Line Association."

All of the presidents and vice presidents of Coast Line companies gathered at the Coast Line office at the Chamber of Commerce in Baltimore on January 26, 1887. Present were William T. Walters, Benjamin Newcomer, Robert Bridgers, Fred R. Scott, president of the Richmond & Petersburg; A. F. Ravenel, president of the Northeastern; John B. Palmer, president of the Petersburg, and Henry Walters.

They signed an agreement organizing their several companies into the Atlantic Coast Line Association. Their stated objective was "to effect an organization by which the interests of each and all [of the companies] may be safely guarded, and their management be made harmonious and economic." They declared that the presidents and vice presidents of this group of companies (namely themselves) would comprise the Board of Directors; and, from their number, elect a president, two vice presidents, and an executive committee for the association. They made W.T. Walters, president; John B. Palmer, 1st vice president; and Henry Walters, 2nd vice president; with Benjamin Newcomer, Robert Bridgers and J. B. Palmer constituting the executive committee.

1887 Corporate Structure of
ATLANTIC COAST LINE ASSOCIATION

Administrative Department

Board of Directors

W. T. Walters	B. F. Newcomer
R.R. Bridgers	H. Walters
J. B. Palmer	F. R. Scott
A. F. Ravenel	

Executive Committee

W. T. Walters, ex. officio	B.F. Newcomer
F.R. Bridgers	J.B. Palmer
President	W. T. Walters
First Vice President	J.B. Palmer
Second Vice President	H.Walters

Executive Department

General Manager	H.Walters
General Superintendents- North & South Carolina Divisions	J.F. Divine
Virginia Division	E.T. D. Myers
General Auditor	W.A. Riach
Traffic Manager	Sol Haas
General Freight and Passenger Agent	T. M. Emerson
Superintendent of Transportation	J. R. Kenly

With the exception of Fred Scott, the same men met again in Baltimore on May 11, 1887, and adopted "Rules for the Government of the Atlantic Coast Line Association and the Companies Forming the Same." These rules provided the needed cohesiveness of organization and uniformity of procedure. They spelled out the duties of the general officers of the Association, and established an executive department comprised of these operating officials: general manager, general auditor, general treasurer, traffic manager, general freight and passenger agent, general superindendent, superintendent of transportation and a purchasing agent. The responsibilities of each member of the executive department and of officials within the railroad companies were fixed with clearly stipulated lines of authority. At their stockholders meetings the following autumn, each of the Coast Line Companies rescinded their old bylaws, accepted the rules of the Association, and adopted new bylaws in agreement with the rules.

It was this basic organization *(see chart on previous page)* that managed the Atlantic Coast Line system until the group of companies were consolidated into one corporation. The Executive Committee, with the President, had general financial and policy responsibility. The lst Vice President (Warren G. Elliott, soon replaced by J. B. Palmer) served as legal counsel and head auditor. As 2nd Vice President, Henry Walters ran the railroad system. The official provisions for this position simply describe the work that he was already doing:

> The Second VicePresident shall, through the General Manager, have the general supervision of the Transportation Department. He shall have the management of the Passenger and Freight Departments, and all rates made by these Departments shall be subject to his approval or to that of the President. He shall have special charge of those relations with competing companies and connecting lines that may be associated with the performance of this duty.
>
> He shall exercise a special supervision over the receipts and disbursements of all lines owned and operated, or controlled by this Association, and make from time to time, such suggestions to the President in connection therewith as may, in his judgment, be to the interest of the Company. He shall direct the adoption of such measures, subject to the approval of the President and Executive Committee, as are calculated, in his opinion, to produce uniformity of system in the departments under his charge, or otherwise advance the interests of the Association or of the companies thereof. The nomination of all the clerks in these departments shall be made by the heads thereof to him; and he shall, with the assent of the President, make any addition to the clerical force that may, from time to time, become necessary, and report the same to the Board. He may also at any time direct the discharge of any officer or clerk in these departments if in his judgment, the interests of the Company require it.
>
> He shall have a general supervision of all construction work upon the railroads owned, operated, or controlled by the Association. He shall also have general charge of the construction of all new lines of railroad in which the Association may be interested. The plans, estimates, and contracts for all such work shall be submitted to the President and Executive Committee for approval.

To this should be added the duties of general manager, which included those of purchasing agent — a position that was not filled by a separate appointment.

Promotions and new appointments altered the structure of the Executive Department from time to time. In 1889, John Kenly was promoted to the specially created post of assistant general manager. That position disappeared again in 1891, when Henry Walters resigned as general manager, and Kenly was appointed in his place. After the Associated Railways of Virginia and the Carolinas agreement lapsed in 1890, and Sol Haas was relegated once more to traffic management for the Richmond & Danville, Thomas Emerson gained the title of traffic manager. Whatever his official title, Henry Walters continued to direct railroad operations, and his trusted aides followed him up the ladder.

Radical Changes in Operation

During the first years in Wilmington, Henry Walters concentrated most of his attention on organizing, with John Kenly, an efficient transportation department. With an apparent sense of accomplishment he reported, in November of 1885:

> During the past year, an entire change in the operation of the Transportation Department and in its rules has been effected, not only over the line of the Wilmington and Weldon Railroad, but over all the roads forming the Atlantic Coast Line; and it gives me great pleasure to state that this change, which has been a very radical one, has been effected in the most satisfactory manner . . . Mr. J. R. Kenly, the superintendent of transportation, especially deserves much credit.

The new plan created three operating divisions of the Atlantic Coast Line: one — the Richmond Division, comprising the lines of the R&P and the Petersburg between Richmond and Weldon; two — the Wilmington Division, which was basically the line of the Wilmington & Weldon Railroad; and three — the Southern Division, which included all of the five-foot gauge lines south and west of Wilmington. Each of these three divisions had its own superintendent. With changes of such magnitude, some resentment was inevitable. Major R. M. Sully, Superintendent of the Richmond Division, had run the Petersburg for years without answering to anyone in Wilmington. He was moved to expressions of outrage one June day in 1886, upon hearing that an engineer on his division had promptly reported an accident to the head office in Wilmington without troubling to inform Major Sully. Actually, no one in Wilmington had been notified either. Major Sully apparently adjusted to the new regime, because he served the Coast Line for many years, but we wonder about that engineer.

The new organization made possible much more efficient and economical use of both operating equipment and personnel. Train crews and motive power were now used on a divisional basis, rather than on the more limited miles of one railroad company. Once the gauge difference was eliminated, passenger and freight cars could be utilized over the entire line. To illustrate the improvement, locomotives and service cars owned by the Richmond & Petersburg were no longer restricted to that company's 27 miles of line, but were now run over the 90-odd miles between Richmond and Weldon. After

1885, the several railroad companies served in effect as legal owners of the rolling stock and motive power needed for operation of the entire Atlantic Coast Line. Each company purchased equipment for its divisional area according to its road's proportion of the traffic mileage.

An important related innovation was standardization of motive power. In 1885, all locomotives were assigned Atlantic Coast Line numbers, beginning with numbers 11 to 34 for the Northeastern locomotives, 51 to 79 for the WC&A, 91, 93 to 122 for the Wilmington & Weldon, 150 to 160 for the Petersburg, and 180 to 186 for the R&P. Walters and Kenly decided that henceforth, motive power would be purchased according to need within each division. In addition, they decided to change from Rogers to Baldwin locomotives — the start of a tradition that would persist on the Coast Line until the end of the steam epoch.

This was quite a policy change: Robert Bridgers had obviously been committed to the Rogers locomotive, possibly for reasons that had little to do with the machinery. For one thing, Morris K. Jesup, an important member of the Walters financial group, had begun his business career with the Rogers Locomotive Works and had retained financial ties with the company. It is an interesting coincidence that Mr. Jesup retired from active business life in 1884. For another thing, old Mathias Baldwin had been a very active abolitionist, and his name an anathema in most areas of the South well before, and long after, the Civil War. The only recent Baldwin locomotive on a Coast Line Road was delivered to the Petersburg in the spring of 1884, before that company was wholly controlled by the Walters group. Perhaps this one Baldwin outshone all the Rogers' models on the line.

In June of 1886, nine new Baldwin locomotives were delivered at a price of $7,525 each. Two were assigned to the Northeastern, two to the WC&A, and five to the Wilmington & Weldon (numbers 123 to 127). They were "American" type engines — 4-4-0's, with 18-inch x 24-inch cylinders, 5-foot drivers, and weighing 90,500 pounds. With minor changes from time to time, this was the Coast Line's standard engine for both passenger and freight trains until 1894.

The changeover from wood to coal began with the Baldwin engines. By March of 1888, most of the older wood-burning locomotives on the line were converted, and all passenger trains and freight trains were being pulled by coal burners.

In his campaign for greater operating efficiency, Henry Walters benefited from a general decision by southern railroad leaders to change all their roads to standard gauge. Talk of such a change, to facilitate car interchange with northern roads, had been in the air for several years. Some southern roads, such as the Kentucky Central in 1881 and the Illinois Central lines south of the Ohio in 1884, had already made the change. On February 2, 1886, Coast Line leaders joined representatives of other broad-gauge southern roads at a meeting in Atlanta, Georgia, where a plan for synchronizing the change of gauge was adopted. The time set for the roads east of the mountains was between 3:30 a.m. and 4:00 p.m, on June 1, 1886. Fortunately, only the Coast Line roads south of Wilmington were involved, and much advance preparation had been made for the anticipated changeover. For example, recently acquired locomotives on the WC&A and the Northeastern were built so that their wheels could be easily reset. Still, a prodigious amount of work had to be done to roadway and equipment in the four months before June 1. On the appointed day, road gangs moved one of the rails, on all of the miles of WC&A and Northeastern tracks, three inches inward and set them with enough spikes to allow traffic to resume. The southern roads had actually adopted a gauge that was not quite standard—the 4-foot, 9-inch gauge of the Pennsylvania Railroad. The final slight change to a 4-foot, 8 ½-inch standard would be made quietly around the turn of the century. The truck transfer pit at Wilmington was no longer needed; all Atlantic Coast Line equipment could roll unimpeded from Columbia or Charleston to Richmond. Moreover, a freight car loaded in Pensacola or Jacksonville could be accepted at Charleston, taken to Richmond and sent ever the RF&P and the Pennsylvania tracks to New York City.

Problems Bring Improvements

Progress is usually accompanied by pain, and the Atlantic Coast Line now encountered some, as the connecting line between railroads in widely different stages of technical advancement. On June 29, 1886, J. R. Kenly wrote to C. S. Gadsen, the superintendent of the Charleston & Savannah and the SF&W, informing him that the Coast Line could accept no freight cars without brakes, for destinations north of Richmond. The reason was that the Pennsylvania and other connections north of Richmond refused to haul freight cars without brakes. Gadsen replied the next day with the observation, "This restriction is inadmissible if we are to handle freights northward this season. None of our roads have provided brakes for their cars, and to insist on this condition immediately on change of gauge will ruin our chances for business." The assistant superintendent of the SF&W, G. W. Haines, reacted in a more lively fashion. His message to the head of the transportation department read:

> Please refuse to receive cars from [ACL] without brakes as they say their northern connections will not receive such cars from them. I have almost despaired of securing any business for ACL, as they seem to make a study to find every possible obstacle to put in the way of the northbound traffic, while the Ocean Steamship Company at Savannah takes the business in any kind of cars we may deliver them and does not throw the slightest impediment in the way of traffic. The ACL may succeed in establishing a good system of conducting traffic, but they will at the same time ruin their patronage.

Indignation accomplished nothing. The Plant railroads had to get freight cars equipped with brakes for destinations north of Richmond.

All things considered, the year 1886 provided plenty of challenges for Henry Walters. Early in February, a fire destroyed the company's offices and warehouses in Wilmington, requiring a major rebuilding program. Operating out of temporary quarters, Walters and his assistants coped successfully not only with the change of gauge project and its attendant traffic and operational problems, but also with two destructive floods, one on the Petersburg and one on the Northeastern, a serious earthquake in the Charleston area which disrupted miles of line, and a disastrous wreck when the trestle over the Santee River collapsed under a passenger train. And all of this while the roads were handling substantial increases in passenger and freight traffic.

Henry Walters' leadership undoubtedly hastened many improvements in the Coast Line system. His father and Benjamin Newcomer were inclined to be conservative, and securing their approval for costly improvements would have been harder for a manager less identified with their financial interests. Henry's influence was especially important during this period of rapid technological changes in railroading. In 1885, he got permission to install block signals on a busy section of track shared with the Seaboard & Roanoke at Weldon. However, even Henry Walters occasionally met resistance from the biggest stockholder. At a board meeting in 1887, for example, he proposed that all passenger equipment be fitted immediately with steel-tired wheels. Passenger trains were on faster schedules, and service had been disrupted six times in the preceding two months by broken wheels. The elder Walters insisted that the new type wheels should be installed only as the older ones wore out. A lively discussion ensued. Newcomer broke the impasse between father and son with a motion that was, probably, deliberately ambiguous: "It is the policy of these companies to use steel-tired wheels hereafter." Undaunted, Henry Walters had steel-tired wheels under all passenger cars before the end of 1888.

Soon after the new General Manager took command, construction of branch lines got underway in earnest. Stockholders meetings in 1884 and 1885 authorized several such projects. During the next eight years, the Wilmington & Weldon added 145.6 miles of feeder lines, bringing service to dozens of additional towns in the North Carolina tidewater area. Among these were the Clinton branch, the Nashville branch, the Scotland Neck branch, and extensions of the Tarboro branch. The Manchester & Augusta Railroad Company was organized in 1886 to provide the WC&A with similar feeders in South Carolina. The area beyond Sumter, S.C., was tapped in 1888, and later crosshatched by roads constructed or acquired by the Manchester & Augusta Company. All of these feeder branches increased traffic volume for the Coast Line, as well as consolidating its hold on territory subject to invasion by the Richmond & Danville and Seaboard Air Line systems. But the most important new lines — in their impact on operations, traffic patterns, and the competitive position of the Coast Line — constructed during this period were the Fayetteville Cutoff and a road to Norfolk, Virginia.

The Cutoff

Robert Bridgers was finally able to get started on construction of his Fayetteville Cutoff early in 1885. The first phase of this project was the construction of a 70-mile Wilmington & Weldon branch line from Contentnea (just below Wilson) to Fayetteville, North Carolina. With President Bridgers, himself, in charge, construction of the road and terminal facilities in Fayetteville proceeded rapidly. Service was opened on this line on October 1, 1886. This Wilson-to-Fayetteville branch line saw only limited service for a number of years, because the portion of the cutoff that was to proceed southward from Fayetteville remained unconstructed. The branch road did, however, receive some business at Fayetteville from the new Cape Fear & Yadkin Valley Railroad.

The second stage in building the cutoff came with the organization of the Florence Railroad Company in November of 1886, and the construction of its 24½ miles of line from Pee Dee (a point north of Florence), South Carolina, to the North Carolina state line. This road was placed in service an October 23, 1888. Simultaneously, a three-mile segment of the cutoff was completed from the state line to Rowlands, North Carolina, giving the Florence Railroad a line which, at least, terminated in an existing town. There still remained a gap of 43 miles from Rowlands to Fayetteville, North Carolina.

Robert Bridgers did not see his project completed. His death on December 10, 1888, closed an epoch in Coast Line history. Even though the Wilmington & Weldon had been for years controlled by majority ownership in Baltimore, so long as Bridgers was President, local stockholders and businessmen had been encouraged to look upon it as their railroad. He had been widely liked and respected among North Carolinians, and with him was lost some of the warmth in the relationship between the Coast Line organization and the people of that state.

Mr. Bridgers' legacy to the Coast Line was immense. The very idea of building a railroad system around the through line from Richmond to Charleston had been his; and many of the improvements in that system had been the product of his lively interest, applying new techniques to the business of railroading. One of his policies, which lasted as a Coast Line tradition, was his insistence on filling top positions with men already in his employ. In many ways Robert Bridgers had established the directions for what the Coast Line was to become in later years.

Construction on the remaining segment of the cutoff was delayed until late in 1890. With Robert Bridgers no longer present to push the project, resistance by local stockholders became more determined. They did not want Wilmington bypassed by the main line. It is also likely that the Coast Line financial leaders were trying to buy the Cape Fear & Yadkin Valley Railroad, the line which paralleled the projected route for several miles south of Fayetteville. If this was the hope, it was not realized in time. Henry Walters explained for the benefit of local stockholders:

The completion and opening of this branch has been postponed as long as possible, The absolute necessity for it. . . will be understood when it is known that the construction of the South Bound Rail Road, between Columbia and Savannah, gives one of our competitors (the Seaboard) a shorter route from Washington to Savannah than our present line.

The remaining miles of the Wilson-to-Florence Cutoff were completed during 1892. On January 1, 1893, the fast through freights and all through passenger trains, with few exceptions, began to move over a route that was shorter by 61 miles. The Atlantic Coast Line was once again the "shortest and quickest route."

John Kenly reorganized the operating department in connection with the opening of the Fayetteville Cutoff. The Richmond Division was extended southward to Rocky Mount, North Carolina, where a large freight yard and new shops were constructed. The through route of the Atlantic Coast Line was divided as follows: Richmond Division - Richmond to Rocky Mount, 122 miles; Wilmington Division - Rocky Mount to Florence, 172 miles; and Charleston Division - Florence to Charleston, 102 miles. The total running distance from Richmond to Charleston was now reduced to 396 miles.

The New Norfolk Line

Second in importance only to the Wilson-to-Florence Cutoff was a new line to Norfolk. Beginning in 1887, a 100-mile road was built from Pinners Point (near Norfolk) to Tarboro. Construction was initiated at the northern end by the Western Branch Railway Company, continued by the Chowan & Southern Railroad Company, and completed by the Norfolk & Carolina Railroad Company. On April 1, 1890, the Coast Line began operation of its own road to Norfolk. The route went from Rocky Mount to Tarboro (a 17-mile Wilmington & Weldon branch), then through Hobgood and Kelford, North Carolina, and Suffolk, Virginia, to Norfolk.

The Norfolk & Carolina Railroad did not greatly alter freight movement on the Coast Line, but it did reflect a rapidly changing relationship with the Seaboard Air Line system. The Atlantic Coast Line's main outlet for heavy freight had long been the Seaboard & Roanoke's road from Weldon to Portsmouth. Here cargo was transferred to steamships for transport to ports in the Northeast and in Europe. As recently as 1885, the Seaboard & Roanoke had entered into a contract as one of the "Railroad and Steamship Companies Composing the Atlantic Coast Line." Negotiated at a meeting at a meeting in Baltimore, October 29, 1885, the agreement joined five steamship companies, plus the Seaboard & Roanoke and the Coast Line railroads into one line for freight passing through Portsmouth. An executive committee and a traffic manager (Sal Haas) were empowered to set all rates. Trace and claim agents, as well as forwarding agents, were provided. A Portsmouth Terminal Fund was established to pay salaries and to reimburse the Seaboard & Roanoke for use of its dock facilities.

The interest of both the Seaboard & Roanoke and the Coast Line were served by this arrangement —the Seaboard & Roanoke got more business, and the Coast Line had access to the port of Norfolk. Such cooperation, however, became more difficult in the late 1880's. Organizations which had stabled their relationships with southern railroads (the Southern Pool and the Associated Railways of Virginia and the Carolinas) were stripped of their effectiveness by the Interstate Commerce Act. In addition, the mushrooming growth of the Richmond & Danville system pushed the Coast Line and the Seaboard Air Line into a competitive scramble for the coastal territory. Each was striving for a complete and independent system of connections. The Norfolk & Carolina held the key to this goal for the Coast Line.

After April 1, 1890, most of the Coast Line's bulk through freight for ocean shipping moved via Rocky Mount and Tarboro to Pinners Point, where the Norfolk & Carolina had its own dock and terminal facilities. Coast Line operating and traffic officials subsequently made their own arrangements with steamship companies for freight interchange at Norfolk, and for through rates to northern ports. The Norfolk & Carolina therefore became one of the busiest segments of the Atlantic Coast Line.

Atlantic Coast Despatch Adds Speed to Through Freight

The Coast Line, along with other southern railroads, had to overcome serious obstacles in the 1880's in order to develop a large volume through freight business. They shared a basic disadvantage in that the Southeast's main exports, cotton and forest products, did not normally require fast delivery. Since they could be carried cheaper by steamship, these commodities normally moved by rail only to the nearest port. Stimulation of other big export industries was essential. Added to that, there were technical impediments within the railroad industry itself. For the Coast Line, one of these was overcome by the gauge change, which eliminated the expensive and time consuming reloading of through freight at Wilmington. There still remained, however, the very large problem of freight car interchange.

Railroads in the 1880's were not yet exchanging their cars in large numbers over great distances. One of the best ways for a railroad to lose its supply of freight cars was to send them over foreign roads to far-removed destinations. "Per diem" demurrage had not been adopted, so other railroads often used the cars as needed, recorded the mileage payments they owed in a very casual manner, and returned them in their own good time. The cooperative freight lines that became so numerous during the 1870s (the Green Line, for example) were the prevailing solution to this problem. By contributing cars to such a "line," and accepting the management of a common staff of officials, a group of railroads could exchange long-haul freight business. It was an adaptation of the cooperative freight line arrangement — the Atlantic Coast Despatch — that enabled the Atlantic Coast Line to expand its freight traffic enormously.

On August 1, 1887, the Wilmington & Weldon Railroad Company, the Pennsylvania Railroad Company and the Seaboard & Roanoke Railroad Company, signed a contract establishing a through freight line called the Atlantic Coast Despatch. The Pennsylvania Railroad was to furnish 30 freight cars, and the lines south of Portsmouth and Richmond were to furnish 70 cars. These were to be set aside and to be marked "Atlantic Coast Dispatch." (Interestingly, the spelling was changed to "Despatch" before the cars were marked.) Three-fourths of a cent per mile was to be paid by each company using another company's car. This system of rates agreed upon was differentially higher, for all classes of freight, than those set by the Coast Line railroads for its water connections to New York, Boston and Providence. The contract gave the Pennsylvania Railroad and the Coast Line roads a common interest in prompt return of empty cars, and in the maintenance of fast freight schedules.

Improved speed had a widespread impact. It stimulated a spectacular expansion of vegetable and fruit growing along the southern seaboard and an equally marked expansion of the Coast Line's traffic in these products. Even before the Civil War the coastal area from Norfolk southward had become a "winter garden" for the northeastern states. The soil and the climate were ideal for the growing of early vegetables. As noted in an earlier chapter, Augustus Pope had begun to promote this industry for the benefit of Wilmington & Weldon business in the early '70s. The normal pattern for this traffic had been shipment from Wilmington and other points on the Wilmington & Weldon to Weldon, forwarding over the Seaboard & Roanoke to Portsmouth, and then shipment by water to the northern cities. The movement began in late March or early April and continued in large quantities through June. The change of gauge and the development of the Plant System greatly improved the time frame and, thereby, the volume of such traffic. Fast shipment of fresh produce and fruit from South Carolina, Georgia and even Florida was now physically possible. The Atlantic Coast Despatch contract provided the organization needed for the job.

The Atlantic Coast Despatch service was a tremendous success. A year after its inception, Henry Walters remarked, "The Atlantic Coast Despatch Line has developed a north bound movement of early vegetables and fruits ... beyond the expectations of the most sanguine." Traffic volume stimulated by the Despatch arrangement quickly made the original provision for 100 cars ridiculously inadequate. On December 24, 1888, Thomas Emerson wired Henry Walters from Wilmington, "Forty-three Atlantic Coast Despatch cars from the south tonight. If we can get cars I think my prediction of 50 per day will be verified. Pennsylvania Road has agreed to send 200 of their empties." The Wilmington & Weldon shops could not keep up with the demand for new freight cars, and in 1889, 300 cars were ordered from a Baltimore concern. Virtually overnight the fresh vegetable business became a major source of revenue for the Coast Line.

Refrigeration Heats up Perishables Business

The standard Atlantic Coast Despatch cars were box cars with ventilating louvers for carrying lettuce, celery, potatoes and other fresh garden vegetables. Because of the fast time made by the new freight service, these cars were also used to transport strawberries to Washington and Baltimore. For the two-day run to New York City, however, the ventilated cars could not maintain strawberries in suitable condition. Refrigeration was necessary. The berry business in North Carolina had developed far beyond the point where it could be served by Augustus Pope's little icebox wagons. By the mid-1880s practical refrigerator cars had been developed with insulated bulkheads and floors, and icebunkers at the ends. Their use expanded tremendously during the last decade of the century as a service related to the Atlantic Coast Despatch.

It took some time to work out the proper arrangement for providing refrigerator cars. Initially a few such cars were built and added to the rolling stock of the railroad companies. The Northeastern, with its territory farthest removed from northern markets, had three refrigerator cars as early as 1885. But this approach was too expensive. The strawberry traffic demanded a large number of cars during a brief period of three or four weeks each spring. No single railroad system could make such a heavy investment in specialized equipment which would remain idle during most of the year.

Henry Plant adopted a solution that he regarded as ideal. His Southern Express Company purchased a number of refrigerator cars designed to be included in passenger trains. These offered some definite advantages — they were available to different railroads as needed for seasonal traffic in perishables, and they gave shippers fastest possible delivery time. They also meant a new source of profit for the Express Company, and additional business for the Plant Railroad system. Florida growers of berries and truck crops needed both refrigeration and fast delivery to gain access to national markets. The Atlantic Coast Line and the Pennsylvania Railroad did not share Henry Plant's understandable enthusiasm for express refrigerator cars. They received relatively little revenues from this type of business. The heavy cars made it difficult for passenger trains to maintain their schedules, and express service for perishables tended to depress the rates for regular freight handling of this business. The Atlantic Coast Line, and railroad companies in general, greatly preferred another type of service that evolved about the same time — refrigerator car companies.

The first of these to be used extensively by the Coast Line was the California Fruit Transport Company, also known as the California Fruit Growers Express. On the basis of contract agreements, these companies furnished the railroad with a stipulated number of refrigerator cars at a given time. They serviced these cars with ice, receiving in return a fixed payment for each car serviced ($5.00 per car at one point) and mileage payments for the use of the car. These cars were hauled in freight trains, the railroad companies setting their own rates and collecting directly from the shipper.

The movement of the strawberry crop from North Carolina during 1897 is quite revealing of the trends in handling this business. The California Fruit Transport Company readied an icing station at South Rocky Mount where they could ice twenty cars at a time. At Goldsboro, and other way stations on the Wilmington & Weldon Road, small quantities of berries were arriving on the loading platforms by April 13. Shipments reached top volume during the last week of April, but practically halted by the middle of May. Nearly 130,000 crates of strawberries were shipped during these four weeks, as compared to 11,000 crates the previous year. Only 4% of the crop was transported in ordinary ventilated box cars, these going presumably to relatively near points like Richmond and Washington. During the first week or so of the season, most of the berries were carried by Southern Express Company cars, the shippers paying premium rates for fast delivery of early berries. The use of express shipment then tapered off, so that only about 25% of the total crop was transported in this way (a lower proportion than the previous year). More than 70% of the crop moved in refrigerator cars in regular freight trains. Encouraged by good service and top prices for their crop, North Carolina growers shipped twice as many berries the following year — 856 carloads. This business would stabilize for the Coast Line at about 1100 cars per year by the turn of the century. For the Atlantic Coast Line and eastern North Carolina, the expansion of refrigerator car service and of the strawberry industry were virtually one development.

Refrigerator car service also greatly extended the areas from which perishables were shipped. Truck crops from the Charleston area, watermelons from South Carolina, Georgia and Florida, peaches from Georgia and Florida, pineapples from the West Indies, and truck crops and strawberries from Florida became important items in Coast Line freight business during the 1890's. By 1898, a very large portion of the Florida perishables business was being delivered to Charleston by the Plant Railway System. The refrigerator cars belonged to Plant's Southern Express Company, but had to be hauled northward in Atlantic Coast Line passenger trains. The Southern Railway Company was being similarly imposed upon by Plant deliveries of express cars to the Florida Central and Peninsular Railroad. Early in 1899, officials of the Pennsylvania Railroad Company, the Southern, and the Atlantic Coast Line met in Washington and agreed that they would no longer haul express refrigerator cars in their passenger trains. Henry Plant was not pleased. Particularly he was not pleased with Atlantic Coast Line leaders whom, as he saw it, should have opposed this move as detrimental to "our joint railroad interests." Henry Walters expressed his regret that he was not able to agree with this viewpoint, and the Pennsylvania, the Southern, and the Atlantic Coast Line all stood firm. Refrigerator car service would, henceforth, be restricted to freight trains.

Freight Takes the Lead

With the Atlantic Coast Despatch and related arrangements for transporting perishables, the Atlantic Coast Line came of age as a freight carrier. Beginning in the fall of each year with the shipment of citrus fruits from Florida, the traffic in food stuffs built to a crescendo by the spring, tapered off and ended by late June. As its territory grew in wealth, so did the volume of southbound general merchandise shipments.

The Virginia segments of the Atlantic Coast Line received the full impact of this traffic expansion. Two years after the institution of the Atlantic Coast Despatch, the Petersburg Railroad was carrying twice as many ton-miles of through freight and receiving 56.2% more revenue from this source. The facilities of the little Richmond & Petersburg were literally overwhelmed by the increase in traffic. A serious bottleneck developed at Richmond where, at one point in 1889, hundreds of cars accumulated in the Manchester yards. In 1890, the James River connecting line was built, making it possible to transfer cars directly to the Richmond, Fredricksburg & Potomac outside of Richmond. During the same year, the entire length of the Richmond & Petersburg line was double tracked.

The unprecedented volume of through-freight business had other effects on the Atlantic Coast Line. Not only did it hasten completion of the Fayetteville Cutoff and the new facilities at South Rocky Mount, but it also necessitated heavier rail. The last segments of the Fayetteville Cutoff were constructed with 70-pound steel rails, and by 1890 repairs on other parts of the trunk line were being made with rails of the same weight. The entire main line from Richmond to Florence was 70-pound rail by the autumn of 1896.

The heavier rail, of course, was required by heavier and faster trains. The 16 and 17-inch cylinder locomotives in use in 1884 had all they could do to pull 15 loaded 10-ton cars. The 18-inch Baldwins were a great improvement; they hauled as many as 35 20-ton box cars. President A.F. Ravenel of the Northeastern complained in 1889 that there were not enough of these locomotives available, and that too many of the Despatch trains northbound from Charleston had to be double-sectioned with the lighter engines. The heaviest motive power available had to be concentrated on the divisions northward from Florence, because the through-freight trains grew in length as they moved toward Richmond or Norfolk.

In December of 1893, Walters and Kenly began shifting to still heavier equipment. They ordered from the Baldwin works four Mogul engines costing $9,000 each, which went into service the following March. By the standards of the time, the Moguls were big locomotives with 19-inch x 24-inch cylinders, six 62-inch drivers and a total weight of 123,300 pounds. They pulled trains numbering from 40 to 50 cars, and now some of these freight cars were of 30-ton capacity. An order for 200 such cars, at $516 each, was placed with the Pullman Company in 1894. With these and other improvements in equipment, the vastly increased volume of freight was handled with increasing efficiency.

Beginning in 1887, the Atlantic Coast Line made a major leap into the modern, long-haul, fast-freight business over the next 10 years. The accomplishment was symbolized by the growth of hundreds of ventilated box cars bearing the insignia "Atlantic Coast Despatch."

Coast Line Passenger Service - Best Way to Florida

Improvements in passenger service kept pace with the advances in freight handling. New equipment, faster schedules, and smoother roadways enabled Tom Emerson, General Freight and Passenger Agent, to promote the Coast Line as the best way to travel to Florida.

One of Henry Walters' earliest innovations was to provide good accommodations at important passenger stops. By the end of 1886, the Coast Line had a new hotel and restaurant at Weldon, plus new restaurants at Wilmington and Florence. These were managed with an eye to convincing the public that the Coast Line represented the "ultimate in traveling comfort."

Certainly the Coast Line's claim to excellence as a passenger carrier was strengthened by the *New York & Florida Special*. During the fall of 1887, 12 cars designed to form two integral trains were constructed, under the existing contract with the Pullman Company, for service on the Atlantic Coast Line and the Plant System. The *New York & Florida Special* was introduced on January 9, 1888. It featured one of the earliest electrically-lighted, solid vestibule trains in the country — the first to be operated in the South. Its initial run caused quite a stir. Witness the following accounts detailed in the *Jacksonville News-Herald*:

NEW YORK, Jan. 9, 1888. — When the time arrived for the departure of the new vestibule train to Florida this morning, a large crowd of spectators gathered around the train and discussed its merits.

It was one of the finest equipped trains that has ever left here for the South, and the dining service is said to rival Delmonicos.

The train consisted of six cars and had on board seventy passengers, all of whom seemed delighted at the prospects of a pleasant journey.

At 9:30 a.m. Ralph Myercks, conductor, pulled the bell cord and amid many parting farewells from the bystanders, it rapidly pulled out. Mr. Myercks and his train officials resembled Prussian officers, so gaudy and gorgeous were their uniforms . . .

Advices will be sent from different points on their way down, and the long-looked for vestibule train to Florida will reach Jacksonville at noon tomorrow.

WASHINGTON, Jan. 9, 1888. — The great Flyer, the special vestibule train, passed through here on time at 3:30 o'clock this afternoon. Good judges among railroad men say that it is one of the finest trains ever seen in the Washington depot . . . It left here on time and will reach Savannah early in the morning and Jacksonville about noon. Of the seventy passengers there is not one who will give up his trip and sell his berth to any one from here.

The train consists of four sleepers, a dining car, a combination car and a baggage car. The engine No. 67 that pulled this train was one of several built to order, for this express work, and is a magnificent piece of railroad machinery. The drivers are 6 feet 2 inches in diameter and all the balance of the machinery is on the same grand scale. The maker rode all the way from Ashley Junction in the cab to see that his pet machine worked all right. [Because of the time reference, the reporter inadvertently gives the impression that this one engine pulled the train all the way from New York or Washington to Jacksonville. The reference to Ashley Junction helps to clarify. This was apparently SF&W engine No. 67, a Rhode Island 4-4-0 with 17-inch x 24-inch cylinders and 63-inch drivers, taking the train from Charleston to Jacksonville; later ACL No. 518.] The baggage car is large and fine and finished in oiled woods . . . and next to this is the combination car (the drawing room car). Entering from the front door one passes through a narrow passageway, on each side of which are located the linen closets. Just beyond this are 12 berths or sections. The beauty of the work and finish is what attracts the attention of the beholder at first. The seats are elegantly upholstered in pale blue and in fine style. The sides are finished in Spanish mahogany which gives a very rich setting. The berths and the outsides are finished in birds'-eye maple burnished to the smoothness of glass, which reflects all objects like a plate mirror. The windows are double of fine French glass, and between them is set long, narrow bevel edged plate glass mirrors. The lambrequins over them match the plush of the seats and add a great deal to the appearance. Overhead are exquisite chandeliers with delicate opaque glass globes, and also the pear shaped globes of the incandescent light. The roof of the car inside is a "raised deck" ceiling beautifully carved and decorated in "Queen Anne" style in a most elegant and fanciful way. The ventilators are embossed cut glass of the same general design as the other fittings. At the end of the apartment a door leads into the smoking room through a narrow short passage. At the end of the smoking room is a neat and compact buffet for wine, etc. The smoking room is fitted to match the other portions of the car, save the chairs, lounge, etc., are of light cane manufacture and the plush is cherry and the window lambrequins the same. At the opposite end, an either side of the entrance, are book cases filled with the latest publications, also a writing desk well stocked. Just on further, a recess is made so parties of four or five can sit together in privacy, if desired.

Passing out of this car into the passage way between the cars, one would suppose he would have stepped into an observation platform or room. On each platform are light folding doors on each side. These have large French glass panels, with beveled edges, and fold back so as to be entirely out of the way when open. When shut, a large brass guard bar holds them fast and secure which would lead one to think that it would be a good scheme to put something of the kind on trains in Texas and keep the "stand and deliver" intruder out of the car. Those cars all have the patent platform coupler and improved brakes and levers. The overhoods are extended and are joined by a strong compressed lever, as also the sides by rubber diaphragms strengthened by a metal plate of the same shape. These rubber folds or diaphragms close tight together and adjust themselves to the curves and twists of the cars. They prevent dust from entering and then, by taking up all lost motion, prevent much of the oscillation usual to railroad cars, adding much to their steadiness and comfort. The bottom is covered with rubber mats, making the passageway between the cars practically a hallway, close and secure from rain, dust or wind. Another thing is claimed for this system and that is that the cars thus equipped cannot possibly telescope, as they are held back, bottom and top.

The next car is the dining room, a very important adjunct to the train. First come the closets, then the ice chests with the capacity of one ton of ice and plenty of room for all the supplies; then the dining room proper with seats for thirty to forty people. Everything is arranged with the greatest nicety, and a party of four or eight can dine in strict privacy or en famille. Beyond the tables is a partition across leaving a small doorway, behind which is the kitchen range, etc., all occupying but little space and entirely out of the way of passengers. It is well ventilated so that no odor of the cooking finds its way into other portions of the car, something very essential. The entire car is handsomely fitted up in Nile-green silk plush and the decorations correspond with the others.

A description of one of the sleepers will suffice for all. First come the linen closets, next two toilet rooms for the ladies, then a drawing room section. These are exquisitely fitted up, and have space for three or four people. The windows and pier glass are of heavy French plate glass, while in all the furnishings and decorations good taste is exercised. Beyond this are the sections proper, some of which may be made private by hanging heavy curtains. At the rear end of the car is another drawing room section and two open wash stands. The cars throughout are finished in the most elegant manner possible, and nothing that can be added to the comfort and pleasure of the passenger is omitted.

The lighting of the train is done by a very simple invention of the Pullman Company. In the baggage room is placed a small dynamo of 85 volt power. A rubber belt is connected with the axle wheel of the car, and all the power necessary to run the machine is economically secured. These are 120 lights in the train, 20 in each car. Each car has 32 cells of electrical insulators, in which is stored the surplus of electricity when the dynamo is running. Enough is stored in this way to run the lights four hours if necessary, when the dynamo is not running for any cause. The machine runs at the rate of 1050 revolutions per minute, and easily supplies all the light necessary. The lights (Edison incandescent) are of 60-watt lens, and are equal to 16 candle power. These give a brilliant light. In the dining room the lights are especially noticeable for their soft diffusive radiance. They are all enclosed globes, called "light condensers," a new patent, and give a mellow clean light that is very pleasing.

Every car has its heater, but the steam is secured from the engine. A main pipe, 1½ inches in diameter runs through the length of the train, underneath, through which the steam is forced. Underneath each car is a sort of stove, 2 ½ inches in diameter, which is filled with salt water. This heats the car well and thoroughly, and by means of valves inside, the porter can control it to a nicety. Salt water is used as it will not freeze when exposed to colder weather than Florida's own sunshiny climate. There are many details that add to the perfectness of this car, like enunciators, callwires, etc. . . . . .

The railroad officials aboard are Major T. H. Wisks, Pullman Palace Car Co., Chicago, Ill.; James Martin, Division Superintendent, Pullman Palace Car Co., Philadelphia, Pa.; T. M. Emerson, G.P.A., ACL RR Co.; R. H. Myerks, Conductor of Dining Cars; Geo. E. Burroughs, Pullman Conductor, who had charge of the train all the way through; D. A. Duncan, Assistant Division Steward; Geo. M. Pullman and B. C. Billings, General Eastern Superintendent, The Pullman Palace Car Co., left the train at Philadelphia; W. J. Craig, Superintendent C & S R.R., boarded the train at Charleston.

All of the passengers seemed greatly pleased with their accomodations and spoke highly of the attention they had received.

It was a revelation in Florida travel, they said, and certainly would do much good in the way of attracting the better class of tourist to travel this way.

The *New York & Florida Special* became a regular feature of the Florida tourist season. Service began early in January each year and ended about mid-April. On its first regular schedule, it departed New York at 9:45 a.m., and arrived at Jacksonville at 3:45 p.m. the following day — 1,074 miles in 30 hours.

It began as a tri-weekly service leaving New York Monday, Wednesday, and Friday mornings; the pressure of business soon increased this to five trips per week until March 10, 1888. The service expanded to meet demand in following years. In 1891 the southbound *Special* was scheduled daily (except Sunday) from late January until mid-March, and the northbound, daily from mid-March until early April, tapering off to tri-weekly again until the end of the season on April 20.

The *New York & Florida Special* was designed to appeal to the "carriage trade," and it carried many celebrities of the period, such as Henry M. Flagler, Chauncey M. De Pew, and John D. Rockefeller, southward for their Florida vacations.

In 1888, Flagler opened his splendid Ponce de Leon Hotel at St. Augustine, and in January of the following year, the bridge spanning the St. Johns River at Jacksonville was completed, permitting the *New York & Florida Special* to extend its run to St. Augustine. After construction of the Florida East Coast Railway southward and Flagler's development of tourist accommodations in Miami, the *Special's* service was extended to both Miami and Tampa.

The *New York & Florida Special* brought its share of headaches for Coast Line executives. Its very popularity soon pointed up the lack of flexibility that would plague railroads featuring special unit trains. Adding an extra car meant disrupting the unity of design, overloading the diner, and slowing the train below scheduled speed. Expanding the number of runs was a better way of meeting the demand for reservations at peak season; but the Pullman Company could not always provide extra equipment of the quality expected by *New York & Florida Special* patrons. Also, demand fluctuated sharply with the vagaries of the weather and other unpredictable events. A yellow fever epidemic in the Southeast in 1889, the financial panic of 1893, and unusually cold Florida winters in 1895 and 1897, made these poor years for tourist travel.

The *New York & Florida Special* was well worth the trouble, both in direct profits and in dramatizing the Coast Line's service between Florida and the Northeast; and the rest of the passenger service was not far behind. In 1888 one could board the fast mail train No. 27 departing the Jersey City terminal at 4:45 A.M. and be in Jacksonville by noon the following day, a scheduled time of only 31¼ hours.

Tourism Encourages Improvements

By this time Florida offered new attractions. The tourist traveler might elect to take a short trip down the Jacksonville, St. Augustine & Halifax River Railway to St. Augustine and spend some time at Henry Flagler's luxurious Ponce de Leon Hotel. If he had taken the Pullman buffet sleeping car on train No. 23 from New York, the traveler might go straight through to Tampa over the Jacksonville, Tampa & Key West and the

South Florida railroads. There he might elect to board the steamer *Mascotte* of the Plant Steamship Line for one of its bi-weekly trips to Havana. The vacationer to Florida after January, 1891, would find at his disposal Henry Plant's magnificent Moorish edifice, the Tampa Bay Hotel, with "parlor and music, and dining halls 100 feet in length, and rich in every appointment; apartments en suite — 20 of them, with every comfort of a private mansion, baths, electric lights, and luxury everywhere . . . a veritable palace and home!" Moreover, the Plant Steamship Company, with the addition of the Steamer *Olivette*, now afforded tri-weekly trips to Cuba, and an occasional excursion to Jamaica.

The Atlantic Coast Line was of course vitally interested in all of this development of Florida, and particularly in Henry Plant's projects. As a matter of fact, the Wilmington & Weldon and WC&A railroad companies made payments described as "contributions towards the Plant Steamship Line" to the Plant Investment Company in 1888. On a more prosaic level, the transportation departments of the Coast Line and the Plant System maintained an effective working relationship, Occasionally John Kenly and his Plant System counterpart would reach an impasse over scheduling, in which case Henry Walters or Newcomer would take up the matter with Henry Haines or Plant himself, and a solution would soon be reached.

Cooperation between Coast Line and Plant System operating officials was further stimulated in the early 1890s by competition from the Seaboard Air Line's new road to Jacksonville. The most exciting aspect of this competition was a series of record speed runs, one of which took place in 1894. As later recounted in the Wilmington *Morning Star:*

> The occasion was a trip of Florida Knights of Pythias to Washington for their national conclave. When they requested a special train from Jacksonville, officials of the Plant System and the Atlantic Coast Line saw an opportunity for a record. Preparations were surrounded with secrecy, as the railroad men were anxious to keep news of the proposed run from a combination of competing railroads, which had a record of 19 hours, 30 minutes.

> The train was composed of one combination car, one coach, and two sleepers, with a combined weight of 242,300 pounds unloaded. The five locomotives assigned to handle it over the five different railroads between Jacksonville and Richmond were similar in weight and construction. The special left Jacksonville at 4:20 p.m. Eastern time, August 26, 1894. In its first lap, it made its fastest time — near Savannah it went 75 miles per hour for at least one mile. It arrived in Washington at 8:09 a.m., August 27 . . .

> The distance covered was 780.5 miles. In spite of its taking 2 hours and 59 minutes to cover the 119 miles between Richmond and Washington, the special arrived in Washington 15 hours, 49 minutes after it left Jacksonville (an average speed of 49-plus miles per hour for the entire trip, and an average of 51-plus miles per hour for the Jacksonville to Richmond run).

This was a remarkable record, especially since the locomotives used on the Coast Line divisions were the relatively light 4-4-0 Americans. Such speed was possible, however, only with a special, four-car train.

The very success of the record run pointed up a need which Walters and Kenly had recognized for some time — the Coast Line required locomotives that could pull ten-car passenger trains at constant high speeds.

After months of study and conferences with Baldwin engineers, they settled on specifications for a new standard model. In December, 1894, the first Atlantics were delivered to the Coast Line. The name "Atlantic" honored the ACL as the first railroad to use this wheel arrangement. Two of these engines were placed on the Wilmington & Weldon as Nos. 151 and 152. They were 4-4-2's, with 6-foot drivers, 19-inch x 24-inch cylinders, and a total weight of 125,800 pounds. The new engines performed very well indeed, permitting faster schedules and greater operating economy.

Reflecting all the improvements in passenger service, a new edition of the *New York & Florida Special* was placed in service in March of 1898. The new cars were larger and even more elegant than the initial ones, and the regular schedule for the run was reduced to less than 28 hours.

A new general contract with the Pullman Company was negotiated by Henry Walters in a series of conferences with representatives of the Plant System, the Pennsylvania Railroad Company and the Pullman Company in November, 1897. The conferences were held in the New York offices of R. G. Erwin, vice president of the Plant Investment Company. The new contract, which became effective December 1, 1897, continued the same basic arrangements for securing Pullman equipment for another 15 years. It is notable that the Atlantic Coast Line Sleeping Car Association now had 38 sleeping cars — about three times the number on the line in 1882.

The Atlantic Coast Line's claim to pre-eminence in service to Florida was solidified by the movement of troops and military equipment during the war with Spain. President McKinley chose to travel by Coast Line, in a specially outfitted Pullman car, to inspect military camps in Florida in September of 1898. Henry Walters had every reason to be proud of his railroad system.

Henry Walters — Lifelong Leader

Over the course of the 1890's, Henry Walters became the central figure in Coast Line affairs. He was chosen President of the Atlantic Coast Line Association when his father resigned that post in 1893. With his father's death, on November 22, 1894, Henry became the major stockholder, sharing responsibility for financial and general policy decisions with Benjamin Newcomer.

He was constantly on the move, shuttling between the offices at Wilmington, Richmond, 16 Chamber of Commerce in Baltimore, and, with ever greater frequency, at

204 Broadway in New York City. Beginning in the summer of 1896, Henry Walters made New York his main headquarters, first in a suite at the Hoffman House and later at a private address, No 13 West 51st Street.

Henry Walters' entry into New York financial circles meant that Coast Line policies were affected, more than ever before, by changes in national economic and political climates, perhaps too much at times. For instance, William Jennings Bryan's "silver crusade" campaign for the presidency spread consternation in Wall Street, which Walters shared. He wrote John Kenly on September 9, 1896:

> We cannot contemplate the expenditure of any money for engines, rails, cars, or any other unusual expenditure until after . . . the election.
>
> I have a friend in New York who had a large interest in Street Railways in the Argentine Republic before they adopted a silver basis. Gold there has reached a premium of 200 per cent . . . As a result, his stock, which was paying him fair dividends, has been wiped out . . . the property is bankrupt . . . It would be very foolish on our part to make any expenditure until we know the result of the election.

Fortunately for the railroad, McKinley won the election and John Kenly received authorization to purchase new equipment for the Atlantic Coast Line.

For the rest of his life, Henry Walters would maintain an active interest in operations of his railroad system, never completely losing his identity as "first General Manager of the Line." His attitude toward the railroad was fiercely protective. Persons responsible for malicious damage, such as derailments, were pursued relentlessly often at considerable cost in fees for Pinkerton agents. There was little room for doubt that anyone tampering with Coast Line property, or endangering the safety of its passengers, would be brought to account. There is record of only one instance, dating from his early years as General Manager, when Walters was frustrated in this policy:

> Late one Saturday night, May 7, 1887, a large band of masked men accosted the engineer of work-train Locomotive No. 99, as he was retiring to the shanty car at Rocky Mount, North Carolina. They allegedly forced him, with threats of death if he did not comply, to man his engine and couple on two flat cars. With rain soaking the black-hooded passengers all the way, the engineer was compelled to run without whistle signals or lights through the "Y-junction" at Rocky Mount, down to Tarboro. There more night riders clambered aboard. The next stop was Williamston, where the mob removed from jail a Negro man accused of attempting to rape a white girl. The train then backed down to Tarboro. From a tree close to the fairgrounds, the Negro was hanged. The engineer was permitted to return (still without lights or whistle signals) to Rocky Mount, where the remnants of the mob released him and his train.

Henry Walters was furious. "The object which prompted this mob is of course a matter with which we have nothing to do, but our duty to ourselves and to the public requires some action on our part. It is merely a piece of good luck that we had not an extra train or delayed train running upon our main line or on the Tarboro Branch, in which event loss of life and great damage might have ensued." He directed John Kenly to investigate immediately. All personnel who had any knowledge of the affair, as well as the engineer of No. 99, were questioned at great length the very next day. Being a newcomer to the area, the engineer had recognized no one; he was absolved of responsibility and allowed to resume his duties. Henry Walters reluctantly accepted the advice of a Tarboro attorney and a local Wilmington & Weldon director, that the Railroad Company should allow the whole unfortunate affair to "pass into oblivion as soon as possible."

A picture of Henry Walters as implacable defender of his railroad must be balanced by recognition of his loyalty and consideration for his close subordinates. For Emerson and Kenly, especially, his regard was expressed in many ways, such as anniversary gifts for their wives, use of his private car in family emergencies, and insistence on long recuperative vacations when they were ill. Yet he wrote, in all seriousness, to Emerson one day demanding a refund of $9.60; the freight department had overcharged him for a personal shipment over a foreign road.

Henry Walters accomplished a great deal in the first 14 years of his leadership. In 1884, he had assumed responsibility for a motley aggregation of railroads with 734 miles of line, an optimistic $15,458,828 in assets and $943,244 in net revenues. By the time corporate consolidation began, in 1898, he was directing the operations of a railroad system with 1,635 miles of road, assets listed conservatively at $34,948,181 and net revenues of $2,306,939. Although he was not personally responsible for all the additional miles of road constructed or purchased, most of the expansion was financed out of increased earnings or by funded debt based on the increasing value of the property. The Atlantic Coast Line was meshed by Henry Walters into an efficient, up-to-date railroad system before it was reorganized into the Atlantic Coast Line Railroad Company.

Chapter VI

Fast-Track Finances — 1884-1900

Taking Stock in Other Railroads

During the years when Henry Walters was building the Atlantic Coast Line into an effective railroad system, equally important progress was made on another front. Benjamin Newcomer, W. T. Walters, and in the later stages, Henry Walters himself, increased their financial control of the several railroad companies; and finally in 1900, merged them into one corporation. They began by using the Wilmington & Weldon Railroad Company as a holding company, a move which considerably enhanced their financial leverage.

There were good reasons for their choice of the Wilmington & Weldon as the controlling corporation. Its railroad was the largest and most profitable, and its assets were the greatest of any company in the Coast Line System. Moreover, its charter exempted it perpetually from taxation. Though stocks in other companies were not explicitly mentioned, it also granted broad rights to hold railroad-related properties.

As mentioned earlier, Walters' group of associates had achieved firm control of the Wilmington & Weldon by the spring of 1884. Of the 20,824 shares outstanding in July 1884, W. T. Walters and his associates held over 12,000. W. T. Walters himself held 2,280, Benjamin Newcomer - 1,101, and the Jenkins family - over 1,300 shares. But the real key to their control was the block of over 4,000 shares held by their bank, The Safe Deposit and Trust Company of Baltimore. The bank had received these in trust, in exchange for an issue of bonds recalled in January of 1882. The Wilmington & Weldon's first purchase as a holding company was made in June of 1884, when it acquired a controlling block of shares in the Petersburg Railroad Company.

The next major step in the centralizing process was the lease of the Wilmington, Columbia & Augusta to the Wilmington & Weldon Company. One reason for this move was to avoid the conflict of interests between the two Wilmington companies that construction of the Wilson-to-Florence Cutoff would create. A large segment of the cutoff would be a branch of the Wilmington & Weldon; and when the cutoff became the through-route, 110 miles of the Wilmington, Columbia & Augusta would no longer participate in through business.

A special meeting of Wilmington, Columbia & Augusta stockholders was held on April 16, 1885, at Barnum's Hotel in Baltimore, a location not chosen to eliminate small, local Wilmington stockholders, but to be convenient to the majority stockholders, who were from Baltimore and New York. Walters and Newcomer were particularly solicitous of WC&A stockholder interest, because some of their most powerful financial associates were these shareholders. After considerable discussion of possibilities at this and a subsequent board of directors meeting on April 23, the decision was made to lease the WC&A to the Wilmington & Weldon. Under the terms of the lease, the Wilmington & Weldon Railroad Company would hold the property of the WC&A for 99 years. It would also pay interest on the WC&A's bonded debts, as well as 6% per annum on the WC&A's capital stock. The lease was approved at stockholders' meetings of both companies on June 1, and went into effect the same day.

The day the lease was approved, Wilmington & Weldon stockholders authorized a new issue of 5% first mortgage bonds at the rate of $12,000 per mile of constructed road. $1,200,000 of these bonds to was to be held in reserve by the trustee, The Safe Deposit and Trust Company of Baltimore, to cover bond issues already out. The balance of the bonds was to be used for the general purposes of the company. They also authorized a new, limited issue of stock with the provision that "all who are now stockholders in this company shall have the privilege at any time prior to July 1, 1885, of subscribing for said increase of stock at the price of $110 per share in the proportion of 20% ... of the present holding of said stockholders."

One of the "general purposes of the company" for which the new bonds were issued turned out to be purchasing stocks in other companies. Before the end of the year, Newcomer and Walters arranged for the Wilmington & Weldon Railroad Company to buy a 77.77% interest in the syndicate which owned the following stocks:

6,871 shares of Richmond & Petersburg Railroad Company stock
33 shares of WC&A Railroad Company stock
9,129 shares of Northeastern Railroad Company stock
4,513 shares of Cheraw & Darlington Railroad Company stock

In exchange for this partial interest in the syndicate-held stocks, the company paid $535,000 of its new first mortgage bonds. The source of this peculiar percentage of the Walters syndicate's holdings is not indicated, but it was probably the interest held by Walters, Newcomer, the Jenkins family, and other close associates in Baltimore. They were apparently selling their personal holdings in other roads to the Wilmington & Weldon, and using the proceeds to increase their control of the Wilmington & Weldon.

The Safe Deposit and Trust Company, W. T. Walters, B. P. Newcomer, and most of their close associates, subscribed fully to the new issue of Wilmington & Weldon stock, thereby increasing their proportion of ownership.

A large portion of the new Wilmington & Weldon bonds were sold at good market prices, and the cash was used for the following purchases:

6,320 shares of Richmond, Fredericksburg & Potomac Railroad Company stock
2,000 shares of Virginia & Carolina Railroad Company stock
1,000 shares of Palmetto Railroad Company of South Carolina stock
2,000 shares of Cheraw & Darlington Railroad Company stock

The important item in the preceding list was the 6,320 shares of Richmond, Fredericksburg & Potomac stock. Walters and Newcomer had achieved a real coup when, in May 1884, they acquired this controlling interest in such a strategic road. The RF&P's line ran from Richmond to Quantico, Virginia, where it connected with a line controlled by the Pennsylvania — together forming the only direct railroad connection between Richmond and Washington. For the next 15 years, Coast Line leaders would enjoy the weighty advantage of RF&P control, in their dealings with the managers of other lines feeding northward through Richmond, especially the Richmond & Danville and Seaboard Air Line systems.

Walters' group clearly enhanced its control of the Coast Line system by using the Wilmington & Weldon as a holding company. They also strengthened the system itself, by giving it new management focus and by guaranteeing its connections for through traffic.

In still another matter — construction of new mileage — the Wilmington & Weldon's service as holding company, from 1884 to 1891, proved invaluable. The Fayetteville Cut-off and the outlet line to Norfolk were accomplished under Wilmington & Weldon's auspices, as were the addition of many miles of feeder and connecting branches in the Carolinas. Arrangements for construction of branch lines were made in two ways. Since the Wilmington & Weldon Company had the right, under its charter, to construct branch lines for its railroad, the company usually managed such construction under its own auspices, paid for it directly, and added the new property to its assets. Additions to other roads, by contrast, usually involved chartering a separate company, sponsoring construction of the company's line, and then purchasing all of the stocks and bonds in the new company through the Wilmington & Weldon Railroad Company. The formal arrangements for the Wilson-to-Florence Cutoff illustrate this procedure. The initial segment from Wilson to Fayetteville, constructed in 1885-86, and the segment from Fayetteville southward to the state line, completed in 1892, were simply branches added to the Wilmington & Weldon Railroad. They were paid for by sale of Wilmington & Weldon bonds and stocks. The segment from the South Carolina state line to Florence was another matter. First, a special act of the South Carolina Legislature was secured to permit the incorporation the Florence Railroad Company in 1882. Construction of its line, which did not begin until 1886, was done under contract by a construction firm. Then late in 1888, when the road was completed, the Wilmington & Weldon Company bought 2,000 shares of Florence stock at par, and set it up in business as an operating company.

Another example of how the holding company operated was the organization of the Manchester & Augusta Railroad Company in 1886. The Wilmington & Weldon Company took over a partially constructed line and finished construction of a branch connecting line between Sumter, on the WC&A, and Darlington, on the Cheraw & Darlington. When the line was ready for operation in 1888, the Wilmington & Weldon bought all of its stock (1,000 shares), and Henry Walters placed it in operation. The

Manchester & Augusta subsequently acquired two branch lines of its own at Wilmington & Weldon expense. Later in 1893, it extended its road from Sumter to Denmark, South Carolina, eventually becoming the line that would reach Augusta for the Atlantic Coast Line.

All of these acquisitions, of course, greatly swelled the assets of the Wilmington & Weldon Company. Its balance sheet for 1891 reveals the entire ACL financial structure. The "trustees' sinking fund" was an account containing only important blocks of stock, valued very conservatively, in other Coast Line companies.

Leasing What's Left

One of the avenues for consolidating the Atlantic Coast Line system, explored during these years, was the possibility of leasing the remaining major roads to the Wilmington & Weldon.

Benjamin Newcomer attempted to arrange such a lease of the Northeastern Railroad Company to the Wilmington & Weldon in the fall of 1887, but he was forced to report to Wilmington & Weldon stockholders that the lease had not been agreed upon, "there being some misunderstanding in reference to certain assets." The dispute was probably with Jesup and Plant, who shortly afterwards sold their personal holdings in the Northeastern to the Wilmington & Weldon Railroad Company. The price was a generous $50 per share or $380,000 total for Jesup's 4,200 shares and Plant's 3,400 shares. It was paid in the form of 6% special trust certificates of the Wilmington & Weldon Railroad Company, secured by depositing the same 7,600 shares of stock with The Safe Deposit Trust Company of Baltimore, the trustee. Walters and Newcomer now had complete control of the Northeastern, so they did nothing further about leasing it.

Shortly afterward, Benjamin Newcomer attempted to arrange a lease of the Petersburg Railroad to the Wilmington & Weldon. Once again it proved difficult to manage. At a special meeting on April 28, 1888, local stockholders voted solidly against leasing their road to the Wilmington & Weldon. Even though a law obtained from the Virginia Legislature had changed voting rights in the Petersburg Railroad so that each share got one vote, giving the Walters group clear control, they decided not to override such concerted opposition on the part of the minority stockholders.

The Atlantic Coast Line would have to be integrated by some means other than leasing all the other railroads to the Wilmington & Weldon Company.

The Effect of the Interstate Commerce Act

Attempts to unify the system through leases, as well as some other actions taken at the time, could have been motivated in part by passage of the first national regulatory legislation. Railroad men from over the country had been watching Congress nervously while the Reagan bill in the House and the Cullom bill in the Senate were debated, passed, and finally formulated by a conference committee into the Interstate Commerce Act.

Apparently Newcomer and Walters expected their arrangements for linking the Coast Line companies would be affected adversely by the new law. It seems too much of a coincidence that the Atlantic Coast Line Association was formed on January 26, 1887, just a few days before President Grover Cleveland signed the Interstate Commerce Act.

The creation of the Association had greatly simplified Henry Walters' task of managing the railroad system, and this was undoubtedly one of the reasons it had been formed; but, it also officially relieved the Wilmington & Weldon Railroad Company of policy determination for the entire system. All the Coast Line companies placed themselves voluntarily into the Atlantic Coast Line Association and accepted the leadership of its general officers and executive department. Now, the Wilmington & Weldon Company could not be accused of requiring them to give preferential treatment to its own railroad, nor to one another. As interpreted by the courts, and enforced by the Interstate Commerce Commission, the Interstate Commerce Act had little relevance to the relationships among Atlantic Coast Line Companies. Probably as a consequence, the Atlantic Coast Line Association was not active beyond the organizational meetings in January and June of 1887. The attempts to lease other railroads to the Wilmington & Weldon were abandoned, partly for the same reason.

Pressure from Raleigh

Most of the financial and organizational moves made by Newcomer and Walters during five years or so after June, 1884, pointed toward gathering all their Coast Line properties under the Wilmington & Weldon umbrella. If the Interstate Commerce Act suspended this policy for a time, it turned out to be a false alarm. It was rather some actions by the legislature of North Carolina which caused then to abandon their use of the Wilmington & Weldon as the parent corporation for the Coast Line.

Pressure had been building in Raleigh with each session of the General Assembly for regulation of railroads within the state and for taxation of railroad properties. In March of 1889, an act was ratified which provided for a general tax on all railroad property. State authorities proceeded to assess the branch lines of the Wilmington & Weldon while respecting its tax exempt status on its other properties. The company refused to pay the taxes. Thus began a heated and prolonged dispute between Coast Line leaders and the State of North Carolina.

The conflict really stemmed from the original practice, by this and other states, of regulating railroads by the provisions in their own charters. The Wilmington & Weldon's charter granted the company exemption from taxation, and the right to set its own rates (up to 8 cents per mile for passengers) so long as the profits on its stock did not exceed 15%. Such individualized controls were antiquated and inequitable, and most states by now had some kind of general type of railroad regulatory legislation. Walters and Newcomer were determined, however, to fight any alteration by the State of North Carolina in their company's legal standing, and they had explicit grounds in the wording of the charter for doing so. Their position was somewhat weakened by the fact that the Wilmington & Weldon was actually returning profits well beyond the percentage limit prescribed in the charter. Much of this "excess" profit was being rolled back into the construction of branch lines. The rest was distributed by a means apparently designed to avoid the limitations set down in the charter. Late in 1886, they had issued $2,500,000 worth of "certificates of indebtedness" — each stockholder receiving an amount equal to the value of the shares he held. Annually, 7% interest was officially paid on the certificates of indebtedness, not as dividends paid on stock. The distinction was a rather thin technicality. Nevertheless, every legal measure was utilized to resist state encroachment.

Warren G. Elliott, as president of the Wilmington & Weldon and head counsel for the Atlantic Coast Line interests, carried on extensive negotiations with state officials. When, in the opening weeks of 1891, it seemed certain that the Wilmington & Weldon was going to have to accept some form of taxation, Elliott went to Raleigh with a proposition for the convening General Assembly. He suggested to legislative committees that the Wilmington & Weldon Company would conditionally waive its exemption from taxation in return for grants of new powers and guarantees against excessive valuation of the company's property. The new powers requested probably included authority to hold stock in, and merge with, other railroad companies.

The General Assembly, however, was in a decidedly unfriendly mood towards the Coast Line people. Elliott's offer of conditional waiver of exemption was rejected. The Assembly then proceeded to revoke the Wilmington & Weldon's right to build a branch line that would have invaded the Richmond & Danville's territory northward from Durham. It also passed two other laws: one establishing a board of railroad commissioners with regulatory powers, and another giving this board the responsibility of assessing the property of railroad companies. The Board of Railroad Commissioners proceeded to assess the branch lines of the Wilmington & Weldon for taxation; and the company again rebuffed "the attempts made by the several state officers to collect the taxes based upon these pretended assessments."

After considerable litigation in state and federal courts, the case finally came before the United States Supreme Court, which rendered a decision early in 1893 against the railroad company. Another round of negotiations with the legislative committees ensued, resulting in two acts ratified on, respectively, February 23 and March 6 of 1893. The first of these amended the charter of the Wilmington & Weldon Railroad Company by completely removing its exemptions from taxation and regulation. It also stipulated that the company must pay back taxes to the state and to certain counties and towns for the years 1890 - 1892. The stockholders of the Wilmington & Weldon Company met the same day and formally accepted the terms of the act, including the bill for back taxes totaling $76,248.66. The second legislative act, contingent upon the company's acceptance of the first, gave the Wilmington & Weldon Company the right to consolidate with any other railroad company with which "it may connect either directly or indirectly."

All of this was too much for Walters and Newcomer, who were inclined to be impatient with what they regarded as "government invasions of their property rights." Not only was the Wilmington & Weldon now subject to rate regulation, which turned out to be gentle enough, but it was also required to submit detailed reports of its entire operations and properties and to pay taxes that would reflect in part its assets in the securities of other companies. They prudently terminated the Wilmington & Weldon's service as a holding company months before the taxation issue was settled.

Adam and Eve — A New Holding Company is Born

The search for a more suitable charter for a holding company began when it first became apparent that the State of North Carolina intended to tax the Wilmington & Weldon. Warren Elliott was in charge. To locate and assist in the purchase of a charter, Elliott retained the services of Andrew Brandegee, a lawyer from New London, Connecticut, a state becoming noted for its lenient corporation laws.

On January 29, 1891, Elliott telegraphed Brandegee to proceed with negotiations to buy a charter that he had found was available; and the two met at Hartford, Connecticut, on March 23, to complete the arrangements. On April 11, 1891, Henry Walters joined Warren, Elliott and Brandegee in Greenwich, Connecticut, where they bought from H.W.R. Hoyt the charter of the American Improvement and Construction Company. They proceeded to organize the company on the same day.

The charter for the American Improvement & Construction Company had been in existence for two years before Walters' group took possession. It had been granted to John T. Wait and John H. Keep of Norwich, John Dayton and H.W.R. Hoyt of Greenwich, and Walter L. Wilcox of Norwalk by the January 1889 session of the General Assembly of Connecticut and was ratified on May 29, 1889.

Very broad powers were conveyed through the charter:

> "Said corporation shall have power and is hereby authorized to acquire, build, aid in building, own, sell, convey, equip, lease, or maintain and operate, by steam or other power, any railroads, street railways, tramways, telegraph lines, telephone lines, water-works, canals, bridges, steamship or steamboat lines, wharves, warehouses, docks, dockyards, steamers, lighters, beat, and vessels of all , and the appurtenances thereof; and may engage in transport, manufacture & transmission of gas & electricity, mines and mining, and animal, agriculture, natural and manufactured productions, and guano, phosphates, and fertilizing products of all kinds, and have these dealings and franchises from the government of Brazil, and from other foreign powers, states, territories, governments, or communities, and from the

United States of America, and any states, territories, communities or governments, in the United States, etc. . . . provided, however, that this corporation shall not have power to use or occupy any highways or public grounds in this State, for the purpose of leasing, holding, building, aiding in building, owning, or operating, any railroad, street railway, or tramway, within the State of Connecticut, or the use or transmission of gas or electricity for any purpose, without further special authority from the General Assembly."

The reference to "the government of Brazil" and "other foreign powers" suggests that Hoyt et al had obtained the charter for a foreign investment venture which failed to materialize. In any case, the American Improvement & Construction Company clearly had not been intended originally as a holding company for the Atlantic Coast Line Railroad system, nor was it ideally suited to the purpose. It possessed farranging rights as an operating company, but no specific authorization to act as a holding company. However, the State of Connecticut could presumably be depended upon for a liberal interpretation of the charter or, if necessary, a grant of additional powers.

The initial organization of the American Improvement & Construction Company company in April of 1891 was largely "pro forma," since only Henry Walters, Elliott, and Brandegee were present.

Subscribers to the original $200,000 of stock — first stockholders and officers were:

President	W. T. Walters	1,000 shares, by proxy
Vice President	Henry Walters	1,000 shares, in person
Secretary & Ass't Treasurer	W. G. Elliott	480 shares, in person
Treasurer	B.F. Newcomer	1,000 shares, by proxy
Ass't. Secretary	A. Brandegee	20 shares, in person
	Geo. B. Jenkins	500 shares, by proxy

The same men, except George Jenkins, were also named the directors. The American Improvement & Construction Company was thus in official existence.

The rest of the basic organization for the new holding company was arranged a few months later. On September 16, 1891, Warren Elliott and Andrew Brandegee were joined in New York by Benjamin Newcomer. They adopted bylaws and called a stockholder's meeting for September 21, in New London, Connecticut. Apparently only Elliott and Brandegee attended the meeting, which authorized issuance of $10,000,000 in $50 par stock and sale or exchange of the stock for other property. Another board meeting was held in the Hoffman House in New York City on September 23. W. T. Walters, B. F. Newcomer, and A. Brandegee were elected as the Executive Committee, empowered according to the bylaws to act for the board. The necessary formalities were now accomplished, and the American Improvement & Construction Company was ready for business.

Two points on the cost are noteworthy. First, the $200,000 subscribed in the initial stock issue constituted the sole new capital spent to create a $10,000,000 holding company. Second, the price of the charter and other organizational expenses totaled less than $10,000 ($9,880.35 by year's end, to be exact).

During the six months that followed, the American Improvement & Construction Company, like Eve from Adam in the Book of Genesis, was given life as a holding company from the body of the Wilmington & Weldon Company. The biblical analogy is not perfect, however, because the Wilmington & Weldon lost much more than a rib in the process. First, all the securities in other companies were transferred from the Wilmington & Weldon to the American Improvement & Construction Company. Then majority ownership of the Wilmington & Weldon Company, itself, was given to the new holding company. This was accomplished by a series of transactions made during November and December, 1891:

One: the American Improvement & Construction Company issued to the stockholders of the Wilmington & Weldon Railroad Company 116,000 shares of its stock (four shares for each W&W share held) and paid the railroad company $200,000.

Two: the Wilmington & Weldon Railroad Company paid the $200,000 directly back to the new holding company and transferred to it, at varying valuation, the securities and financial papers it held on other railroads.

Three: the $1,331,700 in Wilmington & Weldon certificates of indebtedness was used by the new holding company to help purchase the entire portfolio of Walters' syndicate, which totaled $2,663,400 of stock in various railroads.

Four (though not necessarily last): the $200,000 in cash, paid to the Wilmington and Weldon Company in the initial transaction, was spent as follows:

Washington, N.C. property and interest to Dec. 1, 1891	$ 63,183.22
300 shares RF&P Railroad Stock @ $123.29	43,151.50
9,000 lst Mortgage Bonds plus interest, town of Washington, N.C.	9,368.14
Hartford Railroad Company. plus interest	25,750.00
83 shares Cheraw & Darlington Railroad Co. Stock @ $23 plus interest	1,941.77
Notes of Jackson and Bell	7,500.00
110 shares East Carolina Land & Development Co.	3,125.37
Expenses on account to date procuring charter, etc.	9,880.35
	$173,984.91

The net effect of these transactions was to strip the Wilmington & Weldon Company of $5,800,000 in assets — mostly securities in other railroad companies — and to terminate its service as a holding company. However, Wilmington & Weldon stockholders were not shortchanged; after all, the Walters group held two-thirds of the W&W stock outstanding. As part of the plan, they were issued four shares of American Improvement

& Construction Company stock for every W&W share they gave up. It is interesting to note that the small, local W&W stockholders received a total of 40,000 shares in this distribution of American Improvement & Construction Company stock, making it at the outset a rather broadly-owned corporation. To this problem Henry Walters and Benjamin Newcomer would address themselves at a later time.

The American Improvement & Construction Company

On March 28, 1892, the American Improvement & Construction Company attained full status as the holding company for the Atlantic Coast Line Railroad System. On that date, it received 20,000 shares (of the 30,000 shares outstanding) of Wilmington & Weldon stock, and gave in payment four shares of its stock for a total of 80,000 shares with a par value of $4,000,000. The Walters group thus completed the transfer of financial control of the Coast Line system to their new holding company, and they held $8,000,000 of the $10,000,000 in stock issued by the new corporation.

Conspicuously absent from the transactions that founded the holding company was Wilmington, Columbia & Augusta stock. Only 32 shares of WC&A stock (a portion of those held by the second Walters Syndicate) were transferred to the American Improvement & Construction Company. One obvious reason was that control of the WC&A was already complete, as it was under lease to the Wilmington & Weldon. Less obvious, but perhaps equally important, a general distribution of holding company shares in exchange for WC&A stock would have weakened the Walters-Newcomer command of the holding company. Other wealthy Baltimoreans and New Yorkers (e.g. Enoch Pratt, Bradley Martin and Morris Jesup) had substantial interests in the WC&A. They would have been independently powerful, even if generally friendly, associates in the new company. At any rate, the initial holding company acquisitions focused almost exclusively on securities owned and issued by the Wilmington & Weldon Company. WC&A stock was left in individual hands, and Benjamin Newcomer and the two Walters were left free of serious challenges to their decisions for their holding company.

The charter of the American Improvement & Construction Company was deficient in some important respects, and it was probably Benjamin Newcomer who insisted that these be removed. After many months of serious illness he was able, by the beginning of 1892, to resume his direction of financial affairs for The Safe Deposit & Trust Company and the Coast Line. On March 22, he replaced Elliott as secretary of the holding company. One thing that needed to be changed was the meaningless name of the corporation: there was no reason to hide its relationship to the Atlantic Coast Line Railroad system. A more serious problem, the authorized $10,000,000 in capital stock was far too limited; it had all been issued in the process of acquiring the Wilmington & Weldon and its properties, leaving none for future capital expansion. Most crucial of all, there was no explicit authorization in the charter for the company to own shares of the capital stock of other companies—that is, to act as a holding company.

Warren Elliott and Andrew Brandagee were set to work on securing the desired charter revisions. In its January 1893 session, the General Assembly of Connecticut passed the following act:

Resolved by this Assembly:

Section 1. The name of the American Improvement and Construction Company is hereby changed to The Atlantic Coast Line Company, and by that name it shall be hereafter called and known; provided, however, that no rights existing in favor of, or against said Co. shall be affected thereby.

Section 2. In addition to the powers conferred by section two of its charter, said Co. shall have the right to acquire by purchase or otherwise, shares of stock in, or the bonds, securities, obligations, or other evidences of indebtedness of, any company incorporated under the laws of this, or any other State, and to transfer, sell, assign or pledge the same or any part or portion thereof.

Section 3. The capital stock of said Co. may be divided into shares of one hundred dollars each, instead of fifty dollars, as provided in said charter, and may be increased to an amount not to exceed thirty million dollars, in the manner now provided in section four of said charter.

Section 4. The meetings of the Directors may be held in this State, New York, or Baltimore, MD; and a majority of the directors, when so met, shall constitute a quorum for the transaction of business.

The act was ratified on May 29, and its provisions adopted for the company at a stockholders meeting held June 20. It would be some years before any of the additional $20,000,000 in authorized stock was issued, but the desired flexibility had been gained. There was no longer any question of the legality of the holding company operation. The Atlantic Coast Line Company was now fully ready for business.

Atlantic Coast Line Company — In Control

In the first 10 years of its existence, the Atlantic Coast Line Company had proved invaluable to its organizers. Of obvious importance, it served as a repository for financial control of their whole railroad system. Benjamin Newcomer and the Walters, however, used it for a variety of other productive purposes. They made it the financial vehicle for organizing new railroad companies, for building their lines, for constructing extensions of existing roads, for purchasing railroads to add to their system, for buying new equipment and rails for the Coast Line roads, and for acquiring land for commercial, industrial, and mining development.

A special example of the holding company's contributions was its purchase of the Charleston, Sumter & Northern Railroad. In the fall of 1894, Newcomer and Henry Walters bought the receivers' certificates and bonds from a bondholders committee, and then the road itself, at a foreclosure sale in February of 1895 — all in the name of the Atlantic Coast Line Company. This amounted literally to seizing and dismantling a portion of the Seaboard Air Line's route to Florida. Portions of the reorganized Charleston & Northern were sold to various Coast Line companies in the area, to be used as branch lines. The whole operation cost the holding company $825,000, for which it gained only $800,000 in bonds in a fragmented railroad, but Henry Walters clearly felt it was worth the expense. He reported to Atlantic Coast Line Company stockholders:

"At the time your company purchased control of the Charleston, Sumter & Northern Railroad, the latter had formed part of a through line from Florida to Washington and Norfolk, via the Seaboard Air Line and the South Carolina & Georgia Railroad. It was beginning to secure a good share of the business of the Atlantic Coast Line from and to Charleston, and was rapidly increasing a diversion of freights and passengers from the Wilmington, Columbia & Augusta and North Eastern Railroads. The road was locally competitive nearly its whole length with the Wilmington, Columbia & Augusta and North Eastern Railroads, and was paying rebates to shippers and cutting rates at all points. Your purchase restored not only the rates, but also immediately restored the business to the Wilmington, Columbia & Augusta and North Eastern Railroads which had been diverted.

Most of the projects carried out under the auspices of the holding company were of a more profitable and positive nature. This was particularly true of the many instances in which the holding company contracted with one of the Coast Line Railroad companies to build a branch or extension line; subcontracted the job to a construction firm; and delivered the completed road to the railroad company for an agreed price in stocks and bonds. For construction of the 17-mile Latta Branch for the Florence Railroad Company (1892-93) the holding company received $10,000 per mile in stock and $12,000 per mile in bonds— over twice the actual cost. An extension of the Manchester & Augusta's line from Rimini to Denmark, South Carolina, was completed in August of 1894 at a cost of $821,613.50 (plus some interest paid during construction); the holding company was paid $1,607,200.00 in stocks and bonds.

There were more such profitable construction projects completed between 1892 and 1899. In most cases the railroad companies which paid such high prices were wholly owned by the Atlantic Coast Line Company, so the Walters' group was only over-capitalizing its own corporations by these transactions. However, at such time as consolidation might be achieved and these small, heavily capitalized corporations would merge with other Coast Line companies, the holding company stood to fare much better than would the minority stockholders in companies, such as the WC&A or the Petersburg.

The Atlantic Coast Line Company diversified its investments into some interesting fields. By the summer of 1894, it owned $154,988.20 in steel rails leased to railroad companies and individuals, and it had contracted with the Florence Railroad Company to procure 150 box cars and 75 Atlantic Coast Despatch cars. A few months later, it subscribed to $25,000 in stock of the North Carolina Land & Lumber Company. In 1897, the holding company acquired a 29% interest in the Baltimore, Chesapeake & Richmond Steamboat Company. A year later it purchased the East Shore Terminal Company of Charleston jointly with the Plant Investment Company. At the same time, it shared one-half the expense of a phosphate mining track built by the Plant Investment Company from Ashley Junction to Magnolia Crossing in South Carolina. Having access to profits returned from all the Coast Line railroads, the holding company could make investments that benefited the entire system. It would retain this unique function until the railroads could be consolidated into one company.

Strengthening Railroad Operations

On December 27, 1897, Henry Walters and Benjamin Newcomer bought for the holding company all the stock in the Charleston & Western Carolina Railway Company. Here, finally, was the Coast Line's entry to Augusta. By this one action alone, the holding company justified its existence; it would carry this investment in an unprofitable railroad for years so that, later, the western segment of its line could be used as a strategic connection for the Coast Line.

In the autumn of 1899, a 26-mile extension of the old Manchester & Augusta (now part of the Atlantic Coast Line Railroad Company of South Carolina) was completed from Denmark to Robbins, on the Charleston & Western Carolina line. On November 1, Atlantic Coast Line freights (and a month later, passenger trains) began to roll solid into Augusta, Georgia. It had taken 20 years, but the loss of the Charlotte, Columbia & Augusta Railroad had now been overcome. The Coast Line had access to traffic with the interior of Georgia, Alabama, and the Gulf Coast.

The Atlantic Coast Line Company was obviously valuable for centralizing financial management of the railroad system. Moreover, during much of the period before 1900, its financial moves were often taken to directly promote the operating effectiveness of the railroad system. As in the instances of the Charleston, Sumter & Northern and the Charleston & Western Carolina purchases described above, it occasionally even took a loss on an investment in order to strengthen railroad operations.

This emphasis on the operation of railroad was especially true after the rise of Henry Walters to full leadership. Failing energies forced the elder Walters to resign his positions in 1893, and Henry Walters was elected president of the Atlantic Coast Line Company June 20 of that year. After his father's death, on November 22, 1894, Henry Walters inherited full authority and responsibility for the Walters' interests. Financial and operational command of the Coast Line system were now vested in one man.

Although the Atlantic Coast Line Company represented only one facet of his activities, Henry Walters' most important decisions for his railroad system were promoted through the holding company, or directly affected its interests. Until consolidation of the railroad companies, Henry Walters' annual reports as President of the Atlantic Coast Line Company described developments within the railroad system almost as if they concerned only this one corporation. Removal of 17 curves from an 11-mile section of the Petersburg, construction of a new freight yard at Florence for the South Carolina roads, and the commitment by the railroads of revenues earned from moving troops and materials during the "Cuban War" to a special improvement fund — such matters as these were reported along with important financial moves that directly concerned the stockholders of the holding company. This identification of the railroad system with the holding company persisted as long as Henry Walters held the presidency, from 1893 to 1902.

In actuality, railroad operations were directed by Henry Walters in consultation with Tom Emerson, general freight and passenger agent, and John Kenly, superintendent of transportation. Similarly, financial and organizational moves were now decided by Henry Walters in conferences with Benjamin Newcomer. Board of Directors meetings, whether of the railroad companies or the holding company, merely added the formal stamp of approval.

Competition and Cooperation

Concurrent with Henry Walters' rise to full command of the Coast Line were some important developments in another southeastern railroad system. The far-flung Richmond & Danville network went through a period of financial crisis and reorganization between 1892 and 1894. Drexel, Morgan & Company, with J. P. Morgan himself taking an active part, gathered the Richmond & Danville and the East Tennessee systems into the 6,000-mile Southern Railway Company. The new company was established in June, 1894, and began operations on July 1, 1894, under arrangements that insured continued control by Morgan, and with Morgan's railroad specialist, Samuel Spencer, as president.

Fortunately for the Coast Line, the management of this huge competitor proved friendly, rather than hostile. In fact, Samuel Spencer and Henry Walters soon began to cooperate actively to the benefit of both lines. In the closing weeks of 1895, they negotiated a contract by which the Southern Railway Company was given trackage rights over the Wilmington & Weldon and Norfolk & Carolina roads from Selma, North Carolina, to Norfolk, Virginia. As part of the deal, the Atlantic Coast Line Company sold a one-third interest in the Norfolk & Carolina to the Southern Railway Company. The Coast Line gained additional revenues and the Southern gained an outlet to Norfolk.

There was much more. The traffic managers of the two lines, Scott and Emerson, conferred repeatedly in order to maintain rates at competitive points. Information was exchanged on design and cost of new equipment and on charges for special services, such as moving refrigerator cars. As noted in the proceeding chapter, the Coast Line and the Southern joined in refusing to haul Henry Plant's express refrigerator cars. Communication between Henry Walters and Samuel Spencer became so significant that, late in 1896, they began using a code to keep the content of their telegrams secret.

Because of the closeness of this alliance, some contemporary as well as later observers naturally concluded that the Coast Line, like the Southern Railway, was under Morgan's control. This was not the case. J. P. Morgan's apparent solicitude for the Coast Line was a direct application of his railroad philosophy to the situation in the Southeast; his conviction that railroads should avoid ruinous competition was well known. The Atlantic Coast Line was a soundly financed, conservatively managed system with a full network of connections in the coastal region south of Richmond. Moreover, it controlled (along with the Pennsylvania Railroad) the existing road from Richmond to Washington. It also had an outlet to Norfolk and a firm alliance with the Plant System south of Charleston. Surely it made sense for Morgan to reach a friendly understanding with Coast Line leaders.

The pattern of events beginning in 1894, suggests the main points in the friendly understanding. The Southern Railway Company would refrain from invading Coast Line territory in the Carolinas. Expansion in Georgia would be based on agreements between the two lines. Operations would be carried on as cooperatively as possible, especially in correlating schedules and maintaining tariffs at points commonly served. Coast Line leaders would give the Southern Railway access to Washington and Norfolk on their lines, and would not block the Southern from entry to Florida via the Plant System. In return, Drexel, Morgan & Company would make their financial resources and influence available to Henry Walters and his associates for their endeavors to organize and expand the Coast Line System.

Conspicuously absent from this arrangement for railroad affairs in the Southeast was the Seaboard Air Line. That J. P. Morgan and his associates regarded the Seaboard as one railroad too many was made abundantly clear by their actions. The most spectacular instance was an attempt by Samuel Spencer to arrange a joint purchase of the Seaboard system by the Southern Railway Company and the Atlantic Coast Line. The episode merits recounting here:

Early in 1896, President Richard C. Hoffman and others in control of the Seaboard system decided to sell their majority interest in the Seaboard & Roanoke Railroad Company if they could get a high enough price. They commissioned General John Gill, president of the Mercantile Trust and Deposit Company of Baltimore, to offer the stock. General Gill arranged a conférence with Samuel Spencer on February 18; they met at the Union Station in Baltimore and traveled together to Havre de Grace. In the course of the interview, Gill offered to deliver the controlling interest in the Seaboard & Roanoke at $150 per share. Spencer was interested, but not at that price. He asked for full financial statements on the company and agreed to consider the matter.

After subjecting the Seaboard & Roanoke and the other railroads it controlled to careful analysis, Spencer and other Morgan associates decided definitely against buying the stock at the price offered. They apparently also decided that the stock could not be sold to anyone else at $150 a share, especially if the Seaboard Air Line was in trouble. They proceeded to make trouble for the Seaboard. By late summer 1896, the Southern and the Seaboard system were joined in a fierce rate war, with freight tariffs reduced to as little as one-third their previous levels at some competitive points. The struggle expanded into damage suits in state courts in Georgia and the Carolinas, and into investigations by State Railroad Commissions. It also exploded into public charges and counter charges by Samuel Spencer of the Southern, and Richard Hoffman of the Seaboard. On September 15, President Hoffman reported to the stockholders of the Seaboard & Roanoke, "The Southern Railway having failed in its attack upon the Seaboard Air Line and its connections to deplete the revenues of your company, . . . have commenced an outrageous assault through the press upon your corporation and the management thereof, evidently intending to deceive you as to the value of your property, and thus induce you to sell them your securities at their own price."

The bitter public controversy had by this time created an impasse for Spencer and the Morgan interests. Hoffman was standing firm against selling out at a lower price to the Southern Railway Company; in fact, he denied that the stock had ever been offered to Spencer. In any event, the Southern Railway Company could not make the purchase now without in effect confirming the general suspicions about the reason for the rate war.

But Samuel Spencer was not a man to be easily discouraged. He contacted Henry Walters early in September and proposed a joint purchase of the Seaboard & Roanoke, with the assurance that Mr. Morgan would supply the necessary funds on reasonable terms. The purchase by the Atlantic Coast Line Company would be official: "If your company is in a legal position to do so, the strongest way is that you shall make the purchase, or that it be done for your account. Mr. Wilmer, of Morgan's legal staff, will explain a suggested method of fully protecting you."

Henry Walters responded enthusiastically, "Mr. Newcomer agrees with me that we can afford to join you equally in making the purchase at any figure up to $100 . . . We are also entirely willing to leave the matter in all its preliminary shaping in your hands." And after a conference with Morgan's aide, Wilmer, he wrote to Spencer, "There are many reasons why it would be more economical in handling the property to have it apparently belong to the Coast Line Company."

Spencer then authorized John Gill to purchase a majority interest in the Seaboard & Roanoke at $100 per share, and Gill made a good try at assembling enough commitments to sell at this price. He did not miss by far, but President Hoffman and others with large holdings in the Seaboard & Roanoke successfully blocked the move. Serious negotiations were revived in late December when a pool committee offered a large block of shares, but at a higher price than Spencer and Walters were willing to pay. By this time the rate war had been ended, first by court injunctions and then by common consent, and the word was out that the Morgan people were still interested in Seaboard & Roanoke stock. It was too late to buy on favorable terms. They gave their final refusal in February of 1897.

The Seaboard Air Line situation was finally settled in December of 1898, when John L. Williams & Son of Richmond and Middendorf, Oliver & Company of Baltimore bought a majority interest. Corporate consolidation of the system was soon accomplished under their control. There were to be three, not two, major railroad systems in the Southeast. Perhaps it was just as well that the attempt at a joint purchase by the Coast Line and Southern had failed; Henry Walters and his associates would have been drawn close to the Morgan power center if they had secured the Seaboard under the conditions proposed.

Solving the Small Stockholder Problem

By the beginning of 1897, affairs were going most auspiciously for the whole Walters railroad enterprise. The Atlantic Coast Line system was essentially complete in construction and up-to-date in equipment. The roads were generally returning a good profit on the investment, and plans were shaping up for consolidating them into one corporation. Requests for enabling legislation from the state governments concerned were being made by January of 1897. The holding company's assets were beginning to reflect the prosperity of the railroad venture — from $10,000,000 in 1892, they now stood at nearly $15,000,000. It had been paying 1½% semi-annual dividends since September of 1895, and these could soon be increased.

At this point, Henry Walters and his Baltimore associates decided on an interesting course of action. They would reduce the capital stock of the Atlantic Coast Line Company by one-half — down to $5,000,000. The reason may be that they wished to eliminate some of the small stockholders so that the company would be more closely held (a move alluded to earlier in regard to the creation of the American Improvement & Construction Company as a holding company).

The sequence of events was:

1. February 1, 1897: A board meeting at the Waldorf Hotel in New York determined to call a special stockholders' meeting for the purpose of approving the retirement of $5 million in stock and the issuance of $5 million in certificates of indebtedness.

2. February 17, 1897: A special stockholders' meeting at the Bridgeport, Connecticut, office approved the plan. The certificates of indebtedness were to be irredeemable, and would pay 5% non-cumulative interest preferable only to the stock. An issue of $6 million was approved, but only $5 million was to be used for retiring a like amount of stock. Each stockholder would have the option of exchanging up to one-half of his stock for these 5% certificates by March 31.

3. March 31, 1897: A directors' meeting in Baltimore authorized the President and the Treasurer to sell the 5% certificates remaining and to use the cash proceeds.

4. October 6, 1897: At the annual stockholders' meeting Henry Walters reported that $5 million of certificates of indebtedness had been issued and an equal amount of capital stock retired. He also expressed confidence that the new semi-annual dividend rate of 2%, which had been paid for the first time in September, could be maintained in the future.

It seems clear that stockholders not closely associated with Walters and Newcomer were encouraged to surrender half their stock (which had yielded little over the six-year period) in exchange for the certificates of indebtedness and a virtually assured 5% return. The remaining certificates of indebtedness were then offered in the open market and the proceeds used for market purchases of the stock at prices reflecting its low yield.

In this one episode, Henry Walters and Benjamin Newcomer came perilously close to emulating the financial "pirates" of the era. They knew full well when they initiated the stock reduction in February of 1897 that the prosperity of their railroad operations would soon permit the holding company to increase dividend payments. They also knew that the planned consolidations of their railroad companies in South Carolina and Virginia would soon enhance the value of many securities among the holding company's assets. They did not wait long to realize their gains. On October 5, 1898, President Henry Walters reported to the remaining stockholders of the Atlantic Coast Line Company:

> "Owing to the consolidations which have been offered during the past year, and to the distribution of a large dividend made by the Norfolk & Carolina, and also to the actual increases in the market values of many of your securities the, [assets of your Company] now have a market value exceeding $15,000,000. Your Management contemplated a distribution to the stockholders . . . of a number of these securities in the way of a dividend, but, upon reflection, have concluded it would be better to retain the securities in the Treasury of the Company and to increase the capital stock of your Company $5,000,000, and to make a stock dividend of this amount to the stockholders."

The 100% stock dividend was approved and distributed the next month, raising the total of capital stock outstanding once more to $10,000,000. Then in July of 1899, the semi-annual dividend was increased to 2½%.

Viewed in the light of these subsequent actions, the stock retirement move of 1897 amounted to a cynical securities manipulation for the benefit of a privileged group of insiders. In the typical spirit of the 1890s, Walters and Newcomer seemed to be garnering the largest possible measure of control and profits for themselves. These actions demonstrate the importance of the Atlantic Coast Line Company for their railroad operation. They had used it effectively to facilitate consolidation of the railroad companies into one corporation — a process already well along and to be completed in the spring of 1900.

Chapter VII

Consolidation

Initial Plans

The holding company was undeniably a great aid to Henry Walters and Benjamin Newcomer for building and centralizing their railroad system, but it was no substitute for actually uniting the railroads into one corporation. Just observing the required formalities for a dozen different companies was difficult enough — arranging the round of directors' and stockholders' meetings posed a real challenge each spring and early summer. Then, there were all the separate accounts and records to be kept and duly reported to stockholders and governments. Worst of all, every important action for the entire rail system called for special efforts to resolve the different interests of minority stockholders in one or more of the railroad companies. Financial management would remain terribly complicated until the railroad companies could be consolidated.

Initial actions toward consolidation were taken early in 1897, when Warren Elliott, president of the Wilmington & Weldon, began negotiating with legislative committees in South Carolina for an act enabling them to do so. It took more than three years to complete the job. All the legal and financial relationships among the several companies had to be sorted out and, even more difficult, the conflicting jurisdictions of three state governments resolved — too much to achieve at one stroke. It was planned therefore, that consolidation was to be accomplished in two stages. First, most of the railroad properties in South Carolina and Virginia were merged in 1898 into one corporation in each of those states. Second, the reduced number of companies were then consolidated in 1900 into one corporation — **the Atlantic Coast Line Railroad Company.**

Stage One - Merging South Carolina

The situation in South Carolina was the most complicated, and it received first attention. In a relatively short time, Warren Elliott obtained from the South Carolina Legislature an act (ratified March 5, 1897) which authorized formation of a new corporation for consolidating the Wilmington, Columbia & Augusta, the Northeastern, the Cheraw & Darlington, the Florence, and the Manchester & Augusta railroad companies. This enabling act was doubly important, for it granted the Atlantic Coast Line Railroad Company of South Carolina rights for leasing other railroads and for merging with other companies whose lines connected with its own.

Formation of the new company was delayed more than a year by litigation, negotiations with minority stockholders, and securing permission from North Carolina for merging the WC&A. Finally on June 20, 1898, a "Board of Corporators" met and organized the new company. Stockholders of the several companies accepted the consolidation plan at meetings on July 15 and 16. The meeting on the latter date took place in Charleston, initially as the last stockholders meeting of the Northeastern, and then as the first stockholders meeting of the Atlantic Coast Line Railroad Company of South Carolina.

At this meeting, stockholders adopted bylaws, elected C. S. Gadsden as president and Henry Walters as vice president, and authorized the issuance of $3,000,000 in common stock, $2,000,000 in preferred stock, and $8,000,000 in 4% bonds secured by a consolidated first mortgage with the Safe Deposit & Trust Company of Baltimore. Of these bonds, $2,500,000 were used for retiring the bonds of the old companies; the remainder of those actually issued ($2,831,000) were sold to finance improvements in the consolidated properties. There was one exception: stockholders in the Wilmington, Columbia & Augusta demanded (or were persuaded to accept) $960,000 in bonds and only $788,000 in stock of the consolidated company. By contrast, the holding company received $1,000,000 in stock as sole owner of the Florence Railroad, which had only 45 miles of line (as compared with the WC&A's 247 miles). The Wilmington & Weldon Railroad Company surrendered its lease of the WC&A, and its stockholders were compensated with $500,000 in stock of the new company. The end result: the holding company received $3,631,900 of the $4,426,000 in stock issued by the Atlantic Coast Line Railroad Company of South Carolina. The new company was firmly controlled by the existing powers.

Though only part of the first stage in the consolidation process, formation of the ACL of South Carolina company helped a great deal. It gave corporate unity to the Charleston Division of the Coast Line system, thereby simplifying management of the 676 miles owned (and an additional 98 miles operated under lease and trackage rights) south of Wilmington.

This interim company also enabled Henry Walters to seize an opportunity to pick up a connection to Atlanta. Morgan and the Southern Railway management were apparently taking little interest in the Central Railroad of Georgia, which they controlled. The Central was in dire frinancial straits, and defaulted on a bond issue partially secured by the Georgia Railroad lease with the Lousisville & Nashville Railroad. On August 9, 1899, Henry Walters and August Belmont, chairman of the board of the L&N, arrived at an agreement whereby the Atlantic Coast Line Railroad of South Carolina acquired the available half interest in the lease. The 307-mile line of the Georgia Railroad was especially important because it ran from Augusta to Macon on one branch of a "Y" and to Atlanta on another branch. The joint lease remained in effect, returning to the Coast Line and to the L&N a modest profit on their rental payments for most of the years.

Stage Two - Virginia Takes it All

Progress toward consolidation went more slowly in Virginia. Dealing with the legislature was not so difficult, despite political pressure from opposing railroad interests and some local stockholders. Warren Elliott had a good bargaining point — the tax exempt status of the Richmond & Petersburg Railroad Company. The act which was approved on March 1, 1898, authorized the Richmond & Petersburg to purchase and consolidate with the Petersburg Railroad Company, and to adopt the name Atlantic Coast Line Railroad Company of Virginia, on condition that the R&P surrender its exemption from state taxes. The Virginia lawmakers insisted, however, that terms of the consolidation must be approved in general stockholders' meetings "by the affirmative vote of those owning or representing at least two-thirds of the entire capital stock in each of said companies." This requirement of a two-thirds majority cost Henry Walters and associates some extra grief and effort.

Following a respectful delay due to the death on May 15 of Frederick Scott, president of the R&P, the Baltimore group completed work on the merger plan in June. They issued calls for general stockholders' meetings of the two companies, to be held at the Coast Line office in Richmond on July 20.

Henry Walters went to Richmond that day, apparently with every expectation that the necessary votes were in hand, and that the plan would be approved. He was grievously disappointed. Some important local shareholders in the Petersburg, including those holding the entirety of the 2,843 shares of preferred stock still outstanding, decided to hold out for a better deal and refused to participate. When the Petersburg meeting convened, only 6,712 out of 12,843 shares were represented — only 400 more than the Atlantic Coast Line Company of Connecticut held, and far less than the required two-thirds. Nothing could be accomplished, so the meetings of both companies were adjourned indefinitely.

The weeks that followed saw a great deal of attention devoted to the situation in Petersburg. Persuasion, bargaining, and purchase of additional shares finally secured the necessary number of votes. The call went out in October and stockholders of the two companies met again in Richmond on November 21. This time the Petersburg meeting saw 10,507 votes cast in favor of the merger plan, and only 297 against. One minority stockholder still insisted that his vehement statement of protest against this takeover of his railroad be inscribed in the minutes of the meeting, which was done. There was no difficulty with the R&P, because the Walters group had held more than two-thirds of its stock all along.

According to the merger plan approved at these meetings, the Richmond & Petersburg Railroad Company simply purchased the Petersburg for the price of $1,952,672.50. Part of the payment was made with $1,500,000 of a new issue of R&P class "B" common stock, of which Petersburg stockholders received 1½ shares for each share of their common stock surrendered. The balance of the payment was in the form of a note for $412,235 plus $40,437.50 in cash, used to pay $157.50 in cash for each share of Petersburg preferred stock surrendered. The Atlantic Coast Line Railroad Company of Virginia assumed all the debts and obligations of the Petersburg, and gave a bonus of ½ share of class "B" stock for each share held by Richmond & Petersburg stockholders.

Several local Petersburg stockholders, convinced that they were getting the short end of the deal or reluctant to see their railroad company disappear, refused to surrender their shares. They were penalized by missing $6 in dividends for each share not exchanged on January 1 and again on July 1 of 1899. A few R&P stockholders received $3 instead of $6 for the same reason. It was not until September 1899 that the last of the hold-outs came around. Benjamin Newcomer must have been enormously relieved to see the books closed on the Petersburg Railroad Company. In retrospect, it seems unlikely that the Atlantic Coast Line system would have ever been put together by the Walters group if all the components had been as difficult to secure as the Petersburg.

The consolidated company thus created — the Atlantic Coast Line Railroad Company of Virginia — operated only 95 miles of line (92 under its ownership, and 3 under trackage rights from the Seaboard at Garysburg). Against a capitalization of $3,000,000, and a bonded indebtedness of $2,308,500, it listed assets amounting to $7,204,164 on June 30, 1899. With a heavy volume of traffic, a large roster of equipment, and a segment of its line in double-track, the Virginia company was exceeded only by the Wilmington & Weldon in its earnings, valuation, capitalization, and indebtedness per mile. The road was a short but strategic segment of the Coast Line, and the final phase of consolidation was soon to make this company the most important one of all. It is somewhat surprising, if not particularly significant, that the company with the shortest railroad in the Coast Line system, the Richmond & Petersburg, was to be the parent corporation of the consolidated Atlantic Coast Line Railroad Company.

The R&P as Parent Company

Why Henry Walters and Benjamin Newcomer decided to use the Richmond & Petersburg Railroad Company as the consolidating corporation for their entire railroad system can only be drawn by inference from the situation they faced from 1897-98. For one thing, the State of Virginia had a decidedly more favorable political climate for railroads than did the two Carolinas. Friends of the carriers had repeatedly defeated attempts in the Virginia legislature to establish an effective regulatory commission. Virginia had only an advisory and information-gathering Railroad Commissioner. It had no power to set maximum rates, or to control the issuing of securities or the merging of railroad corporations, so a consolidation could be arranged, and the enlarged company could operate with little interference from state agencies in the Old Dominion. These were important, perhaps crucial, considerations. All that was needed were grants of new powers for the Richmond & Petersburg Railroad Company from an amenable legislature, with success assured by bartering away the tax exempt status of the R&P. No other company in their system still retained this privilege, and the benefits to be gained would more than justify the modest new taxes to be incurred by its surrender. It seems likely that these considerations contributed to Walters' and Newcomer's choice of the R&P as the consolidating corporation.

Judging from the overall pattern of events, they had probably decided to use the R&P, and had set the main outlines of the entire two-stage consolidation plan by January of 1897, perhaps even earlier. They certainly showed no inclination to integrate their system under the Wilmington & Weldon Company after losing the battle, in 1892, to conserve its privileges to the North Carolina government. On February 4, 1899, however, they did obtain an act from the General Assembly of North Carolina which permitted the Wilmington & Weldon to change its name to the Atlantic Coast Line Railroad Company of North Carolina, and to merge with any company with which its railroad connected directly or indirectly; but it provided for no increase of capitalization to enable the Wilmington & Weldon Company to purchase the rest of the Coast Line system. The act under which the Atlantic Coast Line Company of South Carolina was formed also authorized too little capitalization for consolidating the entire system.

Walters and Newcomer probably intended all along to consolidate under the R&P charter in Virginia. The first stage was made possible, as seen above, by surrendering the R&P's exemption from state taxes. The final stage — consolidating all the roads into the Atlantic Coast Line Railroad Company — was achieved under an act which removed the R&P's exemption from county and municipal taxation. On January 12, 1900, final approval was won for "An Act to Authorize the Atlantic Coast Line Railroad Company of Virginia to Change Its Name, and to Increase the Number of Its Directors and Officers; to Authorize said Company to Increase Its Capital Stock, and to Issue Bonds and Secure the Same by One or More Mortgages, and to Authorize the Leasing by It and the Consolidation Therewith of other Corporations and to Otherwise Enlarge Its Powers."

At a joint meeting of the boards of all the railroad companies involved, held April 18 in Baltimore, agreement was reached on the consolidation plan. The next day in Richmond, a special stockholders meeting of the [ACL] Virginia Company accepted the provisions of the enabling act, ratified the consolidation agreement, and put the plan into effect. The Atlantic Coast Line Railroad Company of Virginia purchased the properties of the other companies and consolidated them into itself according to the following plan:

1. The Norfolk & Carolina Railroad Company sold and transferred its North Carolina properties to the Wilmington & Weldon Railroad Company.

2. The Atlantic Coast Line Railroad Company of Virginia sold and transferred its North Carolina properties to the Wilmington & Weldon Railroad Company.

3. The Atlantic Coast Line Railroad Company of South Carolina sold and transferred its North Carolina properties to the Wilmington & Weldon Railroad Company.

4. The South Eastern Railroad Company (its properties all in North Carolina) merged with and consolidated into the Wilmington & Weldon Railroad Company.

5. The Wilmington & Weldon Railroad Company then merged with and consolidated into the Atlantic Coast Line Railroad Company of Virginia.

6. The Atlantic Coast Line Railroad Company of South Carolina merged with and consolidated into the Atlantic Coast Line Company of Virginia.

7. The Norfolk & Carolina Railroad Company merged with and consolidated into the Atlantic Coast Line Railroad Con.pany of Virginia.

These transactions exemplify the complexities with which legal counsel and corporation secretaries had to wrestle to effect such a consolidation. The first four steps listed were strictly *pro-forma* moves to satisfy prescriptions of North Carolina and South Carolina laws — all the railroad properties in each state had to belong to a company within the state before interstate consolidation could take place. Since the new little South Eastern Company had no authorization to merge with out-of-state companies, it had to be consolidated first into the Wilmington & Weldon.

At this point, the Atlantic Coast Line Railroad Company of Virginia had increased its authorized capitalization by $37,000,000, to a total of $40,000,000 (200,000 shares common, 200,000 shares preferred), and paid for the properties acquired as follows:

1. To the Norfolk & Carolina RR Co.: 37,500 shares preferred, 12,500 shares common.

2. To the Wilmington & Weldon RR Co.: 60,500 shares preferred, 60,500 shares common and $167,000 in certificates of indebtedness.

3. To the ACL RR Co. of South Carolina: 40,821 shares preferred, 40,821 shares common and $2,833,000 in certificates of indebtedness.

Remembering that the Southern Railway Company held a 33$^1/_3$% interest in the Norfolk & Carolina, it is notable that three-fourths of the shares distributed to stockholders of that company were preferred stock, thus giving the Southern an assured income from its modest interest in the ACL RR Co. Also notable was the fact that stockholders in the South Carolina Company received nearly $3,000,000 in certificates of indebtedness, settling for assured income rather than a large controlling interest.

Completing the capitalization, the Atlantic Coast Line Railroad Company of Virginia increased its own stockholders' interest from $3,000,000 to $9,000,000 in the consolidated company by distributing 1½ shares common and 1½ shares preferred stock in exchange for 1 share of ACL RR Co. of Va. class "B" common stock; plus ½ share common and 1½ shares preferred as dividend for each share held of ACL RR Co. of Va. class "A" common stock.

The class "A" common stock that was not exchanged represented tax-exempt shares in the old Richmond & Petersburg. These were retained in original certificate form throughout the consolidations because of their special value to Virginia residents. It seems a small thing, but retaining this tax advantage for Virginians could have influenced Walters' and Newcomer's choice of the R&P as the surviving corporation. Merger arrangements have often been determined by equally small factors.

There were substantial differences in the amount of compensation received by owners of the several companies, though the par value of their holdings increased in every case. Wilmington & Weldon stockholders were rewarded on a 4-for-1 basis, the R&P on a 3-for-1, the ACL RR Co. of South Carolina on a 2½-for-1, and the Norfolk & Carolina on a 2-for-1 basis. These differences reflected a fair evaluation of the properties of the former companies, the differing market strengths of their stocks, and the relative burdens of bonded indebtedness they brought into the consolidation. It was an equitable settlement; if anything, Walters and Newcomer leaned over backward to treat minority stockholders well. The companies in which Walters, Newcomer and their holding company had the largest proportionate interests (the Norfolk & Carolina and the ACL RR Co. of South Carolina) received the least compensation. They were rewarded by seeing the consolidation arrangements stand without serious challenge in any of the three states involved.

New Name - Same Leadership

On April 19, the stockholders approved the name, "Atlantic Coast Line Railroad Company," and elected an enlarged board. The 12 directors represented local stockholders from Virginia to South Carolina, as well as the Baltimore associates.

The initial Board of Directors of the Atlantic Coast Line Railroad Company:

H. Walters	Baltimore
B. F. Newcomer	Baltimore
Waldo Newcomer	Baltimore
Michael Jenkins	Baltimore.
F. W. Scott	Richmond,
D. W. Lassiter	Petersburg, Va.
Geo. Howard	Tarboro, N.C.
E. B. Borden	Goldsboro, N.C.
Donald MacRae	Wilmington, N.C.
T. W. Norwood	Wilmington, N.C.
H. B. Short-Lake	Waccamaw, N.C.
J. J. Lucas	Society Hill, S.C.

The list of officers chosen reflected carry-overs from the leadership of the constituent companies:

President	W. G. Elliott (pres. of the Wilmington & Weldon)
1st Vice President	Henry Walters (v. pres. of all merged companies)
2nd Vice President	Alexander Hamilton (pres. of ACL RR Co. of Va.)
3rd Vice President	C. S. Gadsden (pres. of ACL RR Co. of S.C.)
Secretary & Treasurer	James F. Post
Ass't. Secretary & Treasurer	W. R. Jones (at Richmond)
Ass't. Treasurer	C. C. Olney (at Charleston)
Ass't Treasurer	C. G. Elliott (at Norfolk)

The Executive Department continued in the hands of the same men who had run the railroad system before consolidation, with J. R. Kenly as general manager, T. M. Emerson as traffic manager, and W. A. Riach as general auditor. All in all, consolidation was accomplished with little change in personnel and, consequently, with practically no disruption of railroad operations.

A Strong New System

The Atlantic Coast Line Railroad Company, which began operating under the new name on April 23, 1900, had impressive dimensions compared to its predecessor and constituent companies. The President's report for June 30, 1900, presented the following statistics:

Assets: $63,516,067
Capital stock: $34,280,500
Funded debt: $24,426,500
Miles owned: 1676
Stock per mile: $20,454
Debt per mile: $14,574

At $20,454 per mile of road, the capitalization was up sharply from the average level of the old companies, yet it was still relatively low. It compared with $49,751 per mile for the Southern and $43,291 per mile for the Seaboard Air Line in the same year, and both of these main competitors in the region carried a much heavier debt load. Soon, however, Coast Line earnings justified the stock increase.

Happily, the turn-of-the-century years were prosperous ones, and Henry Walters' railroad system was operating more efficiently than ever. In the two years ending June 30, 1902, operating revenues rose by more than 13% to $4,867 per mile and net income by over 17% to $2,178 per mile. The company was able to pay $5 dividends on its preferred stock from the beginning and to raise dividends on the common stock to $3 per year in 1901. All in all, the company was in sound financial condition.

Slowly but Surely

The Atlantic Coast Line Railroad Company represented more than 30 years of dreams, plans and efforts brought to fruition. In sharp contrast to many fast-moving promotional activities in railroad finance of the time, the Walters group had put their system together in an almost painfully slow and conservative manner. The Southeast had lagged behind other sections of the nation in assembling large railroad systems; and even here the Coast Line's consolidation came late — six years after the Southern Railway's consolidation. The Seaboard, with a much later start in basic construction, consolidated in the same month. On the other hand, Henry Walters could take satisfaction in the knowledge that the Coast Line had grown "naturally." Financial strength for effecting the consolidation had been drawn from the operations of his railroad system and not from massive infusions of New York capital. Now the existence of the Atlantic Coast Line Railroad Company brought, in turn, increased efficiency to railroad operations and additional financial leverage for future additions to the Walters railroad empire.

Sequel to Consolidation

The holding company — the Atlantic Coast Line Company of Connecticut — and its stockholders were major beneficiaries of the railroad consolidation. In exchange for its interests in the several constituent and predecessor companies, the holding company received over 70% of the stock of the Atlantic Coast Line Railroad Company (about $24,000,000 par value). Its listed assets were thereby swelled to about $30,000,000, against a capitalization of only $10,000,000 and certificates of indebtedness outstanding of $5,000,000. The board solved this gratifying imbalance by declaring a 100% dividend, on October 3, 1900, to be distributed in the form of $7,500,000 in new 4% ACL RR Co. certificates of indebtedness, and from its current assets, $2,500,000 in ACL RR Co. certificates of indebtedness. In a quick change of mind, on December 11 the directors authorized sale of various securities from the company's holdings so that $2,500,000 of the new certificates of indebtedness could be purchased and retired. The net effect of all the transactions was to increase the holding company's liabilities by $5,000,000 to a total of $20,000,000 and to reduce its assets (through sales of securities and distribution to stockholders to a matching $20,000,000.) Issuing certificates of indebtedness was by now a time-tested means by which the Walters associates distributed profits without unduly enhancing the attractiveness of a company's stock. Stock dividends were held at 4½% for another two years, and close watch was kept for any market offerings of shares that might be acquired.

Nearly all the transactions mentioned above by which the holding company reduced its assets were sales of securities to the Atlantic Coast Line Railroad Company. Newcomer and Walters were taking advantage of the railroad company's strength to get increased liquidity for the holding company. In every case, however, there was also good reason for the railroad company to make the purchase. For one example, it purchased $500,000 in ACL RR Co. of South Carolina bonds, which it already had borrowed from the holding company, for deposit as security for the Georgia Railroad lease, giving in payment $516,667 in cash and unattached bonds. For another, it bought an interest in the Chesapeake Steamship Company for $440,549, enabling it to deal directly with other railroad companies who were part owners and patrons of the shipping line. In a third instance, it paid $205,268 for 2,000 shares of stock in the Atlanta Belt Line Company, to be disposed of later in exchange for properties more desirable to be part of the Coast Line. In this same group of transactions, all of which were effected early in 1901, the Atlantic Coast Line Railroad Company purchased from the holding company its large interest (8,115 shares) in the Richmond, Fredericksburg & Potomac Railroad Company. This deal had significance far beyond matters of financial housecleaning between Coast Line corporations.

Within a few months the Atlantic Coast Line Railroad Company, in turn, sold the block of RF&P shares as part of a general settlement of the Richmond-to-Washington route. Even in the "community of interest" atmosphere of 1901, this was an arrangement which evoked some amazement. The main points of the settlement were as follows:

1. A proprietary company (the Richmond-Washington Company) with an authorized capitalization of $3,000,000 was formed under a New Jersey charter.

2. Six railroad companies— the Pennsylvania, the Atlantic Coast Line, the Chesapeake and Ohio, the Baltimore & Ohio, the Southern, and the Seaboard Air Line — purchased equal interests in the proprietary company.

3. The Pennsylvania, previously sole owner of the Washington Southern Railway Company (with about 35 miles of line from Washington to Quantico) sold all of its Washington Southern stock to the proprietary company.

4. The Atlantic Coast Line Railroad Company sold its 8,115 shares, and the Pennsylvania its 1,357 shares (together a majority interest), in the R F &P (79 miles of line, Quantico to Richmond) to the proprietary company.

5. The two railroads were thereafter operated as one continuous line from Richmond to Washington (to a connection with the Baltimore and Potomac Railroad at the south end of the Long Bridge over the Potomac River).

6. All six owning companies now enjoyed equal rights and privileges over the line from Richmond to Washington.

To sum it up, the Walters group and the Pennsylvania Railroad Company surrendered their exclusive control of the only existing line between Richmond and Washington to a joint ownership with four other railroad companies — two of which were main competitors of the Coast Line and at least one, a major rival of the Pennsylvania.

At first glance, this was a startling display of generosity. On more careful scrutiny, it was more in the nature of an imaginative solution for a problem that could no longer be ignored.. For years the Seaboard Air Line had been using the RF&P under traffic contracts that reflected the prior claims of the Coast Line to this road; but now the Seaboard management had secured repeal of a Virginia law forbidding construction of a parallel line, and had obtained a charter for a competing railroad. By the above move, "Construction of a parallel road from Richmond to Washington was prevented," according to Henry Walters' own explanation of the agreement.

There were other, much broader forces at work. The Baltimore & Ohio Railroad, which had been shut out of the Richmond route by the Pennsylvania from the beginning, had recently gone through a reorganization that placed it under the protective wing of Drexel, Morgan & Company. Consequently the Pennsylvania, under Alexander Cassat's leadership, had become very cooperative with the B&O, sharing with it, for example, a purchase of a controlling interest in the Norfolk & Western. The Washington-Richmond solution was typical of Cassat's policy of forming "communities of interest" between railroads through interlocking ownership. In view of J. P. Morgan's insistence that railroads should cooperate, and the fact that two companies directly under his control were parties to the agreement, it is difficult to believe that his persuasive hand did not at least help to shape the RF&P settlement.

Further speculation suggests that substantial benefits for the Coast Line may have been linked to Henry Walters' important concession in the RF&P deal. The very fact that consolidation of the Coast Line roads had proceeded smoothly was likely due to an understanding that the RF&P would not be included.

Henry Plant's death on June 23, 1899, had raised another issue to be settled between Walters and Morgan. If Morgan and Spencer decided to acquire the Plant roads for the Southern Railway Company, Henry Walters would be faced with an exceedingly difficult, if not impossible, fight. Instead, the cooperative relationship which had begun in 1894 continued past the turn of the century, and the established linkage between the Coast Line and the Plant System was respected.

In all likelihood, then, the RF&P deal was settled in the context of some amicable, but very high level "horse trading," from which Henry Walters and his railroad system realized some tremendous benefits. The two most important of these gains will be the subjects of the next two chapters.

A Change of Guard

The man responsible for much of the actual management in building the Atlantic Coast Line system, Benjamin Newcomer, died on March 30, 1901. One of the original formulators, with William T. Walters and Robert Bridgers, of the plan to form such a railroad system, Newcomer had lived to participate in consolidating it into the Atlantic Coast Line Railroad Company. As he had been active up to the last months, Newcomer's passing left a large vacuum in the Walters group. Newcomer's son, Waldo, although already a director in the railroad company and the heir to considerable interests in the key corporations, did not move into an active leadership role. It was Michael Jenkins who was elected president of the Safe Deposit & Trust Company, April 4, 1901, and who became financial manager for Walters' enterprises.

In his late fifties at this time, Michael Jenkins was a member of a respected Baltimore family, several of whose members had been stockholders in the Newcomer-Walters ventures since the 1860's. A director of the bank since 1885, and of the holding company since 1895, he had moved into the top leadership circle as a member of the Coast Line's Executive Committee in 1897. Jenkins now became Henry Walters' closest business associate. Possessed of a warm personality, a lively sense of humor, and considerable sophistication, he seemed to be in touch with business and political developments everywhere, especially those that affected the Baltimore financial marts.

Henry Walters valued his judgment very highly. Even though Walters was in New York much of the time and Jenkins in Baltimore, they were in daily, sometimes hourly communication via letter, telegram, and even that newfangled gadget, the telephone. Walters stopped by for a visit in Baltimore whenever he was passing through, and when Jenkins went to New York, they regularly met for a 7:30 p.m. dinner and strategy session at the Roffman House. Each spring, Henry Walters scheduled his railroad inspection trips so that Jenkins could be a member of his party.

It was in company with Michael Jenkins that Henry Walters now moved, shortly after the turn of the century, into some very ambitious projects in railroad finance.

Courtesy Henry B. Flagler Museum, Tampa

No. 5: *Henry Bradley Plant*

Chapter VIII

Florida's Great Railroad Men

Henry Bradley Plant

Tradition has it that Henry B. Plant became fascinated with Florida in 1853, when he brought his first wife south for her health and spent some time near Jacksonville. He had been in the transportation business since boyhood. Taking a humble job on a New York-to-New Haven steamboat, he seized the opportunity and organized his own parcel express business. After selling his business to the Adams Express Company, Plant was put in charge of their New York office, and in 1854, was made general superintendent for their southern division.

As the Civil War approached in 1861, the Adams Express Company "spun off" their southern division, and Henry Plant became president of the Southern Express Company. Under a rather obscure set of circumstances, the company continued its separate existence after the close of the war, with Henry Plant as practically the sole owner. Here was a shrewd, hardworking, and extremely ambitious man, with a business imagination well suited to the time. It was natural enough that his interest in Florida should be translated into a railroad system that linked the markets of the North, in one direction, with commerce in Latin America, in the other.

Since his Southern Express Company stood to benefit directly, Henry Plant took a lively interest in all post-war projects for rebuilding and extending railroads in the South. In 1871 he became a director of the Southern Railway Security Company. But it was in 1879-80, with the country recovering from the depression of the 1870's, that Henry Plant launched his career as railroad magnate. As mentioned in prior chapters, he became associated with the Walters group early on, and had somehow managed not only to accumulate a great deal of capital during the bad years, but also to win the backing of a very wealthy New Yorker, Morris Jesup. So Plant became a major investor in the Walters syndicate, with a particularly large interest in the Northeastern Railroad, the southernmost of the Coast Line roads. He also joined the Clyde syndicate and participated in enlarging its Richmond & Danville system. With an influential voice in these railroads, he was assured of good connections for the system he was beginning to assemble in Georgia and Florida. The association would later prove even more advantageous to Henry Walters.

Ready, Set, Go

Henry Plant secured the parent railroad for his system in 1879, when he gained full control of the Atlantic & Gulf, with Morris Jesup's backing, and reorganized it as the Savannah, Florida & Western Railway Company. The existing railroad had very limited usefulness for his purpose, since its east-west line had been intended as a connection between the Atlantic port of Savannah and the Gulf ports of Pensacola, Mobile and New Orleans. The original objective of this line was attained in 1883, by completion of an extension from Climax, Ga., to Chattahoochee, Fla., where a connection was made with the Pensacola & Atlantic's new road to Pensacola. Plant lines, however, were headed in many other directions by the time this access to New Orleans was achieved.

The SF&W's east-west road was utilized as a suspension line, to which were tied connections to the north and strategic entries into Florida. The most essential connection northward was secured first — the Savannah & Charleston, purchased in 1880, with the cooperation of Walters and Newcomer. Its roadway and equipment quickly improved. Work commenced immediately on the 70-mile Waycross Short Line to Jacksonville, and this most crucial entry to Florida was put into use by May of 1881. Another access to Florida was already in hand. The old Atlantic & Gulf had possessed a short line running southward from Dupont, Georgia, to Live Oak, Florida. Plant now rebuilt this line and pushed construction of an extension towards Gainesville, Florida. For this project he used two small companies (the Live Oak & Rowlands Bluff Railroad Co., incorporated February 23, 1881, and the Live Oak, Tampa & Charlotte Harbor RR Co., incorporated July 23, 1881) to build 53 miles southward to Newnansville.

Having gone this far in building connections for the SF&W, Plant saw dozens of possibilities in Florida for picking up unused charters, companies with partially constructed lines, and small railroads in financial straits — all of which could be welded into an integrated system to feed traffic to the SF&W. In order to capitalize on these opportunities, however, he needed to move quickly. Otherwise, charter rights would lapse, expensive miles of useless or competing line would be built, and worst of all other big planners might get there first.

To gain the desired flexibility and additional capital, he organized the Plant Investment Company in 1882, under a charter obtained in his home state of Connecticut. The Investment Company apparently began with a modest capitalization, with Plant himself by far the largest investor. W. T. Walters, B. F. Newcomer, the Jenkins family, M. K. Jesup and Henry Flagler were among the important minority subscribers. The Investment Company grew rapidly, however, as Plant and his associates, like Henry S. Haines, persuaded investors in small Florida railroads to surrender their securities in exchange for stock in the new holding company.

The tempo of expansion picked up sharply after 1882. Plant had enough influence with the management of the Florida Southern Railway Company to cease the building of a line they had begun northward from Gainesville, and in 1883, to sell their right-of-way to the Plant Investment Company. In March 1884, after consolidating the two companies whose lines had reached Newnansville, the SF&W then completed the few miles from Newnansville to Gainesville, the following month. Meanwhile, with an agreement from Plant that the SF&W would not construct a parallel line, the Florida Southern pushed its narrow-gauge road southward, reaching Ocala in December of 1881, Leesburg late in 1883, and Brooksville by the beginning of 1885. Again by agreement with Plant, the Florida Southern gave a stretch from Pemberton's Ferry (near Brooksville) through Lakeland to Bartow, to a line being completed under Plant's auspices. The Florida Southern then recommenced its construction southward from Bartow, reaching Punta Gorda on Charlotte Harbor in the summer of 1886.

Background of the Florida Southern

The Florida Southern had an interesting independent history. It went back to the incorporation, on June 8, 1876, of the Gainesville, Ocala & Charlotte Harbor Railroad Company. Organization did not take place until much later, possibly 1879, and it was early 1881 before construction was underway. The route stipulated by the charter was to be from Lake City all the way to Charlotte Harbor, with a branch line to Palatka. Fulfillment of this requirement would win for the company a land grant of 2,655,842 acres — a truly handsome inducement.

The first segment of the railroad to be constructed was the 49-mile branch from Palatka to Gainesville. Materials and equipment arrived via St. Johns River steamers at the docks in Palatka. While this project was in progress, a stockholders meeting, on April 9, 1881, changed the name of the company to "The Florida Southern Railway Company" and elected John W. Candler of Boston, Mass., president. Charles Francis, named general manager, was the man in charge locally. On completion of the Palatka branch, about mid-summer, the Florida Commercial Company received $26,000 per mile in Florida Southern stocks and bonds — generous payment for construction of a narrow-gauge railroad. Overcharged for construction, poorly managed, and burdened with debt from the beginning, the Florida Southern had many of the earmarks of a speculative promotion.

On completion of the road to Punta Gorda, and claiming credit for the Plant-constructed interstices, the company seized its land grant. A pamphlet published in 1888 offered land at prices ranging from $1.25 to $5.00 per acre. Mr. L. O. Garrett, Commissioner of Lands and Immigration, asserted:

> "The land grant of the Florida Southern Railway consists of 3,000,000 acres of agricultural, fruit, grazing and timber lands in the State of Florida . . . It offers to the settler and investor rare advantages and unusual inducements . . . It is of great importance to the settler in a new State to locate near an enterprising and progressive railroad, that will push the development of the country, and furnish rapid transportation for his crops to good markets. The Florida Southern Railway offers all of these advantages."

In actual fact, the narrow-gauge Florida Southern did not furnish very rapid transportation over standard-gauge connections to distant markets, and settlement came too slowly in most of its territories to enable it to meet interest payments. It was placed under a receiver in March of 1890, purchased at foreclosure sale two years later by Henry Hyde and F. O. Brown, and reorganized into the Florida Southern Railroad Company, with Henry Plant as one of the directors. Beginning in 1893, its lines were operated as part of the Plant system, but the company retained its separate corporate identity until 1903.

Onward and Upward

While the Florida Southern was building him a captive line reaching the lower West Coast, Henry Plant was busy with other Florida projects. He watched, with impatient interest, as a corporation ambitiously titled "The Jacksonville, Tampa & Key West Railway Company" prepared to build a line along the St. Johns River from Jacksonville to Palatka and beyond to Sanford. Here was another route down the peninsula — one with special interest because it would connect with an existing railroad from Sanford to Kissimmee. Moreover this company's charter permitted construction of a line from Kissimmee to Tampa. Once he saw the JT&KW construction finally begin in earnest in March of 1883, Henry Plant moved quickly. Only two months later, according to one source, the Plant Investment Company acquired a two-thirds interest in the South Florida Railroad Company, which had recently completed its line from Sanford through Orlando to Kissimmee. About the same time he purchased the JT&KW's franchise for building the road from Kissimmee to Tampa. The price was probably reasonable, for the JT&KW had no funds for the project, and the franchise was to expire on January 25, 1884. By the time all this was in hand, Plant had little more than six months to build 74 miles of railroad.

The ensuing project was one of the most spectacular in the history of American railroad building. Since speed was so essential, Plant and Haines decided on narrow-gauge track for the initial construction. Crews numbering from 1,200 to 1,500 men were set to work at each end of the route. Materials at the eastern end were brought up the St. Johns by steamer, unloaded at Sanford, and transported down the South Florida road. At the western end, they came via the Florida Central and Peninsular to Cedar Key, and then by steamer to Tampa. A roistering camp town grew at "end-of-track," 20 miles east of Tampa, later to be named Plant City. Regular train service between these points, with a scheduled time of 1½ hours each way, was instituted on December 10, 1883. It was not until January 23, just two days before the charter would have expired, that the crews from each end met and joined the rails at a trestle near Carter's Kill, just east of the future site of Lakeland.

Henry Plant now had his through route to a port on the Florida West Coast. He and Henry Haines, along with J. E. Ingram, Herbert Drane and John Mahoney (officials of the South Florida Railroad) took a group of local political dignitaries on an inaugural trip from Sanford on January 25. The train consisting of a baggage car, one passenger coach, and Plant's private car, arrived in Tampa at 5 p.m. for a lively round of festivities.

The crucial battle was won, but much remained to be done before the full potentials of the Tampa route would be realized. From a site on the new South Florida division, a place soon to be named Lakeland, two branch lines were begun immediately. One stretched northward to Pemberton's Ferry, the other southward to Bartow; together they formed part of the Florida Southern's route to Charlotte Harbor, as described above.

Plant and Haines must have grown very impatient watching the most strategic connection for their Tampa line, the Jacksonville, Tampa & Key West, inch its way southward from Jacksonville, finally reaching Sanford in February of 1886. Even then, physical connection was not possible, for the JT&KW was five-foot gauge, and the South Florida was three-foot gauge. This handicap was soon overcome when both railroads were changed to standard gauge, along with the general shift of southern roads in June of 1886. Passenger and freight trains rolled unimpeded between Jacksonville and Tampa during the busy season of 1887. Then the Hillsboro River was spanned with a drawbridge, and a nine-mile extension line reached Port Tampa early in 1888, terminating on a long wharf for direct contact with ocean vessels. The Plant Steamship Line, with the steamship *Mascotte* (later joined by the *Olivette*), was soon offering service to Havana, Cuba, and Mobile, Alabama.

A West Coast Route

Tampa now became winter headquarters for Henry Plant, his family, and his associates. He was fully bent on developing it into an unsurpassed vacation center as well as a major port. Determined to compete successfully with Flagler's development at St. Augustine, Plant and his wife designed the Tampa Bay Hotel to be the ultimate in elegance and luxury. The first phase of the hotel was ready for business in the season of 1891.

Plant now improved connections for his Tampa terminus by assembling a "West Coast Route." Much of the traffic for Tampa, and Southwest Florida in general, could be handled faster by using the middle entry to Florida (via Waycross, Dupont, and High Springs) rather than the round-about route through Jacksonville and Sanford. However, the existing route through Gainesville left much to be desired. It meandered down the center of the peninsula and included many miles of the narrow-gauge Florida Southern. Failing to reach an agreement with the Florida Southern bondholders in 1890, Plant found another solution. The Silver Springs, Ocala & Gulf Railroad Company had completed its line through Dunnellon to Homossassa in 1888. Then, of particular interest to Plant, it constructed a branch from just below Dunnellon southward to Inverness. A few months after this line began service, in April of 1891, Plant's South Florida Railroad completed an extension northward from Pemberton's Ferry (later named Croom) to Inverness. Here was the southern end of the desired "West Coast Route"— miles of straight, standard-gauge road from Dunnellon to Lakeland. The segment northward from Dunnellon took longer, possibly because Plant and his associates hoped somehow to gain access to the Florida Central & Peninsular's line from Gainesville to Dunnellon. Finally, in 1893, the SF&W constructed a line southward from High Springs to Archer and began, about the same time, a line from Juliette (just north of Dunnellon) towards Archer. The latter line was finished only 13 miles from Morriston. The Florida Central & Peninsular, apparently responding to the pressure of this paralleling construction, gave Plant trackage rights on their road over the remaining distance to Archer. The use rights went into effect on January 1, 1894, and service over the new lines began on the same day. The "West Coast Route" was accomplished.

Adding to the Collection

The two main routes from Waycross, Georgia, to Tampa, Florida (one via Jacksonville, Sanford, and Lakeland, the other via Dupont, High Springs, Dunnellon, and Lakeland) were the essential parts of Henry Plant's railroad system in Florida. However, he added hundreds of miles of branch and connecting lines, mostly by taking control of small, bankrupt companies. There were many such opportunities, as the railroad business in Florida shared the same hazards that periodically ruined farmers and innkeepers. The yellow fever epidemic of 1888, the nationwide financial panic of 1893, and the disastrous freezes of 1895 and 1897 were some of the causes of bankruptcies in Florida at that time. Small, poorly managed railroads carrying heavy debt loads were especially vulnerable. Some of the railroads Plant collected were definitely useful for his system. For one instance, the Jacksonville, Tampa & Key West (its line from Jacksonville to Sanford forming part of a major route) was purchased by the Plant Investment Company in April of 1899 after being in receivership for six years. For another, the Florida Southern (with its lines from Gainesville to Brooksville and from Bartow to Charlotte Harbor finally widened to standard gauge) came under his control in 1895 after being foreclosed and reorganized.

There were other acquisitions that were probably less useful to Plant than they would have been for his competitor, the Florida Central and Peninsular. He was never able to get an influential position in the FC&P (it finally went to the Seaboard Air Line in 1900), and by 1890 it was a serious competitor at several points, including Tampa. Perhaps this situation motivated him to take control of the Orange Belt Railway in 1893.

The narrow-gauge Orange Belt Railway ran parallel, a few miles to the north, to Plant's line from the Sanford area to Pinellas Point, on the other side of Tampa Bay. Its roadway was so poor that trains managed to traverse it only by staying under 15 miles per hour. An ebullient Russian immigrant named Piotr Dementieff (Anglicized to Peter Demens) promoted construction of this railroad, 157 miles from the western shore of Lake Monroe to Lake Apopka and then across the state to Pinellas Point (renamed St. Petersburg in honor of himself and his native land). From 1885 to 1889, Demens led a group of local and New York associates through a series of fantastic misadventures. They lost titles to rights-of-way for failure to meet construction deadlines. They built across such lands without a title. Construction crews halted work and threatened to riot for back pay. A contract was signed with the owners of Pinellas Point that necessitated building a dock some 3,000 feet out into the Bay. Needless to say, the creditors took control of the road in the summer of 1889. A reorganization placed it under the Sanford & St. Petersburg Railroad Company in 1893.

When Plant took control two years later, he widened the line from Macon (later Trilby) on the West Coast Route to St. Petersburg, but did little more to improve the railroad or to develop St. Petersburg as a port. Two smaller railroads which served as feeder branches — the Florida Midland and the St. Cloud & Sugar Belt Railway — were added under Plant's leadership.

Enter Henry Flagler

There was one other person like him in developing Florida during these decades — Henry M. Flagler. An erstwhile associate of John D. Rockefeller and a multi-millionaire, Flagler established a retirement residence in St. Augustine in 1883. Very much taken with the old town, he set out to make it a major winter resort by building two elegant hotels, the Ponce de Leon and the Alcazar. In the process, he became impatient with the little Jacksonville, St. Augustine, Halifax Railroad for failing to make direct rail connection at Jacksonville. He purchased the road, built a bridge across the St. Johns River at Jacksonville, and by 1887 had trains running directly to St. Augustine. Begun as an adjunct to his hotel ventures, his railroad was soon extending down the East Coast, reaching New Smyrna in 1892 and West Palm Beach in 1894, where he already had the fabulous Hotel Royal Poinciana under construction. On April 15, 1896, the first train arrived at the Miami River, and building of the Royal Palm Hotel commenced shortly after. Flagler and Plant consistently respected one another's territory and cooperated to the extent of forming a jointly-owned steamship line. There was a certain amount of friendly rivalry, however, as they competed for tourist business for their respective coasts. Rumor has it that when Flagler invited Plant to the gala opening of the Royal Palm in Miami in 1897, Plant inquired by telegram, "Where is Miami?" Flagler wired back, "Just follow the crowds."

Plant Dominates the Scene

In the midst of all the activity in Florida, Plant acquired a major connection for traffic to the Midwest — the Alabama Midland Railroad, a 175-mile line from Bainbridge, Georgia (on the SF&W) to Montgomery, Alabama, completed in 1890. A majority of the stock was purchased by the Plant Investment Company, and the railroad began its operations as part of the Plant System. Its connection with the Louisville & Nashville at Montgomery linked the Plant System effectively with the great commercial centers of the Midwest. A less important connecting line was picked up in the late 1880's, when the owners of the Brunswick & Western, after many years of struggling over an unprofitable road, sold out to Plant. The price was modest, and the line from Brunswick to Albany, Georgia, provided additional access to the interior of Georgia and points northward. In the late 1890's, Henry Plant's railroad empire comprised about 2,000 miles of fully owned or controlled lines serving extensive territories in Florida and southern Georgia, and linked to the Atlantic Coast Line at Charleston and to the Louisville & Nashville at Montgomery.

A Little History Lesson

War with Spain, in 1898, brought a tremendous boost in business and in national publicity for the Plant System. Traffic with Havana had suffered since 1895 from the violence of the Cuban insurrection and the equally ferocious repression by the Spanish government. With the sinking of the Battleship *Maine* in Havana Harbor on February 15, 1898, and the subsequent growth of war excitement in the United States, vessels of the Plant Steamship Company were kept busy evacuating U. S. citizens from Cuba. When the United States Consul General at Havana, General Fitzhugh Lee, arrived at Port Tampa at 9 a.m. on April 12, the Plant System had a special train with the general superintendent's private car waiting to take him to Washington as quickly as possible. The Plant System, the Atlantic Coast Line, and the RF&P did well by General Lee. The special train covered the 1,274 miles from Port Tampa to the capital at an average speed of 54½ miles an hour, all of which received enthusiastic coverage in the national press. When Congress took the country into war with Spain a few days later, Port Tampa was immediately designated the major port of embarkation for the forces bound for Cuba. The Tampa Bay Hotel served as general headquarters for the area. Henry Plant may have regarded Teddy Roosevelt as an uneasy type of Republican; even so, the drilling of the Rough Riders at Tampa must have pleased him. Certainly the part played by his transportation network in this war seemed to come as a justifying climax to Henry Plant's business career.

Though Henry Plant began poor, he had now become a very wealthy man. Most of his personal fortune was in the form of equities which gave him command of a large, complex business empire. He still owned the Southern Express Company, deriving much of his capital for other investments from its profits. The Plant Investment Company gave him absolute control of the railroad and steamship lines. Another Connecticut-chartered corporation, the Southeastern Investment Company, held his interests in real estate and other businesses.

By this point, the reader might have the impression, as did many Floridians of his day, that Henry Plant was omnipresent in the Southeast. Actually, his permanent residence after about 1870 was New York City, with a splendid house at 586 Fifth Avenue, and his main business office at No. 12 West 23rd Street. Many weeks of each year were spent at Tampa, of course, and there were frequent stops at Jacksonville and at the railroad offices in Savannah; yet he left operations in the South for the most part to his executives, such as Henry Haines and, later, Bradford Dunham. Most of his railroad acquisitions were accomplished from the New York office in negotiations with other finance offices in the city. The man who bore increasing responsibility for such matters was Robert G. Erwin, a lawyer who had a fine grasp of corporation finance.

Strong to the End

At the approach of his 79th birthday, October 27, 1898, Henry Plant apparently resolved to gather all of his properties under one corporation so that, rather than being dispersed after his death, they would continue to be identified with his name and his accomplishments. He discussed this several times with his closest legal advisor, Lynde Harrison of New Haven, Connecticut. When he returned from Florida the next spring in perceptibly declining health, they made the following arrangements. First, the name of the Southeastern Investment Company was changed to the Henry Bradley Plant Company under authorization obtained from a Connecticut court on April 13. Control of his entire business empire was to be vested in this company. Second, they drew up a codicil to his will providing that ownership of the Henry Bradley Plant Company and all the properties it possessed should be held in trust, not to be divided until the death of his grandson (then four years old) or until his grandson's youngest child reached majority age, which ever should occur later. Discovering that property could not be entailed to this extent under the laws of New York State, Plant decided to change his official residence back to Connecticut, where no such legal impediment existed.

The events which now transpired testify to the force of this man's determination. On June 16, 1899, Henry Plant rose from his sickbed, left his Park Avenue house accompanied by his valet and a housemaid, and took the train to his home town of Branford, Connecticut. There he spent three days visiting with relatives, announcing to all and sundry that he was moving back to Connecticut. Beginning the return journey to New York City on June 20th, he stopped over at New Haven and spent several hours in Lynde Harrison's office. They made arrangements for buying him a house in that city, and for filing the important codicil to his will. Still accompanied by his small entourage, he boarded an afternoon train and arrived at his house in New York City the same evening. Three days later, June 23, 1899, Henry Plant died.

Henry Plant had continued to expand and improve his railroad system in Florida to the end of his life. Although he left much to be finished, he did assemble an essentially complete railroad network in the State of Florida. Whole sections were opened to agriculture, industry, and tourism as his railroad lines made them accessible for the first time. Towns like Jacksonville, Sanford, High Springs, and, of course, Tampa grew, becoming important transportation centers with wharves and warehouses, repair shops, freight yards, and company offices, and bringing unprecedented activity. Henry Plant had both the determination and the resources needed to keep on building during the bad years, when other people gave up on Florida or were wiped out. His achievements made the next chapter in Atlantic Coast Line history possible.

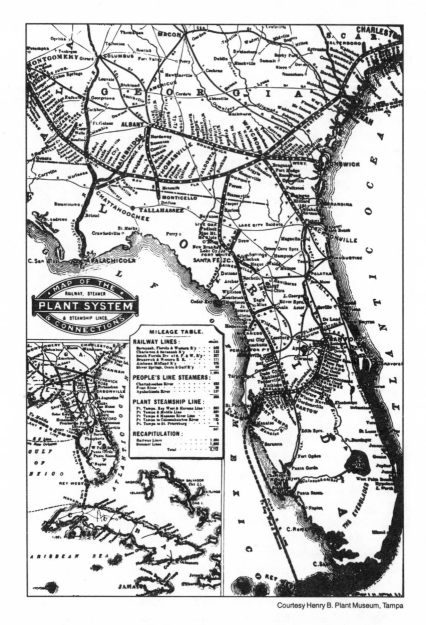

No.6: *Henry Plant's rail empire in Florida opened the door for the Atlantic Coast Line to become a dominant force in the state's development. This map shows the system at the turn of the century.*

Chapter IX

Absorbing the Plant System

Prologue

"Negotiations have been completed under which it is arranged that the Savannah, Florida & Western Railroad companies will, on or before July 1, 1902, be consolidated with and become the property of the Atlantic Coast Line Railroad Company. The negotiations also contemplate that the other railway properties of the Plant System shall pass under the control of the Atlantic Coast Line at the same time."

This matter-of-fact announcement, made on April 4, 1902, by W. G. Elliott, President of the Atlantic Coast Line Railroad Company, and R. G. Erwin, President of the Plant Investment Company, aroused considerable interest on Wall Street and among transportation leaders. At one stroke the Coast Line was acquiring an additional 1,733 miles of road and becoming a railroad system of modern dimensions. It was also establishing itself as the main Northeast-to-Florida route. There was quite a story behind this culminating event.

Henry Plant's Legacy Under New Leadership

Although Mr. Plant had not been able to complete his plan to move to Connecticut, Lynde Harrison did everything possible to carry out his wishes. He managed, apparently with support from Robert Erwin and another of Plant's close aides, G. H. Tilley, to obtain the entirety of the will and to have it probated in Connecticut. This took place in New Haven on June 29, and the widow, Margaret J. Plant, now learned for the first time of the recently executed codicil. In addition to the long-term trust arrangement, it provided that she, along with Morton F. Plant (Henry's son by his first wife), Lynde Harrison, G. H. Tilley and R. G. Erwin, would be the executors. It also provided that Mrs. Plant and Morton would each receive an annuity of only $30,000 from an estate amounting to tens of millions of dollars. Small wonder that she subsequently decided to challenge the will.

Robert G. Erwin now took charge of the Plant Railroad System, occupying the presidencies of the Plant Investment Company and the Savannah, Florida & Western Railway Company. He wasted no time in establishing a close relationship with the Walters group. On the same day as the will was probated, Erwin wrote to Benjamin Newcomer with the news that the other representatives of the estate wanted him to succeed Mr. Plant as president of the Plant Investment Company. Since Henry Walters was in Europe, Erwin had contacted Mr. Newcomer to ask support of the Coast Line leaders, important minority stockholders in his company. Newcomer responded, "If I had been permitted alone to name his successor, this would have been my choice." When Erwin requested, by return mail, a conference to discuss policies for the Plant System, Newcomer answered:

"I have a suggestion to make which I trust will prove mutually agreeable to you and Mr. H. Walters. Mr. Walters sailed on the *Campania* on Saturday last from Liverpool for New

York, and will be due in New York at the end of this week . . . . On his arrival he will find a letter from me asking him to call upon you; and I am sure you will find him much more competent than myself to consider any of the questions of your future policy . . . . He is not only interested in the Plant Investment Co. as a stockholder, but has for some time past been regarding you as the "coming man" for that System, so that a conference with him may result advantageously."

In his letter to Henry Walters the same day, July 3, Newcomer observed, "Knowing, as I do, your desire to keep in touch with him and his management of the Plant Investment Co., I thought it best to put the matter in this shape and open the door for you to have an interview with him as soon after your return as may suit your convenience."

From this point on, Henry Walters and Robert Erwin communicated often, mostly through personal conferences in New York City, where both had their headquarters. Erwin very much needed this outside point of strength to buttress his position, which had a very uneasy base in the Plant estate. Mrs. Plant soon began her legal battle to set aside the will, and the case entered long months of complicated litigation. Under the circumstances it was difficult to get a consensus of the five executors on policy for the railroad system. If the will should be set aside, the whole Plant financial structure would be in question.

Much closer cooperation now developed between the two railroad systems than had existed during Henry Plant's last years. Henry Walters' influence in Plant System affairs was such that Samuel Spencer of the Southern Railway cleared it with him before negotiating a traffic contract with the Plant System. In answer to a complaint from Emerson that Southern traffic agents were soliciting business at Charleston, Walters wrote:

"In the conversations which I had with [Spencer] upon the question of his using the Plant System south of Savannah, I . . . said to him that we would not object to this, but that we would not expect them to change the situation as it now exists at Charleston. This is a matter for a future negotiation, as you understand."

Consolidating the Plant System

By the autumn of 1900, Erwin had a plan formulated for gathering a number of Plant roads into the Savannah, Florida & Western Railway Company and for refunding its debts. He wrote to Henry Walters:

"I enclose a copy of the plan of consolidation, and for the issue of new 4% bonds of the consolidated SF&W Co., about which I spoke to you yesterday. As I told you then, we are not giving this information to anyone outside of our Directors except yourself, and we feel safe in sending you the enclosed knowing that no other eyes but yours and Mr. Newcomer's will see the same."

After studying the plans carefully, Walters assured Erwin that the proposed stock distribution for the consolidation was equitable and the refinancing scheme very sound. He also observed, "The relations which you have established with us, and with the Southern Railway, should be a good guarantee of continued prosperity in the future, and I congratulate you on your scheme, and sincerely hope that you will have no hitch in carrying it out promptly."

Richard Erwin's consolidation plan was approved, although none too promptly, on May 10, 1901. It went far toward clearing up the hodgepodge of corporate relationships produced by Henry Plant's rapid expansion. Capital stock of the SF&W was increased to 250,000 shares ($25,000,000), half of which was 4% dividend, non-voting, preferred stock. SF&W shareholders kept their original stock and received a 75% dividend in new preferred stock. The following railroad companies were consolidated into the SF&W and their owners paid as indicated.

Charleston & Savannah Railway Company — 111 miles of line
common stock exchanged of its par value in SF&W for 10% preferred

Brunswick & Western Railroad Company — 169 miles
common stock exchanged for 1% of par value in SF&W common preferred stock exchanged for 10% of par value in SF&W common

Alabama Midland Railway Company — 207 miles
common stock exchanged for 10% of par value in SF&W preferred; preferred stock exchanged for 20% of par value in SF&W preferred

Silver Springs, Ocala & Gulf Railroad Company — 64 miles
common stock exchanged for 80% of par value in SF&W preferred

Tampa & Thonotosassa Railroad Company — 13 miles
common stock exchanged for 100% of par value in SF&W common

The amounts of new SF&W stock given in exchange for that of the merged companies seem to have been based on fair evaluations of the different   properties. There was, however, a pattern here which worked to the distinct advantage of the Plant Investment Company. The companies in which there were large and troublesome minority interests, e.g., the Charleston & Savannah and the Alabama Midland, received only non-voting preferred stock to distribute to their owners. The consolidation therefore greatly tightened control of the Investment Company over the railroad system. It became effective on July 1, 1901, enlarging SF&W mileage to about 1,600. The process was completed by a secondary consolidation on July 12, which added four more small railroads to the SF&W. They were:

The Abbeville Southern Railway — 27 miles

The Ashley River Railroad — 4 miles

The Southwestern Alabama Railway — 37 miles

The Greenpond, Walterboro & Branchville Railroad — 38 miles

When this second-phase consolidation took effect on September 2, the SF&W grew further to a 1,705-mile railroad. Another 55 miles would soon be added by construction of a cutoff line from Folkston, Georgia, thus shortening the Savannah-to-Jacksonville route by several miles in order to meet competition from the Seaboard Air Line. There were still four railroads (456 miles) controlled and operated as part of the Plant System which were not, for various reasons, included in these consolidations. They were the Florida Southern, the Sanford & St. Petersburg, the St. Johns & Lake Eustis, and the Winston & Bone Valley railroads. Nevertheless, the Plant System was now a model of orderliness compared with its earlier state.

Straightening out the Books

Erwin's new bond plan for the SF&W (approved at the May 10 meeting) was designed to bring a comparable degree of order to the balance sheets of the railroad company and the Plant Investment Company. Henry Plant had collected and constructed his railroads with a cavalier disregard for niceties of corporate finance. He had made advances totaling about $7,000,000 to the Plant Investment Company from the Southern Express Company, from the Southern Investment Company, and from his personal accounts, as if moving money from one pocket to another. The Plant Investment Company, in turn, was carrying about $4,000,000 on its books in construction accounts in railroad real estate, and in loans to the various railroad companies. This interlocking mass of floating debts had not been a serious problem under Plant's one-man regime, but it was now. For the benefit of the other segments of the Plant estate and of the minority stockholders in the Investment Company, Erwin was attempting to order the finances of the railroad system so that the Investment Company could begin to make dividend payments.

The new 4% SF&W bonds would help greatly. They would replace bonds and notes on which the several railroad companies had been paying higher interest. Also, the Investment Company was to receive over $12,000,000 in these new bonds, with which it could pay off its floating debt. The entire issue of SF&W bonds was to be used according to the following plan:

1. Take up bonds and other obligations (held by Plant Investment Co.)
   of railroad companies being consolidated $12,133,000

2. Reserve for acquisition of new rolling stock   1,000,000

3. Reserve for retirement of outstanding bonds of railroad companies as they mature   <u>16,467,000</u>

Total issue of SF&W 4% lst mortgage bonds $29,600,000

The plan was fine, but Robert Erwin had some difficulty with his arrangements to use the bonds for the benefit of the Investment Company. The Investment Company's creditors — the other corporations in the Plant estate — refused at first to accept them in payment for its debts. By this time the struggle over the will had been in the courts for over a year, and relationships among the executors of the estate were strained in all directions. Determined to break the will, Mrs. Plant was probably reluctant to see any more securities deposited with the Henry Bradley Plant Company. Lynde Harrison and John A. Stewart, in charge of the latter company, apparently hesitated to accept low-interest bonds in place of higher-yield notes. Henry Walters went out of his way to help Erwin in these negotiations. He got a favorable quotation on the bonds from a large banking concern, so that Erwin could get them accepted at par value by other administrators of the Plant estate. Agreement was finally reached on this basis in the closing weeks of 1901. Robert Erwin had the Plant Investment Company and its railroad system in solid financial condition.

"Willing" to Sell

Then, in January of 1902, the trust provisions of Henry Plant's will were set aside. The Supreme Court of New York, having heard the case in special session, found that Mr. Plant had died a citizen of _that_ state, and not of Connecticut. The heirs were now free to dispose of their respective shares of the estate as they chose. Mrs. Plant, who received the largest share, apparently wished to liquidate her holdings in the several companies as quickly as possible. The court decision had effectively loosened the grip on the Plant System of Steamships and Railways.

Henry Walters and Robert Erwin began immediately to explore, in confidential sessions, the possibilities of a sale of the Plant System to the Coast Line. On January 15, Walters received from Erwin a list of the railroads and railroad-related properties which the Plant Investment Company held and would sell. They evolved the basic understanding that the Atlantic Coast Line holding company would offer to buy these properties at a price to be negotiated, but in the neighborhood of 90% of par in ACL RR Co. common stock. Also that the Plant railroads would be merged with the Atlantic Coast Line Railroad Company.

For several weeks they worked at developing the agreement in greater detail, keeping the matter absolutely to themselves. As late as February 27, with Erwin in Savannah, they were still exchanging information on their respective railroads. Henry Walters carefully studied the reports on every aspect of the Plant System: location and condition of the roads, amount and quality of the equipment, accounts of earnings and expenses, and capitalization and indebtedness. As a result of this analysis, he reduced the price he was willing to pay to around 75% of par in Coast Line common stock.

When Erwin returned to New York the first week in March, they got down to serious negotiations in a suite in the Albemarle Hotel. The Plant heirs were now consulted, and a question arose that stopped the whole proceedings temporarily. They were not opposed to the sale, or even to the basic terms as Walters and Erwin had developed them, but they (presumably Mrs. Plant in particular) wanted cash for their equities and not ACL RR Co. stock. This posed a real challenge to the financial resources of the Walters group. Henry Walters went to Baltimore on Friday evening, March 7, and laid the whole matter before Michael Jenkins the next morning. Jenkins apparently approved of the whole idea and agreed that the necessary cash could be raised. They traveled together to New York and entered into the final round of negotiations with Erwin and the Plants on Monday. By the next day the group was discussing fine points of wording on a draft of the agreement.

On Wednesday, March 12, the agreement was signed by Henry Walters and Michael Jenkins as president and vice president of the Atlantic Coast Line Company, and Robert G. Erwin and Morton F. Plant as president and vice president of the Plant Investment Company.

The main provisions of the sale were:

1. The Plant Investment Company agreed to sell, and the Atlantic Coast Line Company agreed to buy, all the common stock outstanding ($10,346,200 par value) and $8,708,700 in the preferred stock of the Savannah, Florida & Western Railway Co., plus stock and bonds of all other railroad companies and claims and titles to all railroad-related properties held by the Plant Investment Company.

2. The Atlantic Coast Line Company would pay for these properties $7,837,830 in new 4% gold bonds of the ACL RR Co. and $7,125,000 par value in common stock of the ACL RR Co.

3. The Atlantic Coast Line Company would repurchase the $7,125,000 in ACL RR Co. stock at 85% of par value on July 1, 1902, by paying $1,556,250 in cash on that day, and the remainder in three annual installments of $1,500,000 each.

4. The properties would be delivered, free from floating debt, by the Plant Investment Company on July 1, 1902.

5. The Plant Investment Company would try to obtain from other persons their holdings in SF&W preferred stock, to be exchanged at 90% of par for new ACL RR Co. 4% gold bonds.

6. The Atlantic Coast Line Company would bring about the merger and consolidation of the SF&W with and into the Atlantic Coast Line Railroad Company and would attempt to include the Florida Southern, the Sanford & St. Petersburg, and the St. Johns & Lake Eustis railroad companies in this consolidation.

7. The Plant Investment Company would assist in securing all of the outstanding issue of new SF&W bonds for exchange for new ACL RR Co. 4% gold bonds.

The Agreement is Revealed

Thus far only the four signatories of the agreement, their immediate assistants, and Mrs. Plant knew about the deal. One of the first persons to be told was Samuel Spencer, president of the Southern, to insure against opposition to the merger by J.P. Morgan. Henry Walters had a talk with Spencer a day or two later and "found that it disturbed him very much." Walters gave Spencer a few days to calm down and then offered to let the Southern have a long-term contract for trackage rights between Savannah and Jacksonville. Spencer was satisfied.

Henry Walters next headed southward to get his railroad company affairs in order for the merger. He spent Friday, March 14, in the Richmond office, arrived in Wilmington on Saturday, March 15, and broke the news to Warren Elliott in a meeting in his office Monday noon. It would be Elliott's task, as president and head counsel of the Railroad Company, to make preparations for the merger. They spent three days of intensive work in Wilmington, then traveled together to Baltimore for some sessions with Michael Jenkins. They held a directors meeting of the holding company on Friday, March 21 (probably joined by Henry Walter's nephew, Warren Delano, Jr., to make a quorum), and formally approved the purchase agreement with the Plant Investment Company. Henry Walters then went back to New York and sailed for Europe the following Tuesday, leaving management of the whole affair with Jenkins and Elliott for more than a month.

A Problem Solved

It fell to Michael Jenkins to go to New York in the closing days of March to negotiate an agreement for exchange and cancellation of the new SF&W bond issue. This turned out to be a surprisingly difficult task. It had been arranged that $12,451,000 of these bonds would be issued on April 1, 1902, to be secured by a mortgage on that date with the United States Trust Company of New York. The Walters group simply wanted to provide for exchange and retirement of these bonds so that the mortgage could be canceled before it was recorded. Large portions of the issue were to go to the Plant Investment Company, the Southern Express Company, and Morton Plant, but the largest amount ($4,044,000) was claimed by Mrs. Plant. Michael Jenkins was now confronted with the fact that, as practically sole owners of the SF&W, the Plant heirs would not approve the merger unless these bonds were purchased on their terms. He finally acceded to paying for these in ACL RR Co. bonds on an equal value basis, even though the SF&W securities would have probably sold for less. Still worse, Mrs. Plant, who apparently had seen quite enough of the railroad business, wanted cash for half of her share. He was informed that "her understanding was that in any event, consolidation or no consolidation, she was to receive 90 (cents on the dollar) for $2,000,000 of the SF&W bonds."

After three days of tedious negotiations, an agreement between the Atlantic Coast Line Company, the Plant Investment Company, the Southern Express Company, Morton F. Plant, Margaret J. Plant, and the United States Trust Company of New York was signed at 5 p.m. on April 1, but dated March 31 to antedate the mortgage. Jenkins had the Atlantic Coast Line Company agree (1) to accept some reasonable limitations on the ACL RR Co. bond issue required by the Trust Company, (2) to buy the SF&W bonds on a dollar-for-dollar basis with ACL RR Co. bonds and (3) to repurchase from Mrs. Plant on July 15, $2,022,000 of these Coast Line bonds at 90 cents on the dollar. For their parts, the Plant Investment Company and Morton and Margaret Plant agreed to "use their best endeavors to bring about the consolidation . . . ."

Merger Goes Through

Michael Jenkins retired directly to more congenial surroundings in Baltimore to recuperate and to take satisfaction in the fact that no further obstacles remained. The directors of the Savannah, Florida & Western Railroad Company met on Friday, April 4, and approved the plan for merger with the Coast Line. Immediately afterward, Presidents Elliott and Erwin gave to the press the statement which opens this chapter. They included, at Samuel Spencer's request, the following addendum:

> It is agreed that when the merger of the Atlantic Coast Line and the Plant System takes place, the Southern Railway Company will have trackage rights thereafter for all of its trains, both passenger and freight, over the line between Savannah and Jacksonville, thus making Jacksonville the southern terminus for its Florida service to and from the East and West.

With the essential agreements accomplished, all that remained was the work of carrying out the financial transactions and effecting the merger. There was an interesting twist to the bond exchange agreement. Shortly after the ACL RR Co. bonds were issued in July, the $2,000,000, which the holding company was required to buy from Mrs. Plant at 90 cents, were then sold for 97 cents on the dollar. Michael Jenkins must have found this particular profit rather gratifying.

There now commenced a series of formal steps to complete all the financial transactions, to accomplish the merger, and to clear up some unforeseen details.

April 10: Directors meetings of both railroad companies approved the merger plan and set dates for special stockholders meeting.

May 12: A special ACL RR Co. stockholders meeting approved the merger plan by more than the three-fourths vote required and authorized an increase in capitalization to 188,500 shares preferred, and 231,500 shares common stock.

May 12: The ACL RR Co. made a supplementary agreement with the Plant Investment Company for buying some income bonds of constituent companies in the consolidated SF&W and for covering the construction cost of a new line between Jesup and Folkston, Georgia, thus preventing the issue of more SF&W preferred stock.

May 15: The ACL RR Co. agreed to buy from the holding company nearly all the properties acquired from the Plant Investment Company, and to pay for these with $7,125,000 in par value of its common stock and $10,638,000 in its new 4% bonds.

June 16: A second special stockholders meeting of the ACL RR Co. ratified the purchases made, authorized new mortgage and bond issue of $80,000,000 for funding existing debts of the company and buying the Plant properties, and approved an issue of $25,000,000 in certificates of indebtedness for retiring the outstanding preferred stock of the company. Officers of the consolidated company were elected, with no changes from eight previous ACL RR Co. directors or management.

July 1:   According to provisions of the agreements and actions described above, the Savannah, Florida & Western Railroad became the property of, and its employees the employees of, the Atlantic Coast Line Railroad Company.

A Good Deal

When all the transactions were completed, the Atlantic Coast Line Railroad Company had acquired the 2,235 miles of Plant System railroads by assuming their funded debts of $28,906,500 and paying $17,657,398 ($7,125,000 in its stock at par, $10,532,000 in its bonds, and $398 in cash). In other words, the ACL RR Co. got the Plant System for a total of $46,563,898 in new obligations — $20,879 per mile of the Plant System. Even allowing for the uneven condition of the Plant roads, this was a bargain, especially since a steamship company, many wharf installations, and thousands of acres of land went with the purchase. The values of both railroad systems were enhanced by the merger.

The Plant System was even more of a bargain for the Walters group and their holding company. As discussed earlier, the Atlantic Coast Line Company agreed, on March 12, to buy back the 71,250 shares of ACL RR Co. common stock from the Plant Investment Company for $85 per share (the market price was $87 at the time), or a total of $6,056,250. Once news of the merger was out, the price of ACL RR common rose rapidly, reaching a level between $160 and $170 per share by early July, when the first installment of the payment to the Plant Investment Company was due. The ACL holding company sold 2,000 shares in June at $125 and 7,466 shares subsequently at an average price of $162. After realizing nearly $1,500,000 from these sales, the holding company still retained 61,784 shares of the block of stock in question — securities worth between $8,000,000 and $10,000,000 during the period. The Atlantic Coast Line Company of Connecticut thus made a handsome profit in the course of securing the Plant properties for its railroad system, thanks largely to the Plant heirs' insistence on receiving cash for their interests.

A Good Deal More

Henry Walters arrived back in New York City from his European trip late in April of 1902, in time to preside over most of the final formalities of the Plant merger. His attention was much divided in the following weeks because a spectacular market development in Louisville & Nashville common stock had put control of that strategic railroad system up for grabs. He was not prevented, however, from making management decisions for the takeover of the Plant System. In Wilmington from May 8 to May 11, he spent hours in conference with J.R. Kenly and T.M. Emerson over problems of operations and traffic for the enlarged system. After the big stockholders meeting in Richmond, and a day or two in Baltimore wrapping up financial details, he and Robert Erwin headed for Savannah. They were joined there on Friday, May 16, by their respective executive staffs for a thorough inspection trip over the Plant System. It was nearly a week later before Walters, Elliott, Emerson and Kenly left Florida, greatly impressed by the potential there and the amount of work needed to develop it. No drastic changes were imposed, however, upon the Plant System. Although Kenly, as general manager, headed the Operating Department for all the combined roads, General Superintendent Denham remained in charge south of Charleston much as before. Also, the program of improvements begun by Erwin before the merger was generally allowed to proceed as planned.

The Florida trip resulted in an interesting byproduct. In the course of conversations with Erwin and Henry Flagler, Walters expressed interest in the Peninsular & Occidental Steamship Company, which had been developed jointly by Plant and Flagler. It owned a line of eight steamships offering service between Miami, Key West, Tampa, Havana, and other Caribbean ports. Walters decided to purchase for his holding company the Plant Investment Company's half interest for $350,000. It was a reasonable price for a share in Plant's and Flagler's vision of a complete transportation system linking Florida to much of Latin America.

Reshuffling the Deck

Absorbing the Plant System changed the Atlantic Coast Line Railroad Company in a number of respects. For one thing, it occasioned a reshuffling of top management. Although there were no official changes at the time of the merger, it seems to have been understood all along that Robert Erwin was to be president of the enlarged Atlantic Coast Line Railroad Company. The organizational changes were not made until the annual meetings, November 17, 1902, allowing time for Erwin to close out the Plant Investment Company and also for public interest in the merger to subside. At the same annual meetings, the stockholders created the new office of chairman of the board, and the directors elected Henry Walters to that post.

The officers of the Atlantic Coast Line Railroad Company now were:

Chairman of the Board	**H. Walters**
President	**R. G. Erwin**
First Vice President	**Alexander Hamilton**
Second Vice President	**C. S. Gadsden**
Third Vice President & Traffic Manager	**T. M. Emerson**
Fourth Vice President & General Manager	**J. R. Kenly**

Warren Elliott, who had resigned as president to make way for Erwin, was given the presidency of the holding company — the Atlantic Coast Line Company of Connecticut. Related to these organizational changes was the opening, in July of 1902, of a finance office in New York City, at Number 71 Broadway. This office served henceforth as Henry Walters' business headquarters, and Robert Erwin divided his time between this address and the general offices in Wilmington.

Maintaining the Giant

It would take years to get all the Plant properties fully integrated with the Coast Line. The separate little companies, however, were quickly consolidated into the ACL RR Co. Possession of the St. Johns & Lake Eustis Railroad, the Sanford & Lake Eustis, and the Florida Midland railroads was secured on July 1, 1902. Then, after some lengthy bargaining with their bondholders, the Sanford & St. Petersburg (the Orange Belt) and the Florida Southern railroads were consolidated effective April 1, 1903. Following these actions, the Atlantic Coast Line Railroad Company owned 3,999 miles of line and operated a total of 4,140 miles. Construction of a 28-mile line to Fort Myers, Florida, and of various new spurs increased the mileage operated to 4,229 by June 30, 1904.

The Atlantic Coast Line was now a large railroad, a fact now reflected in its geographic organization. There were two Main Divisions, each divided into three districts:

The First Division, corresponding to the pre-merger Coast Line, included the Richmond, Norfolk, and Charleston Districts;

The Second Division (the old Plant System) was comprised of the Savannah, Jacksonville, and Montgomery Districts. The total locomotive complement in 1903 had grown to 451, and the complement of freight cars to nearly 14,000.

The roads and equipment in the Jacksonville District remained for a time markedly below the standard maintained for the rest of the Coast Line. With the panic of 1903 coming hard on the heels of the ambitious financial commitments made during 1902, Henry Walters insisted on strict economy for the entire railroad operation. Consequently, no improvements to the Florida lines had been made since consolidated into the Coast Line. By 1905 this was becoming a problem that could no longer be ignored. Freight tie-ups repeatedly developed at Jacksonville during the busy seasons. Prominent tourists were shocked at the primitive nature of some of the transportation they encountered in Florida and did not hesitate to convey their reactions to Coast Line officials. Local patrons, especially businessmen engaged in tourism, became insistent and sometimes strident in their requests for improvements. For example, a letter from one P. Isaacs, president of the Fort Myers Board of Trade, had this to say to Coast Line officials about the line from Lakeland to Fort Myers, the Charlotte Harbor Division:

"The Board [has] resolved that the proper officials be requested to investigate, at once, the condition of the roadway, engines and cars that are being operated on this division, with the request that they put same in a safe condition at the earliest possible moment. The belief has become general, as a result off requent wrecks and mishaps, that this track is unsafe to passengers . . . .

We are reliably informed by some of the employees of your road that in many places the cross ties are so rotten that the spikes can be pulled out with the fingers, and in many instances the connecting bars of the rails have no bolts in them. Further it is a provable fact that the coaches are allowed to go on duty in a very dirty and dusty condition, often times being indecent and almost intolerable for ladies to be compelled to ride in, being in continual service without interim for cleaning same. Furthermore, these coaches are many times practically without lights, and it is a common occurrence for them to be without drinking water of any kind, and in our judgment such a condition is against the traveling public's health, safety and convenience.

We feel that our grievances are well founded, and that your company should make extraordinary efforts to remedy these evils without further delay.

The Board of Trade makes these requests in the kindest spirit, believing that your company will consider them in the same spirit . . . as our interests are mutual for the upbuilding of this section."

Fortunately, by the time this letter was written, an ambitious program for improvements in Florida was already in progress. The national business climate in 1905 inspired optimism, and Henry Walters was impressed by the growing volume of traffic south of Jacksonville. After making an especially careful inspection tour of the Florida lines in late January and early February of 1905, he wrote Michael Jenkins an unusual six-page letter, from St. Augustine. A new set of Coast Line policies for Florida is expressed in the following excerpts:

We made a mistake in not insisting upon your taking with us the trip which we have just finished, in order that you might understand more accurately the situation in Florida. It has truly been amazing to me, because I have gone to the section of Florida which I was not familiar with, and have seen the great development taking place upon our lines which I never fully realized and which must be provided for.

You will recall that we rather looked slightingly upon the Sanford and St. Petersburg, originally a narrow-gauge road, which has now been changed to broad-gauge. The development upon it is enormous, and it will be among the most valuable feeders of our long haul. The little town of St. Petersburg has now a population of about 6,000 in the winter. We have already authorized an expenditure of $7,000 for land upon which to erect a new freight station and a small yard (at St. Petersburg), all of which will be done as promptly as possible.

The development of tonnage in the last three years in this State has been simply enormous, and we have done almost nothing to provide for its transportation.

It is several years now since we have bought any but 19-inch cylinder engines. Our main line in Florida has four bridges on it too light to carry such engines. As a result, the division south of Jacksonville has received no new engines at all since we purchased the Plant System, we having sent down here only our second hand lighter engines. The result is, our motive power is much too light for the business, and is in anything but first class condition . . . .

As a result, we have lost much prestige, and the Seaboard Air Line has secured a great deal of business that should have come to us . . . . We must bend every energy, and spend every dollar necessary, to be ready for next fall's business.

Mr. Kenly, Mr. Emerson and Mr. Erwin were with me, and we have laid out a series of improvements, all but one to be finished by next November.

Attention Turns to Florida

The Florida area's increasing importance was reflected by the fact that, by this time, it constituted the Third (or Southern) Division of the Coast Line. Included in the program of improvements for Florida were replacement of the four light bridges between Jacksonville and Sanford; construction of a large freight yard at Jacksonville to serve large port installations already in progress; extensive rebuilding of the lines with heavier rail; construction of some new phosphate spur lines; development of large shops ("all the tools to be new and run by electricity") at Waycross, Georgia, and smaller shops plus a freight yard at Lakeland; and purchase of 30 new engines, 20 passenger coaches, and 1,500 new freight cars.

Walters had visited Henry Flagler in Palm Beach on an inspection tour of Florida. His own expansive plans for the area may have been inspired to some extent by the magnitude of Flagler's projects. He observed:

"Mr. Flagler has decided to build all the way to Key West, extending his present line down the mainland until opposite Key Largo, when he crosses the water to that island, and then skips from island to island until he reaches Key West. Of the 107 miles of road that he will have to build from the mainland, 30 will be water, which it is estimated will cost $200,000 a mile. The balance will probably cost $20,000 a mile, so that his extension will cost him about $7,500,000.

"Mr. Flagler intends to have two big ferry boats built, each of which will carry 18 freight cars, to run between Havana and Key West. I think Mr. Flagler believes that this road will be the means of creating an intimacy between Cuba and the United States which will be of great benefit to our country."

The general air of optimism and excitement surrounding the development of Florida in this period was infectious, and the enormous prospects for tremendous expansion of traffic from the area could not be ignored. The Atlantic Coast Line would now concentrate increasingly on the long-haul business to and from Florida.

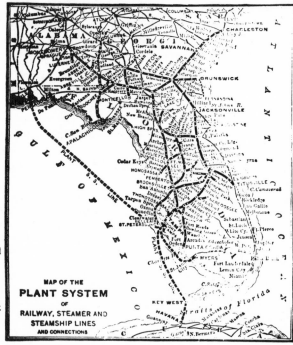

:: The _____
Plant System

The Favorite Route to the Favorite Resorts beyond the Frost Line.

The Finest Hotels.

ﺽﺽ

The Best Shooting.

ﺽﺽ

The Finest Fishing.

ﺽﺽ

The Most Enjoyable Boating, Sailing and Bathing are found on the West Coast of Florida.

MAP OF THE
PLANT SYSTEM
OF
RAILWAY, STEAMER AND
STEAMSHIP LINES
AND CONNECTIONS

The West Coast of Florida is the Health and Pleasure Seekers' Paradise.

ﺽﺽ

The Lines of the **Plant System** reach the Finest Health and Pleasure Resorts of Florida.

5,088 Miles of Perfect Passenger Service.

Luxurious Passenger Trains with Pullman's Finest Sleeping Cars Attached Between All Points.

H. C. McFadden,
Asst. Gen. Pass. Agt.,
Savannah, Ga.

J. J. Farnsworth,
Eastern Pass. Agt.,
261 Broadway, N. Y.

L. A. Bell,
West'n Pass. Agt.,
312 Marquette Bldg.,
Chicago, Ill.

H. B. PLANT, President.

B. W. WRENN, Passenger Traffic Manager.

No. 7: Henry Plant promoted the West Coast of Florida in his ads and posters.

Chapter X

The Louisville and Nashville Purchase

While the Cat's Away

On April 29, 1902, Henry Walters arrived in New York City after a trip to Europe. Waiting for him was a letter from Samuel Spencer, president of the Southern Railway Company. Coming, as it did, from one of J. P. Morgan's associates, the message was very significant:

> You have no doubt seen that the control of a majority of the capital stock of the Louisville & Nashville has been deposited by Gates and his associates with J. P. Morgan & Co.
>
> This deposit was solely the result of Gates' purchases and the cornering of shorts to an extent which threatened trouble in the street, and from any railroad standpoint was entirely unpremeditated.
>
> I may say to you confidentially that no plans have been matured for dealing with it, and it is this that I desire to discuss with you as soon after your arrival as practicable.

Walters and Spencer got together on Saturday morning, May 3, for a long conference. Spencer disclosed the details of the situation and proposed, judging from later communications, that the Southern and the Atlantic Coast Line Railroad companies jointly purchase control of the Louisville & Nashville. Thus began Henry Walters' involvement in one of the most exciting financial episodes of the time.

Bulls Upset the Balance

A highly successful stock speculation venture touched off a series of events that put control of the L&N up for sale. In January of 1902 a group led by John W. "Bet-a-million" Gates had quietly begun to buy L&N common stock on the New York Exchange. At some point they were joined by Edwin Hawley and certain associates, who had been pursuing the same course independently. The L&N listing was a prime target for a bull raid, as the shares were relatively underpriced, at just over $100, and were widely held in small lots. The buying campaign was carried on very skillfully so that only a modest increase in volume and a slight firming of prices, in the $103 to $108 range, were discernible through February and March.

Then the directors of the Louisville & Nashville made a fateful decision. Wishing to take advantage of the favorable market to finance some new construction projects and acquisitions, they authorized August Belmont, their chairman, to sell 50,000 shares which had been in the company treasury. August Belmont & Co. placed these shares on the market on April 5, 1902. They must have been unaware of the market situation, because a new Exchange regulation prohibited delivery of the new certificates until they had been listed for 30 days. The effect was spectacular. Gates and his associates stepped up their rate of buying to keep the large new offering from depressing the price; consequently, Belmont & Co. were unable to borrow shares to cover their technically short position. They were forced to enter the market and attempt to buy enough (at higher prices than received for the new stock) to escape the corner. The price of L&N rocketed from 107$\frac{1}{8}$ on Monday, April 7, to 133 on Monday, April 14, when about 124,000 shares changed hands. The Gates syndicate now held about 51% of all L&N outstanding common stock, and maintained their corner on the market. A group of speculators had garnered control of a first-rate railroad system.

The mysterious market behavior of L&N common stock had been displacing the weather and horse racing as topics of conversation in Louisville barbershops, as well as in New York brokerage offices. Amateur pundits offered a variety of explanations, among them that J. P. Morgan was in the market to capture the L&N. As word of Gates' victory and Belmont's plight circulated in New York financial circles on April 14, there was widespread fear that the market disorders of the Northern Pacific corner of the previous year might be repeated. Railroad leaders worried about the fate of the L&N; it was hard to picture "Bet-a-million" Gates as a responsible manager of a strategic railroad property.

One theory holds that Gates and his colleagues were not interested in owning the L&N, but were manipulating the stock to corner the market and force Belmont and others to come to them to cover their positions at their price. However, there was no stock to be had, and the Gates group ended up owning a railroad that they had no desire to run. In other words, they ended up owning the L&N by accident.

In the Catbird's Seat

Meanwhile, J.P. Morgan & Co. came to the rescue. Morgan persuaded the Gates syndicate to deposit all their holdings (306,000 shares) with his company and to give Belmont time to deliver the shares he was still short. It was a very expensive rescue operation. Morgan & Company signed two contracts on April 15, one with Harris, Gates & Co. for 206,000 shares and another with Hawley & Davis for 100,000 shares. Morgan agreed to buy one-third of the stock for $130 per share and to endeavor to formulate an acceptable plan to dispose of all the stock within six months. Failing this, he reserved the right to buy the remaining two-thirds at $150 per share.

On the face of it, Morgan went out on the proverbial limb in this agreement. He was undertaking to find a buyer for the entire block of L&N stock at the very high price of $150 (in effect for a broker's fee of $16.67 per share), and he was committing his company irrevocably to the deal by purchasing one-third of the stock in advance. Turning the remainder of the stock back to Gates would be an unthinkable blow to Morgan's prestige, and it would be exceedingly awkward if his firm had to purchase the entire block. He must have had a likely customer in mind.

The next day, Wednesday, April 16, J. P. Morgan & Company informed the press:

At the request of Messrs. Harris, Gates, and Company, who on their own independent account have recently made large purchases of Louisville and Nashville Railroad stock, Messrs. J. P. Morgan and Company, as bankers, have consented to take control of the stock so purchased and to receive the same on deposit. They have so consented solely to relieve the general financial condition, and not for the benefit of any railway company. The Southern Railway has no interest, direct or indirect, present or prospective, in the stock or its purchase or deposit. Messrs. J. P. Morgan and Company are acting with the cordial consent of Messrs. August Belmont and Company.

August Belmont issued a statement concurring in the arrangement that was restoring peace to the market in L&N stock. Presidents Spencer of the Southern and Williams of the Seaboard Air Line both published disclaimers as to any interest on their parts in acquiring control of the L&N. Then the whole affair disappeared from public view for six months.

The L&N episode had stimulated endless gossip at the time and, naturally enough, it has been remembered in many divergent versions. One tradition has it that Morgan sent one of his junior partners (some say Charles Schwab, others George Perkins) to Gates' room at the Waldorf to wake him up in the middle of an April night with an insistent offer to buy the L&N stock. Gates responded that if Morgan & Co. wanted it so much, they could have it for $10,000,000 above its cost to him and his associates. They allegedly met his terms on the spot.

The tendency of many persons to believe the worst of J. P. Morgan had given rise to a persistent story that Morgan actually bought the stock from Gates at $120, thereby making a huge profit for his firm by selling it at $150. As reputable a writer as John Leeds Kerr perpetuated this version in his sketch of the Louisville & Nashville's history.

J. P. Morgan & Co. were assuredly tough-minded bargainers, but they were not given to practicing out-and-out fraud. They had made it clear at the outset of their negotiations with Henry Walters that they had bought one-third of the stock at $130 and that at least $150 would have to be paid Gates for the balance. They even handed Walters copies of their contracts with the Gates-Hawley syndicate.

Morgan's Plan

Morgan & Company had evidently intended to dispose of the L&N control within the South, rather than have it attached to any one of the big northern systems. In May, shortly after taking control, Morgan's people worked out a joint purchase, by the L&N and the Southern Railway, of the "Monon" — the Chicago, Indianapolis & Louisville Railway. Had they contemplated selling the L&N stock to a northern railroad, J. P. Morgan & Company would not have insisted that the L&N acquire this line to Chicago. Morgan had two obvious objectives in any disposition of the L&N stock: (1) to stabilize railroad relationships in the South, and (2) to make a profit on the transaction. The answer, therefore, was to bring about some kind of attachment to the Southern, the Seaboard Air Line, and/or the Atlantic Coast Line.

In spite of Samuel Spencer's public denial of any interest on the part of his company, the possibility that the Southern Railway might share in the purchase was explored for a time. In fact, beginning with their initial conference on May 3, Spencer and Henry Walters studied the L&N together and developed a plan for a joint purchase. By the end of the month Walters was prepared to close the deal on this basis; but the joint purchase transaction was delayed and then, about mid-June, discarded altogether — no doubt to Spencer's great frustration.

There were two good reasons why Morgan could not sell control of the L&N to the Southern Railway. First, it would have raised a storm of criticism and probably serious challenges from regulatory agencies and the courts. After all, the Southern competed with the L&N at several points, and any combination of the two roads would have confirmed widespread suspicions that Morgan had engineered the market attack on the L&N. Second, the Southern Railway Company simply could not afford to make the purchase. It was carrying a very heavy load of fixed charges, and, although it had recently begun to pay dividends on its preferred stock, dividends on the common stock were still many years away. By contrast, the dividend-paying Atlantic Coast Line carried a light debt, and it was in the process of gaining more financial strength through its absorption of the Plant System. It was a better customer in every way.

After withdrawing Spencer and the Southern Railway, Morgan assigned one of his finance specialists, George Perkins, to the L&N "case." Perkins had the task of devising, with Henry Walters, a plan by which the Atlantic Coast Line would be able to take control of the L&N, and which would also be acceptable to the Gates and Hawley group.

Perkins' Plan

The first avenue Walters and Perkins explored together was a merger of the Atlantic Coast Line and Louisville & Nashville railroad companies. At a meeting in Morgan & Company's offices on Thursday, July 3, 1902, Perkins presented a scheme with the following essential points:

1. The consolidated company would issue $120,000,000 in 5% non-voting preferred stock and $30,000,000 in common.
2. For each 100 shares of L&N, 150 shares of preferred stock of the consolidated company would be paid.
3. For each 100 shares of ACL RR Co., something in the order of 120 shares preferred and 30 shares common stock of the consolidated company would be paid.

4. For settlement with the Gates-Hawley group and other expenses, $5,000,000 in common stock would be used.
5. Another $5,000,000 would go to J. P. Morgan & Co. for fees.
6. Still another $5,000,000 of common stock would go to Henry Walters personally for conducting the negotiations.
7. An underwriting pool would receive $8,000,000 in common stock to provide cash to buy at $150 any L&N or Coast Line stock which would not exchange.

The Bout Begins

Walters found the plan unacceptable in some aspects, particularly in that too much of the common stock in the new company would go to other parties. At the end of the day, he communicated his reactions to Michael Jenkins:

"I have had a siege today with Perkins . . . and finally convinced him that if anything was to be done the Atlantic Coast Line stock must be considered to be of equal value with the Louisville & Nashville.

This afternoon I had to go over the whole thing again with Belmont, which was much harder because he does not know much about his own property, and would not talk except in generalities, but at last he agreed to the even proposition.

When I talked with you, I told you that I had said to Perkins that we would not trade unless in some way the control of the joint property was to be in such shape that it could not pass from our hands, so long as 5% dividends were paid on preferred stock.

The idea still is, that the preferred stock is not to have a vote so long as the dividend is paid upon it. We both agree that the dividend . . . will have to be 5%, but Perkins wants the voting power to become effective if 5% is not paid, and I think that this is too much and that we ought to fix it that the voting power for the 5% preferred stock becomes effective if 4% is not paid.

In order to pay 4% on the preferred stock both the Atlantic Coast Line and the Louisville & Nashville must pay 6% [on their present capitalization].

I propose now to devote myself to getting as even a trade as possible, and manage somehow to get the control of the common stock in our hands.

You can appreciate that there will be great difficulty in dealing with Gates, for unless Morgan offers him something that he thinks will sell for more than $150, he is going to demand $150 in cash. If he takes the securities, he will look after them in the market and keep the price up. If, on the contrary, he takes cash he will probably run them down, and whilst we have no particular interest in this, Morgan's people have a great deal, as they want to get their money out."

In negotiations early the next week, July 7 and 8, Walters and Perkins resolved their points of difference in the merger plan. Perkins then presented the plan to the

Gates-Hawley group, presumably on the basis that they would receive payment largely in the form of preferred stock in the consolidated company. They summarily rejected his proposal. Two revisions of the plan met with the same reception over the following two weeks. The Gates-Hawley group wanted <u>cash</u>.

The L&N stock definitely could not be purchased from Gates with stock in a consolidated company. Morgan, for his part, did not wish to buy all the L&N shares in question and thus end up with a huge block of non-voting preferred stock. The Walters group could not raise enough of the $45,900,000 in cash to buy the stock outright. Consequently the idea of securing control of the L&N by merging it with the Coast Line had to be abandoned.

At the end of July, the whole deal was at sixes and sevens. George Perkins was casting about desperately for some means of putting the L&N in the hands of the Walters group, on terms they could meet. One possibility considered was for Morgan & Company to buy as much of the balance of the stock as would be necessary to satisfy the Gates crowd, and then to lease the L&N to the Atlantic Coast Line Railroad Company for a yearly rental of 6% on the stock. This was discarded when Perkin's lawyers reported back that the L&N had no clear legal authority to lease itself. Henry Walters described the whole situation to Michael Jenkins on July 31, ending with the observation,

> "I write you these facts to show you how mixed up the thing is, but I was also very much impressed today with the idea that Mr. Perkins is very anxious to bring the combination about, and I still believe that some method will be found to accomplish this."

Round Two

The next alternative studied was that the Atlantic Coast Line Railroad Company might purchase the majority block of L&N stock with a new issue of its bonds. Having rejected this notion at the outset, Henry Walters came around to it very slowly and reluctantly. "I cannot believe that it would be judicious for us to agree to purchase the $30,600,000 of stock and pay for it with bonds," was his comment to Jenkins. He wrote again on August 2, "The more I think of it, and the more I talk with them, the more difficult a proposition I find it."

It was indeed a difficult proposition. Perkins was suggesting that the Atlantic Coast Line Railroad Company pay for the L&N stock with $50,000,000 in 4% gold bonds, to be secured by placing the 306,000 L&N shares in trust as collateral. By adding these and an additional $23,000,000 in new bonds (which certificate holders would have the right to claim) to its bonds already outstanding, the ACL RR Co's. funded debt would be ballooned to $139,000,000 against a capitalization of only $23,150,000. Even less appealing to Walters, control of the ACL RR Co's. stock was to be placed in a voting trust — Morgan to name one trustee, the Walters group another, and both parties to agree on a third. Here was a typical Morgan arrangement: the interests of the bondholders in a heavily indebted company would be protected by Morgan control of its management. Henry Walters wanted very much to get control of the L&N, but not enough to accept such onerous conditions.

The Southern Railway and the Seaboard Air Line were very interested parties on the sidelines throughout these negotiations, and Morgan's people kept Walters reminded of their presence. Perkins threw in the possibility again at this point that the Southern might take a one-third interest in the purchase.

Then there came a proposal by John Skelton Williams, president of the Seaboard, who suggested that a proprietary company be formed to lease the L&N at 7%, the new company to have a capital of $15,000,000 (invested and held as guarantee against the lease), with the Seaboard, the Coast Line, and the Southern each contributing one-third.

The Final Round

Henry Walters ignored these pressures in the conviction that Morgan was committed to a deal with the Coast Line interests. He left for a two-week cruise on his yacht, the *Narada*, obviously agreeing with Michael Jenkins' statement, "They will have a better proposition to submit when you return . . . ."

On Monday morning, August 18, Walters was back in his New York office, chafing somewhat at the absence of both George Perkins and J. P. Morgan. He had evidently worked out an acceptable solution in his own mind while on his cruise. In any case, he and Perkins arrived at essential agreement on a plan later in the week, with Michael Jenkins giving his concurrence in a conference on Friday morning. The plan provided that (1) the bond issue by the ACL Railroad Company would be limited to $35,000,000 providing (at 90 cents on the dollar) about $31,500,000 of the purchase price, (2) an additional $10,000,000 in cash would be raised by subscription sales of ACL RR Co. stock, and (3) 40,000 shares of Coast Line stock would be paid directly. The $45,900,000 total price of the L&N stock would thereby be covered. From Henry Walters' standpoint this scheme offered the advantages of keeping the bonded indebtedness of the ACL RR Co. within reasonable limits and of leaving majority control of its stock firmly in the hands of his holding company. He and Perkins were ready to close the deal on Saturday, August 23.

J.P. Morgan was not ready. He withheld his approval while he digested the important departures from the earlier proposal. At an interview the following Tuesday, Walters found Morgan still had reservations. He was apparently having difficulty accepting the idea that his firm would have no control over the L&N - Coast Line combination. Relinquishing control called for special care that the Coast Line was paying a high enough price and that it could bear the resulting financial burden. He may also have been engaging in a war of nerves by letting both Walters and Gates worry about the

The L&N Purchase Agreement

New York, September 25, 1902

Messrs. J. P. Morgan & Co.,
New York.

Dear Sirs:

If, on or before December 31, 1902, you will deliver or will cause to be delivered to the Atlantic Coast Line Rail Road Company, a Corporation of Virginia, transferable certificates for 306,000 shares of the common stock of the Louisville and Nashville Rail Road Company, the said Corporation, upon tender thereof, properly endorsed so as to pass a good and unencumbered title thereto, will receive the same, and will issue to you, or upon your order, in payment therefor, on or before December 31, 1902, cash and securities as follows, for the aggregate par value of $50,000,000, viz:

(1) $35,000,000. Collateral Trust 4% 50-year gold bonds of the said Corporation, to be secured by a pledge of the said 306,000 shares; the form of the bonds and of the indenture securing the same to be satisfactory to you, and the Trustee to be designated by you. Such bonds to be declared redeemable by the Corporation at its pleasure at 105% and accrued interest on any interest day.

(2) 50,000 shares of the Capital Stock of the said Corporation of the par value of $100 each.

(3) $10,000,000 in cash.

The condition of said Corporation at present is approximately as follows:

Capital	$23,150,000
Preferred stock	$ 1,000,000
Certificates of Indebtedness	$22,500,000
Bonds	$ 66,000,000 outstanding

(There are $5,500,000 Certificates of Indebtedness convertible into said bonds.)

This condition, in case of your acceptance of this offer, and until the consummation thereof, is to remain unaltered except to the extent necessary to carry this offer into effect by the issue of said Collateral Trust Bonds, and 50,000 shares of stock, and such further shares of stock as shall be necessary to provide said $10,000,000 cash.

This offer is made to you as a basis for your communication thereof to Mr. Edwin Hawley or John I. Harris as Umpire under your agreement of April 15, 1902, with Harris, Gates & Co., and Hawley & Davis, and is irrevocable after acceptance by you.

THE ATLANTIC COAST LINE RAIL ROAD CO.,
by W. G. Elliott, President.

approach of the October 15 deadline. At any rate, Morgan prolonged negotiations for another month. He placed a lower valuation on the ACL RR Co. stocks and bonds than had Perkins and insisted that an additional 10,000 shares of its stock be included in the payment. Henry Walters finally agreed to the increased price.

The last details of the purchase plan were settled by Walters and the Morgan people on Tuesday, September 23. Acting as the executive committee of the ACL Railroad Company's board, Walters, Jenkins, and Elliott then tendered a contract letter. (preceding page)

The Board of Directors of the Atlantic Coast Line Company of Connecticut sent a letter the same day guaranteeing, as majority stockholder in the Railroad Company, performance of the commitments made in its purchase offer.

And the Winner is . . .

At 1:00 p.m. on Saturday, September 27, the final documents were signed: a statement of personal endorsement by Walters and Jenkins, a letter of acceptance of the offer by J. P. Morgan & Company, and a letter of confirmation from the Atlantic Coast Line Railroad Company. Formal announcement to the press was made by Morgan early the next week.

Morgan had presented the plan to Gates and Hawley in a manner well calculated to tempt them. He described the extra 10,000 shares of ACL RR Co. stock that he had successfully demanded from Walters as being in "special consideration of the service and responsibility required from us in case we shall have to form a syndicate to make a cash purchase of 204,000 L&N shares." In other words, this block of shares represented an over-payment which would be kept by Morgan & Co. if Gates and Hawley insisted on cash. If, however, they accepted the plan, they would receive ACL securities which (figured at par) combined with the cash portion of the parent to total $163.40 per share of L&N.

Even computed very conservatively, as shown below, the Atlantic Coast Line Railroad Company was paying more than the pre-set price for the L&N shares:

$35,000,000 bonds at 90¢ on the dollar	$31,500,000.00
50,000 shares of stock at $125/share	6,250,000.00
Cash	10,000,000.00
Total paid for 306,000 shares L&N	$47,750,000.00
Amount paid per share of L&N stock	$156.05

Actually, the ACL common stock was trading at $180 per share at the time, reflecting market excitement over rumors of the L&N purchase. In spite of all the inducements, the Gates-Hawley group still insisted on payment in cash. Some of them were probably overextended and in no position to hold or dispose of large blocks of bonds. Morgan undoubtedly had their answer before closing the deal with Henry Walters on September 27; his underwriting syndicate for buying the ACL RR Co. bonds was ready by then. He had the cash gathered to pay the Gates group in entirety on October 15.

The Gates-Hawley group turned a handsome profit on their speculation in L&N stock. They had accumulated their holdings at prices ranging from about $103 per share in January and February to around $130 in the last hectic days in early April. An average price in the neighborhood of $112 is probably a fair estimate. Calculated on this basis, they realized $18 per share on the 102,000 shares purchased by Morgan at $130 in April and $38 per share on the 204,000 bought at $150 in October — a total gain of about $10,000,000. Perhaps in the lusty atmosphere of turn-of-the-century Wall Street, this was not an unreasonable fee for gathering and delivering control of a fine railroad system.

Morgan's profit on the L&N transaction was more modest than the Gates syndicate's, yet substantial enough. First, his $20 commission on 102,000 shares amounted to $2,040,000. Second, valuing the ACL RR Co. bonds at 90¢ and its stock at a conservative $125, he received $156 per share for an additional profit of $1,836,000. Third, he organized an underwriting syndicate by which the $10,000,000 cash portion of the payment was raised by the ACL RR Co. His company, as syndicate managers, accepted subscriptions for 85,000 shares of ACL RR Co. common stock at $125 and received a commission of about $500,000 for the service. J. P. Morgan & Co. thus made total profits of $4,376,000 on payments from the ACL RR Co. Any further profits from sale of the securities received were necessarily limited or postponed by the market decline that commenced shortly after the deal and deepened through 1903.

By and large, J. P. Morgan had attained his objectives to a high degree in the L&N transaction. He had realized a good profit for his firm, and he had placed control of the L&N — a major competitor of the Southern Railway — in cooperative hands. Certainly the solution contributed to the stability of railroad relations in the South.

Walters In — Morgan Out

Since it was control of the L&N for which a premium price was being paid, Henry Walters lost no time in making it clear that he expected to receive this in full measure, especially where J. P. Morgan & Co. was concerned. He and Michael Jenkins bristled at the first sign of interference from Morgan's direction. As he wrote Jenkins on October 23:

"I am a good deal worried about the way in which Morgan's people talk about M. H. Smith. I have taken the stand very positively, however, that we are to be the judge of whether he is to be retained, and I can see that this worries them a little."

Milton H. Smith, the capable and outspoken president of the L&N, had incurred the enmity of Samuel Spencer and Morgan's whole establishment by opposing some of the policies introduced during their interim control of his company. Now, in the awkward interval between the purchase agreement and actual transfer of all the securities, Morgan & Co. were attempting to participate in Walters' arrangements for the L&N. Michael Jenkins' reacted forcefully:

> "I have read with much concern your letter of October 23 . . . about the talk of Mr. Morgan's people relative to Mr. W. H. Smith's future position; it is well enough to confer with them, and meet their views where possible, but it should be positively understood that we are to be the judge as to whether Mr. Smith is to be retained, and as to his future position. This stand is to be taken not only in reference to him, but to others holding important positions in the L&N."

The actual takeover of the L&N went smoothly enough. Walters let August Belmont hold the regular annual stockholders meeting on November 5, get approval for some improvement projects, and adjourn the meeting to December 17. With final arrangements for payment completed on December 1 and with proxies (from the Trust Company) for the 306,000 shares in hand, Henry Walters and Robert Erwin went to Louisville with August Belmont on Monday, December 15. They had an opportunity for a short tour of the road and some talks with Milton Smith before the stockholders meeting on Wednesday. They elected H. Walters, W. Delano, Jr., W. G. Elliott, R. G. Erwin, D. P. Kingsley, and Michael Jenkins as new members of the board. August Belmont remained chairman until the January meeting of the board, when he was replaced by Henry Walters.

These delayed actions were arranged to keep public interest in the changes to a minimum, as well as to postpone the official takeover until effective control was in hand. At one point Henry Walters considered passing up the trip to Louisville altogether, confessing, "I have looked forward with a good deal of uneasiness to our visit there, for fear that some attempt at entertainment and public demonstration and newspaper interviewing would take place."

There was no further problem of interference from Morgan & Co. in the affairs of either the L&N or the Coast Line. Milton H. Smith remained as president of the L&N for many years, his management justifying Walters' confidence throughout. Partly because of Smith's strength Walters did not take as active a part in management of the L&N as he continued to do in the Coast Line. He was chairman of the board for each railroad company, as well as of the holding company, but he kept these three hats, so to speak, scrupulously separate. The holding company took no action directly affecting or even communicating with the Louisville & Nashville Railroad Company.

Cool and Calculated

The times were such as to call for caution. Theodore Roosevelt was President, the ICC and Congressional committees were taking great interest in financial interrelationships among railroads, and the famous Northern Securities Company case was in the courts.

Henry Walters kept management of the two railroad companies absolutely separate, permitting their respective officials to communicate directly only on matters that would arise between any two railroads. On questions affecting their common interests, policies were formulated in separate consultations between Walters and the officials of each road.

Prudent as he was in financial matters, Henry Walters doubtless regarded the L&N stock as a safe investment for the ACL RR Co., and he probably even expected that it would be a profitable one in years to come. His primary concern at the time of the purchase, however, was to gain control of the L&N. It was his motivation for spending the "long, hot summer" of 1902 in negotiations with George Perkins. The full meaning of this can be understood only in terms of turn-of-the-century sentiment among railroad financiers.

Since the Interstate Commerce Act had outlawed pooling and "gentlemen's agreements," the solution for eliminating or at least limiting competition was to concentrate control of railroads in fewer hands. Mergers, consolidations and interlocking stock investments were the rule of the day. If a competitor could not be absorbed, he could be reduced as a threat by attaining a full set of controlled connections for one's own road. In fact, the competitor could often be persuaded to be more cooperative if he also needed some of the same connections. Henry Walters repeatedly justified the L&N stock purchase in later years with references to the danger that the L&N would otherwise have been leased to the Seaboard Air Line and this important connection lost to the Coast Line.

Seaboard Air Line Panics

Whether this was a real danger or not, its significance was expressed by John S. Williams' agitation in the fall of 1902. A crucial connection for his Seaboard Air Line system had fallen under the control of its chief competitor. Williams' initial reaction to the news was a rather bitter statement to the press containing some ominous references to new lines that the Seaboard might have to construct. On October 25, he addressed the following inquiry to Elliott and Walters:

> "The Louisville & Nashville Railroad has, for a long time past, been an important connection of the Seaboard Air Line System. The interchange of business between the two properties at Atlanta, Ga., Montgomery, Ala., and Chattahoochee River Junction, Fla., has been considerable, and profitable, I believe, to both companies. May I inquire whether the recent acquisition by the Atlantic Coast Line Railway of a majority of the stock of the Louisville & Nashville Railroad will serve to interrupt or to affect adversely . . . the relations which have heretofore existed between the Louisville & Nashville system and the Seaboard Air Line system, or to interfere with the free interchange of business between these two properties? If so, I beg that you will advise me in what way and to what extent these existing relations are likely to be changed."

Henry Walters responded with some reassuring words:

> "It is not the desire or intention of the Atlantic Coast Line Railroad Company to take any action, as the majority stockholder of the Louisville & Nashville Railroad Company, which would disturb or interfere with the interchange of business between the Seaboard Air Line and the Louisville & Nashville Railroad. On the contrary, the Atlantic Coast Line Railroad Company, as such majority stockholder, hopes to aid in maintaining not only the pleasant and profitable relations existing between the Seaboard Air Line and Louisville & Nashville Railroad, but also hopes, both as such stockholder and for itself, to continue that fair and friendly competition between the Seaboard Air Line and the Atlantic Coast Line, which has, for the past two years, been so mutually beneficial, and made it possible to give the public so much increased and improved service."

In spite of these and other cordial exchanges on the subject, the Seaboard Air Line management could not abide a situation which placed them at the mercy of the Coast Line. They soon had a line under construction from Atlanta to Birmingham which, when completed in 1906, gave the Seaboard other connections to the Midwest. The panic of 1907 caught the Seaboard financially weakened by this project and put it into receivership. Control of the L&N was obviously a matter of considerable importance.

To put the whole matter of connections in proper perspective, it should be noted that nearly ten percent of the Coast Line's total freight revenues during twelve months ending with November of 1902 was derived from traffic interchanged with the L&N. While retaining this volume of business was not exactly a life-or-death matter for the Coast Line, it was an important consideration. Moreover, the freight tonnage interchanged with the L&N increased in actual volume and relative importance in the following years. On March 24, 1910, Tom Emerson wrote to Henry Walters:

> "I am sure you will be pleased to know that our interchange of traffic with the Louisville & Nashville Railroad is in more satisfactory shape than ever before. The traffic departments of the two roads are working in thorough harmony, and our Freight Traffic Manager stated to me this morning that he now considers the L&N one of our most satisfactory connections."

Trouble in Paradise

The L&N transaction did not stand without some challenges. Hetty Green, known to some of her contemporaries as the "Witch of Wall Street," allegedly tried to make trouble by accusing August Belmont of being in complicity with Walters or Morgan from the beginning. Walters reported to Jenkins on December 15:

> "I learned today that Hetty Green is seeking some means of black-mailing either August Belmont & Co. or ourselves, on account of the $5,000,000 of L&N stock issued last spring, claiming it is part of the stock which we have purchased."

On a more serious level, the general resentment and suspicion in Louisville congealed into hearings into the matter by the Kentucky Railroad Commission. Apparently concluding that J. P. Morgan was dominating the whole southern railroad complex, the state body charged the Atlantic Coast Line, the L&N, and the Southern Railway with being in illegal combination and requested an investigation by the Interstate Commerce Commission.

At the ICC hearings held in New York City in January of 1903, Morgan, Perkins, Belmont, and Walters — all the principals in the L&N deal excepting the Gates group — were called to testify. The statements by Belmont and the Morgan people praised Henry Walters and those associated with him in control of the Coast Line, and now the L&N, for their record of solid and responsible management. They also emphasized that Morgan had in no way constrained Walters to buy the L&N stock or gained a voice in Coast Line and L&N policy making. The ICC took no further action.

Several years later, however, one member of the Commission publicly criticized the transaction. At a meeting of the Economics Club at the Hotel Astor, January 28, 1910, Judson C. Clements charged that Morgan had arranged the L&N sale to eliminate competition; that the Coast Line had paid too high a price; and that "this added amount in stocks and bonds was taken out of the pocket of the public in increased rates."

Commissioner Clements was exaggerating somewhat in his "stumping" for more effective regulatory legislation. The Southern and the L&N were still competing, if within limits; rates had not been increased, although generally maintained. In any case, expanded powers for the ICC would eventually settle this question.

Clements was, however, right on one count — the Atlantic Coast Line Railroad Company had indeed paid a high price, at $156 per share, for the L&N stock. Market prices for the issue had averaged about $100 during 1901; they ranged from $130 down to $95 during the market slump in 1903 and from $101 to $148 in 1904. It was nearly seven years after the purchase — the summer of 1909 — before the market price of L&N stock attained and firmly held the level paid by the Coast Line. Whether appraised in terms of market performance, yield, price-earnings ratio, or the intrinsic value of the property, L &N common was worth no more than $120-$125 per share in 1902. If $123 is taken arbitrarily as the price, then the ACL RR Co. overpaid $33 for each of the 306,000 shares purchased — a total of $10,000,000. The increment of value for which this $10,000,000 was paid was, of course, control of the L&N.

Worth the Price in the End

Was control of the L&N worth $10,000,000 to the Atlantic Coast Line Railroad Company and its stockholders? If it was not, then the portions of the new issues of bonds ($7,350,000) and common stock (28,350 shares) that went for this "overpayment" constituted a devaluation of stockholders' equity in the ACL RR Co. This would hold true for the big stockholders who subscribed to the new issue and even more for the small stockholders who did not. The benefits of L&N control to the Coast Line were for many years largely intangible, such as the assurance of dependable connections to the Midwest and the relative advantage over the Seaboard in this regard. If the L&N gave any preference to the Coast Line in such areas as scheduling passenger train connections or priority handling of freight, this was necessarily done very discreetly and on a limited basis. There was, of course, the advantage of added prestige for the Coast Line, buttressed by speculation down through the years as to whether the two companies might be merged. It is very difficult to assess such factors and to say with assurance that control of the L&N was worth $10,000,000 or any set amount to the Atlantic Coast Line Railroad Company.

It would not be until the 1930's, after Lyman Delano succeeded to leadership of the Walters railroad empire, that active cooperation between the L&N and the Coast Line developed under the concept of the "Family Lines." Until this time, the traffic departments of the two railroads pursued independent courses, and their representatives often argued conflicting positions before regulatory agencies. In 1932, the two companies agreed that "none of the 'family' lines will undertake any action of comparatively minor benefit which will cause a hurt to any member of the 'family' lines greater than said benefit." In 1938, a program of reducing costs by housing the soliciting forces of "Family Lines" in the same offices in many cities was begun. The gains to both companies from these policies were concrete, if rather limited.

The L&N stock eventually proved to be a fair investment for the Coast Line in terms of monetary return, even though this was not true at first. A normal 4% yield on the investment of $50,000,000 in cash and par value securities would have amounted to $2,000,000 per annum. With L&N dividends at $5, the Coast Line received only $1,530,000 in each of the first two years. It was not until 1910, eight years after the purchase, that the Louisville & Nashville increased its dividends to $7 and began paying the Coast Line as much as $2,000,000. From that time forward L&N dividends were usually high enough to constitute a good profit; and in only two years (1931-33) did the income from this source fail to cover at least the interest payments on the $35,000,000 in bonds.

In the summer of 1944, F. D. "Frank" Lemmon, secretary of the ACL RR Co., analyzed the history of this investment and discovered that (1) the L&N stock purchase had cost his company $102,167,988 in interest on bonds, dividends on stocks, and related losses on other securities over the 41½-year period, and (2) dividends received from the L&N stock during the same period totaled $110,863, 800. The net income of $8,695,812 for such a long term was hardly a bonanza, but it represented a solid and almost constant contribution by the L&N to the Atlantic Coast Line Railroad Company's balance sheet.

A Footnote

The Walters railroad empire was essentially completed with the great financial ventures of 1902 — the Plant System merger and the L&N purchase. It was only eighteen years since Henry Walters had become General Manager of the little Wilmington & Weldon and a few connecting lines in Virginia and the Carolinas. Now he presided over a combination of railroads operating more than 9,000 miles and serving the entire Southeast. His family and a few associates in the Safe Deposit & Trust Company of Baltimore held all but a small percentage of the stock in the Atlantic Coast Line Company of Connecticut. The holding company, in turn, owned a large majority interest in the Atlantic Coast Line Railroad Company, which had in its treasury 51% of the Louisville & Nashville Railroad Company's common stock. It was an effective combination. For nearly three decades to come, Henry Walters, as Chairman of the Board, would govern the management of all three corporations.

Modernization at the Turn of the Century

Proceeding with Caution

A general market decline in 1903, following on the heels of the ambitious Louisville & Nashville purchase, gave Walters and his Baltimore associates some particularly awkward months. Atlantic Coast Line common stock traded for as low as $101 per share in October and L&N shares for as little as $95. While this shrinkage created no great difficulty for Walters personally, it did make for uneasy relations with other stockholders. Some had extended themselves late in 1902 to subscribe to Coast Line railroad stock at a privileged low price of $125, only to see the actual market price soon drop well below this level. The price of $156, which they just paid for the L&N shares, seemed very high indeed now, during the months when they were trading for around $100.

Henry Walters stood firmly on his earlier moves. He observed to Michael Jenkins, "I see no reason whatever why we should put ourselves in the breach. We have never asked our stockholders to do anything we did not do ourselves, and it is not to be expected that we will be able to do more than stand our own shrinkage in value at the present time."

Fortunately, earnings from railroad operations actually improved during the financial crisis, which was relatively mild, short-lived, and limited primarily to banking and the securities markets. Gross earnings for the ACL were $20,544,975 for the year ending June 30, 1904, as compared to $19,682,456 for the previous year. ACLdividends stayed at $5.50 straight through this period. The L&N also showed higher earnings for 1904. A decision to raise L&N dividends, however, was probably delayed until 1905 by concern over the financial slump.

The same concern motivated Walters to insist on stringent thrift measures in railroad operations. Some changes were beneficial, bringing lasting efficiencies in the transportation and roadway departments. Others were unfortunate deferrals of needed improvements. Neglect of the Florida District, for example, was due largely to preoccupation with the financial squeeze in 1903-1904. After the huge financial commitments of 1902, the Walters associates were in no position to allow the ACL to pass dividends; but they need not have worried.

Profits Belie the Plunge

Events soon showed the newly consolidated and essentially complete Coast Line to be a very profitable railroad — profitable enough to carry easily its enlarged burden of debt. Actually, the Coast Line still had a relatively low capitalization. As compared with the Southern Railway's $52,648 per mile in stocks and bonds and the Seaboard's

$50,190, the Coast Line's burden was only $41,258. As operations became steadily more profitable, this relatively conservative capitalization became even lighter and showed up in better dividends for stockholders. The railroad was also operating efficiently. Operating ratios were in the low 60's — 64% for 1903, 62.4% for 1904, and 63.8% in 1905.

Another distinctive characteristic of the Atlantic Coast Line was its unusual traffic mix. For freight business it relied on lumber, naval stores, fertilizer, cotton, cattle, fruit, and garden produce. Very little coal, a basic source of revenues for many northern and western roads, was carried by the Coast Line beyond that needed for its own consumption. Even among Southeastern railroads, the ACL had a thin territory and low freight density. In 1904, for a point of comparison, the Southern Railway, with an average mileage worked of 7,164, had a freight density of 449,227 tons per mile of road. The Seaboard Air Line, with 2,611 miles, had a freight density of 296,626. The Atlantic Coast Line, with an average mileage of 4,307, had a freight density of 256,463. The Coast Line had a high proportion of branch line mileage in sparsely populated, low traffic areas. Consequently it was hauling its freight in smaller train loads than most major railroads at that time. However, it was getting higher rates per ton-mile and showing higher net earnings per revenue train-mile than most carriers. The Coast Line's traffic mix included a high proportion of "high quality" freight tonnage and, of course, an extraordinary high percentage of revenues from passenger business. A 1905 comparison with the Southern points up marked differences.

	Southern Railway	Atlantic Coast Line
Revenue train load	190 tons	157 tons
Freight earnings per train-mile	$1,771	$2,095
Average ton-mile receipts	.993 cent	1.33 cents
Net earnings per revenue train-mile (includes passenger trains)	39.6 cents	69 cents

Performance Merits Improvements

A major reason for the Coast Line's thin territory and its distinctive traffic was Florida. The entire territory of the old Plant System was relatively undeveloped; and most of south Georgia and Florida were almost frontier. The towns, where they existed, were mostly tiny hamlets, and the hastily built roads stretched most of their lengths through piney woods, palmetto scrub, jackoak sand hills, and swamps. On the other hand, there were the winter resorts drawing the lucrative tourist traffic, many miles of vegetable- and fruit-producing farmland, plus tremendous potentials for the lumber and phosphate mining industries.

A basic tendency to caution, plus the sobering market slump of 1903, had caused Henry Walters to take a "wait-and-see" stance on Florida development. His strict economic policy for the entire railroad meant that the roads and equipment in the Jacksonville (Florida) District remained for a time markedly below the standard maintained on the rest of the Coast Line. It was not long before Florida growth required a change of policy. Immigration into the state had been going on fairly steadily, with much of the settlement following the railroads as they opened new territories during the 1880s and 1890s. Now, during the first decade of the twentieth century, Florida's growth swelled with scant notice of financial problems in Wall Street. Some of the tiny hamlets of 1890 were turning into substantial towns. A sampling of a number of municipalities served by the Coast Line reflects the accelerating growth rate in turn-of-the-century Florida.

	1890	1900	1910
Jacksonville	17,201	28,429	57,699
Lake City	2,020	4,013	5,032
Live Oak	687	1,659	3,450
Gainesville	2,790	3,633	6,183
Ocala	2,904	3,380	4,370
St. Petersburg	273	1,575	4,127
Tampa	5,532	5,839	37,782
Lakeland	552	1,180	3,719
Fort Myers	575	943	2,463

This growth in Florida meant prosperity for the Coast Line. Its tourist and perishables traffic would continue to expand, but the increase in permanent residents would bring more year-around business. Southbound general merchandise traffic would fill increasing numbers of the freight cars that used to be deadheaded to Florida loading platforms. More and more, the Atlantic Coast Line would be oriented to a very profitable long haul, carrying freight.

Fixing up Florida

Large expenditures for new equipment and physical improvements in Florida were authorized. Some things had already been done. New frame passenger and freight depots had recently been finished at many points. The line from Sanford to Trilby (most of the old Orange Belt Line) had just been widened to standard gauge to match the already widened segment from Trilby to St. Petersburg. Walters observed:

> You will recall that we rather looked slightly upon the Sanford and St. Petersburg, originally a narrow gauge road, which has now been changed to broad gauge. The development upon it is enormous, and it will be among the most valuable feeders of our long haul. The little town of St. Petersburg has now a population of about 6,000 in the winter. We have already authorized an expenditure of $7,000 for land upon which to erect a new freight station and a small yard [there], all of which will be done as promptly as possible."

Actually, a good-sized new passenger station was included in the improvements at St. Petersburg, and the new buildings were ready early in 1906. Passenger stations were rushed to completion at many other Florida points. By the summer of 1905 there were new frame structures at DeLeon Springs, Wauchula, Punta Gorda, Alligator Creek,

Tice, Samville, Fort Myers, Walkill, and Moffetts, plus a new freight depot at Live Oak. More were planned or in progress.

The four inadequate drawbridges between Jacksonville and Sanford that Walters noted during his trip were soon replaced with sturdy steel structures. And the new motive power began to arrive before the end of 1905. There were thirty new engines purchased especially for the Southern Division. They were 20-inch Baldwin ten-wheelers (4-6-0s), which were just being introduced as the standard freight and passenger locomotives for the Coast Line. No fewer than 1,500 freight cars and 20 passenger coaches were purchased to meet the need for rolling stock on the Southern Division.

Additions and improvements were planned; contracts were let; and work was begun in all departments. Dock terminal installations were already underway at Jacksonville. These were now developed into a major project for large export docks and warehouses, plus an ample new freight yard with a capacity of 1,200 cars. Freight yards were to be enlarged and rearranged at many points, including a good-sized one at Lakeland and a major one at Waycross, Georgia, to handle car movement to and from points in Florida and western Georgia.

To maintain all the additional rolling stock, small new shops at Lakeland would complement the ones already at Sanford and High Springs, while major new shops at Waycross would serve the entire southern portion of the Coast Line for heavy repairs. Plans for the Waycross shops , including "all the tools to be new and run by electricity," were ready and construction contracts were signed by the end of February, 1905. Work was also commenced on rebuilding many miles of roadway in Florida, with raised grade levels, reduced curvatures, and heavier 85-lb. rail for the main lines and 60-lb. and 70-lb. rail for secondary routes and branches.

Management Problems Overshadow Projects

John Kenly, as general manager, was the executive in charge of all the improvement projects, and he pushed them hard with characteristic attention to every detail. Perhaps he overdid it. At any rate, toward the end of the year, with many of the lesser projects completed and the rest in full swing, he fell seriously ill.

Coast Line management was further disrupted by the loss of several key executives within a short period. Most crucial were the resignation of Robert Erwin as president in November, and his death soon after, on January 13, 1906. The man whom Walters had valued as his top finance specialist was gone. Moreover, the two men next in line for promotion were both unavailable due to ill health. Warren Elliott, who had stepped aside as president so that Erwin could have the post, was in the grip of a long, terminal illness that would finally take his life the following September. John Kenly, probably Walters' first choice, was out for an indeterminate period. The situation was difficult for

Chairman Walters, who greatly valued continuity in his associations. He confided in Michael Jenkins that he had been "so upset by the changes which we are contemplating" that he was unable to concentrate on other items of business.

Characteristically, Walters settled on another close associate from the early Coast Line years —Thomas M. Emerson — as the new president. Shortly afterward, on March 23, 1906, President Emerson's brother Horace died. Horace Emerson had also been with the Coast Line's traffic department for years, and had been promoted to the post of general traffic manager, on his brother's promotion to the presidency. These were critical losses in top personnel to absorb in such a short space of time.

Now the circle of trusted colleagues and lieutenants grew smaller and tighter. Fortunately, John Kenly recovered and resumed his duties as general manager of railroad operations during the early months of 1906. He and Tom Emerson would be in charge of running the railroad. Walters, with Michael Jenkins' assistance, would tend to financial matters and set general policy.

New Friendship Formed

The loss of both Erwin and Elliott meant that Henry Walters took more active charge of the New York office. Even as president of the ACL Railroad Company, Erwin, a corporate finance specialist, had spent much of his time in New York. Now the presidential office moved back to Wilmington, where Tom Emerson was in charge of day-to-day administration of railroad business.

Emerson did get to New York more often during his years as president, and Walters treated him warmly as the close friend he was. When Emerson asked to borrow Walter's Rainier limousine for a family trip in New York state in August of 1907, Walters responded, "Delighted to have you use my machine. Have already instructed chauffeur to post himself about the roads." He often played the host to Emerson and Kenly when they were in the city on business, at least one occasion for dinner on his yacht, the *Narada*, when it was moored at the foot of East 23rd Street.

Their relationship was easy enough to admit competitive joshing. On October 19, 1911, he wrote Emerson:

> "I was highly pleased to receive your check . . .for the value of a new suit of clothes, the result of the . . . bet that the cotton crop of last year would exceed 11½ million bales."

Perhaps Emerson had been over optimistic in this one instance, but business was generally very good during these years. Tom Emerson was a genial friend and a competent railroad executive. He also had the good fortune to be president of the Atlantic Coast Line Railroad during one of the most prosperous periods in its history.

Back to Work

The modernization program continued, of course, in the hands of the several capable superintendents, and John Kenly was able to give increasing direction in the early months of 1906.

The new shops and 315-car freight yard at Lakeland, Florida, were readied for use about this time. The huge shops at Waycross, Georgia, which were to make that town a major railroad center in the Southeast, took much longer; they were not opened for full use until January of 1909.

New stations in Florida were completed at an impressive rate. Combination freight and passenger frame depots at Pine Mount, Tarpon Springs, Winter Garden, Kathleen, and Juliette were in use by mid-1906; and there were new passenger stations at Leesburg, Dunnellon, Doctors Inlet, Apopka, Newberry, Satsuma, Duke, Edgar and Homeland within the following year. Palatka's handsome new brick station also was completed.

The ambitious projects at Jacksonville took much time, money, and effort. Part of the dock and warehouse space went into use on January 1, 1906, and the big freight yard the next fall. Completion of the export terminal facilities, including dredging a deep enough approach channel in the St. Johns River, took about another two years. Roadway improvement all over Florida was pushed at a great rate until late in 1907.

Mining Makes an Impact

A category of business that received much attention in Florida during these years was phosphate mining and hauling. The Plant System had made some modest beginnings in this traffic by the turn of the century. Walters now pushed its development to a major item in the Coast Line's revenues in Florida. Mining enterprises and construction of railroad spurs were necessarily locked together in opening new territories in the central and southern parts of the state. The Winston and Bone Valley Branch, an old logging road which swung southward from a point just west of Lakeland, gave access to one of the busiest mining areas. Construction of phosphate spurs and negotiation of traffic contracts with mining companies proved one of the liveliest arenas for competition between the Coast Line and the Seaboard Air Line. For example, Henry Walters wrote glumly to Emerson on September 28, 1906:

> "I have just learned that Peters, White & Co., at a meeting in Baltimore last week, made a contract with the Independent Phosphate people . . . for a total of 120,000 [tons] per year, for six years . . . . I presume every ton of these 120,000 will move all rail by the Seaboard Air Line."

Competition for phosphate hauling caused the railroads themselves to invest in mining enterprises. In so doing, they contributed necessary capital for initiating mining operations while guaranteeing themselves all the hauling business from such companies. In the period from 1902 to 1910, the Coast Line made important investments in the Dutton Phosphate Company, the Prairie Pebble Phosphate Company, and the Atlas Phosphate Company.

The Coast Line entered into a number of partnerships with mining operators, sometimes supplying up to two-thirds of the capital needed to develop a new location. The actual vehicle for making these investments was at first the ACL RR Co. - Connecticut Company (the holding company). Beginning in 1904, this role was transferred to the Atlantic Land and Improvement Company, organized as a subsidiary of the Railroad Company primarily to handle the Florida real estate acquired from the Plant System. This was a logical change, since phosphate mining involved land rights, and some of the land was owned by the Atlantic Land and Improvement Company.

In 1904, the Improvement Company received from the Connecticut Company 6,667 shares of stock and $650,000 in bonds of the Dutton Phosphate Company. Following the expansion policies set early in 1905, the Improvement Company, under Alexander Hamilton as president, enlarged its investments in phosphate mining. It soon held over $1 million in the securities of the Prairie Pebble Phosphate Company.

This arrangement was disrupted by the United States Congress. The Hepburn Act, enacted in 1906 at Teddy Roosevelt's urging, strengthened and enlarged the powers of the Interstate Commerce Commission in several ways, including the provisions of the "commodities clause." This prohibited a carrier from transporting, through interstate commerce, articles which it had produced or in which it had an interest. Although the prohibition was intended primarily to end abuses created by railroad ownership of coal mines, it was probably illegal now for the Coast Line to be transporting phosphate rock produced by companies controlled by its wholly-owned subsidiary. To counter this, in the spring of 1906, the Atlantic Land and Improvement Company sold to the Connecticut Company over $3 million in stocks and bonds of various phosphate enterprises. The Railroad Company was thus relieved of any official responsibility for the mining companies.

Other moves were made to stimulate this traffic. The dock facilities at Jacksonville contributed greatly, since there was considerable demand for dried phosphate in Europe. The loading installations at Port Tampa were also enlarged, and a large volume of phosphate and other rock moved through that port. Special rolling stock was designed and acquired for this business. The Coast Line had 115 phosphate cars by 1904, and increased the number sharply to 325 in 1907. Most of these later cars were of an improved design developed by R. E. Smith, General Superintendent of Motive Power. Nearly 39 feet long and with 40-ton capacity, they were fitted with loading doors in the top half of the sides and hopper doors in the bottom for unloading. By 1911, the Coast Line was moving around 1.5 million tons of phosphate each year.

Wrapping up Renovations in the South

Aside from new spurs to mines and factories, little roadway construction was initiated in Florida during this period. The line from Punta Gorda to Fort Myers, which had been started as an extension southward from Bartow by the old Florida Southern, had been completed and in use since May 10, 1904. Also in 1904, the Jacksonville & Southwestern was officially consolidated into the ACL Railroad Company. This company's line from Jacksonville to Newberry had been serving as the Coast Line's main line to Gainesville and Ocala, as well as southward from Newberry to West Coast points, since 1899. Now it was extended from Newberry westward and northwestward, reaching Wilcox in the spring of 1907 and Perry in 1909. Henry Walters obviously intended this extension from Wilcox to Perry as one segment of a complete West Coast route to Thomasville, Georgia, which would greatly improve the Coast Line's service to Chicago. The segment between Dunnellon and Wilcox would be started in 1912, but the line from Perry northward to Monticello, Florida, and thence to Thomasville, Georgia, would be postponed until the mid-1920's.

During this first decade of the century, the Coast Line's main efforts in Florida were bent toward improving the service on existing lines. Thanks to the helter-skelter growth of the Plant System, there were plenty of existing lines.

Construction Booming All Over

The modernization program begun in 1905 was not by any means limited to the Southern Division. Many millions of dollars were spent on new equipment and improvements for the entire system. Traffic volume was rising from year to year, and it required expanded capacity. One innovation was the "doubletracking" of strategic sections of the main line between Richmond and Jacksonville. The growing number of trains and their higher speeds were creating bottlenecks, especially in the Richmond District and at busy junction points farther south. Installation of second track began on a modest basis in 1904, with five-mile stretches near Richmond and Charleston; by 1908 there were 86 miles of double track in use. A few new-style signal towers and related interlocking plants for controlling switches were installed in 1903 and succeeding years. Then, in 1907, many new signal towers and related interlocking plants of improved design were installed and the earlier ones were all rebuilt to higher standards. Introduction of the automatic block system of signaling began about the same time.

Heavier rail was part of the modernization program. The advantage of the new 85-lb. rail in carrying the faster and heavier trains of the day caused Henry Walters to insist on a crash program for installing it. Delivery of the huge tonnage ordered took awhile; but for the peak year, fiscal 1906-1907, John Kenly reported that 46,989 tons (352 miles) of this heavier rail were laid. The 70-lb. rail thus released was used for improving lighter traffic lines and branches.

In order to cope with the growing volume of freight movement, yard capacity had to be expanded. In addition to the ones already mentioned in Florida, the following important new freight yards were constructed as rapidly as possible:

South Rocky Mount, N.C.	Completed October, 1907	2,609 car capacity
Wilmington, N. C.	Completed May, 1908	1,812 car capacity
Chadbourn, N. C.	Completed 1908	597 car capacity
Florence, S. C.	Completed September, 1907	1,887 car capacity
Southover Junction	Completed March, 1908	1,072 car capacity
(near Savannah, Ga.)		
Waycross, Ga.	Completed 1908	1,842 car capacity

Some of these new yards replaced (with doubled or tripled capacity) old yards at the same points; others as at Chadbourn and Southover Junction, were totally new facilities. The yard at Chadbourn was built especially to accommodate the seasonal movement of fresh strawberries from the area.

It was not only towns in Florida that boasted new freight and passenger depots; there were 25 completed elsewhere on the line between 1904 and 1908. Many were in relatively new territory in Georgia, as at Valdosta, Quitman and Thomasville. The most ambitious structure was the Union Station at Charleston, occupied jointly with the Southern Railway on November 10, 1907. There seemed to be construction everywhere. An additional story was built atop the office building at Wilmington, and adjoining passenger facilities were enlarged.

A prosperous Coast Line could give its patrons handsome accommodations. Passengers were also treated to comfortable new cars. Between 1904 and June 30, 1908, the company bought 92 new passenger coaches at a cost of $685,813.

Purchasing Cars

The Coast Line acquired rolling stock at a startling rate during these years. Looking at freight car needs during the planning sessions of February 1905, Henry Walters decided that Coast Line shops could not supply a significant number; they had plenty to do just keeping up with car repairs. The thousands of cars needed would all be purchased on contract from car builders. A large order for 30-ton capacity boxcars was placed with the South Baltimore Car Works late in 1905. These cars were of superior strength thanks to new, steel underframe construction. A few months later, another large order was given to the Standard Steel Car Company of Butler, Pennsylvania. In fiscal 1907 alone, the Railroad Company bought 5,522 freight cars at a cost of $5,365,332. Damaged and worn-out cars were retired at the rate of 500 to 600 per year, their loss was scarcely noticed except in the gratifying decline of equipment failures. The freight car complement expanded from 13,157 on July 1, 1902, to a total of 24,668, according to the Annual Report for June 30, 1908.

In the course of the three-year program, 242 new locomotives were purchased for a total of $3 million. Some of these were yard engines, but the Coast Line had 30 of the large (20-inch cylinders) 10-wheelers by June of 1905, 157 by 1907, and no fewer than 193 by 1908. The freight version of these cost $12,500 in 1905 and $13,300 by 1907; the higher-speed passenger variation cost about $800 more. Just after absorbing the Plant System in 1902 the Coast Line had boasted a motive power roster numbering 451. When locomotive deliveries came to a halt early in 1908, it totaled 672, and most were in splendid condition.

In High Gear

These were halcyon years for Henry Walters' railroad. There seemed to be no end to the prospects for business improvement. Operating revenues swelled from $20.5 million in 1904 to $26.8 million in the year ending June 30, 1907. Earnings remained about the same; but they were expected to rise sharply once the huge improvement and modernization program was accomplished. The Coast Line was being brought to a handsome condition. Particularly in Florida, newspapers and distinguished travelers expressed their appreciation of the marked year-to-year improvements.

President Emerson reported in 1907 that the Railroad Company had spent in the preceding three years $15.8 million on new equipment and about $6 million on property improvements and additions, and the program was still going at a great rate. The final year is impressively outlined in the Annual Report for 1907-1908.

On July 1,1907, there remained unexpended appropriations for authorized work of $6,168,792.06. During the year, additional expenditures were authorized to the amount of $686,085.98, making aggregate of $6,854,878.04. The total amount expended for the year was $5,247,559.01.

These huge outlays coincided embarrassingly with the onset of a business downturn in 1907. Most of them represented deliveries of equipment and completion of work on contracts let months before. The program was nearing completion, and it was too massive in any case to be halted instantly as revenues slackened.

Applying the Brakes

The Panic of 1907, a nasty crisis that struck the financial markets of the nation in the fall of the year, was accompanied by a business slump that started a few months earlier and continued through much of the following year. It began a two-year leveling off of Coast Line operating revenues — certainly a disappointing pay-off for the great modernization program.

Noting signs of slackening business activity in the late summer, Henry Walters directed President Emerson to make sharp cutbacks in the improvement program where possible and to reduce operating costs. Orders for new rail were halted. Roadway gangs were laid off, and even operating crews on freight trains were reduced.

The financial crisis hit in October and November. As a result of sharp market declines, Michael Jenkins and Henry Walters became concerned over some of their associates' holdings of margined stock in the Connecticut Company and the Railroad Company. Walters observed, however, "About all that we can do is to hold onto our stock and not let that come upon the market. I do not see what else we can do."

At Wilmington on Monday, November 4, Walters conferred with the bankers there and encouraged them to secure enough currency from New York City banks to meet the Coast Line payroll in cash. He feared a devastating run on the banks if the ACL workers had to be paid by check or special certificates.

Tightening the Belt

The currency shortage, with bank clearings and currency payments suspended for a time, put a new, sharper edge on Walters' economy drive. The Coast Line, in concert with other Southeastern railroads, reduced wages and salaries in January of 1908. Hourly wages were reduced wherever possible, and beginning February 1, officers and employees receiving more than $3,000 "submitted willingly" to a reduction of about 10 percent. Wages of roadway gangs working on the improvements in Florida were reduced from $1.10 to $1.00 and then to 90¢ per day. The year-end dividend on Railroad Company stock was paid in certificates of indebtedness in lieu of cash.

The situation certainly looked bad enough in January, when the hard line policy on economy was laid down. The financial panic had halted much construction activity, so lumber and other building materials movement was down sharply. Freight business in general and passenger traffic dipped ominously. The Seaboard Air Line went into receivership, and the cash position of even the Coast Line was disturbingly low. Banks were buying scarce currency at a 3% premium, and gloom was thick on Wall Street. ACL Railroad Company common was selling in the low $70's.

Out of the Slump

As it turned out, the great panic of 1907 did little damage to the Coast Line. It was mostly a financial crisis, and the business decline in Coast Line territory was neither as deep nor as long as Henry Walters feared it would be. In fact, even as the drastic economy measures were taking effect in February, Coast Line traffic moved again at an encouragingly high level. Florida had a good tourist and perishables season. By mid-February, Walters decided to take advantage of appealingly low prices to buy 10,000 tons of steel rails in Baltimore. Not all railroad companies were in a position to do this, for business improvement moved slowly across the nation. As late as June, Walters observed from his New York vantage point, "The whole country is wearing its old hats and its old shoes and patching them when they get holes in them. . . . The railroads have absolutely stopped buying."

Most of Walters' pessimism, however, was soon dispelled by very healthy reports on Coast Line revenues for the spring. Michael Jenkins told him: "I fully approve the proposition to restore all salaries of the officers of the ACL and L&N to what they were prior to the cut last February, and I would certainly include those of the Presidents and Chairman. Glad to see May net showing a good increase." The late summer of 1908 was a particularly slack season, but fall would bring a lively upturn. For the year ended June 30, 1908, ACL freight revenues were down only 4%, and passenger revenues were actually more than 3% higher than the previous year. Operating profits, however, were down rather sharply. Behind that fact was a larger story than the Panic of 1907.

The financial and business slump came at an awkward time for the Coast Line when earnings were already being squeezed by rising costs and reduced rates. Operating costs jumped from 64% of revenues in 1904-1905 to a ratio of 76% for the year 1906-1907. Some of this increase resulted from charging huge improvement expenditures to operating costs, but wage hikes also contributed. The railway brotherhoods were achieving bargaining strength nationwide during the first decade of the century, and the Coast Line was paying more to the men running its trains and repairing its machinery. The bitterest blow of all, however, was the general reduction in passenger rates imposed by the individual states within Atlantic Coast Line's territory. New problems loomed on the horizon.

Chapter XII

Government Regulations — A Fact of Life in 1900s

States Exercise Muscles

Regulation of railroads by state governments had been intensifying for several years. The movement struck with particular speed in the South around the turn of the century, where several states adopted new constitutions and, impelled by comparably strong contemporary sentiment, established strong commissions to regulate business corporations in general and railroads in particular.

There was widespread populist resentment of railroads stemming from a general awareness that big shippers often got preferential treatment, and, of course, long-term resentment over the differential between long-haul and short-haul rates. The Interstate Commerce Commission was doing little, so the states moved determinedly into railroad regulation.

All of the states in ACL territory, with the exception of Virginia, had established commissions with some degree of mandatory powers over railroads before 1900. Now these commissions were being assigned more powers, and they were applying them more energetically.

Legislatures in some cases were going beyond the recommendations of commissions in passage of harsh restrictive legislation. North Carolina, where Coast Line relations with the Railroad Commission were amicable for years, had attempted to impose sharply lowered passenger rates on only the Wilmington & Weldon in 1898, and had then, in 1902, applied a standard schedule of passenger fares to all roads in the state. The South Carolina commission attempted to get powers to set commodity rates. Georgia had established in 1879 one of the earliest effective railroad commissions. It was reorganized with extended powers in 1907. In Florida, a once impotent commission reduced intrastate passenger rates from 4 cents to 3 cents a mile in 1903, and imposed a lower schedule of freight rates on the Coast Line and the Seaboard Air Line, effective July 1, 1904. The Alabama Railroad Commission received enlarged legal powers from the state legislature in 1903. Finally, the Virginia Constitution of 1902 replaced a powerless railroad commissioner with a strong new Corporation Commission, which immediately set out to formulate a uniform freight classification for regulating rates of the railroads operating in the state.

State railroad regulation was by no means confined to rate questions. In their new constitutions, by actions of their commissions, and/or in legislative enactments, the states prescribed conditions for all aspects of railroad operations, with, of course, many variations from state to state. They required hostile railroads to cooperate with one another in providing service to the public. They prescribed equipment for trains, especially for the safety and comfort of passengers, but even to the extent, for example, of setting minimum candle power for locomotive headlamps. They demanded more frequent trains to be operated according to regular, posted schedules. They set conditions and hours for railway labor. Most states limited the speeds of trains within cities, and some forbade the running of freight trains on Sunday. Worst yet, Jim Crow laws in one southern state after another forced the railroads to provide separate passenger accommodations for "Negroes." Politicians even vied with one another to gain reputations as fighters for the people against the railroads. In so doing they sometimes passed unreasonable laws.

Comply if you Can

Henry Walters viewed much of this as unwarranted encroachment on private property rights. Yet, with some encouragement from members of his legal staff, such as Alexander Hamilton, he directed Coast Line management to cooperate as much as possible with state commissions.

State regulatory matters became an increasing burden for ACL officers. In March of 1905, Tom Emerson complained of being occupied for weeks with "almost continuous performances" before the railroad commissions of the various states. On occasions when government encroachment seemed to go too far, the Coast Line contested new regulations. One of the most spectacular instances was the bitter passenger rate controversy of 1907-1908.

With Virginia leading the way with an enactment in 1906, the southern states all joined in a "crusade" against railroad fares that swept the country in 1907. President Emerson reported to ACL Railroad Company stockholders:

> Since our last report the following named States, either through their Legislatures or Corporation Commissions, have taken such action as will greatly reduce your passenger rates: [Virginia, North Carolina, Georgia, and Alabama.]

> We are now operating under these reduced rates, although we believe them to be confiscatory, and their legality is being tested in the Courts; in the meantime the Company is suffering irreparable loss pending final decisions.

Fight if you Must

The Coast Line, along with several other affected railroads, elected to fight this dictation of lower rates, especially in Virginia and North Carolina where the cuts were deepest. They refused to issue mileage books to patrons at 2 cents per mile, as required by the 1906 act of the Virginia Legislature. When hauled before the Virginia Corporation Commission, ACL officials successfully challenged the constitutionality of the legislation. Then, when the Commission set the same low intrastate rate of 2 cents per mile, the ACL and five other carriers began court challenges that lasted for many months. As a result of a compromise arranged by Governor Swanson, they agreed to operate under the low rates until the litigation was settled. This was done with the understanding that the Commission would later evaluate the effect of the reduction, should its powers be upheld by the courts.

The situation in North Carolina was more crucial for the Coast Line, as well as for the Southern and the Seaboard Air Line because they had far more intrastate passenger traffic in this state.They obtained injunctions from the United States Circuit Court forbidding state officials from enforcing the new 2¼ cent rate law. When several railroad ticket agents were indicted, tried, and sentenced in state courts for refusing to obey the law, the federal court directed their release. After much excitement and some heated oratory about the sanctity of North Carolina law, the financial panic impressed officials on both sides with the need for a reasonable settlement. President Finley of the Southern Railway negotiated, on behalf of the carriers, directly with Governor Glenn. The railroads offered, as inducement, mileage books with which North Carolinians could travel at 2 cents per mile. The carriers' traffic men had concluded that such books might actually increase travel and reduce ticket agents' expenses enough to compensate for the lower fare. By offering the mileage books, plus a maximum interstate rate of 2½ cents, Finley got first Governor Glenn, and then the legislature, to accept an intrastate rate of 2½ cents.

Press Influences Public Support

Throughout the months of litigation and negotiation, the railroad companies carried on a lively publicity campaign, stressing the terrible hardship that the business depression was visiting upon them. Information about the cost-cutting moves undertaken by the Coast Line was given to the press for maximum public impact. News releases reiterated the theme: "The railroads are not making any money." Friendly press treatment sometimes linked the business depression directly to legislative attacks on the railroads:

> The people of the South are beginning to realize that railroad officers were sincere when they prophesized that the legislative attacks on the railroads would hurt the people of the South. The receivership of the Seaboard Air Line has had some effect in bringing about this change, but even before that happened, the effects of the industrial depression were being sharply felt in the South and it was obvious that the attacks on the railroads had been one of its principal causes. The future of the Atlantic Coast Line rests largely with the people of its territory. The officers of the road are doing their best . . . to be fair in their treatment of the public. They ask in return justice; no special favors, but an understanding by the public of the facts and difficulties of railroad operation; and the passage of laws based in fairness on these facts.

Settlement Accepted

As it finally developed, the North Carolina agreement of December 1907 set the pattern for a general settlement of the passenger rate conflict. The carriers accepted the reality of a 2½ cent interstate rate and strove to get intrastate rates at least that high.

The carriers succeeded in all the southeastern states, using the experiment of the lower-rate mileage books as inducement. President Finley, conferring directly with state governors as well as commissions, achieved the speediest and most amicable settlements in South Carolina and Florida (which accepted the highest rate: 2¾ cents). Virginia came around last. Its Corporation Commission finally granted the 2½ cents rate when, during 1908, it observed that large numbers of people were crossing into Virginia from surrounding states to buy their through tickets at the uniquely low fares prevailing there.

Henry Walters had some misgivings about the new mileage books, but he concurred in the settlement as probably the best that could be won under the circumstances. He and President Emerson informed Coast Line stockholders in 1908, that the new rate arrangements were costing them an average of $50,000 per month in passenger revenues.

It is interesting that Walters' other railroad, the L&N, followed a policy that contrasted sharply with the conciliatory approach of the Coast Line; in fact, the L&N was unrelenting in its opposition to every rate reduction by a state government. It fought the Florida Commission's initial reduction in passenger rates from 1903 until 1908 before giving in; it refused an interim compromise in 1907 in Virginia; it did not accept the 2½ cent passenger rate set by the 1907 law in Alabama until 1913, when every last avenue of legal resistance was exhausted. It was almost as if the ACL had been assigned the "good guy" role and the L&N the "bad guy" role.

The general passenger rate settlement of 1907-1908 lasted until after World War I. Although the Coast Line now carried more passengers more miles per dollar of fare, the new rate structure did not depress passenger revenues as Henry Walters had feared. In fact, passenger revenues were actually up more than 3% for the year ended June 30, 1908, and 8% higher still by the end of the 1910 fiscal year. Higher volume of business overcame the negative effects of the lower rates.

Short-Lived Truce

The Coast Line enjoyed a few years respite from state assaults on revenues, but the war was not yet over. Later conflicts with states tended to concentrate on freight rates. Beginning in 1911, there was repeated agitation in Georgia for lower rates between the port cities and points inland in the state. The Coast Line and other major roads, with their trunk lines running North-South, were not interested in building business to and from the Georgia ports, and they resisted this change successfully.

More serious were developments in North Carolina. In 1908, the Corporation Commission began exploring the sharp differential between rates to cities in its state and rates to neighboring Virginia cities. The Commission won some modest changes in successful cases brought before the ICC in 1908 and 1912. One solution adopted by the Commission was to reduce intrastate freight rates so combination rates to northern cities would be lowered. This, however, brought little relief to North Carolina towns close to the Virginia border; besides, by 1913 the intrastate rates had been reduced as far as was feasible. ACL management complained to the stockholders:

> The attack on rates charged by your company (ACL), especially intrastate rates, is assuming alarming proportions, but your officers, trusting in the fairness of the people of the States through which your line is located, express the hope for final action less drastic and destructive than now threatens.

Its patience exhausted by the spring of 1913, the North Carolina General Assembly set up a special committee with the explicit charge of formulating an acceptable schedule of interstate freight rates to and from North Carolina points. Faced with the likelihood of drastic legislative action, officers of the Coast Line and other railroads met with the legislative committee, the Governor, and the Council of the State of North Carolina and offered a set of proposals for reducing interstate rates to selected points in the state. The legislative committee rejected the proposed changes as too modest. The Corporation Commission then stepped in as peacemaker. It held a long series of intensive informal conferences with railroad representatives, and finally secured the carriers' reluctant agreement for most of the rate reductions demanded by the legislature. The General Assembly accepted the agreement in special session. The ICC approved some exceptions to its rate rules, and the new rates took effect on July 23, 1914. The change cost the large railroads serving North Carolina an estimated $2 million per year in interstate freight revenues.

ICC, the Winner

The worst effects of the onset of state railroad regulations were experienced in this period before World War I. There would be more sharply disputed issues and an occasional maddeningly absurd statute, but state regulatory commissions tended to grow more sophisticated and reasonable. Moreover, the Interstate Commerce Commission assumed jurisdiction over an increasingly broad range of railroad problems as it grew in power.

The Hepburn Act of 1906 enlarged the ICC and gave it effective control power over accounts and records and maximum rates. The Mann-Elkins Act of 1910 gave the Commission power to require advance approval of new rates and greatly strengthened its authorization for ending long-haul vs. short-haul discrimination. Armed with these new powers, the ICC became an effective regulatory agency.

Coast Line officials complained, in 1908, about an ICC reduction of rates on fruit and vegetable shipments from Florida. In 1911, both the Coast Line and the Seaboard Air Line were fined $2,000 by a federal court in Savannah for violations of the commodities tariff schedules between Philadelphia and Jacksonville.

In general, however, ICC actions affecting the Coast Line were reasonable. It accepted, for example, the contention that the thin territory of Southeastern railroads called for relatively high rates to offset costs — a principle applied especially to "end-of-the-line" Florida points. The ICC was also friendly, when, in 1912, Congress prohibited railroad control of competing steamship lines, subject to exceptions in the public interests and, of course, regulation by the ICC. In December of 1915, the Commission finally decided that the Coast Line and the Florida East Coast Railway could retain control of the Peninsular and Occidental Steamship Company (serving Jacksonville, Miami, Key West, and Havana). A few months later, it upheld continuance of Coast Line and Southern Railway interests in the Old Dominion Steamship Company (serving Norfolk, Baltimore, and New York).

Government intervention in the railroads was now a fact of life. Coast Line leaders were concerned mainly that regulations be imposed in a responsible and consistent manner. They had generally little quarrel with the actions of the Interstate Commerce Commission; however, taxes by state and local governments went up almost 16% in just the two years from 1910 to 1912. Coast Line leaders were therefore highly sensitive on the subject of taxes already when the federal income tax went into effect in 1913. Their reaction to this innovation included a dramatic recapitalization of their holding company and a distribution of a huge chunk of its assets.

Income Up

Once the effects of the 1907 downturn subsided, Coast Line revenues resumed their upward march. A pronounced upswing in business commenced in 1909-1910 and continued until the outbreak of war in Europe disrupted trade in the fall of 1914.

Operating revenues swelled from $26 million in 1907-1908 to $36.8 million in 1913-1914. Net operating revenue improved from $7 million to $10.6 million in the same period, hitting a peak of $11.5 million in 1912-1913. Net income swelled spectacularly from $2.8 million in 1907-1908 to $7.3 million in 1913-1914.

The Holding Company in Clover

The Atlantic Coast Line Company of Connecticut (the Connecticut Company) had existed since 1891 as a holding company to bring together the components of the Coast Line. It had served its main purpose by the end of 1902, with ACL Railroad Company consolidation, and the Plant System and L&N purchases completed.

At this point, Henry Walters considered terminating the Connecticut Company. It was an additional corporate entity to manage; and moreover, the public and the Federal Government were becoming hostile towards holding companies. Walters observed to Michael Jenkins, in February of 1908, "As you know I have for some time been disturbed over the change in public sentiment towards holding companies, and a year ago last

September I suggested winding up the Connecticut Company. At that time, it probably could have been done, but I do not think we could do it now, except at enormous sacrifice."

As noted earlier, the Connecticut Company had acquired a new usefulness as repository for Coast Line investments in phosphate mining enterprises. By 1910, it held more than $4 million in phosphate company securities. It also held various other securities, such as the Coast Line's stocks in the Old Dominion Steamship Company. So the Connecticut Company was kept alive, with Michael Jenkins serving as its president, as a convenient storehouse for assorted Coast Line investments, and as continued locus for the Walters group's financial control of the railroad empire.

As the railroad system prospered, so did the Connecticut Company and its stockholders. Dividends were increased to $10 per share in 1909-1910, reflecting higher dividend payments from the Railroad Company. Distribution of profits was further increased by selling 50,400 new shares of stock to stockholders at $100 par (a real bargain as the market price was around $250); the proceeds of the sale being used to retire nearly $5,000,000 in 4% certificates of indebtedness. In effect, the stockholders exchanged about $5,000,000 in $4-yield securities for a like amount of $10-yield securities. By June 30, 1911, the net income for the year had grown to $2,151,825; and even after payment of the enlarged dividend, another $387,825 surplus had accumulated.

The balance sheet was a veritable picture of financial health. Net income swelled by $394,462 the following year to a total of $2,546,287, and dividends were increased again to a $12-per-year rate in March of 1912.

The Party's Over

Then came the Federal Income Tax Law, passed by Congress in 1913, following ratification of the 16th Amendment. This new law provided that not only personal income, but also dividends received by corporations, would be taxed.

For the year ending June 30, 1914, the Connecticut Company was accordingly taxed about $2,100. The levy was hardly an insupportable burden for the holding company, but Henry Walters felt that such a tax was grossly unfair. Viewed from his position, his antipathy is understandable. The L&N would now pay income tax on dividends received from its subsidiaries, the ACL Railroad Company on dividends from the L&N, and the holding company on dividends from the Railroad Company. Finally, stockholders in the holding company would pay personal income tax on their dividends from that company. Surely, it was felt, something should be done to combat this multistage taxation.

The Federal Government would use these increased revenues in part to expand its regulation of railroads, while states were taxing and borrowing to build public highways for autos and trucks. Interest, however, on state bonds was tax-exempt income.

Much of the discriminatory impact of such taxation could be reduced by distributing a large portion of the Railroad Company's stock held by the Connecticut Company directly to the stockholders of the latter company.

A plan to accomplish the distribution was adopted at a board meeting held January 14, 1914, and ratified at a stockholders' meeting on February 20, 1914. The stockholders of the Atlantic Coast Line Company of Connecticut surrendered their 176,400 shares of $100 par stock, receiving in exchange an equal number of $50 par shares and 176,400 shares of ACL Railroad Company stock. The holding company's capitalization was thereby reduced from $17,640,000 down to $8,820,000; its block of Railroad Company stock was reduced from 362,306 shares down to 185,906 shares. The Connecticut Company now had only a 27% interest in the Atlantic Coast Line Railroad Company, but control of the Railroad Company was not affected because Henry Walters and his Baltimore associates (the major stockholders of the holding company) received most of the distributed stock.

Public announcement of the action caused a stir in the financial community. Some Wall Street sages saw it as the first step in the dissolution of the holding company; others were unaccountably certain that the Coast Line was preparing to surrender control of the L&N.

Henry Walters refused to make any public explanation of the move, answering all questions from reporters with one laconic written reply: "No further changes contemplated." And he meant just that. The Connecticut Company still served a useful purpose, and it would be continued.

Prosperity Ahead

Despite all the preoccupation with increased taxation, regulation, and operating costs, these were marvelously prosperous times. Railroad Company dividends were increased from $5 to $6 annually in 1910 and again to $7 in 1911. Income represented a return of nearly 6½% on property investment during the years 1910 to 1913. General business conditions contributed much to such profitable operations, but so did management achievements in the areas of increased operating efficiency and traffic promotion.

The Coast Line had also become very active in promotional efforts under President Emerson. From its inception in 1905 the Agricultural and Immigration Department was charged with increasing the number of Coast Line patrons and generating more traffic for the road.

In order to bring new settlers to Coast Line territory, the department placed advertisements in farm magazines and newspapers in northern towns. Some of its agents took a display car to several state fairs in the North each year. to acquaint farmers with opportunities awaiting them in the Southeast, and inform produce buyers of the products of the region. In 1914 the display car even went to the Canadian Exposition at Toronto.

The A&I Department directed prospects to land-selling agencies, and aided immigrants and new business ventures in getting established. In 1912, for example, the department reported that 3,844 heads-of-families engaged in agricultural pursuits, and 215 new industries had located on the Coast Line in the space of a year. Drawing on the resources of universities, state agriculture departments, and the U.S. Department of Agriculture, demonstration trains were sent through the territory to give farmers up-to-date information on crop growing and livestock raising. It particularly pushed for introduction of new crops, to get southern growers to diversify. Tom Emerson, first and always a traffic man, was particularly insistent on the importance of this department's work.

A Door Closes

In the midst of all the prosperity and all the challenges of the time, the Atlantic Coast Line Railroad, and Henry Walters, experienced a deep loss over the death of Thomas Emerson, president of ACL, on November 25, 1913. Walters expressed his sorrow over "the loss which Mr. Emerson's death is to me personally [after] knowing him for 30 years and working side by side . . ."

Tom Emerson had been an excellent top manager for the Railroad Company. He had also served for three decades as its head salesman. He had been effective in communicating with the public and with government commissions during the recent controversies. It would be a long while before anyone performed these last functions equally well for the Coast Line.

In some ways President Emerson's death marked both the culmination and the passing of an era. The railroad lines of the United States were essentially built and enjoying unchallenged supremacy as a transportation mode. They were also encountering some hostile and restrictive actions from government. Doubtless they needed some restrictions. There were, for one thing, far too many accidents. President W. W. Finley of the Southern Railway was killed in an accident on his own road within a few hours of Emerson's death. Another significant passing was that of Henry Flagler on May 10, 1913, after seeing his great construction project completed to Key West.

The lusty, free-wheeling days of railroading were passing. From now on, there would be growing stress on careful management and efficient operation, and in these respects the Coast Line was outstanding.

No. 8: *John R. Kenly, Atlantic Coast Line president from 1913 to 1928.*

Chapter XIII

World War I — Progress In Spite of Problems

Under New Management

The death of Tom Emerson in 1913 had left a vacancy at the top level of ACL administration, and no one was surprised when John Kenly was elected President of the Atlantic Coast Line Railroad Company. He had been Henry Walters' most trusted manager of railroad operations from the beginning of the latter's active role in Coast Line affairs. Their life experiences were closely parallel. Kenly, too, was born and raised in Baltimore, although he attended the public schools for his short formal education. He, too, was a southern sympathizer, joining the Confederate army when only 16. He preceded Henry Walters by a few years in getting his initial railroad experience with the engineering department of the Pittsburgh & Connellsville Railroad. Kenly became a well-qualified civil engineer by the time he went to work for the Union Railroad of Baltimore as roadmaster. He was appointed superintendent of the Richmond & Petersburg Coast Line road in 1882. Henry Walters encountered him there, a year later, while inspecting the Coast Line railroads in preparation to taking over as general manager. They had been closely associated ever since. Now, surveying the small number of old friends left at the corporate meetings in the late autumn of 1913, and viewing the challenges facing him and Kenly, Henry Walters remarked, "I wish he and I were 20 years younger." The sentiment is understandable, but, Walters, at 65, and Kenly, close to 67, were to serve as top officers of the Coast Line for many more years.

Repeatedly during its history, the Coast Line seemed to get the particular kind of leadership it needed at the time it was needed. Tom Emerson, a traffic man, was president during an especially difficult time for government regulation of rates and other traffic matters. Now, at a time when operating effectiveness and sound physical condition would be tested, the Coast Line got a president who was interested especially in its transportation, machinery and roadway departments — John R. Kenly.

John Kenly had been striving for years to keep these aspects of operations abreast of the current technology. If he had a shortcoming as a leader during this period, it was his whole-hearted agreement with the careful conservatism that characterized Chairman Walters. After all the years together, they tended to see eye-to-eye on most questions. An impressive list of officers served at that time:

H. Walters	Chairman of the Board	New York, N. Y
J. R. Kenly	President	Wilmington, N.C.
Alexander Hamilton	First Vice President	Petersburg, N.C.
C.S. Gadsden	Second Vice President	Charleston. S.C.
Lyman Delano	Third Vice President	Wilmington. N.C.
H.L. Borden	Fourth Vice President	New York, N.Y.
James F. Post	Treasurer	Wilmington. N.C.
W .N. Royall	General Manager	Wilmington. N.C.
W. J. Craig	Passenger Traffic Manager	Wilmington. N.C.
James Menzies	Freight Traffic Manager	Wilmington. N.C.
H. C. Prince	Comptroller	Wilmington. N.C.

Certainly the most portentous name in the above roster was that of Lyman Delano, nephew of Henry Walters. Following in Walters' footsteps, Delano had been in Wilmington for several years, learning the Coast Line from the roadbed up. In 1911, he was given the title "Assistant to the President," and in 1913, "Third Vice President." Delano came along quickly, first under Emerson and now under Kenly, assuming increasing responsibility for general administrative matters at Wilmington. Before long, policy decisions for the Coast Line would be made in three-way conferences between Henry Walters, John Kenly and Lyman Delano.

Recession and Recovery

It was only a few months after John Kenly became president of the Coast Line that the European powers began the sequence of belligerent actions that were the commencement of World War I. From the fall of 1914 to December of 1917, when the railroads were taken over by the United States government, Coast Line management had to contend with the profound effects of the war in Europe, and then of America's entry into the hostilities.

The initial impact was a very sharp economic recession. The onset of war in Europe disrupted international trade, greatly intensifying a business downturn that had already begun in the United States.

Particularly hard hit were southern agricultural, forest, and mining industries, which temporarily lost their overseas markets. During the year ending June 30, 1915, the Coast Line suffered declines in freight tonnage of 6.5% in agricultural products, 41.5% in livestock and animal products, 16% in forest products, and 33% in products of mines. Phosphate tonnage was only half that of the preceding year. Freight forwarded revenue from Norfolk was down 17%, from Wilmington, 25%, and from Charleston, 38%. To combat the decline, Walters and Kenly instituted another economy drive, slowing construction projects and equipment purchases, plus cutting back salaries by as much as 10%. Dividend payments were reduced to $5 from the level of $7 per year that had been maintained since 1911.

Recovery came quickly, as the American economy began to respond to huge demands for goods from Great Britain, France, and their allies. The boom really arrived in full force during the summer of 1916, when Coast Line operating revenues began to run a good 20% ahead of the year before. The dividend rate was restored to $7 by 1917.

By April of 1917, when the United States declared war on Germany, the problem for Coast Line executives was no longer that of promoting traffic, but rather of coping with the enormous volume of business.

Demands for More Motive Power

The drastic dip in business during the year 1914-15 was peculiarly ill-timed for the Coast Line, as for most American railroads. It slashed earnings at a time when they were already being squeezed by tight rate regulation and rising costs. Several important railroads went into receivership in 1915, many were seriously under-maintained, practically all cut investments in plant and equipment. Only months later they would all be scrambling to acquire desperately needed motive power and rolling stock in order to meet the demands of a war-stimulated economy.

With its careful management, conservative capitalization, and still-expanding territory, the Coast Line did better than most railroads. A substantial improvement program was carried on through the prosperity swing of 1910 to 1914, reduced temporarily during the recession, and resumed full scale in 1916. As a result, its roadway was brought to fine condition, and there were great improvements in transportation equipment, especially in motive power. Many new locomotives of more powerful design were purchased, and the tractive power of many engines on the line was boosted by the introduction of "superheaters." However, as General Superintendent of Motive Power R. E. Smith kept telling his bosses, they were not buying enough new locomotives.

After a three-year pause following the Panic of 1907, the Coast Line had begun to order locomotives again in 1910. The first ones were the 20-inch 10-wheelers that had been the road's standard for new engines for several years. Forty-nine more of these were added to the roster by mid-1913. The switch to new types began in 1911. Following much study and discussion, in which not-yet-president Kenly, Chairman Walters, and Superintendent Smith all took an active part, the company placed an order April 15, 1911, with the Baldwin Works for 15 Pacific-type passenger engines and 20 Mikado-type freight engines.

The immediate need for more powerful passenger engines was to maintain schedule speeds on mainline runs when the weight of the new steel Pullman cars was added to train complements. The Baldwin Pacific type, already in use on several other railroads, was in the next evolution of high speed locomotives used on the Coast Line. Its tractive power was 23% greater than that of the standard Coast Line te10-wheeler. Some minor defects were corrected, and superheaters added to the design, increasing further the efficiency of the engines by giving higher tractive power in relation to weight and boiler size. The Waycross shops, already a Coast Line showplace for up-to-date equipment, received a Hartz flue welder in 1914 for installing superheaters on older locomotives.

Choosing motive power for freight was more complicated because of the diversity of freight handled on the Coast Line. The need for the 20 Mikado locomotives seemed clear enough. It was large by ACL standards and well suited to haul slow and heavy freights like coal, sand, rock, etc. Changing to heavier locomotives for regular fast freights proved more difficult. Henry Walters liked the 10-wheelers. He felt that his railroad's freight business called for the fast movement of relatively short trains, which did not need larger engines. Finally Kenly and Smith persuaded him that larger cars and growing traffic volume called for heavier motive power on mainline freights, and Baldwin Pacifics were also chosen as the new standard freight engine. It differed slightly from the passenger version only in having 64-inch drivers instead of the 72-inch size of the passenger model. There were 83 Pacifics, freight and passenger models, in service by 1917.

Bigger and Better Rolling Stock

Rolling stock was also so generally up-graded from 1910 to 1917. Some 12,600 freight cars were put on the line, and nearly 25% of the equipment owned in 1910 was replaced, bringing the total inventory to 30,377. Most of the box cars purchased were larger and many were specialized, reflecting new traffic patterns. Increases in the demand for coal, the growing automobile industry, international requests for foodstuffs and a booming livestock industry necessitated purchases of a variety of freight cars of new design.

The larger locomotives and improved freight cars boosted efficiency. The average tonnage hauled by the Coast Line more than doubled between 1910 and 1917 — from 160 tons to nearly 346 tons per train mile. This success was accomplished by using longer trains and the fullest possible loading of each and every freight car. For freights moving northward, the optimum was a payload of 2,100 to 2,200 tons in 55 to 65 fully loaded cars.

Passenger trains, especially through trains, grew in length, too. Many new coaches of larger capacity were purchased — 75 of them from 1910 through 1917. These were now up to 83 feet long, and had the strength and safety features of the steel underframe that had become standard. Again, Henry Walters had at first resisted this change, but in the end he bowed to progress.

Safety and speed for passenger trains were greatly increased by improvements to the line. By 1917, some 335 miles of the Richmond to Jacksonville main line were double track. Train movements over almost all of those miles were protected and controlled by automatic block signals. More powerful locomotives, heavier rail, and double track with block signals all contributed to faster schedules.

New Roadway Construction

From 1908 until halted by the materials shortages of World War I, the Coast Line carried on a fairly active program of constructing new lines. Although the system was essentially complete in 1902, there were some new areas to be tapped in Florida, some points of dependency on other railroads to be removed, and a need for better access to the coal fields.

The Winston-Salem Southbound Railway was the Coast Line's solution for carrying soft coal from the Pocahontas region. By spanning the 88 miles southward from Winston-Salem to Wadesboro, North Carolina, and connecting there with the northern terminus of the old Cheraw and Salisbury, the new road would give the Coast Line the shortest possible coal route to Florence, Charleston, and other points south. The project was first initiated jointly with the Southern Railway, but the officers of the Southern decided that the project was of marginal benefit to their road and withdrew in March of 1909, with the suggestion that the Norfolk & Western should take their place. The Norfolk & Western already had a line running directly southward from Roanoke, Va., to Winston-Salem. Henry Walters reached a basic agreement with President L. E. Johnson of the Norfolk & Western on March 9, and Michael Jenkins completed the negotiations during April.

Construction of the road was underway by July of 1909, and it was opened for light through traffic on March 6, 1911. Although jointly owned with the Norfolk & Western, the Winston-Salem Southbound was operated under ACL management for some years.

The new route was part of a general push to expand coal-hauling business. The very limited supply of 31 coal cars owned in 1903 was by 1911 enlarged to 647, and by the end of 1917 to 733. During the first full year that the Winston-Salem Southbound was in use, the Coast Line's bituminous coal tonnage increased from 673,000 tons to nearly 790,000 tons. The tonnage was 830,000 for 1917. In spite of all efforts to promote coal consumption in its territory, the Coast Line's coal traffic remained at a modest 5½% to 6% of its revenue freight tonnage.

The new roadway constructed for the ACL Railroad Company itself was mostly in Florida. The most ambitious project was the Haines City branch. The first segment of this line, running from Haines City (a point about halfway between Orlando and Lakeland), 47 miles southward to Sebring, was begun in October of 1910 and placed in service in June of 1912. The Haines City branch opened virgin territory for rapid development of new lumber, mining, citrus, and tourist business.

Amid the prosperity of 1916, a plan was adopted to extend this line southward a full 81 miles to the town of Immokalee, using a drawbridge to cross the Caloosahatchee River. There would also be a branch going from Harrisburg eastward to Moore Haven, on the western shore of Lake Okeechobee. The road was completed to Harrisburg and the branch to Moore Haven by April, 1918. Shortly afterward the project had to be suspended due to war shortages. The remaining line to Immokalee, and subsequently still further southward to Port Everglades, would be constructed some years later.

The other mileage constructed in Florida during this period included a 50-mile stretch from Dunnellon to Wilcox — a segment of the eventual "west coast route" referred to earlier. There was also a 20-mile line built from Archer to Morriston. When completed on October 15, 1913, it ended the Coast Line's dependency on the Seaboard for trackage rights between those two points. Somewhat earlier, the Coast Line had completed a short but expensive line between Weldon and Garysburg, North Carolina, including a bridge over the Roanoke River, which ended use of the Seaboard's road there under trackage rights that dated back to 1884.

New Post-War Stations

During the year following addition of the Plant System, the Railroad Company had owned 3,999 miles of line, and operated 4,139 miles. On December 31, 1917, it owned 4,693 miles and was operating 4,787 miles of line. Henry Walters' railroad was very close to being complete. Two great passenger stations would soon add another measure of fulfillment. The station at Richmond, at the northern end of the Coast Line's main stem, and the other at Jacksonville, at the southern end, would give tangible witness to the railroad's maturity and greatness. Their designs would be fitting in style and scale, conceived in all the grandeur of Roman basilicas. Henry Walters attended the opening ceremonies of the great Pennsylvania Station in New York City on August 1, 1910, and found it "simply stupendous!"

The New York example doubtless influenced his aspirations, for he began discussing the need for better terminal facilities at Richmond. It was, however, two years later before an agreement was worked out between the ACL Railroad Company and the Richmond, Fredericksburg & Potomac for proceeding with an ambitious project for a new station. Another year passed before architectural plans were ready for consideration. It was 1916 before the jointly-owned Richmond Terminal Railway Company purchased the old fair grounds and some adjoining land and began construction. A contract was also let for construction of a new upper bridge across the James River. The station itself was to be a handsome stone edifice. The whole project was to be completed in 1918, but war shortages and various other obstacles delayed construction almost a year. Broad Street Station finally opened for service in Richmond at noon on January 6, 1919, without ceremony of any kind. The post-armistice public mood was not receptive to fanfare about a splendid new railway terminal. Also, there was a certain amount of resentment in Richmond at changes in local passenger service and the conversion of Byrd Street Station entirely to freight use. Still, the new station at Richmond was a grand introduction to the Coast Line for southbound travelers.

The increase of Florida travel had rendered the existing station in Jacksonville obsolete shortly after the turn of the century. Much local sentiment, if not clamor, had built up by 1916, when the Jacksonville Terminal Company bought additional land adjacent to West Bay and Lee Streets and let contracts for a new terminal complex. The

Terminal Company was owned by five railroad companies: the Atlantic Coast Line, the Seaboard Air Line, and the Florida East Coast Railway with a fourth interest each; and the Georgia Southern & Florida and the Southern Railway, with an eighth interest each. Consensus took longer, but the cost would be mercifully distributed more widely. A good thing, because the bill for the entire project came to $1,300,000; the station alone cost nearly $750,000.

Here, too, there were delays, so that it was not until late 1919 that the new passenger gateway to Florida was ready. On Sunday, November 16, the public was invited to come and admire it. Although the station opened for business at 12:01 the next morning without ceremony, the facilities made quite an impression. The facade featured a colonnade of 40-foot columns. The main waiting room was 180 feet long with a domed ceiling 75 feet high, marble wainscoting and tile floors. A 400-foot main concourse gave access to 8,000 feet of passenger loading platforms, almost all covered with butterfly sheds. Switching of the many miles of yard tracks was all controlled by the latest in automatic interlocking systems. All in all, the new Jacksonville Terminal was grand in design and efficient in engineering. It was hailed in the local press as the "finest south of Washington." The station was finished none too soon; there were 110 trains and an average of 20,000 passengers daily flowing through the terminal in its first months of use.

Employee Relations

The Coast Line's policy toward labor had been a conservative one over the years, with great emphasis on two-way loyalty between the company and its employees. To dismiss the policy simply as paternalism would be to ignore the special quality of solidarity that characterized a railroad "family." The strong insistence on promoting from within the ranks has been mentioned often. Provision of medical care by the Relief Department was another way that the company cared for its own.

The Coast Line was one of the first railroads in the country to organize a special medical and hospital program for its employees. Patterned after plans just introduced on the Pennsylvania Railroad and the Chicago, Burlington & Quincy, the Relief Department was established by the Wilmington & Weldon Railroad Company late in 1898 and joined shortly afterwards by all the separate companies then comprising the Coast Line. Dr. George G. Thomas of Wilmington was appointed as superintendent and chief surgeon of the department, a post he held until 1920. The program simply continued as a department of the consolidated ACL RR Co. Then, with some changes in regulations late in 1902, the Plant System's medical program was amalgamated with the Coast Line's.

Hospitals at South Rocky Mount and Waycross, staffed with Relief Department physicians, afforded no-cost care to employees of the railroad. The service was supported by both employee and company contributions to the fund. About half of Coast Line employees joined during the first year of the program, which was strengthened in 1902 by stricter requirements on participation.

Employee benefits expanded soon after the beginnings of the Relief Department to include a pension plan. To be sure, the benefits were at first quite modest: retirement (voluntary at 65, compulsory at age 70) at no higher than 10% of active income. Under the initial rules, disability pensions were not permitted before age 61. This was liberalized in 1909 to enable an employee with 20 years of service to be pensioned at a younger age, "provided that his disability is reported as permanent by the examining surgeon, and not arising from vicious life or due to immoralities . . ."

In keeping with a movement throughout the nation, the Atlantic Coast Line cooperated with the YMCA in furnishing another employee benefit. Three YMCA hotels were located on the line, affording good away-from-home housing to railroaders at very reasonable rates, a particular boon to train crews. The Annual Report presented to stockholders in November, 1911, explained the arrangement:

> At the sole expense of the Railroad Company, brick buildings, equipped with modern conveniences, are now in course of erection at Rocky Mount, N.C., Florence, S.C., and Waycross, Ga. They are leased to the International Committee of the Young Men's Christian Association, and are to be operated under the supervision and control of the Association for the accommodation of the employees of this Company. This Company will pay the salary of the Secretaries; all other expenses of operation will be borne by the Association.

Union Power

Labor difficulties intensified for the Coast Line as the pressures of war business increased. John Kenly had been entrusted with settling disputes with the operating hands since the 1880s when he was assistant general manager. Now, as president, he found this responsibility a heavier one, because relationships with wage employees were changing profoundly.

The various new benefits for Coast Line employees were being provided in the midst of a general climate of growing awareness of the rights, and organized power of the working man. The opening years of the century saw much labor organizing activity, and the Coast Line came in for its share of conflict with the new brotherhoods and their negotiating committees. Most of the categories of operating trainmen, led by the locomotive engineers, had won recognition for their organizations by the turn of the century. Shopmen, maintenance-of-way workers, and other categories of railway labor were harder to organize effectively; and the Coast Line, along with other southern roads, was slow to accept their unions.

The company signed an agreement with the Brotherhood of Maintenance-of-Way Employees in December of 1902, which amounted to limited recognition of the union.

However, John Kenly balked at improvements in the work rules and wages advanced by the union's board in January of 1904. He ordered his roadmasters to discharge all employees who would not agree to stand by the company. John T. Wilson, president of the Brotherhood, responded by calling a strike, effective February 11, with the men voting almost unanimously in support. The company demonstrated that it meant business by firing a number of striking section foremen, and evicting them from company housing. The strike was ended, and most of the men back on the job, in three weeks.

There was trouble, too, with various categories of shopmen. A strike of car repairers on the Second and Third Divisions of the system began early in 1907 and dragged on for many months, with the railroad replacing the striking workers as best it could.

By 1910 Coast Line management was dealing regularly with negotiating committees representing most categories of skilled railroad workers, including shopmen, yardmen, engineers, trainmen, and telegraphers. In some cases these committees represented only a class of Coast Line workers, not a branch of a national brotherhood; yet Chairman Walters and his executives were acknowledging the new power of labor. They were certainly aware of its effects. The wage increases agreed to in the course of 1910 alone added more than $1 million to operating costs.

The company encountered the full force of union power in another way when, early in 1916, President Kenly attempted to introduce a new system of train auditing. The Coast Line contracted with an outside company, White's Train Auditors, to furnish auditors who would ride Coast Line freights and record tonnage hauled, car complements, car mileage, etc. It was part of the determined drive to increase tonnage hauled by each freight train, mentioned earlier.

The Coast Line conductors objected to bringing in outsiders to look over their shoulders. In mid-February, they voted, almost to a man — over 570 of them — to back the Order of Railway Conductors in a posture of absolute rejection of outside train auditors. The company backed down and dismissed White's Train Auditors, reserving the right to assign auditors who were company employees. The conductors accepted this as the basis for settling the dispute. As it turned out, the Coast Line conductors also accepted the new duty of turning in special reports on cars and tonnage carried in each train run. The Coast Line increased its freight train loads without the use of special train auditors.

During the same weeks, the operating brotherhoods were commencing their push for an eight-hour day. It was a bitter, hard-fought struggle. It took all the pressure of war-stimulated business, two calls for nationwide strikes (one for September 4, 1916, and another for March 19, 1917), an act of Congress (the Adamson Act), and a decision of the United States Supreme Court in favor of the Adamson Act to force the railroad executives to agree to this change.

Coast Line management, although as reluctant as most, accepted the resulting jump in operating costs with relatively good grace. It was a drive to organize the clerks on their railroad that really raised the hackles of Coast Line leaders and produced the most spectacular labor conflict the company had yet experienced.

Walters and Kenly, as old railroad men, could accept the relative prestige and definite labor status of the men who ran the trains, but not of the men who worked in their offices. The firing of a clerk in the Richmond freight agency became the *cause celebre* in a union organizing campaign.

On October 16, 1917, 36 clerks walked out of the Richmond freight agency and yard, whereupon the company replaced them with newly hired personnel, and announced that any clerk who joined the union would be fired.

There were many other walkouts at other points on the system as the dispute intensified. A union leader declared in a public meeting at Wilmington that he would tie up all the railroads in the Southeast if necessary in order to protect a clerks' union on the Coast Line.

On November 16, the port at Norfolk was practically shut down by a sympathetic strike of railway and steamship laborers. Kenly went to Washington on November 17 in response to a call for a conference by William B. Hale, acting for the Council of National Defense. He agreed to suspend the policy of firing union members, to reinstate those clerks whose positions had not been satisfactorily filled, and to meet with a committee of striking clerks. The meeting took place in Wilmington on November 22 and 23. The clerks demanded reinstatement without pay loss for all those fired. Kenly refused.

The threat to vital communications was so great that the President of the United States now intervened with a direct request that the company give in. Only after the second telegram from President Woodrow Wilson reached him, on November 27, did John Kenly give his reluctant concurrence as spokesman for the Coast Line.

It was a very painful episode, one that dramatized the profound changes in the status of labor taking place under wartime conditions. On a less spectacular level, labor was absorbing a larger portion of operating expenses — it was the main reason that the Coast Line's operating ratio climbed to 72.7% for 1917. With 760 of the company's regular employees in military service by the end of the year, it was harder and harder to fill positions with people who could do a good job.

Traffic Challenges

The Coast Line handled a tremendous increase in traffic during 1917, in spite of labor troubles and materials shortages. Southern producers of food, fiber, and livestock shipped much more northward, and southbound merchandise traffic boomed. Men and supplies were transported hurriedly to military training camps at various points in the Southeast. Freight ton-miles rose nearly 20% from the previous year and passenger miles nearly 25%.

The most critical equipment shortage in meeting the challenge was in motive power. The railroad got only seven new road engines, mentioned earlier, during 1917. They were all that was delivered of 20 Pacifics ordered from Baldwin in November of 1916 and another 20 ordered in March of 1917. The orders were placed too late to beat the rush. The Baldwin works and all other builders were swamped with orders and running way behind on deliveries. The seven Pacifics received were put on the line in the fall of 1917. Failure to get all the new locomotives that were ordered was especially critical because they were to replace 40 old light engines that Superintendent of Motive Power R. E. Smith determinedly scrapped during the year, an awkwardly timed move.

Even so, the Coast Line was better off than many railroads. Its north-to-south main line was not caught by the main flow of war traffic. Most of the movement of men and goods was in one direction eastward to the Atlantic ports. It proved to be too much for the trunklines east of Chicago and St. Louis. For one thing, there was no precedent for an operation of such magnitude, and there was no organizational structure capable of administering a coordinated plan.

A voluntary organization, headed by a five-man Railroads' War Board, attempted to lead the nation's railroads into operating as if they were a continental railway system. John Kenly was in Washington, D. C., for the meeting on April 11, 1917, of the railroad leaders who approved the organization. In spite of the best efforts of Chairman Fairfax Harrison, president of the Southern Railway, the War Board failed. It had no authority to enforce its decisions, and railroad managements were obliged by law and position to pursue their separate companies' interests.

In addition, the country's railroads were not in top physical condition. Among various deficiencies they had too few freight cars, and too many of the cars they had were in bad order. They were straining, and none too successfully, to keep up with transportation demand even before the U. S. entry into the war. There was a national shortage of 145,000 freight cars by March 31, 1917, which increased to 158,000 cars by November. Traffic jams developed on eastern lines, as their port terminals proved inadequate to permit rapid unloading of cars. An estimated 180,100 freight cars were crammed near the eastern gateways, and the railroads involved simply did not have the terminal facilities to get them unloaded or the motive power to clear them out. The situation on the Pittsburgh Division of the Pennsylvania Railroad was one of the worst. Writing as Chairman of the Railroads' War Board, in early December, Fairfax Harrison informed Henry Walters:

> The congestion of the Eastern railroads is giving us the greatest concern. Our General Operating Committee at Pittsburgh has certified that the Eastern railroads require five hundred more engines to clean up the congestion. They have secured the use of one hundred

of the engines built for the United States service in France, for which shipping is not yet available, and are negotiating for the use of some of the engines built for Russia. They have also called on the roads west of Chicago and St. Louis to provide one hundred engines for use in the territory east of those cities. They may call upon the Southern roads for help in cleaning up the congestion at Potomac Yard and other Southern gateways.

The Federal Government Steps In

The problem was soon taken out of Mr. Harrison's hands. By Christmas time, the situation had deteriorated still further. By proclamation of President Wilson on December 26, the Atlantic Coast Line and 384 other major railroad lines were placed under the control of the United States government to begin at noon on December 28, 1917. Centralized management would now be provided for the "continental railway system."

Chairman Walters and President Kenly viewed the commencement of government possession as a definite millstone for their railroad. The Atlantic Coast Line Railroad now had a new boss: William G. McAdoo, Secretary of the Treasury, and now also Director General of Railroads. There was also a regional director at Atlanta (at first Charles Markham, later B. L. Winchell) to whom ACL management reported directly. The United States Railroad Administration was officially in possession of the railroad from December 28, 1917, until March 1, 1920.

President Kenly was relieved of his command and Lyman Delano was named Federal Manager, on June 26, 1918. Henry Walters served on the Director General's staff, being particularly active in Washington through May of 1918. He and Kenly, however, kept constantly in touch with ACL matters, and he regularly communicated helpful suggestions to Delano from the sidelines, so to speak.

Not being in the most critical area, the Coast Line was not terribly disarranged in its operations under Federal control. In the face of a drive to cancel all unnecessary "frill" service, Lyman Delano even succeeded in keeping the *Florida Special* run as an added passenger service each winter season. He persuaded the regional director at Atlanta and the central staff in Washington that an additional, regularly scheduled train during the months of heavy passenger traffic cost less than running extra sections of other trains to meet extraordinary demand. So it was decided that the luxury train, the *Florida Special*, was not a luxury after all, especially if its name were not mentioned in the announcements. For the duration it was presented on schedules simply as Train No. 87 southbound and Train No. 88 northbound.

There was, however, considerable intervention in questions of motive power. Lyman Delano was informed that the ambitious ACL schedule of locomotive scrapping, on the part of Superintendent of Motive Power Smith, should be halted. The people in the Director General's office took a very dim view of this behavior, since everyone was crying for more motive power. Coast Line officials were busied for a time keeping track of their engines as some of them were assigned to other railroads. Under persuasion of the "War Board" in December of 1917, three ACL Mikados were leased to the Chesapeake & Ohio, then returned the next spring. In another instance, some of the Pacific engines built by Baldwin under order for the Coast Line were sent to other roads — four to the Baltimore & Ohio and four to the Erie Railroad. In April and May of 1918, eight decapod engines intended for export to Russia for aid in her war effort were sent to the Coast Line for temporary use. McAdoo's staff was shunting equipment around to points of greatest need, while keeping locomotive builders working full tilt turning out engines of U. S. standard models.

As production caught up with need, the locomotive shuffling ended. By early 1919 the Coast Line had received 20 more heavy Pacifics and 10 new huge Midako freight engines, which had been ordered by the company before government control. The Railroad Administration purchased and assigned to Coast Line 45 new U. S. Standard Light Pacifics (with 25-inch cylinders) before the year was out. The railroad was getting fairly well supplied with motive power, although the pressure of business was great and keeping up with repairs almost impossible.

The Outcome

The Coast Line was kept very busy during the war and the subsequent months of continued Federal control. The traffic and mileage statistics for the years in question indicate the extent of the challenge that the road's operating personnel had to meet.

Revenues increased as a result of all the business, but not as much as one might expect. Railway rates, compared with the price of practically everything else, went up very little. Still, the Coast Line's operating revenues for 1918 were an impressive $56,992,329 and for 1919 an even more impressive $63,559,015. Unfortunately for the United States Treasury, expenses rose even faster. So net operating income actually declined from $11,685,220 in 1918 to only $7,218,193 in 1919. Yet Lyman Delano and the rest of Coast Line management deserve credit for keeping the income from operating their railroad so high. On many American railroads in 1919, expenses exceeded revenues. The U. S. Railroad Administration almost broke even during its operation of the Coast Line. It paid to its owners an annual compensation, or "standard return," of $10,185,942.34, not so very much more than the actual operating profit. The total deficit on other lines was so great that Congress had to appropriate over $900,000,000 to meet "standard return" payments.

The Atlantic Coast Line Railroad Company was one of the many railroads that accepted Congress' provision of a guaranteed income, at the standard return rate, for the first six months of private operation. The Transportation Act of 1920 (the Esch-Cummins Act) was solicitous of the railroads' well-being in various ways, since Congress recognized that the end of Federal operation was leaving them in all kinds of trouble as private enterprises. In consequence, the ACL Railroad Company received the following payments from the United States Government during the transition year of 1920:

Standard return for January and February	$1,684,187.36
Additional compensation for betterments	5,316.89
Guarantee for six months, March 1 to September 1	5,478,458.01
Adjustments of standard return	252,014.87

In addition, the United States Railroad Administration paid the Company $5,442,744.42 in claims for under-maintenance and various kinds of damages incurred during the period of government operation. Another claim for damages suffered during the guarantee period would be settled in 1923 for a very modest sum. All in all, the ACL Railroad Company fared quite well in compensation payments.

From the standpoint of Chairman Walters and President Kenly, considerable compensation was in order. The U. S. Railroad Administration was returning to them a railroad with its physical plant greatly in need of repairs, a labor force under sharply altered work conditions and costing 200% more than before the war, and an operating ratio right at the 90% level. Given the uncertainties of the post-war scene, they had grounds for concern. There was much to be done.

Chapter XIV

The Roaring '20s — A Return to Excellence

Triple Header

Soon after World War I, the U.S. Railroad Administration disbanded the "continental railway system" that had placed the major railroads under government control for the war effort. When the Atlantic Coast Line Railroad returned to its corporate owner on March 1, 1920, it remained under the administrative direction of Lyman Delano. Only his official title changed. He had been federal manager for the government; now he was made executive vice president by the company.

It was Lyman Delano who had day-to-day responsibility for running the railroad, and many decisions were made in communications directly between him and his uncle, Chairman Henry Walters. Their relationship was an affable one. "Uncle Harry," as Lyman called him in private, enjoyed his visits at the Delano household in Wilmington. They were scrupulously formal, however, in the conduct of railroad business, and there was never the slightest question that any change of policy or practice would be taken up with Chairman Walters and that the final determination would be his. President Kenly was consulted on most policy matters, and he kept active as spokesman for the railroad company, especially at hearings before state and federal regulatory agencies. The Coast Line was run during these years under a congenial and effective executive triumvirate.

Wilmington Railroad Museum

No. 9: *Lyman Delano led ACL as chairman during the Depression and into World War II.*

Postwar Recovery

The immediate objective for Coast Line executives was to restore the railroad to profitable operations. Expenses were running so high — the operating ratio for the year was 93% — that net operating income (after taxes) amounted to only $1,497,364 in 1920. Even with non-operating income, including the substantial dividend payments from the Louisville & Nashville Railroad, the Coast Line was not making enough profit to pay the interest on its debts. Of course, federal payments raised final income to "standard return" level for the first two months of the year and for the additional six-month guarantee period, thereby keeping the accounts in black ink. Drastic changes were obviously required for the time when, after September 1, 1920, the Atlantic Coast Line was once again completely on its own as a private enterprise.

The federal government made an important contribution to the campaign to restore profitability. The Interstate Commerce Commission cleared nationwide raises in railroad rates in July of 1920. These gave the ACL freight rate increases of 25% within its territory and $33^1/_3$% on shipments to other regions, plus a boost of 20% in passenger rates. Full benefits of the higher rates were delayed, however, by resistance from some state governments. A number of states, Georgia and Florida among them, attempted to keep intrastate passenger fares and freight rates below the new level of interstate rates approved by the ICC. This naturally had the effect of nullifying the higher interstate rates. In 1920, through precedent-setting decisions involving New York and Illinois, the ICC asserted its power to prevent discrimination by states against interstate commerce. The decrees for lower freight rates and passenger fares by various state commissions were set aside, and the new higher rates finally were fully in effect by December. U. S. courts supported the ICC in subsequent test cases. As late as 1923, however, South Carolina still challenged federal dominance in the matter by trying to reduce Coast Line passenger fares, and to forbid a surcharge in its sleeping cars. A U. S. District Court enjoined the state's railroad commission from enforcing its orders.

Another Economy Drive

The situation in 1920 obviously called for some drastic cost cutting. Coast Line officials overlooked no possibilities. They called for price reductions from their suppliers on everything from journal bearings to paint — and got them. They drove hard bargains with producers of crude materials such as cross ties, which were lowered in price from $1.60 to 50¢ each in less than six months.

The greatest cost burden of all was the swollen payroll. The new Railroad Labor Board granted a generous wage hike to rail workers, effective retroactively to May 1. As a result of this, and all the earlier wartime changes, labor costs were up sharply — from a monthly payroll of $1,432,702 for 19,305 employees in 1917, to a monthly payroll of $3,713,067 for 25,215 employees in 1920. This was the cost category that got the most determined attention. General Manager P.R. Albright and his superintendents were charged with restoring efficiency and cutting payrolls drastically in all departments. They did. By March of 1911 the Coast Line had only 21,980 employees and a monthly payroll of $2,968,814.

There was finally some federal government assistance in this matter, too. The Railroad Labor Board abrogated, effective July 1, 1921, the wartime National Agreements which had established work rules and conditions so favorable to labor. Thus freed, the company set out to cut wages, to reduce still further the number of employees on its rolls, and to restore many prewar work rules. President Kenly and

General Manager Albright were especially interested in improving the work organization in their repair shops. The U. S. Railroad Administration had done away with piecework pay and had established the eight-hour day. Kenly complained that shop efficiency had been reduced by at least 30%.

New urgency was lent to the economy drive by the postwar depression, which saw prices and business activity dip sharply during the last half of 1920 and stay at a low level through 1921. Agricultural interests, so important in Coast Line territory, were particularly hard hit. In the six states served, the value of farm products declined, according to the U. S. Department of Agriculture, from a wartime average of about $1.8 billion to $1.4 billion in 1920, to only $925 million in 1921.

Not all areas of trade were down so much, but the railroad's operating revenues for 1921 declined to $66.4 million, off 10% from the previous year. Fortunately, the economy drive was very successful. Operating costs were pared from $68.9 million in 1920 to $58 million in 1921 and again to $52 million in 1922.

Labor Rebels

Coast Line management was remarkably successful in eliminating hundreds of jobs and reducing wages substantially without serious conflict in most categories of operation. A painful exception was the company's experience with the nationwide shopmen's strike in 1922. The impasse developed in the course of many months of disputes. Many railroads attempted, as did the Coast Line, to reinstitute pre-war work rules and pay scales in their repair shops, and the unions resisted the changes. The Railroad Labor Board studied the dispute and ordered, effective July 1, 1922, a reduction in shop workers' wages. It also authorized some of the work rules changes that the railroad companies desired.

The shop crafts unions saw the board's decision as unacceptable. They responded with a nationwide strike, beginning 10 a.m. on Saturday, July 1. Over 90% of ACL shopmen joined the walkout.

The company took the position that the strikers were placing themselves outside the law by defying the Railroad Labor Board and that they consequently were surrendering all rights to their jobs. As General Manager Albright put it,

"The strike . . . is between the shop employees . . . and the American public, acting through its representatives on a federal board delegated by the Transportation Act to decide such matters."

Albright and his superintendents proceeded to reorganize their shops. They reinstituted the piecework system, and hired as many new men as they could find to replace the strikers. By mid-August they had hired 2,793 new men, and had the shop forces up to 64% of full complement. The operating brotherhoods stayed on the job, so the trains kept rolling. The railroad made 93% of its scheduled passenger runs during July and managed to deliver all perishable freight on time. The numbers of cars and locomotives that fell into bad order increased, of course, as the strike wore on.

Much more serious was the violence the strike brought on the Coast Line. The strikers apparently resorted to desperate acts, as they saw their jobs being filled by "scabs." Air hoses were cut on locomotives and cars, reportedly 350 of them in just one night. A pumphouse at the Lakeland shops was dynamited, and there was an attempt to blow up the dormitories for shop employees at Tampa. On the night of August 16, dozens of rifle and shotgun rounds were fired into the Waycross shops, resulting in the assignment of a National Guard machine gun detachment to guard the place. The company hired many special guards to protect shop installations and non-striking workers. A large crowd kidnapped 13 such guards from a public place in Rocky Mount one night, then took them to remote locations, and subjected them to severe personal abuse. Four of the men were reportedly never found. There were no fewer than 152 cases of injury to persons, and 49 instances of substantial damage to property, connected with the strike, according to later testimony of General Manager Albright.

The strike ended on most American railroads in mid-September, when the federation of shop crafts unions accepted defeat. Responding to a "call" by President Warren G. Harding, the workers agreed to return. Most carriers hired back all the workers who were not guilty of violence; and, eventually, most restored workers' seniority.

Coast Line management, however, refused to hire returnees except for vacancies not filled by new men. It also refused to recognize as an organizing or bargaining agent any affiliate of the national union that had called the strike. The whole affair left a legacy of bitterness in some of the Coast Line service towns that took a long time to die. The repair shops everywhere on the system were now restored to the efficient old practices that management preferred; and as business picked up, the shop workers were given modest increases ranging from 1 cent to 3 cents per hour in the fall of 1923.

The Coast Line was taking a tough stance in its dealings with labor organizations in the postwar period. Its officers were clearly intent on rolling back many of the gains made by labor during the years of federal control. These gains — in wages, work rules, and organizational power — had been especially striking in the South. As Federal Manager, Lyman Delano had felt the impact of the wartime changes first-hand. Now, in his continued active leadership at Wilmington, he seemed to be at least as firm on the issue of property rights as were his uncle, Henry Walters, and President Kenly.

When the ACL telegraphers union asked for a raise in pay in 1923, the management countered with a proposal to the Labor Board that those at small stations should receive a 4¢ per hour reduction. There followed many months of fruitless negotiations until, in October of 1925, 1,184 Coast Line telegraphers voted to go out on strike. Enough stayed on the job, however, that the company was able to maintain vital communications. Delano and Albright "locked out" the union telegraphers, held a supervised election, and recognized a committee of cooperative men as negotiators for Coast Line telegraphers. During the early months of 1926, the strike was effectively broken. The telegraphers union no longer had a contract on the Coast Line. It was getting unequivocally established that the Coast Line was a railroad company that did not respond in a kindly fashion to a strike.

Repairing and Refurbishing

The railroad was in rather rundown condition when the company resumed control from the government in March of 1920. The roadbed and track needed much attention. Wartime steel shortages had cut rail replacement to about half the normal rate during the heaviest traffic period ever. Maintenance of way work had been intensified during 1919, but it had to be cut back now in the attempt to get costs under control. The condition of the motive power and rolling stock was even worse. About 30% of the locomotive complement and 11% of the freight cars were in unserviceable condition.

Roadway maintenance, where the labor situation was most flexible, picked up first. Unit expenses dropped sharply in late 1920 and 1921, as wages and costs of materials went down. A record 216 miles of track were re-laid with new rail in 1921, reflecting a general push in roadway improvements. It included an ambitious program of replacing wooden trestles with culverts and earth embankments.

Rehabilitation of rolling stock took longer, since cost-cutting came more slowly in the shops. Repair costs obviously were very high and slow to come down. The work force was reduced, and this meant that needed repairs were not getting done fast enough. It would take long and painful months to get the Coast Line repair shops running again on an efficient and economical basis.

The postwar depression permitted another solution for bad-order equipment — scrapping. During 1921 and 1922, an unprecedented total of 68 locomotives were destroyed or sold, as were some 2,000 freight cars. Scrapping, plus purchasing of modest amounts of new equipment, gradually brought the number of unserviceable engines and cars down to manageable levels.

The supply of new, high-performance engines was comparatively good. The U.S. Railroad Administration had acquired for the Coast Line a few new heavy locomotives, for slow freights, and 70 new Pacific passenger locomotives.

The Pacific-type (4-6-2) passenger locomotives were of the standard design adopted for all the Light Pacifics built for the Railroad Administration. The first 10 put on the line, Class P-5, had 73-inch drivers, 25-inch x 28-inch cylinders, and a total weight of

278,000 pounds. The remaining 60, Class P-5-As, were equipped with coal pushers, stokers, and other equipment, which increased the weight of some to as high as 281,000 pounds.

One of these Class P-5-A locomotives, No. 1504, survived the age of steam, and was placed in front of ACL's new headquarters building following the relocation to Jacksonville in 1960. In 1988, No. 1504 was donated to the city and moved to the Prime Osborn III Convention Center in Jacksonville, commemorating the millions of miles of service performed by Coast Line Pacific-type road engines.

Similarly, a 1910 Baldwin "Copper Head" 4-6-0, No. 250, which served more than 40 years, was retired in 1953 and displayed at division headquarters in Tampa. This 10-wheeler was moved from Tampa to Wilmington, N.C., in 1983, where it was put on display at the Wilmington Railroad Museum.

By early 1922, General Superintendent of Motive Power R. D. Hawkins, had developed some modifications of the Light Pacifics that, early in 1922, Chairman Walters approved as the design for a new standard road engine. The changes adapted the Pacifics for fast freight as well as passenger service. The most important alteration reduced the diameter of the driving wheels from 73 to 69 inches, increasing the tractive force substantially. The new engines, Class P-5-B, were larger than earlier Pacifics on the Coast Line. They had 25 x 28-inch cylinders, and they weighed 275,950 pounds, carrying 166,770 pounds on their drivers.

The initial order placed with Baldwin was for 45 locomotives, but the total would reach 135 by the end of 1926. The first 20 were delivered before the end of the year. Another 50 arrived in the course of 1923.

The New & Improved

In the spring of 1923, Walters, Kenly, and Delano shaped up a plan to bring their railroad to a high level of excellence. Business was definitely on the upswing. The worst postwar readjustment problems in their operations had been overcome; and government payments, owed from the period of federal control, were comfortably in the treasury. New settlers and businesses were once more moving into the Southeast. Nationwide, railroad executives were mounting a drive for greater operating efficiency. Coast Line leaders participated in a meeting of rail executives in New York City in April of 1923, held under the auspices of the Association of American Railroads. It addressed various problems, especially car shortages caused by the shopmen's strike in the summer of 1922. An unusually severe winter had convinced many rail executives that increased efficiency of operations should be a nationwide goal. One course agreed upon was more extensive and effective use of the Car Service Division of the recently formed Association of American Railroads. Another was enlarged expenditure for new motive power, rolling stock, and trackage facilities.

Hard on the heels of the New York meetings, the Coast Line management announced a $26 million improvement program, of which $10 million would be spent for new equipment. Shop facilities would be expanded, and many new sidings and yard tracks put down. Doubletracking of the entire 661-mile main line, Richmond-to-Jacksonville, would be finished by the end of 1927, with all those miles provided with automatic signals. In a letter to stockholders, President Kenly and Chairman Walters explained, "Your company has pledged itself, with the other railroads of the country, to do its utmost to furnish adequate service to the public."

Much of the investment went for new motive power and rolling stock. Large additional orders were placed with Baldwin for the Class P-5-B Pacific-type locomotives described earlier. Nearly $5 million was spent for 102 new road and yard engines in 1923 and 1924. The Coast Line was ahead of the national drive to increase freight car complements, with huge orders already placed the previous autumn. As a result, no fewer than 4,630 new units of freight equipment — most of them 4-ton and 5-ton box cars — were put on the line during 1923. The roster of freight equipment swelled to a record 32,616 cars at the end of the year.

Expansion of refrigerator car service took place at the same time, with the Fruit Growers Express Company expanding its complement to nearly 17,000 cars. Walters and Delano were vitally interested in this development, not just because of the Coast Line's 27.26% share of ownership in the refrigerator car company, but also because shippers were changing from ventilated cars to refrigerator cars for long-distance movement of perishables.

Spending for improvement to the fixed plant was comparably high — close to $10 million in the two years, 1923 and 1924. Signalling was improved over large segments of the line. An experimental automatic train control program, under direction of the ICC and in cooperation with the Association of American Railroads, was instituted in the Richmond District. Many station and office buildings were renovated or replaced. Nearly $1 million in new equipment and buildings was added to repair shops and engine houses all over the system.

Introduction of heavier rail came as part of the big improvement program. Beginning in 1923, replacements for worn rails on main line track, as well as all the new miles of second track, were laid with rail that weighed 100 pounds per yard, instead of the 85-pound rail that had been the standard since 1905. In just the first two years, over 400 miles of 100-lb. replacement rail were put down, and the pace would be accelerated in the mid-1920's.

The objective was to get the entire main stem, Richmond-to Jacksonville, plus mainline stretches in the Jacksonville, Tampa, and Montgomery districts in the heavier rail. It was needed, because locomotives and cars were heavier, and trains were moving faster.

The Coast Line was being brought rapidly into excellent physical condition. A very happy aspect of the improvement program was the fact that it was not adding to the debt load. Except for an issue of $6 million in trust certificates in 1921, all the improvements were financed out of an improving cash flow, including of course the substantial amounts tendered by the federal government in closing the accounts for the period of federal control. Still clearly in effect was the long-standing Walters policy: curtail expenditures for improvements quickly when earnings decrease; expand them generously as earnings increase. The formula worked wonders for keeping the debt burden light.

Promoting an Image

Coinciding significantly with inception of the big improvement program was the formation of a new executive department — the Department of Public Relations. Following the example set by the Illinois Central under its President Charles Markham in 1920, many railroad companies were hiring professionals to tell their stories to the public. The Coast Line became one of the early participants in this trend, by appointing, in May of 1923, John L. Cobbs, Jr. as Director of Public Relations.

John Cobbs became prodigiously busy telling America about the Atlantic Coast Line Railroad. He went all over Coast Line territory giving talks to chambers of commerce and civic clubs; and he provided useful compilations of information for other Coast Line spokesmen. By the end of the year, he was publishing and distributing weekly pamphlets entitled *Timely Railroad Topics*. These conveyed information about the efforts being made by the Coast Line to improve its service and, of course, insights about the various obstacles, such as taxes, government regulation, and highway competition that were preventing the railroads from doing their best. He also mailed articles to newspapers and magazines about Coast Line accomplishments and innovations. After some months of getting organized, Cobb's office published more ambitious coverage of the Coast Line, dealing with its history and many facets of its operations. Examples were two handsomely illustrated booklets entitled *It Didn't Just Happen* (1926) and *Florida & the Coast Line* (1928). Together they gave pictorial testimony to the excellence of Henry Walters' railroad at the height of the prosperity of the 1920s.

Chapter XV

The "Standard Railroad of the South"

Building Boom

The Atlantic Coast Line Railroad was not only attaining splendid condition in the post-war years, it was still growing. It was extending its lines into new territory with new construction projects, especially in Florida.

In 1917, the Haines City Branch reached Harrisburg, with a branch swinging eastward to Moore Haven, on the shores of Lake Okeechobee. As materials became available in 1919, it was pushed southward again to the hamlet of Goodno, on the south bank of the Caloosahatchee River. Resumed again in October of 1920, the project was extended another 26 miles southward to Immokalee. A few years later, impressed by the lumbering and agricultural development of the territory, Chairman Walters approved completion of this line all the way to the lower Gulf coast. This was accomplished by construction of another 27 miles of road to Deep Lake, in 1926-27, and by purchasing the existing 14-mile line of the Deep Lake Railroad, which terminated in the coastal town of Everglades. Here the Coast Line reached as far south as was physically possible without invading the territory of the Florida East Coast Railway, a move that was apparently never seriously contemplated. The Moore Haven branch of the Haines City line did provide another junction with the Florida East Coast Railway, though hardly one that would ever rival Jacksonville as a connection for interchange of business. In 1925, the ACL Railroad Company bought the stock of the Moore Haven & Clewiston Railway Company and leased its 14-mile road as an extension to Clewiston. This line was built eastward another 10 miles, to make junction with the FEC at Lake Harbor in 1929 — the last of the Florida expansion of the 1920s.

The west coast of Florida was the scene of active construction, stimulated both by boom development in the state, and by competition from the Seaboard Air Line. Two subsidiary companies were used for completing the west coast system — the Tampa Southern and the Fort Myers Southern. The Tampa Southern project began in 1919, with construction of 34 miles of road from Uceta to Palmetto, with the short distance remaining to Bradentown (as it was then spelled) accomplished in January of 1920. A major use for this new line was to reach phosphate mines just to the east of Palmetto, which was accomplished in 1921 with the little "Ellenton Belt Line" looping inland from Palmetto and Gillett. The extension southward to Sarasota was deferred for a time, then pushed to completion in 1924. Seldom has a new rail line been rewarded with a more sudden rush of travelers. To avoid the limitations of a terminus here, Delano and Walters decided to build this line 40 additional miles southward to a junction with the Charlotte Harbor line, at Southfort. When completed in 1927, this connecting line permitted routing trains through Bradentown (Bradenton) and Sarasota, on their way to Fort Myers.

The Fort Myers route was the scene of lively construction competition with the Seaboard Air Line. Work commenced on the line of the Fort Myers Southern in 1924, with service established 24 miles to Bonita Springs early in 1925, and another 12 miles to Naples (the southern terminus of the Seaboard's paralleling line), in 1926. Finally, in 1927, the road was completed to Collier City on Marco Island. The Coast Line thus reached its two termini on the lower Gulf Coast — Everglades and Collier City — in the same year.

The railroad was still growing along with its territory. As a result of all the construction in Florida, the Coast Line increased its mileage appreciably, at a time when American railroads in general abandoned more miles of line than they built. Excluding lines added through later mergers with subsidiary companies, the Atlantic Coast Line Railroad Company attained its all-time high point in mileage owned (4,849.91) and mileage operated (5,161.68) in 1930. These figures contrasted with 4,758.26 miles owned and 4,893.65 miles operated at the outset of the 1920's.

Aquiring Railroads for the System

Although the decade of the 1920's was hardly a time of aggressive railroad empire building, the Coast Line acquired control of some substantial new properties during the period. A very modest beginning was the purchase of controlling interest in the Rockingham Railroad, in the summer of 1922. This little ten-mile road served to extend the Bennettsville, S.C. branch northward from Gibson, on the North Carolina side of the border, to Rockingham, N. C. The Coast Line thereby moved into erstwhile Seaboard Air Line territory and deprived the Seaboard of a potentially useful connecting line.

More significant was addition of the Clinchfield Railroad to the system. In mid-May of 1923, word leaked out of this coup by Henry Walters. The 309-mile system operated by the Carolina, Clinchfield & Ohio and its subsidiaries, was to be leased to the Atlantic Coast Line and the Louisville & Nashville, jointly for 999 years. CC&O officials confirmed the reports in Louisville on May 17. The Interstate Commerce Commission indicated approval, initially, as did officials of most affected states. Even so, final approval came hard. The Seaboard Air Line, and banking interests friendly to that system, carried on a determined campaign against the Coast Line's take over of the Clinchfield, delaying the official grant of authority for the lease for more than a year. When the ICC finally released its favorable report, dated June 3, 1924, it attached some conditions Walters and his associates found hard to accept. Particularly objectionable were the Commission's requirements that the ACL and the L&N must allow their competitors — notably the Southern and the Seaboard — to continue interchange of business with the Clinchfield, as in the past, and must permit these and other connecting carriers to establish through routes over the Clinchfield with no discrimination in rates and charges. The effect was to keep the line of the Clinchfield an open route between the Northeast and the Southeast. ACL and L&N leaders objected strenuously, but they were obliged to accept these requirements as conditions to the lease.

The main line of the Clinchfield ran from Elkhorn City, Kentucky, (on the northern slopes of the Cumberlands) some 287 miles southward through western Virginia, eastern Tennessee, and North Carolina, to Spartanburg, South Carolina. The road was primarily a coal carrier, and a very well-built one. L&N officials saw it as a valuable artery for opening up their company's eastern Kentucky coal fields. They immediately launched a project to make a connection with the Clinchfield by building a short but expensive line from Norton to just south of St. Paul, Virginia. As for the Coast Line, the new arrangement offered two positive prospects: first, an assured and plentiful source of coal for itself and its patrons in the Southeast and, second, another through route (thanks to the new connection with the L&N) to the Midwest. In the last expectation, the parties to the lease were disappointed. The traffic departments of all three railroads cooperated in efforts to promote through-business, but with very limited successes. The Clinchfield remained valuable mainly as a coal originator and carrier.

The Coast Line's connection with the Clinchfield at Spartanburg actually went through the line of its subsidiary, the Charleston & Western Carolina Railway, which now took on added value to the system. To improve connections even more in the area, Walters and Delano got control of still another railroad — the Columbia, Newberry & Laurens. This little railroad had been the object of a tug-of-war between ACL and Seaboard leaders since 1891, when each had bought a one-third interest in its company. Now, in 1926, with approval of the ICC, the Atlantic Coast Line Railroad Company bought a controlling share of its stock and took over its management. The 75-mile railroad, true to its name, ran from Columbia through Newberry to Laurens, South Carolina, where it made a junction with the Charleston & Western Carolina. Here was another useful connection for carrying Clinchfield coal to Carolina points, especially to Charleston.

Far and away the most ambitious and expensive addition to the system was the Atlanta, Birmingham & Atlantic. In late February of 1926, Coast Line leaders and bondholders' committees of the bankrupt AB&A announced agreement on a financial reorganization plan that would place this railroad under Coast Line control. The Coast Line was intensifying coverage of its territory by acquiring a railroad that owned 637 miles, and operated 640 miles, of line in Georgia and Alabama. It was not, however, exactly a smashing financial triumph.

A Tale of Woe

The AB&A's short history was a story of deficit operations, bankruptcies, receiverships and reorganizations, liberally punctuated with other sorts of grief. The

Atlanta, Birmingham & Atlantic was a well constructed mainline railroad without adequate connections for through traffic. Dependent on the traffic it could originate in its sparsely populated territory, with no feeder branches and tough competition at many points, AB&A had little chance for profitable operations. It was put together early in the century, apparently by people with terminals in search of a railroad. A group of promoters acquired good terminal properties both in Birmingham and Atlanta, but failed to get any of the railroads serving those points to use them. There did exist in Georgia a rather unlikely railroad pointed in the right general direction —northwestward toward Birmingham. This was the Atlantic & Birmingham, which had a line from Waycross to Montezuma, with branches from Nicholls to Brunswick, and from Fitzgerald down to Thomasville. So they organized, in 1905, the Atlanta, Birmingham & Atlantic Railroad Company to build a 241-mile line to Birmingham from the terminus of the Atlantic and Birmingham at Montezuma, plus a 75-mile branch to Atlanta from Manchester, Georgia. They rescued the struggling Atlantic & Birmingham and consolidated it into their new company. Construction of the line to Atlanta was completed in 1907; the longer one to Pelham, Alabama, in 1908. L&N trackage rights were used into Birmingham. The newly completed system promptly went into bankruptcy on January 2, 1909.

It was not until 1915 that a reorganization was accomplished. A new company bearing a slightly altered name — the Atlanta, Birmingham & Atlantic Railway Company — took possession on January 1, 1916. The new company actually operated the road at a modest profit for two years prior to federal wartime control. The railroad recorded big deficits, however, under government control, and was unable to meet its interest payments once federal support payments ceased. It went again into receivership in February of 1921.

It was a very unhappy time indeed for the AB&A. Its operating ratio in 1921 was a disastrous 145.57%, which was reduced by fierce cost cutting to, a still-discouraging, 91.2% in 1924. There was talk of junking the railroad as a hopeless enterprise. Protracted labor strife added to the grimness of the situation. In response to wage reductions in February of 1921, the union workers on the AB&A struck, with the backing of the 16 national brotherhoods, with which they were affiliated. The AB&A went into receivership. The strikers failed to comply with certain procedural requirements, so the National Railroad Labor Board and the federal courts refused to recognize their case. The management, under Receiver B. L. Bugg, declared that the strikers had forfeited all rights to their jobs, and hired replacements as they could. The strike dragged on for many months, to the accompaniment of bridge-burnings, derailings, and imprisonment of strikers found guilty of such acts. The union leaders still voted in January of 1923 to go on with the strike. By the following autumn, AB&A officials had arranged to settle questions with the road's employees by allowing them to choose representatives through their recognized Benefit Association. Receiver B. L. Bugg thus succeeded in effectively "locking out" the unions. The AB&A became the largest railroad in the country with no union employees — a distinction that it would retain for many years.

All's Well that Ends Well

Even with its labor problem overcome, the AB&A remained in trouble. It simply did not generate enough revenue to cover its obligations, much less to show a profit. As a measure of the carrier's weakness, it was defaulting on rather light interest payments — the funded debt amounted to less than $14,000 per mile of road. As month after month of deficit operations went by under the receivership, AB&A bondholders became increasingly anxious for a solution that would salvage some of their investment. Consequently, they grew more modest in their expectations. So it was that the Coast Line got control of the property at what seemed a bargain. The price might have been even lower, had there not been some rumored bidding competition from the Seaboard Air Line and other railroads. After some months of dickering, committees representing the two classes of bondholders accepted an offer from Henry Walters and Lyman Delano to pay them 60¢ on the dollar for their bonds. Payment would be in the form of guaranteed 5% preferred stock in a new company. So the bondholders foreclosed and reorganized into the Atlanta, Birmingham & Coast Railroad Company, which took control of the property at midnight on December 31, 1926. On January 4, 1927, the Atlantic Coast Line Railroad Company took possession of all the AB&C's common stock (150,000 shares), guaranteed $5,180,000 in non-voting preferred stock to the bondholders in the old company, and paid or assumed close to $4 million of obligations of the old company and the receiver.

Thus, the Coast Line picked up controlling ownership of a 640-mile railroad, and kept it out of the Seaboard's hands, for only $4 million in out-of-pocket costs. Even so, it was in the nature of a financial rescue operation for the Coast Line to take over this railroad. If Walters and Delano expected earnings from the AB&C to cover the dividends they had guaranteed on its preferred stock, they were sadly disappointed. With the exception of a very modest profit in 1936, the AB&C would operate at a loss until the heavy traffic years of World War II.

It is questionable whether having the AB&C as part of the system was worth the $4 million paid initially, plus the $259,000 in yearly dividends that had to be covered by the Coast Line. It was used very little as a through-line, because the Coast Line already had superior routes to both Birmingham and Atlanta via the Central of Georgia from Albany. Yet, the AB&C did connect with the L&N at Birmingham and Atlanta, and with the Coast Line at Waycross. Both of the big Walters' roads now benefited from more interchange of traffic with a controlled AB&C; plus, the Seaboard had not been permitted to add this competitive mileage to its system.

Taken altogether, the new railroads acquired significantly strengthened the Coast Line's position in the Southeast. Even the AB&C contributed to more extensive coverage of the territory. Especially valuable in the context of the 1920s was control of the

Clinchfield, for it meant a new and assured access to the coalfields. Both railroads, moreover, provided new connections with the L&N. As a result, Henry Walters' rail empire not only grew with these acquisitions, it was also welded more firmly together.

Come On Down!

Coast Line fortunes in the 1920's were affected more by the population and land development boom in Florida than by any other single factor. Beginning in 1923, and reaching a crescendo in the summer and fall of 1925, millions of Americans swarmed to Florida to look around, to settle, and/or to "get rich quick" in land speculation. Some three years of extravagant publicity about the miracles of Florida land values provided the stimulus for the great migration. Realty syndicates developed subdivisions, and placed ads in New England and Midwestern newspapers. Some of the larger ones promoted interest by holding lavish invitational balls in selected northern cities, and by offering interested prospects free bus or train trips to Florida to view the splendid lots available. Stories of spectacular overnight profits teased the imagination, and millions of Americans caught the Florida contagion.

Many made the trip by auto. From many parts of the country and diverse walks of life they came in rickety farm trucks, in luxurious touring cars, in Ford Model-T's, and in buses. They crowded the Dixie Highway by day, and its wayside campsites by night, leaving, as one writer described it, "a trail strewn not with whitening bones, but discarded inner tubes and empty salmon cans."

Many others, however, came by train. As a result, the Coast Line enjoyed repeated gains in passenger mileage and revenues during these years, when most American railroads were experiencing losses. Everything necessary and imaginable was done to accommodate all these travellers and to persuade them to "go Coast Line." New trains with exotic names were added, schedules were improved, and equipment was upgraded to make the service to Florida as attractive as possible.

Fancy Names — Fancy Trains

At the onset of the decade, the Coast Line had four scheduled passenger runs between the upper East Coast and Florida: the original *ACL Express*, the *Havana Special*, the *Palmetto Limited*, and the famous winter season train, the *Florida Special*. A new New York-to-Florida train, the *Everglades Limited*, was initiated for the 1920-21 tourist season. A second section of this train was added later, an all-Pullman train entitled just the *Everglades*. In 1926, two additional trains were put on the New York-to-Florida run: the *Florida West Coast Limited* and the *Florida East Coast Limited*. For the following season this latter train was given all new Pullman equipment, rescheduled as a one-night-out service to Miami, and billed as travelling "1,388 miles, doubletrack all the way!" Its time from New York to Jacksonville was just under 26 hours; to Miami, it took only 36 hours, 15 minutes. To further handle the massive movement to Florida, the Coast Line revived, for a time, the old *West Indian Limited*.

At the height of the Florida boom, the Coast Line had no fewer than nine through-trains daily to and from the Northeast. Five were year-round, and four just for the Florida winter season. The earliest of the seasonal trains commenced in late November, while the last made its last run about May 1. The four tourist season trains, along with the *Havana Special*, were all-Pullman trains, emphasizing luxury for patrons who liked to travel in style. The *Florida East Coast Limited*, for example offered such amenities as barber, maid, and valet service, with "accommodations en suite," if desired.

Service from Chicago and other Midwest points was expanded even more. Of course the Coast Line, in cooperation with other railroads, had provided through-Pullman service for years between Jacksonville and Chicago and St. Louis. Now these runs also developed into name trains. The *Florida Seminole*, the *Southland* and the *St. Louis-Jacksonville Express* were long established runs that received their eye catching names after World War I. By 1923 the *Floridan* was added as a tri-weekly, solid Pullman train service between Chicago and Jacksonville. In 1926, this train was expanded to a daily express service to Miami — only 34$\frac{1}{4}$ hours, Chicago to Miami.

The *Dixie Express* was another train that began modestly, and grew to a major through run. In 1923 this train was basically an Atlanta-to-Jacksonville coach train which was being used as a second section of the *Dixie Flyer* and the *Southland*. By 1926 it was a full-scale Chicago-to-Jacksonville daily, with coaches, sleeper, observation car, and diner service. The *Dixie Limited* was another new full-service train that ran between Chicago and most Florida points by 1926. A new through train between Detroit and Florida was instituted also in this period. Called the *Flamingo*, it provided daily service with coaches, sleepers, observation car, and diner from Detroit to Miami, Tampa, and St. Petersburg. Its scheduled time was 46 hours, 10 minutes to Tampa, and 46½ hours to Miami. The Coast Line had eight major trains running daily between the Midwest and Florida in the tourist season of 1925-26.

There were two basic routes used for the Chicago-to-Florida trains in those days. One route traveled over the Chicago & Eastern Illinois to Evansville, Indiana, the L&N through Nashville to Atlanta, Georgia, then the Central of Georgia to Albany, Georgia, and finally the Coast Line to Jacksonville. The other Chicago-to-Jacksonville route went via Illinois Central through Paducah, Kentucky, Jackson, Tennessee, and Corinth, Mississippi, to Birmingham, then via Central of Georgia to Albany (or alternately the L&N to Montgomery) and on to Jacksonville.

These splendid new passenger services were not achieved without some difficulties or even failures. One persistent headache during the early 20s, for both the passenger traffic department and the transportation department, was the undependable performance of the Florida East Coast Railway. The boom caught this road with a singletrack line and insufficient equipment. The FEC repeatedly delivered Coast Line trains late at Jacksonville. The northbound , for instance, arrived late at Jacksonville 91 times of its 108 runs in the 1924 season. At one time, critics said "ACL" stood for "Always Comes Late." Lyman Delano now pointed with pride to the fact that Coast Line crews made up the lost time before Richmond in 70 of these cases.

Attracting Attention, Profits & People

The passenger traffic department under W. J. Craig actively promoted Florida trains, both new and old, keying advertising themes to the names and particular routes. They published a small handbook of Spanish vocabulary and pronunciation in the fall of 1923, as a service to prospective patrons of the *Havana Special*. The opportunity to laud this marvelous train and other Coast Line service was not, of course, missed. Another booklet appeared about the same time. *Tropical Trips* was a guide to hotels and recreational facilities in Florida and Cuba, as well as to schedules of Coast Line trains that would take the traveler to the desired locations.

Little was overlooked that might impress the traveler with the advantages of going Coast Line to Florida and Caribbean resorts. To dramatize the excellence of the service and, perhaps more important, to demonstrate that the Seaboard's line to Miami was a slower route, the Coast Line and its cooperating connections staged a special speed run in January of 1926. They set a new record of 36 hours, 20 minutes from New York's Pennsylvania Station to Miami. Seaboard's competing run was in fact somewhat slower.

All this Florida travel showed up nicely in revenues, which rose to nearly $10 million from through passengers in 1923, and then to almost $14.5 million in 1925. It just seemed as if the people would never stop coming. As it turned out, it was easier to provide for the movement of persons than for the transportation of the articles and commodities they demanded.

The population of Florida swelled by an estimated 1.5 millions in 1925 alone. Substantial portions of this influx settled points along the Gulf Coast, as in the Tampa Bay area, but the truly spectacular scene was on the lower East Coast. In just five years, Miami grew from a modest city of 30,000 to an excited locus of 150,000 to 250,000 people, depending on the enthusiasm of the estimator. Coral Gables, with its 16 square miles of tropical terrain, and some $50 million in development investment, was the most amazing of many planned communities springing up to house fortunate sun-seekers.

People descended on Miami from trains, buses or their autos, and bought binders on lots from hucksters on street corners. The plats were invariably handsome, but sometimes the land was in a swamp or did not even exist. More often, the project was located several miles out in the Everglades and improvements were not yet started. It mattered little, because the real objective was to resell the binders as prices rose. True stories circulated about people who put down a few hundred dollars in 1923 or 1924 and resold for many thousands a few months later. Everyone seemed to be saying, "Buy anywhere; you can't lose."

Everywhere there was construction — streets, houses, and store buildings, along with elegant apartments and luxurious resort hotels. It seemed impossible to get enough men, equipment, and materials to do it all soon enough, but the developers were trying. Then there were all the creature needs and wants of those hundreds of thousands of new people. The challenge proved too much for existing storage and transportation facilities.

Too Much of a Good Thing

There was not enough terminal and dock space to handle the shipments coming in by train and ships, partly because there were not enough auto trucks or horse-drawn drays to remove goods from loading docks, or enough warehouses in the boom communities to receive the goods.

Speculative builders ordered huge backlogs of materials and simply used freight cars as warehouses until they were ready to use the materials. When shippers encountered delays in rail deliveries, they turned to steamship lines, and some of the larger development companies even chartered vessels to get building materials to the lower East Coast of Florida. The dock facilities were soon overtaxed, and some vessels lay outside Miami for long weeks, waiting to be unloaded. Rail spurs, sidings, and freight yards began filling up during the spring and early summer of 1925 at Lakeland, Tampa, and St. Petersburg on the ACL , and in the Miami area on the Florida East Coast. The Seaboard was having the same difficulty. The congestion backed up toward the northern part of the state, as hundreds of additional freight cars jammed through the Florida gateways. The Florida East Coast Railway was hardest hit. Construction of double track had not gotten far enough to help much in clearing the enormous volume of empty freight cars from its line. It began refusing to accept cars destined for the Miami area from its connections at Jacksonville, which meant that the Southern and the ACL had to stack cars on their sidings and yards in Georgia and the Carolinas. They in turn placed embargoes on carload shipments bound for the busiest points in Florida. Since all traffic destined for points on the Florida East Coast Railway, and most freight for other parts of the state, passed through Jacksonville, a serious bottleneck had developed there by late summer.

It was clear that drastic measures were needed. The situation was so bad that even such unfriendly competitors as the ACL, the Seaboard, and the Southern were compelled to cooperate. On October 29, 1925, representatives of these railroads and of the Florida East Coast Railway held a meeting in Jacksonville, presided over by an official of the

Association of American Railroads. They estimated that some 7,000 carloads of freight for Florida destinations were being held at Jacksonville and points north. It was imperative that this backlog be cleared away before the late fall and winter movement of perishables began.

They agreed to impose a general embargo on carload shipments to all points in Florida. Exceptions were made for livestock, fertilizers, perishables, petroleum products, foodstuffs, and packaging materials for fruits and vegetables. In addition, the railroads could issue permits for other traffic, depending on their abilities to handle it and the willingness of consignees to unload shipments immediately on arrival. The embargo took effect on October 31, by which time many more carloads accumulated. There was a further lag of several more days when all the shipments initiated before the embargo gathered on Florida-bound lines. The situation peaked about mid-November, with southbound movement of freight to Florida nearly paralyzed.

Long Term Solutions

The embargo was a drastic expedient for dealing with a crisis situation. A more basic and positive, long-range solution was to increase capacity, and this the railroads were doing as fast as they could manage. The Florida East Coast Railway, which got the main onslaught — an increase in traffic volume of more than 70% in a two-year period — rushed to complete its program for double-tracking its entire line from Jacksonville to Miami.

The Coast Line also needed to enlarge its capacity, in spite of the huge expenditures for improvements made in the preceding years. The program for double-tracking the entire 661-mile main line from Richmond to Jacksonville (begun in 1923 and scheduled for completion in 1927) was speeded up as business intensified, and pushed to completion in December of 1925. The last large segments were a 41-mile stretch from Java to Lanes, S. C., one of 49 miles from Drayton Hall to Yemassee, S. C., and a third of 38 miles from Burroughs to Altamaha, Ga. Train movements of greater density and higher speeds would now be possible. Two short, high-density stretches of the line between Jacksonville and Tampa were also double-tracked at this time. One extended about nine miles south of Jacksonville, from Moncrief to Yukon, and another nearly 11 miles north from Sanford.

The work force was expanded for these construction projects and also for operating trains and maintaining equipment. There were 28,000 persons working for the Coast Line by the end of 1926. Freight yard capacity was expanded repeatedly at points all up and down the main stem, and throughout Florida. The yards at South Rocky Mount and at Waycross had been enlarged during the major improvement program; they got additional tracks in 1926. Huge new terminal yards at Savannah and Charleston were finished during 1925, helping to absorb the Florida-bound cars backing up on the main line. At Savannah they were enlarged again in 1927. In Florida, freight yards were expanded at

Jacksonville, High Springs, Palatka, Lakeland and Tampa. Shaken by the experience of the freight congestion of the fall of 1925, Coast Line officials kept a major program of yard expansion going through 1927. Eighteen new switch engines helped to handle the press of car movement in the yards. New road engines and rolling stock were needed, even beyond all the equipment bought since 1920. Forty-five more Class P-5-B Pacifics were put on the line during 1925, and another 30 in 1926. The Coast Line also got its first Santa Fe-type locomotives at this time for handling its heavy freights.

The Santa Fe's (2-10-2s) were bought to replace the Mikados, that had been handling the heaviest freight runs in the Montgomery District, where the line had grades up to 1.65%. They were basically the U. S. Railroad Administration's design for heavy Santa Fe's, built by Baldwin with a few minor modifications specified by the Coast Line. They had 63-inch driving wheels, 30 x 32-inch cylinders, and a total weight of 391,980 pounds, with 303,060 pounds on the drivers. They developed a tractive force of 75,700 pounds, 28% greater than the Mikados, they were replacing. Designated ACL Class Q-1, fifteen were placed on the line in November of 1925 and another five the following year.

Rolling stock was added at a comparable rate — over 1,000 box cars in the two frenetic years, and no fewer than 2,250 steel gondola cars in 1926. These last were to handle the huge press of business in road-building materials, such as sand, gravel, and limerock.

To maintain the larger concentration of equipment in Florida, Kenly, Delano and Walters now decided to build major new shops, capable of doing heavy repairs, at Uceta, near Tampa. Most of the buildings were completed and much of the machinery installed by the end of 1926. The Tampa shops would take their place, along with those at Waycross and at Rocky Mount, as a major repair center on the Coast Line. The repair shops would keep stock in good rolling condition, but the locomotives needed coal to make them roll. To speed up fueling operations, new electrically operated coaling stations, many of them of 500-ton capacity, were installed at points from one end of the line to the other between 1924 and 1926. Some of these were in Florida, at Moncrief (Jacksonville), Tampa, High Springs, Wilcox, Palatka, Ocala and St. Petersburg.

Thanks to the restraining effects of the embargo, and to the increased capacity resulting from all the improvements, the railroads serving Florida began to clear out the jam during the early months of 1926. Reporting in April, President Kenly asserted that the situation was "steadily improving and everything possible is being done to bring about normal conditions, but it will take time." In June he observed, "We are beginning to get the advantage of the high pressure improvement work of last year. Our roadway and equipment are in excellent condition."

It was a good thing, for the Coast Line was being kept busy with an unprecedented volume of business. Its freight tonnage swelled from 20.7 million in 1924 to 27 million in 1926; its ton-miles increased from 3.7 billion to 4.8 billion. Freight revenues increased from $57.3 million for 1924 to $68 million for 1926; total operating revenues from $81.8 million to $97.1 million. Freight revenues peaked at a record monthly high of $7,454,912.86 in March of 1926. Mileage of passenger cars increased from 68.5 million to 84.2 million for the same years, while mileage of loaded freight cars rose from 226.7 million to 260.1 million. The Florida boom was perhaps too much of a good thing, but it did wonders for revenues while it lasted.

Filling in the Gaps

There was also another important construction project for speeding the movement of traffic in and out of Florida — completion of the West Coast route. As described earlier, Henry Walters had started, in 1906, to build a line up the west side of the peninsula that would give the Coast Line a direct run from South Florida points to its east-west line across Georgia. Once connected there, the West Coast route would give a short line route to Atlanta or Montgomery, and then on to the Midwest and the West. The old Jacksonville & Southwestern had been extended from Newberry to Perry, reaching there by 1909. Then, in 1914, a 50-mile stretch was opened from Dunnellon to Wilcox, affording a straight line run paralleling the Gulf coast from Lakeland to Perry — and there it stopped. The line of the Live Oak, Perry & Gulf did make a connection of sorts, so that with a jog eastward to Live Oak, trains could be routed northward to the old junction at Dupont, Georgia. It was, however, hardly a suitable substitute for the distance-saving route nearly completed between Perry and Thomasville, Georgia. The gap between Perry and Monticello, Florida, grew more frustrating and awkward with each passing year. The pressure of business during the Florida boom made it intolerable.

Plans were completed in the autumn of 1925 for construction of the 40-mile Perry-to-Monticello cut-off. No more than this was needed, because an existing line from Monticello to Thomasville, Georgia, would complete the new Florida gateway. Construction contracts were let early in 1926. The Perry-to-Monticello cut-off was finished the following December. The frustrating gap in the West Coast route was finally closed.

Other improvements were pushed to completion to gain maximum advantage from the new route. The West Coast route would be a major traffic artery, taking much pressure of train movement away from the Jacksonville gateway, which had demonstrated that it could become a bottleneck. So that train movement from Tampa would not have to go eastward all the way to Lakeland before turning northward, a short-cut connecting line between Tampa and Dade City (actually constructed between Thonotosassa and Vitis) was readied for use by the summer of 1927. The whole project was completed by double-tracking a 60-mile stretch between the Vitis junction, south of Dade City, to Dunnellon. The roadbed was improved and heavier track was laid on older segments of the line.

The completed West Coast route was a reality by mid-1927. Through freights now rolled from their formation in the Uceta (Tampa) and Lakeland yards, directly to the connection with the L&N at Montgomery, Alabama, or with the Central of Georgia at Albany. Of the through-passenger trains from the midwest, only the *Southland* was routed beginning January, 1928, to take advantage of the Perry cut-off. It still came via L&N to Atlanta and then via the Central of Georgia to Alba.., ; but now it ran from Albany straight southward through Thomasville, Perry, and Dunnellon to Trilby, Florida. Here one section of the train took the line to St. Petersburg, while the remainder continued on to Tampa and Sarasota. The fastest Coast Line service from Chicago to Tampa in 1926 took 40 hours. Using the new route, the trip in 1931 could be made in a little under 36 hours. Though completion of the West Coast route was impelled by the Florida boom, it was available for full use, unfortunately, only after the boom had ended. It would, however, serve henceforth as a vital segment of the Coast Line.

Boom Gone Bust

Unfortunately, just about the time the railroads began to catch up, to carry successfully the huge volume of business, the Florida boom collapsed. By the early weeks of 1926, there were already many worried people on the Gold Coast — people who held binders on lots for which they could not keep up the payments — people who were anxiously searching for suddenly scarce buyers. Defaults on land payments became widespread during the spring and summer, and lots in new subdivisions found no takers. A general and exceedingly painful devaluation of land values now began.

A natural disaster hastened the economic one. A great hurricane smashed ashore in the Miami area on September 18, 1926, wreaking terrible destruction. It deposited steam vessels on city streets, ruined hotels and apartment buildings, and strewed mud and debris over many a handsome development community. It literally pushed the waters of Lake Okeechobee over its western banks, and nearly wiped out the town of Moore Haven. Hundreds were killed; thousands injured; and tens of thousands were left homeless in south Florida. The greatest loss of life was at Moore Haven. Coast Line officials gave the American Red Cross and other rescue and relief organizations every possible assistance in this area — sending in special trains and putting stations and other facilities at their disposal. As for its own condition, the Coast Line had a few washouts to rebuild, but little more.

The Florida boom was over. Abandoned, partially built communities — some with only streets, sidewalks, and lamp posts — remained as monuments to the speculative folly and the attendant disaster. Population movement changed direction, and development projects halted in the boom towns. Bank clearings in Miami fell from a high of $1,066,528,000 in 1925 to $260,039,000 in 1927, and again to $143,364,000 in 1928. The downhill slide was less precipitous on the Gulf Coast, where the speculative expansion had been less extreme; yet St. Petersburg, Sarasota, and Fort Myers, for example, had their shrinking pains, too. The boom ended in a general business contraction for Florida and for the railroads that served the state.

Looking Back

Seen in retrospect, the collapse of the boom brought the Great Depression early to Florida and, consequently, to the Coast Line. Revenues sagged sharply, as traffic to and from Florida ebbed as suddenly as it had swelled, in 1924-26. Further griefs added to the downturn. There were more devastating storms in 1928, visiting widespread damage in Georgia and the Carolinas, as well as in Florida. It was a particularly bad crop year, with markedly lower agricultural shipments. An infestation of the Mediterranean fruit-fly then brought more crop damage, and led to a marketing disaster for many Florida growers of citrus and some vegetables in the 1928-29 season. Florida and extensive areas of the Southeast simply did not participate in the national prosperity of the closing years of the decade.

It seemed to Coast Line officials that the times were thoroughly out of joint, as one bad blow after another fell. The Interstate Commerce Commission made its contribution, too. Rate revision had been underway since the ICC's Southern Class Rate Investigation of 1925. As a result of its findings, the Commission threw out the old Jacksonville-based combination rates and insisted on a schedule of joint through-rates to Florida points which were substantially lower. President Kenly observed pessimistically, "Effective January 15, 1928, the railroads in the Southeast, by order of the Interstate Commerce Commission, were required to put into effective new class-rates based, to a much greater extent than heretofore, upon distance carried. In some cases the new rates are higher, but in the aggregate in your company's territory they will produce a material decrease in revenue."

A New Competitor

A touch of unpleasant irony was added by another factor contributing to the loss of business. The automobile had played an important part in the Florida frenzy; concurrently a federal highway building program in the South had been giving the railroads a large boost in bulk hauling business. This program now tapered off toward completion in 1927, and the Coast Line's tonnage in clay, gravel, sand, and stone fell sharply, as did the number of autos and motor trucks carried. The highway, of course, would turn out to be a long-range competitor to rail.

There was now a marked decline in passenger business, with the slump in travel to and from Florida compounded by the constant inroads private autos and bus lines were making into the short haul passenger business. The automobile, of course, had been cutting into railroad passenger business since World War I. The first serious losses were felt in local travel, as increasing numbers of Americans climbed proudly into their new autos for business or pleasure trips to neighboring towns. Coast Line officials got ICC permission to cancel several local passenger runs as early as 1924. They cited bus competition as a major cause.

In 1923 revenue for passenger through traffic was $9,726,277, and for local traffic $8,268,806. By 1930, with fluctuations in business conditions, revenue for through traffic was still at a respectable $8,393,186; but local traffic had plunged to $2,145,155. The average distance each passenger rode in 1920 was 63.90 miles; and in 1930, it was 169.95 miles. It was obvious that passengers now regarded train travel as a long-distance mode of transportation.

The Coast Line fared better than most railroads, thanks to all the travel to and from Florida. An expedition from New York to Tampa or Miami in a 1923 model touring car was an adventure for only the hardiest and most enthusiastic motorists; most people still preferred the speed and comfort of the trains for such long jaunts. Highways and automobiles improved tremendously during the 1920s, until they were even making serious in-roads to the Coast Line's through business. Now, in the late 1920's, the movement to Florida contracted sharply. Revenues from passenger business, which had contributed between 21% and 25% of the Coast Line's operating income in the decade before World War I, and nearly 26% in 1920, dropped to 17.5% in 1930.

The Coast Line fought hard to keep its long-distance patrons. Schedules of through trains were improved repeatedly. The fastest time from New York to Jacksonville was 30 hours in 1920; this was reduced to 25½ hours in 1926, and again to $22^2/_3$ hours in 1930. Many niceties of service and appointments were added in order to keep people going Coast Line to and from Florida. The Passenger Traffic Department composed messages designed to influence travelers to choose train transportation. In the 1930-31 season , a Coast Line dining car menu bore an article called "Avoiding Highway Dangers," which cited horror stories about automobile travel. It suggested that by using Coast Line's new plan for shipping autos to Florida, "the traveler by rail is insured against injury to himself and to his car, does not have to worry about bad weather, slippery roads, detours, hotel accommodations, or hold-up men." The American Automobile Association was moved to expressions of outrage at this "invoking the psychology of fear," but the fight to retain passenger business was no casual game for the Coast Line.

The loss to motor trucks during the decade was relatively light. Trucks were carrying less than 4% of the nation's intercity freight ton-miles in 1930. However, the Coast Line's freight traffic manager, J. W. Perrin, put the loss to his railroad much higher. He calculated that in 1930, motor trucks carried freight tonnage that formerly brought nearly $5 million per year in revenues. In any case, the combined inroads of automobiles and trucks on the Coast Line's business were substantial.

Under pressure from so many negative trends, earnings dropped substantially. Equipment purchases ceased, maintenance programs slowed, and the number of employees fell from a high of 28,326 at the close of 1926 to 24,015 two years later. With expenses pared, however, operating income began to improve. By the summer of 1929 business was up again, and the future looked bright. A few months later, of course, events were in progress that would make 1928 look, in retrospect, like a halcyon year, even for the Coast Line.

All Dressed Up and Nowhere to Go

The financial crash and the ensuing spiral of business depression terminated with brutal finality the last stage of dynamic physical growth and an era of unequalled prosperity for the Atlantic Coast Line. Here was a splendid railroad that would have less and less to carry — a sad waste. For its traffic density, Henry Walters' railroad was probably unsurpassed, in the late 1920s, in roadway quality and maintenance level. The entire main stem, Richmond-to-Jacksonville, was double-tracked, except for three bridges and a stretch of paralleling lines between Jesup and Folkston, Georgia. Between those points one line ran through Nahunta and the other through Waycross several miles to the west. Together they served as a double-tracked line. Grades had been reduced to a minimum all over the system, and ballasting and crossties were at peak condition. At the end of 1927 there were 1,034 miles of first track and 331 miles of second track in 100-lb. rail. In 1931, this reached the extent of 1,612.5 miles of first track and 519 miles of second track.

Another indication of quality was the level of equipment maintenance. The percentage of bad order cars was kept to 5% or below, an enviable accomplishment among American railroads. Coast Line shops did even better with motive power. By 1928 they had the percentage of unserviceable locomotives down to a startlingly low figure of 7.2%, and, thanks to the opportunity to scrap a few of the oldest ones, they had the figure still lower in 1929. It was, of course, largely because the peak levels of business that it was readied to carry had fallen off, but the Coast Line was regarded by some as an over-maintained railroad. Henry Walters' splendid railroad was poised for another surge of expansion in Florida and the Southeast. It became painfully clear, as the decade ended, that much of this fine capacity would go unused.

The End of a Dynasty

In passage of leaders, as in profound change of conditions, an era was ending for the Coast Line. John R. Kenly died on March 1, 1928, having been actively involved with the railroad even longer than Walters himself. He was replaced as president by George B. Elliott, a graduate of Harvard Law School, who had served as general counsel since 1916. The son of the first president of the consolidated company, Warren Elliott, George Elliot represented a traditional Coast Line family. Several other members of the older generation of officers were lost in a short space. R.A. Brand, vice president for traffic, and W.J. Craig, passenger traffic manager, both retired toward the end of the decade. James Menzies, freight traffic manager, died in 1929, and John T. Reid, treasurer, in the following year.

Henry Walters, himself, seemed indestructable. As he turned eighty he still maintained his active leadership role. Whether it was selecting, in correspondence with Lyman Delano, a new design for emblems on freight cars or settling some financial matters through a stroll down Broadway for a chat with the Morgan people, Chairman Walters stayed on top of things. He was not spared, therefore, the experience of seeing his railroad empire wracked by the onset of the Depression.

After a very brief illness, on November 30, 1931, Henry Walters died at the age of 83. It was certainly the closing of an era for the Coast Line. He, more than anyone else, had built the railroad into a major system. He had held a substantial share of its ownership as his personal property; and he had directed its management to the end of his life. It was difficult to imagine the Atlantic Coast Line without Henry Walters at its head.

Until his death in 1931, Henry Walters had presided watchfully over the affairs of his railroad, the Atlantic Coast Line. A picture of his entire rail empire would, of course, include the Louisville & Nashville system.

L&N affairs, however, remained a separate story a while longer. Henry Walters had made this so, by keeping management of the two railroads so separate that paying dividends and providing cooperative connections to north central points were practically the only L&N actions which directly affected the Coast Line. Walters had also given President M. H. Smith of the L&N a much freer hand than he did Coast Line executives.

The years from 1902 to 1917 were ones of tremendous growth for the Atlantic Coast Line Railroad Company. Although essentially complete in 1902, the railroad subsequently added many miles of branch and connecting lines. Its equipment and physical plant were increased and repeatedly improved to the latest standards of railroad technology. It prospered with, and in spite of, government controls.

In many respects, the period from the turn of the century to World War I was the heyday of all American railroads. Their operating systems and technology matured while their revenues soared. The country was growing in all respects, and the railroads were right in the center of the general economic expansion. With no serious competition yet from the automobile or the motortruck, much less the airplane, the railroad was "king of the road."

If railroad was "king," the Atlantic Coast Line Railroad was certainly a jewel in the crown — and Henry B. Walters, its "crown prince." Walters had played a major part in building the Atlantic Coast Line Railroad. He had come up through the ranks of its management, and for the remainder of his long life, not only controlled it as principal owner, but also served actively as its top executive. It seems fair enough to characterize the Atlantic Coast Line as "Henry Walters' railroad."

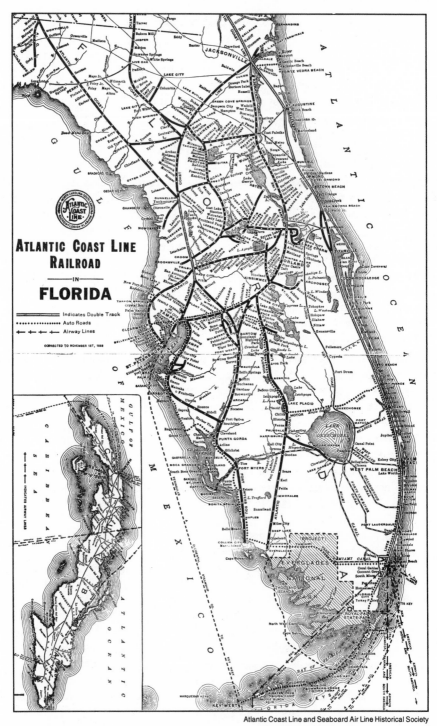

No.10: *Map of the Florida system in 1938.*

Chapter XVI

Lyman Delano and the Great Depression

Legacy of Leadership

When Lyman Delano moved to the New York office in December of 1931, and took over as chairman of the board, it was a change that really meant continuity. The Walters' fortune continued intact as the basis for Delano's financial control of the Atlantic Coast Line Company (the "Connecticut Company") and thereby of the railroad empire. As the heir-designate to Henry Walters, who died November 30, 1931, Delano had been actively involved in Coast Line management since 1910, and a director of both the ACL and the L&N for more than a decade. Now, he made it clear that established policies and executive relationships would be maintained. He let President Elliott of the Coast Line and President Cole of the L&N know very explicitly that all policy questions affecting the two railroads would be taken up with the chairman, and not directly between the presidents. The structure of Henry Walters' railroad empire would continue intact, and Lyman Delano, Walters' nephew, was very <u>definitely</u> in charge.

No significant management changes were imposed on the Atlantic Coast Line Railroad Company. As executive vice president, Delano had been acting as *de facto* president for years; he continued to do so after becoming chairman. He retained the office of executive vice president, directing operations from New York by telephone and telegraph, and by making frequent trips to Wilmington. George Elliott, a lawyer while representing the company in many public contexts as titular president, concentrated mainly on the duties of general counsel. Percy Albright, vice president of operations, had to assume more responsibility for day-to-day management now. Yet, his subordinates, such as the director of transportation and the assistant to the general superintendent of motive power, often reported directly to Delano when the latter was interested in a problem. Champion McDowell Davis, vice president of traffic, was especially highly regarded by Delano, and gained prestige at Wilmington with each passing year.

Drastic Decline

December of 1931 was a terrible time to be taking charge of almost any business enterprise in the United States, and the Coast Line was no exception. Many railroads were already in the hands of receivers — the Seaboard Air Line (December, 1930) and the Florida East Coast (September, 1931) among them. The plight of the Coast Line through the first few years of Delano's administration presented a real challenge to financial management. Happily, he was well qualified for the task. A few earnings figures for the period reveal the drastic situation:

	1929	1930	1931	1932
Total Operating Revenues	$72,371,894	$63,019,957	$54,088,005	$37,268,564
Net Operating Revenues	18,940,305	13,334,497	10,899,534	4,997,687
Net Income	9,332,457	3,784,310	2,020,858	-6,685,229

Harsh Times — Strict Measures

Delano's problem was intensified, somewhat, by the fact that financial policies had not been changed quickly enough to meet the sharp loss of earnings. Perhaps Chairman Walters had been unwilling to recognize the full enormity of the Depression in his last months. Dividend payments had been continued too long, and Delano moved quickly to halt this outflow of funds. The established rate of $10 per year ($3.50 regular and $1.50 extra, paid semi-annually) on the railroad company's common stock had been continued right through 1930. The company paid out in dividends $5 million more than it earned that year — cash that was sorely missed a few months later. The extra dividend was finally omitted in the spring of 1931; and the regular semi-annual dividend was reduced to $2 at the end of the year. Under Delano's control, dividends on the common stock were suspended, except for small payments in 1936 and 1937. They would not be resumed consistently until the end of 1941. Dividends on the small issue of preferred stock had to be omitted in the fall of 1932, and for all of the next year. They were declared again in November of 1934, and maintained thereafter, except for one semi-annual payment in 1939. Even the modest interest payments on $135,100 in certificates of indebtedness had to be suspended in 1932 and 1933. Thus stockholders, large and small, lost their incomes from this source as the railroad moved into hard times.

The steepness of the traffic decline at the onset of the Depression, though too real to be ignored, was almost too much to be believed. The Coast Line's freight tonnage had slumped from its record high of 27 million tons in 1926, to 19 million tons in 1929. In 1930 it shrank to 16.8 million tons, and in 1931, to an incredibly low 13.8 million tons. Chairman Delano and President Elliott expressed their conviction that this had to be the bottom. The following year, however, it was down still more to a sickening 9.2 million tons. Although 1929 had hardly been a banner year for the Coast Line, 1932 made it look great in retrospect. In 1932, as compared to 1929, less-than-carload freight tonnage was down 51%; phosphate rock, 41%; lumber, 68%; fertilizers, 60%; soft coal, 35%; citrus, 30%; and tobacco leaf, 59% (reflecting the results of a bad crop year).

Not surprisingly, freight revenues for 1932 were little more than half those for 1929. Passenger business was down too, and, due to sharp reductions in fares, the loss of revenues from this source was even sharper. At $4,622,457, passenger revenues for 1932 were only 39% of the amount received in 1929.

The Coast Line was hit harder by the Depression than were most American railroads, and for that matter, harder even than most railroads in its section of the country. There were a number of reasons for this. One was the very high peak of the Florida boom, from which the downhill slide in Coast Line business began. Florida, where the ACL had more mileage than any other railroad, was a particularly depressed area during the 1930s. The Coast Line suffered also as a carrier of food and fiber. Agricultural prices were terribly low and market demand for the products greatly reduced. Moreover, competition from highway trucks in perishables traffic now became serious, as they carried ever larger proportions of the crop movements. The Coast Line also had a special vulnerability to another kind of competition — coastal shipping. At a time when price considerations loomed so large, speed became less important for movement of many commodities. Moreover, some ships were now equipped with refrigeration; so that they could carry citrus fruits and vegetables from Florida ports to northeastern cities. Consequently, steamers now made substantial inroads even into the Coast Line's perishables traffic.

One response to the terrible loss in freight revenues was to fight the competition with better service and reduced fares. Rates were lowered repeatedly to combat truck competition, but with little effect. The truckers generally moved their charges still lower. The Seaboard and the Coast Line both reduced their rates on citrus shipments drastically in 1932, and again in 1934 without recapturing a significant portion of the traffic. One reason, of course, was the comparative flexibility and therefore, speed of highway truck service, factors that counted heavily both in perishables and in merchandise traffic. Early in 1936, the southeastern roads introduced a new service for their customers — free pickup and delivery service for less-than-carload freight, effective February 7. They resorted to contracts with local truckers to match the store-to-store service provided by intercity truckers. To combat the coastal steamers, the railroads tried, in 1935, "shipping day rates" — special low rates that matched those of water carriers to the eastern ports on those days of the week when vessels normally sailed from Florida points with citrus lading. This move did recapture some of the citrus movement to northern cities. Each rate reduction meant, of course, less unit revenues from the lading carried. The traffic people under Vice President Champion Davis were working hard to get the business, but there was a close limit to the potential gain from this direction.

Layoffs and Lowered Wages

The only real solution lay in cost-cutting, particularly in the long months of the Depression downswing. As revenues shrank, operating ratios soared from 74% in 1929, to almost 87% in 1932. Lyman Delano responded with economy measures that showed him a worthy heir to the Walters' dynasty.

The Coast Line had employed some 28,000 people in 1926. By 1930, the number was reduced to little more than 22,000. As traffic and revenues plunged further in 1931, another 3,000 men were laid off — hard-core, long-term ACL people by now. In the grim months of 1932, the cuts went even deeper, leaving only 15,276 persons on the payroll at the end of the year. More slowly thereafter, by refraining from filling vacancies left by retirements, the rolls were reduced to their low point. In 1935, the company averaged only 13,423 employees. The successive layoffs had a devastating effect on towns like Waycross and Rocky Mount, where such a large proportion of the people worked for the Coast Line. Employment was sporadic, and shopmen waited for the company work calls that were issued when enough essential repairs accumulated. (The new year was brightened a little for 750 men who were recalled to the Emerson Shops in South Rocky Mount for 16 days scheduled work in early January of 1933.)

That the Depression cost fully 9,000 Coast Line people their jobs was certainly the worst part; but even those retained felt the effects. Chairman Delano decreed successive cuts in pay for everyone. Salaries of officers and supervisory employees were cut by 10% on January 1, 1932, again by 10% six months later, and then by an equivalent of two days pay per month on February 1, 1933. Wages and salaries for all other employees were cut by 10% on February 1, 1932, and for clerical employees the reduction of two days pay per month took effect a year later. All these pay cuts remained in effect through 1933. The resulting savings were substantial. The annual payroll fell from $30,904,021 for 1930 to only $18,469,445 in 1933, the lowest year. Even though the work force declined further, gradual restoration of wages and salaries commenced in 1934 and the total payroll rose modestly from then on.

An employee-related safety drive that began under Delano's administration during the 1920s, helped to keep costs down now. In 1923, the Coast Line had an unenviable record of nearly 27 casualties to employees per million man-hours worked. Persistent and energetic education and exhortation by a special safety organization got results. Every employee was actively enlisted in the effort to achieve perfect safety records. The casualty rate was down to 1.66 per million hours in 1930 and to 1.10 in 1931. It continued low during the 1930's, saving on insurance, labor, and Relief Department costs, and won National Safety Council awards for the railroad. Perhaps this campaign was pushed too hard, for an ICC investigation team found, some years later, that Coast Line officers and employees were sometimes overzealous in interpreting injuries as too slight to justify a report.

A Halt to Spending

Chairman Delano and the board really clamped the lid on equipment purchases. Of course, the Coast Line had been left with an oversupply of rolling stock and motive power by the collapse of the Florida boom. The company now used this resource and ignored modernization trends through most of the Depression years. Not one new engine or passenger car was bought from 1926 until 1938. From a high of 1,042 locomotives in 1927, the motive power complement was reduced year by year through scrapping or sale until, in 1937, the Coast Line had only 742 units. The last substantial purchase of freight cars was an order for 200 phosphate cars delivered in 1928. A few assorted cars were constructed in company shops in 1929 and 1930. From then on, the railroad made do with the equipment it had. In the opening years of the decade this was no hardship, for, as President Elliott observed, "there was a large surplus of power and cars in first class condition."

Operations were pared in all departments, resulting in savings of fuel, materials, and equipment, as well as in payrolls. There were naturally many fewer freight runs as business slackened. Freight train miles totaled only 5,536,708 for 1932, as compared to 7,398,961 for 1929. One passenger train after another was discontinued as travelers were either kept at home by lack of money or stolen away by autos and buses. General Manager Albright and his superintendents were charged with making every train mile count for as much revenue as possible.

Chairman Delano and the directors halted several projects already approved, or in progress. A little connection line between the Charleston & Western Carolina and the Clinchfield at Spartanburg, South Carolina, had been planned in 1930. The object was to end dependency on the Southern Railway's line there, to interchange cars between C&WC and the Clinchfield, and to get a more satisfactory operating situation. With right-of-way, engineering plans, and ICC approval all in hand, the project was postponed in 1931. The Coast Line could not afford to let either the C&WC or the Clinchfield spend the money. In 1929, the Coast Line had commenced a five-year program of installing automatic signals on main line stretches in Georgia and Florida; this, too, was suspended in 1931. Even the program of relaying track with 100-lb. rail tapered off to practically nothing. Actually, most of this job was done by the end of 1932, with 1,695 miles of first main track and 519 miles of second main track in the heavier rail. Still, the 19 miles of 100-pound rail laid in 1933 was a far cry from the 411 miles put down in 1926 or even the 198 miles in 1930.

Innovative Economics

Chairman Delano had been interested in one potential economy measure for years, and he finally pushed his transportation and mechanical department officers into working it out in the mid-1930's. This was the lengthening of engine runs.

Delano was struck by the wasteful aspects of assigning a locomotive to just one engineer, and limiting the service of both to only one division. It was a practice hallowed by long tradition and the pride of enginemen in their machines. Coast Line operating officials were loathe to tamper with it. Delano insisted, however, that a variation should be given a trial. On March 16, 1936, he ordered that the two engines on the *Palmetto Limited* be run through, between Richmond and Savannah. When this experiment proved successful, he soon directed F. W. Brown, director of transportation, to extend the practice to two more trains, one of them the *Coast Line Florida Mail*. These ran their engines the entire length of the main stem from Richmond to Jacksonville. Five engines were saved through this innovation on only three trains, northbound and southbound. By the end of the year, it was regular practice to run engines all the way between Richmond and Jacksonville, on all through passenger trains.

The economy campaign was not without its failures, frustrations, and omissions. For example, a proposed lease of the Charleston & Western Carolina, which would have eliminated management expenses for maintaining that separate company, was blocked by the Interstate Commerce Commission. Abandonment of unprofitable lines was unfortunately deferred by the ICC until 1939, and much obsolete mileage was carried through the Depression. There were some unavoidable expenditures of scarce money for keeping the passenger service competitive with bus lines and other railroads. Finally, the federal government began to force expenses up by the mid-1930's, with minimum wage laws and the new Social Security and railroad pension programs that imposed higher tax payments and contributions on railroad companies.

With a few such exceptions, the economy drive was thorough and effective. The figures show clearly just how effective:

	1929	1931	1932	1933
Operating Expenses	$55,966,059	$43,188,471	$32,270,877	$29,127,630
Additions & Improvements - Road	3,374,517	1,251,218	691,084	347,673
Additions & Improvements - Equipment	551,334	9,921	20,386	912

Delano's economy drive resulted in drastic reductions in overall expenditures. It made a big contribution toward keeping the company solvent.

The Money Squeeze

During the first year or so of his command, Lyman Delano lived with the possibility that the Atlantic Coast Line Railroad Company might not be able to meet its debt obligations. The company had enjoyed a strong cash position at the end of the Florida boom — a cash balance of $19.3 million, within current assets of $34.8 million, at the end of 1927. It was frightening how quickly this strength eroded. The cash balance was only $11 million at the end of 1931, and a meager $4.5 million (within current assets of $13.1) at the end of 1932. The company ran a net deficit of nearly $6.7 million in 1932, leaving the cash assets too low to cover another such year. With the money markets so uncongenial, a repetition of 1932's results would likely have forced default on some bond coupons.

Fortunately, while 1933 was another terrible year for business, it produced much better final results for the Coast Line. Operating revenues were actually up a little; but the real key to averting disaster was Delano's strict economy drive and financial management. Operating expenses were pushed so low during 1933 that the railroad earned enough to cover all interest payments with a net deficit of only $2.4 million; and the company received no dividends whatsoever from the L&N.

By dint of careful money management in all areas, the cash position was practically unchanged at the end of 1933, in spite of the deficit. The years 1932 and 1933 were the lowest of the Depression, and the most dangerous for Coast Line finances. Luckily thereafter, the L&N Railroad did well enough to pay some dividends every year — a crucial factor in the Coast Line's income. The business recovery, however, was discouragingly slow, and expenditures could not be kept down to the level of penury achieved in 1933. The earnings picture remained in red ink through 1935 and very bleak through the entire decade.

There were cash drains in many directions. The company had lost over $200,000 in bank failures by March of 1934. The lease of the Clinchfield Railroad represented a deficit during several Depression years, while $252,095 in guaranteed dividends had to be paid every year for the money-losing AB&C.

Maturing bonds created some awkward moments. On April 1, 1934, $6.5 million in old Savannah Florida & Western bonds matured, and the funds had to be borrowed from some very reluctant banks on short-term notes. Another $4 million in Wilmington & Weldon Railroad Company bonds would mature on July 1, 1935, and still another $1.5 million in Charleston & Savannah bonds on January 1, 1936. There was no chance of covering all these obligations out of current assets and income. Delano and the New York office attempted to raise the cash by selling $12 million in authorized bonds of the railroad company in the spring of 1935, but the bond market was so bad that they could not be sold at acceptable terms. An alternative solution was worked out, whereby $12 million in 10-year collateral trust, 5% notes (secured by $25 million of the company's bonds) brought a reasonable price. By this, the Coast Line stayed solvent without adding to its total debt burden.

Light at the End of the Tunnel

The worst was past. A pickup in business was perceptible in 1936, and substantial in 1937. After a discouraging fall-off in 1938, recovery was definitely underway as the decade ended. It was scarcely a boom, to say the least! The Coast Line's revenues and net earnings for 1939 were still below those for 1931. Total assets had shrunk to under $365 million, as compared with over $390 million in 1929; but there was a gratifying $8.3 million in cash in the treasury.

The Atlantic Coast Line Railroad Company survived the Depression intact primarily because it had been capitalized relatively conservatively in its formation, and because it was managed very tightly during the bad years. It is true that it did not earn enough from its own operations during the 1930's to cover fixed costs, and dividend payments from the L&N were essential for covering interest payments on all the bonds. On the other hand, it is also true that part of its fixed costs — $1.4 million in interest on $35 million of its bonded indebtedness — had been incurred to purchase the L&N stock in 1902. Annual dividend payments on the L&N stock averaged considerably more than $1.4 million, in those years. On balance, the financial connection with the L&N was a source of some strength for the Coast Line during the Depression.

On the Lighter Side

Grim as they were, the Depression years were punctuated by events that kept life interesting—sometimes too much so. An example was a bizarre misadventure with local law in Florida.

On Saturday afternoon, April 12, 1930, Sheriff Oscar Wolff, of Highlands County, seized Train No. 191 at Sebring, preventing completion of its scheduled run from Haines City to Lake Placid.

This "wild west" action grew out of a Depression-related tax dispute. The Coast Line, along with other railroads in the state, had protested the assessment levels set by the state's Railway Assessment Board for 1929, and was withholding payment of all its real estate and personal property taxes pending settlement of the question. At the same time, there was a totally unrelated taxpayers' revolt afoot in the state. Faced with high tax bills to pay out of shrinking incomes, many Floridians were joining a "Taxpayers' Association," and threatening to default. Surveying the list of taxpayers delinquent after the April 1 deadline, worried officials in Highlands County apparently concluded that the Atlantic Coast Line Railroad Company was a participant, if not a ringleader in the taxpayers' strike. Failing to get satisfactory reassurances from local Coast Line officials, the local government chose a line of direct, forceful action. The County Commission, under Chairman I.C. Pearce, ordered seizure of ACL's property.

On the fateful Saturday, County Attorney J.M. Lee and Sheriff Wolff first served a warrant on the station agent at Avon Park. They took possession of the Coast Line's depot and other structures there, plus its 60 miles of right-of-way and track in the county. Their strategy, as to trains, was to avoid the ire of travelers and the federal government by allowing the mail-carrying passenger trains to pass through; but they would seize the three freight trains expected (two regular and one fruit extra). Accordingly, they let passenger train Number 191 go on southward after its stop at Avon Park, and waited at the freight depot for the fruit extra that was due a few minutes later. ACL local officers responded with a highball signal. The fruit extra roared through Avon Park without so much as slackening speed. Lee and Wolff quickly altered their plan. They charged southward on U. S. Highway 27, covering the nine miles to Sebring at a rate that did credit to that town's fame as an auto racing center. Catching Train Number 192 standing in the Sebring depot (the end of its mail run), they affixed notices of attachment to the locomotive and all except Pullman cars, and ordered the engineer to leave the train standing there. Dispatchers halted other trains short of the Highlands County line. A mail train was allowed through that night, but nothing else moved on the Haines City branch.

However outraged they may have been, Coast Line leaders handled the affair calmly enough. President Elliott declined public comment while sending F.E. Franklin, of his general counsel's staff from Fort Myers, to meet with Highlands County officials. When Franklin arrived on Sunday, he found County Attorney Lee actually preparing an official notice for a sheriff's sale of the attached Coast Line property. He got Lee to suspend these proceedings by assuring him that the railroad company had no part in a taxpayers' strike; that it expected a settlement the very next day in a meeting with the assessment board in Tallahassee; and that it would then pay its taxes promptly. He obtained release of the train and the rest of the property temporarily, so that Train No. 192 could make its run northward to Haines City.

On Monday, April 14, W. E. Kay, the Coast Line's general solicitor at Jacksonville, did conclude a compromise agreement with state officials, having obtained a somewhat reduced rate on personal property. On learning of the settlement, Highlands County officials set aside the attachment. Happily, such dynamic initiatives by county governments were rarely encountered.

There were many good things done by, and for, Coast Line people. One of the warmest stories of the period involved a run of a *Presidential Special* in December of 1937. Hearing that President Roosevelt was to be making a trip northbound on the road, engineer J. B. Weymess requested assignment to the special run. Weymess was about to retire at age 71, after 52 years of service, and he wanted this as his last run. His request was granted. Weymess was at the throttle on the Florence-to-Rocky Mount leg of the trip, demonstrating that he was proud of his life's work, and that the Coast Line valued its old-timers.

There were acts of heroism performed by people in the most modest positions. Station Porter Will Gibson risked his life in order to snatch a four-year-old boy from the path of an ACL train at Dothan, Alabama, on February 9, 1940. His deed received national recognition that spring, when he was awarded the Bronze Medal of Honor.

Luring Passengers

An area of operations that remained lively in spite of the Depression was passenger service. Competition from bus lines and other railroads forced innovations, sometimes to the frustration of Delano's economy policy.

The inroads from buses were combatted by cutting fares and speeding up schedules. Coach fares were reduced first to 2¢ per mile in November of 1933, and then, forced by prior action of the Southern and the Seaboard, down to 1½¢ per mile the following month. The fastest schedule time, New York to Jacksonville, was cut to 21 hours in 1932, and again to 20 hours and 35 minutes in 1937. Buses continued to undercut fares, but they could not match the speed.

The traffic and transportation men put together a new service in 1931, which grew in popularity through the 1930's. By purchasing three tickets, two people could travel to Florida and have their auto shipped as baggage.

Interestingly, the "top varnish" service drew heavy patronage in this period. The *Florida Special*, maintained as an aristocrat among trains, was particularly successful. In January 1932, it ran on a new "world record" schedule of 29 hours and 40 minutes from New York to Miami. The following season the train featured a recreation/entertainment car, with a three-piece band, a dance floor, bridge tables, a miniature gymnasium, and hostesses who presided over games for adults as well as children. Organized festivities were expanded for the golden jubilee year of the *Special*, the 1937-38 winter season. Regular movie programs were added the next year. The train was so popular that many of its runs had to be double-sectioned, year after year.

Responding to Stiff Competition

The Coast Line was repeatedly pushed into providing better service by competition from the Seaboard Air Line. The Seaboard was quite aggressive under its receivers, in its drive for a larger share of passenger business. In the summer of 1932, when the Coast Line sharply curtailed its passenger service, the Seaboard maintained its regular schedule, thus gaining a larger proportion of the through-passenger business. In response, the Coast Line was forced to keep a full schedule of service during the summer of 1933.

In 1934, the Seaboard again jumped out ahead by offering air-conditioning in many of its summer trains. Lyman Delano had vetoed the idea of installing air-conditioning in passenger cars, but he now felt compelled to give way. The Coast Line had air-conditioning in a few of its diners for the 1934 season, throughout some of its through trains the following summer, and in nearly all its top-quality coaches for the summer of 1936. Almost $600,000 went grudgingly into this improvement during the three years.

In the 1935-36 tourist season, the Seaboard began the operation of the air-conditioned and air-cooled *Florida Sunbeam* between the Midwest and Florida, a train that became so popular that two sections were run the following season. Then, in 1937, the Seaboard introduced trains equipped with modern deluxe coaches, again drawing customers away from ACL trains in droves. The situation in 1937 definitely called for a change.

By the spring of 1937, business had picked up enough that Chairman Delano decided to relent and buy some new equipment. The company's cash position was still so tight that an equipment trust was used. Under a 15-year trust, financing was secured for $5,201,555 worth of new equipment, which included:

- 12 passenger steam locomotives
- 15 steel passenger coaches with air conditioning and lounges
- 400 steel automobile box cars
- 100 steel furniture-automobile cars
- 100 steel rack-equipped automobile cars
- 100 steel phosphate cars, and
- 15 steel express cars.

The amount of money and new rolling stock was modest enough; still, it seemed like a momentous occasion after more than a decade of famine.

The number of automobile-transporting cars reflected partly the Coast Line's combination passenger-auto service from the Northeast to Florida, but mostly the expanding volume of auto sales.

The new coaches, which were delivered by the Bethlehem Steel Company in the spring of 1938, drew considerable interest. Although traditional in design compared with the new lightweight streamliners being introduced by some roads, they had features that were innovations on the Coast Line. There were divided reclining seats for 66 passengers, and extra-large lounges at each end of the car, reflecting their intended use for overnight service on through trains.

A special new train using these coaches was introduced late in 1938. This was the all-coach *Vacationer*, which made its inaugural run on December 15. It departed Pennsylvania Station in New York daily at 1:45 p.m., in combination with the *Gulf Coast Limited*; made up into a separate train with additional coaches at Washington; and arrived at Miami at 6:10 p.m. the following day. The handsome new air-conditioned coaches, in combination with the prevailing low coach fares, made the *Vacationer* a very popular winter season train. It often comprised 20 coaches, with every seat taken from Washington south. Another attractive feature of this train was the diner, in which economy priced meals were served. Unfortunately, this train ran in competition with the Seaboard's new all-coach streamliner, the *Silver Meteor*. Introduced the same season (February 2, 1939), Seaboard's train was much more advanced in design. However, the Seaboard management had ordered equipment for only one train, so the schedule was limited to a departure from New York every third day.

Running Full Steam

The fast schedule of the *Vacationer*, and speedier schedules for the *Florida Special* and other winter trains, were made possible by the introduction of some new motive power. It was none too soon. Maintenance of even the relatively modest 48 mph schedule of the *Special* was difficult with Pacific-type locomotives. In fact, double-heading was necessary for keeping the schedule of all the ACL all-Pullman through trains when their length reached 15 or 16 cars. This was happening repeatedly on the *Havana Special* and the *Tamiami* by 1937. In choosing a more powerful passenger locomotive, the Coast Line management decided to stay with steam power rather than changing to the new diesel-electrics. Superintendent of Motive Power James Paul and General Manager J.N. Brand preferred keeping the traditional type locomotive. Lyman Delano, following his conservative bent, accepted their recommendation. It proved to be a costly decision.

The locomotive chosen — the last model steam engine to be built for the Coast Line — was a 4-8-4 type. Twelve of these were ordered from Baldwin in 1937. At a cost of $158,834 each, these engines were still considerably cheaper than enough diesel-electric units to match their power would have been. On delivery in April through June of 1938, these Class R-1s were first run down to Waycross for inspection in the shops there; then assigned to freight runs for a week or so for breaking in. The 4-8-4s were truly immense locomotives. They had 80-inch driving wheels, 27-inch x 30-inch cylinders, a weight of 263,127 pounds on their drivers, and a total weight of 460,270 pounds. The tender alone weighed 435,500 pounds when loaded with its capacity of 24,000 gallons of water and 27 tons of coal. The wheel base length of engine and tender combined was just one inch under 98 feet. Powerful enough to exert a starting tractive force of 63,900 pounds, they were intended to haul trains of 20 or 21 heavy Pullman cars at speeds well over 60 mph. They proved capable of doing it; their huge tender capacity was designed specifically to enable them to run straight through from Richmond to Jacksonville. The age of steam was culminating on a grand scale.

It was several months before these engines could be used to full advantage. When they were run at high speeds, an improper balancing of their huge driving wheels caused severe pounding of the rails. To prevent serious track damage their speed had to be limited until, after extensive road testing, the right level of balancing for the reciprocating weights was discovered. This problem corrected, the speed limit was raised to 80 mph, and eventually 90 mph

The new engines were first put to regular work handling the *Havana Special* and the *Tamiami* on the 648-mile run between Jacksonville and Richmond, the latter making its 10-stop run in 13 hours and 15 minutes. As the R-1s were corrected for full speed use, schedules were improved. When the *Miamian* replaced the discontinued *Tamiami* on December 15, 1938, the southbound time was reduced to 11 hours and 45 minutes for a four-stop run. An identical time was set between Richmond and Jacksonville for the non-stop for the winter season.

Billed as the "largest engines in the South," the 4-8-4s kept the Coast Line's passenger runs competitive. However, the combination of the break-in problems, the complicated maintenance routines, and their voracious appetite for fuel and water made them very costly motive power.

Considerable interest and even pressure was building in railroad circles to woo passengers back to the railroads with modern streamlined trains. The diesel powered Burlington *Zephyr* had made its famous run to the Chicago World's Fair in May of 1934, and the Union Pacific and the Santa Fe had introduced their streamliners soon after. By the close of 1936, the stainless steel cars of the *Super Chief* were speeding from Chicago to Los Angeles in only 39 hours. The Illinois Central had no fewer than 11 trains, including its *Green Diamond*, that averaged 60 mph over their total runs. The fastest Coast Line trains were averaging somewhat less than 50 mph, and not a streamliner among them. Granting that the travel needs and the competitive situation were somewhat different in the Southeast, the Coast Line was still lagging far behind the transcontinental lines.

Story of a Champion

Introduction of the first of the Coast Line's fleet of streamliners, the *Champion*, came in the closing weeks of 1939. It was an event of considerable moment in the history of the railroad, so it merits recounting in some detail. The process by which the innovation was decided tells much about Coast Line management at the time, particularly about the rising importance of Champion McD. ("Champ") Davis.

By the late spring of 1939, the traffic people under Vice President Davis were chafing about the gains the Seaboard was making with its new train, the *Silver Meteor*. The shiny stainless steel cars and sleek diesel locomotives of the *Meteor* were really attracting the travelers. The train was sold out weeks in advance, after its introduction on February 2, 1939. Then, in May, came word that the Seaboard would order enough additional equipment to offer this streamliner service daily for the next winter season.

Champ Davis got very busy. He suggested to General Manager F. W. Brown that he and General Superintendent of Motive Power F. S. Robbins should study (keeping the matter confidential) the relative merits of the new types of locomotives, especially diesel-electrics and the so-called "turbo-electrics." The latter burned coal to turn steam turbines, which generated the electricity to power the locomotives. They were newly developed by the General Electric Company and were being used to pull the Union Pacific's fleet of streamliners. Robbins and Brown soon concluded that diesel-electrics offered more in prospective fuel economy and power applications. Davis concurred. He regarded the turbo-electrics as still too much in the experimental stage.

With the question of the best motive power settled, Davis began in early June to point out to Chairman Delano the need for quick action to head off an enormous gain by the Seaboard. He sent Delano several lengthy statistical reports, detailing the striking success already scored by the *Silver Meteor*, in taking passengers away from Coast Line trains. He stated his position forcefully: "I have come to feel that we must give immediate consideration to means of meeting the Seaboard's competition afforded by its diesel service, or we will inevitably and quickly lose our prestige, and with it a substantial share of our business."

At first he recommended just the purchase of enough streamlined diesel locomotives to power the *Vacationer* and the *Florida Special*, as the minimum for keeping the Coast Line competitive with the Seaboard's new service. Such locomotives would have considerable glamour appeal and they could maintain faster schedules. He probably despaired of getting Delano to purchase anything beyond this. Passenger traffic officials under George P. James were not satisfied with this solution. They pointed out that the public was very much taken with modern trains, and that the appeal of a whole shiny streamlined train should be exploited. It was also true, as information from equipment manufacturers showed, that the new locomotives could haul much larger payloads in the new lightweight stainless steel cars. As more data became available, Davis concluded that the Coast Line should offer year-round, daily streamlined coach train service to Florida. During the last week in June he pressed upon Chairman Delano the importance of ordering very soon the equipment needed to institute such service.

The main pressure for immediate action was the five-month lead time required for the new equipment to be built and delivered in time for the winter tourist season. The decision for the Coast Line was aided greatly by the Florida East Coast Railway. The receivers for that road, Davis informed Delano, were in the process of ordering two streamlined, seven-car trains from the Budd Manufacturing Company, one of which might be used in conjunction with a proposed new Seaboard-FEC Service to Miami. Delano, thereupon, contacted Scott M. Loftin, co-receiver of the Florida East Coast, and got a firm commitment that one of the FEC's streamliners would be available for combining with two ACL trains in a daily, New York-to-Miami service. Then he found (with Davis' assistance) that the Budd people could build two more seven-unit trains of the same design, make the December 1 delivery on all the trains, and give both railroads a reduced price because of the larger order. That did it! Delano closed the deal in a telephone conversation with S. M. Felton of the Edward G. Budd Manufacturing Company during the noon hour on Friday, June 30, 1939. He also called Paul R. Turner of the Electro-Motive Corporation and ordered two 2,000-horsepower diesel-electric locomotives to be delivered by December 1. Shortly afterward he sent a wire to Scott Loftin of the FEC:

> We are proceeding in line with our understanding on the phone last night to construct two streamlined trains similar to yours, with further understanding that, regardless of what action the competitor may take, you will supply additional unit for the through operation between New York and Miami. It will be necessary to provide sleeping quarters for the crew in the head-end car and automatic train control for operation over the Coast Line and RF&P.

The same afternoon he released to the press an announcement that the Atlantic Coast Line Railroad would begin daily streamlined coach service between New York and Miami early in the next Florida tourist season; and that the new trains would be powered by diesel locomotives south of Washington. Such was the genesis of the *Champions*.

Idea into Action

Now a prodigious investment of attention and effort began in preparation. Passenger and mechanical men from the Coast Line and the FEC painstakingly went over specifications for the trains in conference with Budd specialists. Coast Line passenger representatives rode the Seaboard's *Silver Meteor*, quietly observing details of the competitor's new service. Agreements for handling the new trains had to be thrashed out with the Pennsylvania, the RF&P, and the FEC railroad companies. There were some difficult issues to be resolved over division of fares, apportionment of expenses, payments of car mileage, and scheduling. Just the fact that one engine would now pull a-train over three different railroads from Washington to Miami caused long and tedious negotiations with the RF&P and the FEC. Men from the transportation and maintenance departments had to get acquainted with diesel locomotives. Superintendent of Motive Power F. S. Robbins sent a succession of road foremen of engines from the several divisions, as well as machinists and electricians from his shops, to learn about running and maintaining diesel-electrics at the Electro-Motive factory in LaGrange, Illinois. Two of his officials, S. M. Lynch and W. D. Quarles, General Mechanical Instructor, spent much of the summer and fall in the Midwest, observing at LaGrange and riding the diesels of other railroads, particularly those of the Chicago & Northwestern. Several equipment "extras" were selected for the locomotives, the most expensive of which was automatic train control gear. Another was the Mars signal light, which was being hailed enthusiastically by operating men on the C&NW and the Rock Island. This new device threw a warning beam from side to side in a figure-eight pattern, greatly impressing motorists at grade crossings. The Coast Line engines had to have it. The "extras" finally added nearly $10,000 to the $175,000 base price of each locomotive.

One additional cost on both locomotives and passenger cars resulted from a ruling from Commissioner Patterson of the ICC, who found that an economical pneumatic brake specified in the original agreement by the Budd Company would not be adequate. There ensued much debate over who was to absorb the additional expense. More serious, for a time it looked as though this required change in equipment would cause a five-week delay in delivery of the trains. It was finally arranged that the Budd Company would install the required electro-pneumatic brake system as far as they could, without delaying delivery; the installation to be completed on the railroads as time permitted. Commissioner Patterson approved, with the suggestion that a speed limit of 70 miles per hour be observed until the better brakes were fully operational.

The schedule for delivery of the train cars became a very hot issue, with Edward Budd and his production people the focus of more attention than they probably wished. The Seaboard's two new trains had also been ordered from Budd, and at just about the same time. Consequently, the slightest indication that one road's equipment might be delayed, giving an early-start advantage to the competitor, evoked fierce protests. Delano and Davis were unrelenting in their pressure on the Budd Company to finish the trains in time for a December 1 inaugural. They even sent Coast Line mechanical officers to plants of Budd's suppliers, such as of brakes and air-conditioning apparatus, to make doubly sure that no hitch was developing anywhere.

Meanwhile, the traffic department was mounting a lively publicity campaign. One facet was a contest, in which some 102,000 persons from all over the country submitted their entries for a name for the new train. The winner was a secretary from Pittsboro,N.C., Miss Betty Creighton. Miss Creighton, reportedly inspired by the broadcast of a championship boxing match, won $300 and a vacation trip to Florida for her suggestion, the "Champion." It seems too much for mere coincidence that this dynamic appellation was also the first name of the man rising to top leadership at Wilmington. Apparently Chairman Delano and other Coast Line officials chose to honor "Champ" Davis in this special way.

By the first of November, the Coast Line had many things ready. The *Champion* had not only a name, but also a schedule. It would leave Pennsylvania Station each afternoon at 12:30 as part of the Pennsylvania Railroad's Train No. 125, becoming ACL Train No. 1 south from Washington, and arriving in Miami at 1:30 p.m. the following day — 25 hours, New York to Miami. Train No. 2 would leave Miami at 8:15 each morning and get to New York 25 hours later. Tickets for the first runs sold out early in the month. It remained now to get the equipment in time for the event.

As good as their word, Electro-Motive Corporation had the Coast Line's diesels ready with days to spare. General Manager Brown was in LaGrange inspecting them as they neared the end of the assembly line on October 16. The first ACL diesel locomotive was delivered at Harrisburg, Pennsylvania, the night of November 21; it arrived at Richmond 11:30 a.m. the next day. F. S. Robbins had his men check it out thoroughly, including a simulated *Champion* schedule run northward from Jacksonville on the night of November 28-29. It made the run at schedule speed without the slightest difficulty, hauling cars equivalent to the weight of the new train. The second diesel engine arrived on the property on November 28.

Meanwhile the Budd Company was pushing assembly of the new cars on a round-the-clock production schedule, and finished just in time. They turned over to the Pennsylvania Railroad one Coast Line train on November 29, and the second one, the next day. The Pennsylvania got the trains to New York with a few hours to spare for hurried mechanical checking and servicing.

The Debut

The events of Friday and Saturday, December 1 and 2, were all that a traffic man could wish for. If the passenger officials overlooked anything, it escapes the imagination. The entry gate to Track 3 at Pennsylvania Station was decorated with palms and Spanish moss. In response to huge newspaper ads, more than 10,000 people pressed through to view the *Champions* on display there, 10 a.m. to 12 noon and 2 to 4 p.m. Perhaps it was more of an embellishment than a detraction to have the Seaboard's new *Silver Meteor* sitting in comparable splendor on adjoining Track 2. There were movie stars, dignitaries, and many members of the press present for the inaugural ceremonies, during which Chairman Delano handed a huge bouquet of flowers to the name-contest winner, Betty Creighton. To his regret, Delano had time only for a short ride to Philadelphia. There was a christening ceremony at Washington, D. C., where the *Champion* was finally made up as a separate and complete train headed by one of the new Coast Line diesels. Miss Creighton broke the ceremonial bottle of champagne over the nose of the locomotive.

Delayed by the festivities in its departure from Washington, the *Champion* made up the time over the RF&P. A small difficulty with watering put it, 17 minutes behind schedule when it started its run down the ACL line from Richmond. Road Foreman of Engines J. A. Holdren was at the controls. Crowds lined the tracks during the evening to catch their first glimpse of a streamliner at towns along the line — Weldon, Rocky Mount, Fayetteville. Taking over the controls in turn ,as the train reached their division points, were road foremen B. D. Sweeney at South Rocky Mount, J. M. Boylston at Florence, and G. F. Baker at Savannah. Each time the train fell behind schedule, usually due to small malfunctions of new equipment. The time was easily made up in the next hours by the steady 70-mile-per-hour speeds the diesel held past all the watering and fueling stops the steam engines normally made. Railroad writer E. L. Thompson, riding the diesel's cab and timing the run, concluded that there would be plenty of slack in the *Champion's* run for a faster schedule, especially when the 70 mph speed limit was lifted.

The arrival at Miami was spectacular, as was fitting for the event. At Fort Lauderdale, the *Champion* was joined by the FEC's new streamliner for Jacksonville-to-Miami service, the *Henry M. Flagler.* Side by side, the two trains flashed along the Gold Coast in the bright mid-day sun at 75 mph, heralded by twin smoke trails from two preceding airplanes. They glided to a stop in Miami at exactly 1:30 p.m., to be welcomed by the mayor, the University of Miami's band, and a crowd of thousands. No fewer than six newsreel companies covered the run down the FEC and the ceremonies at Miami. All in all, the *Champion* was impressively introduced to the traveling public.

The *Champion* was indeed an attractive addition to the roster of American streamliners, its sleek, shiny exterior trimmed with a stripe of Coast Line purple on the cars' letterboards. The seven-car consist included one combination car (crew dormitory, baggage, and passenger), four coaches (three 60-seat and one 52-seat, with hostess berths), a diner, and a tavern-lounge-observation car. They were handsomely and comfortably appointed. All coach seats were reserved in advance, and the price was right. One-way fare from New York to Jacksonville was only $18.07, from New York to Miami only $23.57. One could get a substantial breakfast in the diner for 50¢, a tasty lunch or dinner for 60¢.

The ride was the smoothest ever experienced on the Coast Line. If anything, it seemed to improve at speeds above 60 miles per hour. Lyman Delano approved elevation of the maximum speed of the train to 80 miles per hour in late January 1940, after the revision of the brake system required by the ICC was completed. Still, the *Champions* were kept on their 25-hour schedule between New York and Miami until 1943. The Coast Line segment of this schedule required averaging 56.4 mph, including three intermediate stops, over the 848.4 miles between Richmond and Jacksonville. The slack in this easy schedule was used to deliver the *Champion* on time to the FEC or the RF&P with almost unfailing regularity.

Popularity Plus

The *Champions* were phenomenally successful in drawing travelers. They ran as seven-car units through December of 1940, with a very high rate of occupancy. They contributed much of the 21% increase in passenger-revenues enjoyed by the Coast Line in 1940. For the 1940-41 season, enough new cars and diesels were bought to double the size of the trains to 14-car units. The new equipment was also built by the Budd Company, with some refinements in the design of the coaches that reduced their seating capacity to 56. The biggest change was in the new tavern-lounge cars, which had squared-off ends fitted with vestibule connections so that they could be placed anywhere in train consists. The rounded ends of the first ones, though appealing to the public, had proved a real nuisance to the transportation department. The enlarged *Champions* began their runs in January, 1941, filled to capacity on many trips and actually showing a higher rate of occupancy for the season than had the smaller trains. During the summers this service was modified by adding sleepers and running some sections to St. Petersburg and Tampa, all the trains billed as the *Tamiami Champions*. On December 12, 1941, the *Champions* were restored to their regular New York-Miami runs as all-coach trains, now with as many as 17 cars per run. At the same time an eight-car *Champion* was introduced as a daily service on Florida's west coast, New York to Tampa, with a connection to St. Petersburg.

The *Champions* were just part of the breakthrough in modern trains. In December of 1940, a daily streamliner service between Chicago and Miami was instituted, as a cooperative venture by several railroads. The Pennsylvania's new *South Wind*, the FEC's *Dixie Flagler,* and the Illinois Central's *City of Miami* departed Chicago on successive days. Using somewhat different routes, they made the trip in 29½ hours. The Coast Line handled the *South Wind* from Montgomery to Jacksonville, the *City of Miami* from Albany, Georgia, to Jacksonville, and the *Dixie Flagler* from Waycross to Jacksonville (after its subsidiary, the AB&C ran it from Atlanta to Waycross). These trains also afforded vastly improved Coast Line connections between Chicago and points in central and western Florida.

The *Florida Special* regained its "top of the schedule" status in December of 1941, when it commenced a new season equipped with diesel locomotives and a schedule that was faster by 2¼ hours — only 24 hours, New York to Miami! The Coast Line had moved fully into the era of modern trains, as the nation climbed out of the Depression.

Chapter XVII

A New Decade — A New Leader — A New War

Champ Enters the Ring

As the new decade began, Champion McDowell Davis ascended to the top leadership role in the Atlantic Coast Line Railroad Company in Wilmington. In April of 1940, Chairman Lyman Delano and the board appointed Davis executive vice president. Actually, he had been acting in that capacity for many months, as Delano entrusted him increasingly with day-to-day administrative responsibilities. His energetic leadership soon proved indispensable in meeting the challenges of a reviving economy and the nation's military buildup.

Champ Davis was neither a young man, nor a newcomer to the Coast Line, when he officially took command of operations at age 61. He had started his career as a messenger boy in the main freight office of the Wilmington & Weldon, way back in March of 1893. Except for some months of wartime service with the U. S. Railroad Administration office at Atlanta, he had been with the Coast Line ever since. He was a freight traffic man most of the way up. Davis was designated chief clerk in the freight traffic department in 1902, an assistant general freight agent in 1906, general freight agent at Savannah for lines south of Charleston in 1911, and general freight agent of the entire system in June 1917. On his return from Atlanta, he was appointed, in January of 1921, assistant freight traffic manager and finally, in August of 1925, freight traffic manager. In December of 1928 he was named vice president of traffic. The respect that Chairman Delano had for his judgment is indicated by his election as a director of the company in 1934.

Davis was one of those rare tough-minded executives who could be congenial with his associates. He was also known as a person who would do his best to carry out any task or responsibility entrusted to him. Davis was explosive. Confronted with an unexpected problem, large or small, he would vent his displeasure in a few minutes of lively fulmination; but then he would set to work calmly and deliberately on a solution. He was capable of attention to detail, and unsparing in expenditure of time and effort in his work. The Coast Line was already his life; now he had a position that could give full scope to his energies. A specialist in traffic matters, Champ proceeded to spend several weeks in each of the other departments, becoming acquainted with every aspect of the railroad's operations. He prided himself eventually on being able to deal knowledgeably with practically any problem in any department.

When President George B. Elliott announced his decision to retire, the choice of his successor was a foregone conclusion. Champ Davis became president of the Atlantic Coast Line Railroad Company on October 15, 1942. The operation was in good hands.

George Elliot died on February 20, 1948, and was buried in Wilmington, where he had lived for 42 years.

There were also promotions for the men Davis wanted in charge of various offices. In 1940, Frederick W. Brown was named vice president of operations; F. L. King, general superintendent of transportation; J. B. Brantly, general traffic manager; R. Doss, general freight traffic manager; and George P. James, general passenger traffic manager. Two years later, he arranged for the promotion of R. J. Doss to vice president of traffic, following the death of J.B. Brantly, and of C. G. Sibley to general manager, in recognition of his effectiveness in assisting Fred Brown with the operating departments.

Whipping Freight into Shape

The Coast Line came alive as a competing carrier about the time Champ Davis assumed administrative leadership at the Wilmington headquarters. The revival was due partly to the increase in business that began slowly in the late 1930s and accelerated in 1940-41; yet a large part must be credited to Davis' influence.

We have already seen the innovations in passenger service for which he pushed. There were concurrent programs to secure new rolling stock of all types, to improve freight service, to upgrade maintenance of the property, and to abandon unprofitable branch lines. The Atlantic Coast Line had retained its financial integrity through the Depression. Now as business picked up, Champ Davis strove to put it in the front rank of the industry.

Despite Delano's propensity for economizing, abandonment of unprofitable lines was delayed by the ICC until 1939. Low density branches all over the system were now subjected to cost/revenue analysis. More than ample evidence indicated that hundreds of miles had been rendered obsolete by modern highways.

Thinning Down

The first line abandoned was an excellent example of the problem. It was a tiny 3-mile line from Tavares to Lane Park, in the heart of central Florida's orange and lake country. Running parallel to a new state highway, the line had generated only 10 carloads of freight, and less than $600 in revenue, in 1938. Taxes alone were averaging over $400 per year; needed repairs were estimated at $16,000. Clearly, here was a money-losing situation. The Interstate Commerce Commission authorized abandonment in June of 1939.

From this modest beginning, the abandonment program moved very slowly. Some of the branches abandoned were in early Coast Line territory, like the 20-mile line from Latta to Clio, South Carolina, on which service was discontinued in December 1940. Most of the mileage abandoned was in Florida, where some fairly long branches were taken up within the 32-mile line from Fincher to Fanlew, in the northern part of the state. The Atlantic Coast Line Railroad Company, and its integrated subsidiaries, abandoned

181 miles of line during the years 1939 - 1945. Some minor trackage was added, so that the total miles operated shrank only from 5,103 at the end of 1938, to 4,930 at the end of 1945. The loss of mileage, of course, would be greater had it not been for the demands of World War II, which began on December 7, 1941.

Toning Up

Freight service was improved in various ways. Champ Davis persuaded the transportation men to speed up freight train schedules by raising the speed limit on Coast Line freights from its long-standing maximum of 35 mph to 50 mph. In mid-November 1938, almost a full day was lopped off some of the perishables runs from Florida to Philadelphia and New York. This special service featured third-morning delivery in New York, while regular fourth-morning service continued to accommodate later carloadings.

New types of service were introduced. Containerized service for less-than-carload merchandise freight was initiated on May 1, 1939. A coordinating rail-truck service in Virginia and North Carolina was proposed to the ICC, but did not gain approval until 1942. The railroads of the region won a reduction in refrigeration charges, which helped to make rail perishables service more competitive with highway trucks.

Classifying and dispatching was speeded up in the yards, and all categories of freight began to move faster. By the Spring of 1941, the Coast Line had several fast overnight freights serving Carolina points to Atlanta, in one direction, and Norfolk and Richmond, in the other. Trains now averaged 34 mph between Augusta and Richmond. Regular freights on the Jacksonville-to-Richmond runs did even better.

Traffic increased substantially in the course of 1941, and the Atlantic Coast Line got its full share. Engines and freight cars that had been standing idle for years were run through the shops and restored to service. President Davis got the board to authorize large orders for new cars — solid steel boxcars, automobile cars, gondolas for coal, and large hopper cars for phosphate. Some of the new boxcars were fitted with shock-resistant springs for fragile lading. All told, 2,193 new freight cars were put on the line in 1940-41. Another 2,430 were ordered in time to be constructed before wartime restrictions on production took effect. The railroad seemed to have freight equipment enough in December of 1941.

Wartime Challenges

The American entry into World War II handed the country's railroads a prodigious hauling task almost overnight. Following years of Depression starvation, the railroads were generally ill-prepared, their roadways undermaintained and equipment rosters depleted. Yet they were soon carrying more passengers and lading than ever before.

The Atlantic Coast Line was no exception. In fact, its special situation drew a larger traffic surge than most other American railroads experienced. There were two main reasons for the disproportionate gain in ACL's business: (1) the cessation of coastal water transport, and (2) the tremendous expansion of military and business activity in its territory.

The Coast Line's route into Norfolk became a crucial link to that strategic port. In addition to all the naval installations there, dozens of military bases were reactivated or newly established all along the tidewater, and into Florida.

The railroad was called upon to carry millions of additional passengers, the total reaching a high point of nearly nine million in 1944, as compared to fewer than two million in 1940. Many were armed services personnel traveling under orders to new bases, to embarkation points, or to and from leave locations. Many others were civilians forced onto public conveyances by gasoline rationing. Most were traveling longer distances. The passenger mileage recorded for 1942 tripled, and for 1944 quintupled the figure for 1940.

The increase in freight movement was just as spectacular. There was much more traffic, and a larger portion of it moved by rail. Coastal water shipping almost entirely ceased, because of the danger that ships plying the coastal lanes were literally "sitting ducks" for submarines. Moreover, every vessel capable of making Atlantic crossings was needed for that use. Though they had been fierce competitors during the 1930's, the ships would have been welcomed as helpers by Coast Line people at times during the war. The difference tended to show up especially in bulk commodities, a large proportion of which normally moved by water.

The railroad's tonnage of phosphate rock and fertilizers nearly doubled from 1940 to 1943, while lading of construction rock more than tripled. Citrus car-loadings almost doubled in the same period, and for the same reason. Sugar and petroleum went Coast Line in unprecedented quantities, from Port Tampa up the eastern seaboard. Even the banana traffic was diverted to this route for several months early in the war.

Answering the Call

The most important cause for the sharp rise in traffic was, of course, the rapid expansion of military and industrial activity in the Southeast. The category of manufactured goods and general merchandise showed the largest increases of all — from 189,543 carloads in 1940 to 427,416 in 1943. The railroad was also entrusted with movement of military supplies and equipment, including many thousands of carloadings with record of the lading censored. To guard against possible sabotage, some Coast Line personnel had to wear identification badges.

It all added up to a huge amount of freight hauled during the war years. Total freight tonnage swelled from 18.8 million tons in 1940, exceeding for the first time the boom record of 1926, to a high point of nearly 40 million tons in 1943. Freight ton miles tripled from 1940 to 1943. Atlantic Coast Line freight trains logged 12.5 million miles in 1943, compared with only 7.7 million in 1940. It seemed as though they would run the wheels off their equipment.

Motive power was in short supply. The shift to diesel power for freight trains started too late to help much with the war traffic. Nine 5,400 h.p. diesel-electric freight locomotives (each a combination of two 2,700 h.p. units) were ordered late in 1942, but the War Production Board decreed a long wait for these. Only four were received before the end of 1943.

Pouring on the Power

President Davis soon reported that these new diesel locomotives "have proved very satisfactory, and have demonstrated a marked economy in fuel cost as compared with steam locomotives." Maintenance costs were also substantially lower — less than 12 cents per mile for all the Coast Line's diesels in 1943, compared with nearly 24 cents per mile for steam locomotives. Davis and other ACL executives were convinced. They ordered new diesels as fast as the War Production Board would allocate them. The railroad had a fleet of 87 diesels by the end of 1944, including switching locomotives, passenger units and freight units.

Although the diesels contributed much hauling power by 1945, the backbone of the road's motive power during most of the war months was its 500 steam road engines, 318 of them Pacific types dating most recently from the 1920s. The need for motive power was so great that the Coast Line enlarged its complement with secondhand locomotives from other railroads. The company bought five used Mountain-type (4-8-2) locomotives for $55,369 each from the Delaware, Lackawanna & Western Railroad in 1943. These were used largely for passenger runs on the Southern Division. In addition, 25 steam locomotives and 33 conventional passenger coaches were leased from other, less busy, railroads and returned after the war.

In spite of the timely pre-war purchases, there were too few freight cars. The railroad had only 18,354 freight cars in December of 1941 in contrast to a complement of more than 34,000 in the boom year of 1926. The War Production Board suspended production of boxcars for a time, and limited allotments of all kinds; so the company was able to secure only 5,200 by the end of 1944. One answer to the problem was to keep the cars they had in good repair, rebuilding them as necessary.

Making the Most of It

President Davis put Coast Line shops on a 48-hour week as early as July 1941, and he kept them working at more than full capacity in the months that followed Pearl Harbor.

As a result, bad-order cars were cut from 16.2% in 1940, to only 2.9% by the end of 1943; 2,371 freight cars were rebuilt ; and, after all the millions of ton-miles of use, only 2.2% of the railroad's 23,402 freight cars were out for repairs at the end of 1944.

There were several reasons why the Coast Line was able to surpass the tonnage records of the mid-1920s with only about two-thirds the number of cars: movement, car size and speed. Not many cars were deadheaded during the war — movement tended to be heavy in all directions, and car accounting and exchange procedures were vastly improved. Also, the cars were larger—many of the new ones were of 50-ton capacity, and some of the new phosphate hopper cars were the 70-ton size. A crucial factor was faster train movement. The Coast Line raised the speed limit on its passenger trains to 90 mph, and its freight trains to 60 mph, so each car made more trips during the war months. Net ton miles per freight car day rose from 449 in 1940 to an unprecedented 951 in 1943. Particularly impressive, as a measure of improved operating efficiency, was the increase in the average tons carried per freight train mile — 808.2 in 1943. ACL was getting the most out of its equipment.

Wartime Efficiency

With higher speeds and improved car handling, the Coast Line now offered three day citrus delivery service, south Florida to New York, on a regular basis. It was an impressive operation. A typical fruit train began to form at Fort Myers, Florida, as cars were loaded and iced, on Monday morning. Northward movement began at a modest pace, with cars added at Punta Gorda, Arcadia, Brownsville, Wauchula, and Bartow. Delivered to the yard at Lakeland, the cars were re-iced as needed and put in "blocks" for assignment to new consists at major points up the line — Waycross and Potomac Yard. The freight train became longer on its evening run up the West Coast Route, stopping briefly for pickups at towns like Dade City and Trilby. At High Springs, there was a longer stop, while ice bunkers were refilled and a few cars of perishables from the Gainesville area were put on. The overnight trip then commenced, non-stop through Dupont, Georgia, for Tuesday morning arrival in Waycross. At this major concentration and diversion point, cars bound for Mid-western cities were separated from those for eastern destinations, and trains were made up with a consist limit of 50 cars. In the early afternoon many of the original cars from Fort Myers, their ice bunkers replenished, were in a 50-car train that started the 591-mile run from Waycross to Acca Yard at Richmond. Headed by one of the Pacific-type freight engines, the train kept to the 60 mph maximum speed limit for long stretches. There were stops at such points as Southover Yard (Savannah), Florence, and South Rocky Mount for setting out cars; yet the citrus special averaged around 40 mph for the entire mainline run. With pre-dawn arrival at Richmond, the Coast Line turned the train over to the RF&P, which probably ran it intact to Washington. In Potomac yard by mid-morning, the cars were again iced and re-classified. The Pennsylvania Railroad got them to Jersey in time for the oranges and grapefruit to be sold in the New York produce market on Thursday morning. Wartime or peacetime, this service was a Coast Line hallmark.

The Downside — Accidents

Wartime demands and strains on roadway, equipment, and personnel took their toll in accidents. The higher incidence of wrecks began in 1941 and worsened. Some were instances of pure bad luck, as when the northbound *Champion* hit a cow near Ludowici, Georgia, on July 12, 1941. The impact opened a switch, derailing the train and injuring 17 passengers. More typical were several other serious wrecks during the same year that resulted from broken rails. It was discovered that high-speed train movements were "burning" the rails, causing them to fracture internally, but escaping detection in visual inspections. The number of wrecks from track failures increased with the density of high-speed wartime train movement.

The worst wreck in the Coast Line's history happened at about 1:30 a.m. on December 15, 1943. Just before midnight, the southbound *Champion* (*West Coast*) was halted on the main line between Buie and Rennert, North Carolina, when a broken rail threw its last three cars — two sleepers and a diner — off the tracks. These were left many yards behind the rest of the train and tilted so sharply that two of them blocked the adjacent tracks for northbound traffic.

Trains were not yet equipped with radio-telephones, and telegraph wires were down from a snowstorm; so there was no dispatcher notification of other trains. The flagman trudged northward in the deep snow and successfully flagged down a following freight train. The crew at the head end found a coupler failure a few cars back that seemed to explain why the brakes had automatically stopped the train. They apparently did not even learn that part of their train was separated, or that the adjacent tracks were fouled. In any case, they were lax in providing signal protection. The fireman walked southward with lanterns and one fuse, rather than the ample supply of fuses and torpedoes prescribed by the rules.

According to his own account, when the fireman saw the oncoming headlight of northbound train Number 8, the *Champion* (*East Coast*), he hurriedly tried to light the fuse, but he slipped on the snow-covered ballast rocks and broke the device in his fall. He then signaled with his red lantern, but to no effect. Train No. 8 roared by at 85 mph, its engineer blinded by the headlight of the standing train. He saw the track blockage too late for his brakes to take hold. Number 8 slammed full tilt into the standing cars — its diesels stopped nearly dead by the impact; its cars buckling and telescoping behind them.

It was a nightmarish scene of destruction and death. The second and third cars of the northbound *Champion*, in which most of the fatalities occurred, were utterly demolished. The conductor survived and walked three miles into Rennert to telephone for a rescue train from Rocky Mount. It was late the next afternoon before all the injured were removed from the scene. The casualty count was dreadful: 72 dead, many of them servicemen on leave; 160 passengers and 27 employees injured. It was a terrible tragedy and a very black mark for a railroad that had taken pride in its low accident record.

The transportation department rehearsed its train crews on their knowledge and strict observance of emergency procedures, but that did not stop the derailments. Forty-seven of the railroad's own track laborers were killed in a mishap near Stockton, Georgia, on August 4, 1944. The coach in which they were riding on westbound No. 57 was thrown, by a broken rail, against the engine of an eastbound freight. Investigating this accident, the ICC noted that the Atlantic Coast Line had reported between January 1, 1940, and June 30, 1944, no fewer than 61 accidents caused either directly or indirectly by broken rails. The ICC concluded that "excessive stresses are being exerted upon the track structure." This was scarcely news to Coast Line executives.

Many railroads with greater pre-war traffic density already had their main lines laid in heavier 115-lb. or 131-lb. rail. The Coast Line's shift to heavier rail commenced in the latter part of 1943, when a program of relaying the mainline track with 131-lb. rail began. The work was done first in the heavily traveled segments south of Richmond and north of Jacksonville. With wartime shortages and traffic conditions, the changeover was necessarily slow. There were only 191 miles of the heavy rail in the main line by the end of 1944. High speed movement of trains continued on marginal tracks. The actual accidents, and the risk of more, were hard facts for railroad men to live with, but speed was the key to the wartime transportation achievement.

Achievements and Financial Rewards

American railroads remained under private control during World War II, with the exception of a few days of formal government seizure to avert a strike at the end of 1943. Technological advances in communication and signaling, larger cars and better provisions for car interchange contributed to a vastly more efficient performance than during World War I. The Coast Line, as we have seen, did its full part in the overall achievement.

Financial rewards for the good service were handsome. Although rate increases were limited and expenses climbed sharply, all the traffic brought soaring revenues and vastly improved earnings. Operating revenues for 1942 were double the figure for 1940; at the end of 1943 they had tripled. Showing what full use of plant and equipment could do for a well run railroad, the operating ratio dropped from 79% in 1940 to less than 55% in 1942-43. Nothing to equal this record had been seen since the days of the old Wilmington & Weldon.

The profit picture improved correspondingly. Even with high wartime taxes, net income reached record levels in 1942 and stayed very high through 1944. Not only was the ACL operating at a healthy profit; the L&N was also doing well — its dividends swelled total income for the "parent company." From the $1 paid in 1941, the Atlantic Coast Line Railroad Company raised annual dividends to $2 in 1942, and to $3 in 1943.

The financial condition of the company was strengthened greatly during these years. Delano and Davis had embarked on a debt retirement campaign as early as 1939, and they retained large portions of the profit-surge to accelerate their program. The $11,789,000 in collateral trust notes, that were used to get past the financial squeeze of 1935, were redeemed in 1942. Equipment trusts were retired on schedule, while much new equipment was bought for cash. In 1945 alone, nearly $25 million in bonded indebtedness was retired. L&N stock was sold in an amount that reduced ACL's ownership, so that the ACL Railroad Company held the L&N stock free from indenture. The company's long term debt was reduced from $158.3 million in December of 1941 to $102.6 million at the end of 1945. There had been a remarkable simplification of Coast Line financial structure. Granted, the property had been "mined" of much of its value by heavy wartime use, but the company had its reward in a greatly lightened debt load.

Closing Another Door

The man who had done the most to keep the Coast Line solvent through the lean years lived to see his railroad contribute substantially to the war effort, and to regain its strength. Lyman Delano died on July 23, 1944, at the age of 61. Although he had relinquished administrative command of the railroad to Champ Davis in the late 1930s, he had remained in active policy control as chairman of the board. He left no heir to take his place; and with his passing, the personal stewardship of members of the Walters family over the Atlantic Coast Line was ended.

The financial structure of the railroad empire, however, was undisturbed. The ACL Railroad Company retained its controlling block of L&N shares. The "Connecticut Company" remained the biggest and effectively controlling stockholder in the Atlantic Coast Line Railroad Company. The largest concentrations of Connecticut Company shares were deposited in trust accounts with the Mercantile Safe Deposit & Trust Company of Baltimore.

Henceforth, the most influential voice among Coast Line and L&N directors tended to be that of the president of the latter institution. As World War II drew to a close, however, the dominant figure among Coast Line executives was President Champion McDowell Davis.

An Appreciation of

Champion McDowell Davis

by the Board of Directors of
Atlantic Coast Line Railroad Company

On July 1, 1954, Mr. Champion McDowell Davis will celebrate his *seventy-fifth birthday*. For more than sixty-one of these years, he has given his energy, his thought and his devotion in the service of this Company. Since October 15, 1942, he has served as President.

Rare is such a close association of man and institution over such a wide span of years. This historic milestone in the life of Mr. Davis affords a worthy opportunity to his colleagues and associates to register their recognition and to express their appreciation of the outstanding quality of his life and service.

Under his dynamic leadership as President of the Company, the Atlantic Coast Line Railroad has been modernized and almost completely rebuilt to the highest standards of railroad properties. These accomplishments have earned for the Railroad high prestige in the railroad industry and among investors as well as with the public generally. This notable accomplishment is largely the product of the vision and foresight of President Davis, supported by his unwavering courage, untiring energy and an abiding faith in the future of the Coast Line Railroad and of the area it serves.

Not only his outstanding accomplishments as a railroad executive but his magnetic personality, his warmth of friendship, his kindness and his thoughtfulness of others have earned the respect and esteem of his associates and countless friends; his integrity, patriotism and acceptance of civic and religious responsibilities have won for him an eminent position in his home State of North Carolina and throughout the country.

The Directors of Atlantic Coast Line Railroad Company welcome this opportunity to attest their admiration and affection for Mr. Davis. They felicitate him upon his coming anniversary and for his long, faithful and productive service to the Company.

Ordered this May 20, 1954, by resolution of the Board of Directors, that this testimonial be delivered to Mr. Davis with the deep and earnest wish for his health, happiness and continued success in all his endeavors.

No. 11: *Resolution honoring ACL President Champ Davis on his 75th birthday on July1, 1954, and his 61st anniversity of service with the railroad was seen as a gentle hint from the board that it was nearing time for him to retire. He retired three years later.*

Chapter XVIII

Davis' Quest for Perfection

"Mr. Coast Line"

For a dozen postwar years, the Atlantic Coast Line Railroad was dominated by the stewardship and personality of President Champion McDowell Davis. Without a strong, central figure exerting financial and policy direction from the New York office, the board tended to support Davis' policy initiatives from Wilmington. F. B. Adams, chairman of the board, was prevented by other responsibilities from taking the active leadership role of his predecessors, Delano and Walters. A. Lee M. Wiggins, who became chairman in 1948, devoted himself to financial management enabling President Davis to carry out his programs. Although he had much help, it was Champ Davis who brought the Coast Line to a standing of unsurpassed excellence between 1945 and 1957. By the end of his tenure as president, he was very definitely "Mr. Coast Line."

Davis was truly a phenomenon in the amount of time and attention he devoted to the job. He spent most weekdays on the go — inspecting the property; conferring with officials and supervisors all over the system; attending meetings of railroad executives; and appearing before government agencies. His fierce dedication to the railroad, his energy and expertise made him one of the most respected railroad leaders in the nation. He participated actively in the affairs of the American Association of

Wilmington Railroad Museum

No. 12: *Champion McD. Davis*

Railroads and other railroad organizations. He also made a point of maintaining affable relationships with the members of the Interstate Commerce Commission, a connection that brought the Coast Line a sympathetic hearing on many questions. For most of the normal working week, his office car was both home and headquarters. He typically got back to Wilmington on Friday afternoon and charged into the week's accumulation of paper work, keeping his executives busy all weekend in the headquarters in Wilmington. Under Champ Davis, it was more than the trains that ran seven days per week.

It is said that for an evening "social" for his executives, Davis would announce to his male-only "guests" that it was time to leave. As for working on Sundays, one new vice president purportedly told Davis, "If you need me on Sunday mornings, sir, you can find me at St. James Church."

The Work Begins

The railroad company that Champ Davis led into the postwar era had its mileage considerably enlarged through merger of subsidiary companies. During 1944, the organizational structure was simplified by merging the Washington & Vandemere and the Moore Haven & Clewiston companies into the parent company. This added 40 miles of branch line in North Carolina and 24 miles in Florida to the property of the Coast Line.

A much more significant merger was that of the 640-mile Atlanta, Birmingham & Coast. President Davis and the ACL Board took a hard look at the AB&C in 1945. Even the busy war years had not enabled this subsidiary road to wipe out the red-ink balance in its profit and loss account. After a four-year respite from deficit operations. the AB&C was facing an imminent return to money-losing operations; and the Coast Line was facing the prospect of continuing an annual outlay of $259,000, in guaranteed dividends on AB&C preferred stock, for a decaying railroad. The AB&C had either to be junked, or revitalized, and made a useful part of the Coast Line system. Davis and the board chose the latter alternative.

The AB&C's physical condition was considerably below the Coast Line standard for secondary main lines, so the decision to retain and rebuild it meant committing a substantial portion of the funds available for postwar improvements to this segment of the system. At least a modest savings lay in eliminating the separate corporate organization. Formal merger moves commenced in July of 1945, and, with ICC approval, the properties of the AB&C were taken over by the Atlantic Coast Line Railroad Company at midnight on the following December 31. The AB&C retained a fairly high degree of operating autonomy for many years thereafter as the Western Division of the Coast Line. It did, however, see increased use as a through freight and passenger route.

Thanks to these moves of organizational streamlining, the Atlantic Coast Line Railroad Company owned 5,334 miles, and operated 5,573 miles, of line at the end of 1946. Other important parts of the system, however, still operated under separate companies. They were the Charleston & Western Carolina, the Georgia Railroad, Atlanta & West Point Route, Western of Atlanta and the Clinchfield (the latter two leased jointly with the L&N). The Coast Line/L&N rail empire was still quite complex.

A Custody Battle Begins

The most ambitious postwar acquisition and merger venture was destined never to be accomplished. President Davis set out determinedly in 1944 to get the Florida East Coast Railway for the Coast Line. This placed him on a collision course with a formidable opponent — Edward Ball, trustee of the Alfred I. duPont estate. The result was a struggle of heroic proportions.

The FEC had been in the hands of the courts for a long time — first in receivership, beginning in 1931, and then under title 77 of the Bankruptcy Act, in 1941. Coast Line executives had considered acquiring the FEC toward the end of the Depression decade. They had studied the value of the property, and had made an offer to A. M. Anderson, of J. P. Morgan & Company, for a majority of the first and refunding mortgage bonds. When Anderson, as head of a bondholders' committee, asked a higher price, Lyman Delano refused; so, Edward Ball acquired this block of bonds for the duPont estate trust. Reorganization proceedings had already begun under the Federal Bankruptcy Act in 1941. The bonds were subsequently placed with the St. Joe Paper Company, the largest corporate organization in the Florida duPont empire. An ICC examiner recommended approval, in 1944, of an amended St. Joe Paper Company reorganization plan. It seemed as though Ed Ball would soon take over the Flagler railroad.

Upon receiving assurances of cooperation and support from some minority bondholders, President Davis and the board decided to contest ICC approval for control of the FEC. Supporting a petition of S. A. Lynch Corporation, the Atlantic Coast Line Railroad Company appealed to the ICC on December 11, 1944, to reopen the Florida East Coast Railway reorganization case, and to consider a plan whereby the ACL would purchase 60% of the stock in a reorganized company. Early in January, the ICC gave its refusal to reopen the case. Again it looked as though the matter was settled.

A few months later, however, the commission reopened the case for the purpose of receiving an entirely different Coast Line plan. Ralph M. Jewell, the assigned examiner, heard several days of testimony in Washington and West Palm Beach in November, 1945. He studied the case for several months, and then recommended that the commission adopt the St. Joe Paper Company's plan. There was another long wait until May 20, 1947, when the ICC voted five-to-four to reverse the recommendation of its examiner and to approve the Atlantic Coast Line's plan for merger of the Florida East Coast.

Opponents registered a storm of protests. The Southern Railway and the Seaboard Air Line objected. The city of Fort Pierce had second thoughts about its support of the ACL plan, as did most of the minority bondholders groups, including the one led by S. A. Lynch, who wanted more money. The duPont trustees declared that they would continue the fight "regardless of time and cost."

The ICC heard arguments pro and con from all interested parties early in January, 1948. A little over two months later it announced its decision (by a 6 to 5 vote) affirming its earlier finding that the Florida East Coast Railway should be merged with the Coast Line.

The majority of the commission had become firmly committed to a true "railroad man's solution" for the FEC. They agreed with Champ Davis that a FEC-Coast Line merger would strengthen both roads and best serve the public interest. They also subscribed to U. S. Senator Claude Pepper's contention that control by the Florida duPont interests would lead to discrimination against other shippers and carriers. The battle lines were drawn on this division of interests: the ICC backing Champ Davis and a "good railroad solution" for the FEC; Edward Ball and others representing an overwhelming majority of the creditor rights resisting vigorously and seeking redress in the federal courts. It was destined to be a long struggle.

The court proceedings included three sessions in Federal District Court, two trips to the 5th and 6th Circuit Court of Appeals, the denial of certiorari by the U. S. Supreme Court, and one full-scale proceeding in the Supreme Court, which included the rare allowance of one full day for argument before that court.

In the initial proceeding in Federal District Court in Jacksonville, the duPont side "rolled up the heavy artillery" — its position was argued by former Secretary of State and Supreme Court Justice James F. Burns. Judge Sam Sibley recognized him by saying "I don't know whether to call you Governor, Senator, Mr. Secretary, Mr. Justice or Mr. Assistant President, so I guess I will just call you 'Jimmy'." The Coast Line's position was ably presented by New York attorney Edward W. Bourne, and ardently supported by Senator Pepper.

The struggle would go on for years. Meanwhile, there was a railroad to run.

Davis' Great Improvement Program

No matter how urgent other affairs might seem, President Davis fixed his main interest unswervingly on the aim of building and running the best possible railroad. In the course of broadening his expertise beyond traffic matters he had become engrossed with the physical aspects of railroading. Such aspects as equipment design and maintenance, roadway engineering and construction, signaling and communications, yard layouts and procedures, and train operation drew his active attention. He had initiated a campaign to rebuild and modernize the property, the moment he assumed the duties of executive vice president in 1939; but he had at first been closely limited by the slowness of business and by Delano's conservatism. Then he had been obliged to lead an underprepared and shortage-plagued railroad through the unprecedented demands of the war years. Now Davis was determined to bring the Coast Line to a level of physical excellence that would be second to none in the industry. In the dozen years from 1945 to 1957 he did just that.

The great rebuilding program got underway immediately at the end of World War II, in 1945. The word went out that the Atlantic Coast Line was engaged in probably the largest roadbed and track rehabilitation program in the country. Bridges were strengthened, dips and rises removed, the roadway regraded and reballasted throughout with crushed granite, millions of old cross-ties replaced by new and longer ones (a nine-foot standard was adopted in 1940), and the mainline track re-laid with 131-pound rail. The double track main line between Richmond and Jacksonville would truly be a "speedway of the South."

Secondary main lines and branch lines would receive comparable attention, although with lighter rail — a new 115-pound rail or 100-pound relay rail, according to traffic density. Station buildings and bridges were repaired and repainted, new signals installed, and every mile-post on the railroad replaced. Practically the entire fixed plant was rehabilitated.

The work initially progressed very fast — 326 miles of 131-pound rail were laid in mainline tracks in 1945 — leading to optimistic forecasts that the program would be essentially complete by the end of 1947. As it turned out, the timetable extended considerably beyond that date, partly because the modernization program grew more and more ambitious, and partly because postwar problems delayed and sometimes suspended improvements.

Rising Costs Slow Progress

The immediate postwar years brought various developments that slowed railroad reconstruction. For one thing, wartime shortages carried over into peacetime. Just as millions of Americans had to wait for their new automobiles, railroad companies "stood in line" while manufacturers worked through their order backlogs for diesel locomotives and cars. Steel producers, limited by under-capacity and labor strife, were unable to meet demands of equipment manufacturers for structural materials and of railroads for rails. Coast Line officials placed orders for enough rail to lay 447 track miles in 1945, and a like amount in 1946; but little more than two-thirds of the tonnage was received.

A number of factors combined to put the company in a cash squeeze that forced postponement of purchases, even when materials and equipment became available. Prices of all items soared as government controls were lifted. The lightweight passenger coaches bought for the first *Champion* in 1939 cost about $70,000 each; comparable coaches were priced at nearly $80,000 by the end of 1946 and over $90,000 in 1950. Thanks to mass production efficiency, the cost of diesel-electric locomotives stayed about the same; but everything else went up sharply.

Higher unit costs combined with postwar slackening of business to squeeze profits; operating income per mile of road shrank from $3,652 in 1944 to only $990 in 1947.

The most serious category of increased cost was higher wages. Wartime wage increases on the Coast Line had been somewhat higher than the national average of 33 percent. At war's end the payroll really began to skyrocket. Coast Line employees returning from the armed forces got their jobs back, while hundreds of new maintenance-of-way workers were hired for the rebuilding program. The railroad had averaged only about 20,000 employees during the busiest months of the war. The figure for 1945 rose to 22,392. The addition of AB&C employees hiked the figure to 23,842 during 1946. Railroad brotherhoods won successive rounds of postwar wage increases, beginning with an important nationwide settlement in 1946. The impact on payrolls was spectacular. The Coast Line had paid out only $43.7 million in 1943 to an average of 19,526 employees; by contrast it paid $69.3 million in 1946 to 23,842 workers, and more than $72.5 million in 1948 to 20,893 employees.

Under pressure of these rising costs and a serious business slump, the company laid off more than 4,000 employees in 1949. Then came another round of wage settlements and higher employment during the Korean War. The company paid $83 million to an average number of 19,761 employees in 1952. Thus, cost of labor practically doubled in the less than ten years from 1943 to 1952. This was true not only on the basis of cost per employee, but also in relation to transportation produced. The railroad carried about 17% more tons of freight in 1952 than in 1943, but the totals for ton-miles were very nearly the same, while only one-fourth as many passengers were carried in the later year. Thus wages as an increment of operating expenses became an item of greater concern than ever before.

Improving the Cash Flow

The Atlantic Coast Line Railroad Company's money position was tight enough in the late 1940's and early 50's that it sometimes took careful and creative management to pay all the bills and keep the improvement program rolling. Ironically, the wartime accomplishment of reducing the debt load had left the company too short on treasury cash for comfort.

An unenthusiastic market for railroad securities made Chairman Wiggins uneasy about the fact that $51,187,000 of first consolidated bonds were due to mature on July 1, 1952. He developed a plan in 1949 by which bonds would be issued as needed against a new general mortgage to retire all older bonds at maturity. Advance exchange of new bonds for the ones maturing in 1952 absorbed some $27 million (over half) of the old consolidated bonds; the remainder were paid off easily when due with cash raised by sale of more new general mortgage bonds. The eventual result of the plan in the mid-1960's would be a few series of bonds with comfortably spaced maturities, all secured by one general mortgage — a funded debt situation that contrasted sharply, in both lightness and orderliness, with that of many railroad companies.

With the long-term debt structure arranged in this way, the main financial problem that remained was to find adequate cash for rehabilitating and modernizing the railroad. Happily, earnings were high enough during most postwar years to cover much of the bill. Dividend payments, which totaled $3,302,093 in 1946, and grew only to $4,948,332 in 1956, were kept well within the company's non-operating income. In effect, Coast Line stockholders contented themselves with a modest yield from dividends received from the L&N, so that earnings from their own railroad could be reinvested in the property.

There was another matter that concerned minority stockholders more directly than did financial management of the company — market volatility of Coast Line stock. A relatively high-priced stock with a "thin float" trading on the exchange, ACL common saw some sharp price fluctuations, as institutional investors began to bid for substantial blocks. A price run-up of 18 points during November of 1944 finally convinced President Davis that splitting the stock would be advisable. The board and the stockholders gave the necessary approval, and two additional shares were issued for each old share held (effecting a 3-for-1 split) on February 23,1955. The railroad company now had 2,470,281 shares of no-par common stock outstanding, with 705,600 of these owned by the holding company, the Atlantic Coast Line Company of Connecticut.

All in all, the railroad was strengthened by resourceful but still conservative financial management during the postwar period. Keeping funded debt at a manageable level continued to pay off for the Coast Line. The whole financial arrangement, including the modest dividend pay-outs, freed President Davis to apply huge amounts of generally healthy operating revenues (through high charges to maintenance), and virtually all of operating income, to improving the railroad.

New Traffic in a Growing Territory

In the final analysis, rebuilding of the Coast Line was made possible by economic expansion in the Southeast and the surge in traffic and revenues that resulted. President Davis had an early vision of postwar prospects for the region, and for the Atlantic Coast Line.

In the spring of 1944, obviously confident of allied victory even before the Normandy landing, Davis began to discuss openly the opportunities that industrial development in its territory would pose for his railroad. "Your company believes," he declared, "that a great expansion period lies ahead for the South." Events proved him right.

The movement of new industries into the region continued after the war, greatly changing the railroad's traffic mix. Pulp and paper mills multiplied dramatically; and other types of manufacturing, from chemicals to heavy machinery, kept pace. As a result, miscellaneous and manufactured items accounted for 44% of ACL freight revenues in 1952, compared with only 28% in 1938. There was enormous expansion of phosphate mining in ACL territory, generating a hauling business for which trucks could not compete. Phosphate rock became the most important single commodity handled, with tonnage increasing to produce 8.8% of total freight revenues in 1956. The general economic expansion required electrical power; consequently many new generating plants were built, sharply boosting the Coast Line's coal carrying business.

Although many military bases were closed or cut back, there were some new federal projects begun in the area. In 1951, the Atomic Energy Commission began constructing its huge Savannah River Plant in Aiken County, South Carolina. The site was served only by the Coast Line. Actually, it was on the line of the subsidiary Charleston & Western Carolina, which experienced a tremendous boost in bulk lading from the project, initially in construction materials, and then in coal and other commodities needed for operations. Thus one of the quietest segments of the Coast Line system was galvanized into lively activity. Nearly $2 million in roadway improvements and new equipment had to be poured into the C&WC during 1951 alone. This was a phenomenal situation, of course, but it epitomized the postwar experience of the Coast Line.

The high relative growth rate in its territory — all along the tidewater and extensively in Florida — provided the railroad with an expanded traffic base and reduced its dependence on agricultural and seasonal business. It also gave the Coast Line relatively healthier revenues than most American railroads enjoyed during the period. There were, of course, some lean times, such as during the immediate postwar years, in 1949 and again in 1954, when business slumps constricted the company's cash position and slowed improvements. In general, however, economic growth in the Southeast pushed the Coast Line's tonnage and revenues back up to the record levels of World War II, which necessitated and supported President Davis' ambitious program of rebuilding the railroad.

A Railroad Second to None

There was money enough for Champ Davis to realize his ambition for the Coast Line: namely to bring it to a level of physical excellence unsurpassed in the industry. The top-priority job of rebuilding the main line track with 131-132-pound rail was essentially completed, Richmond-to-Jacksonville, early in 1950. Then came a push to get all secondary main lines relaid with 115-pound rail. This program was finished from Jacksonville to Tampa in 1953 and was duplicated on other parts of the system. Rebuilding of the Western Division (the old AB&C) was largely finished in 1952, with all its lines, Waycross to Atlanta and Birmingham, re-laid with cropped and reconditioned 100-pound rail. The new Coast Line tracks, everywhere, rested on a rebuilt roadbed. Extensive regrading eliminated many dips, rises and curves. By the end of 1952, no fewer than 70 curves had been modified in the main lines, and 29 of them had been totally eliminated. Year after year, section gangs placed millions of new cross ties and hundreds of thousands of cubic yards of new ballast in the roadway. Nothing but the best — crushed granite — would do for the heavy duty main line. Toward the end of 1951, President Davis boasted, probably accurately, "There is no better track structure, roadway and riding track in the United States than that of the Coast Line, particularly the Richmond-Jacksonville line."

There was much more. Passing tracks were being lengthened to accommodate the longer freight trains of the times. For the same reason, freight yards were being enlarged at many points, with more and longer classification tracks. Bridges and buildings were renovated with repairs and paint. Annual charges to "Additions and Betterments — Roadway" averaged around $10 million in the late '40s and early '50s, while still larger amounts were being charged off to operating expenses. Late in 1951, President Davis reported that gross expenditures on way and structures since he had taken command late in 1939 had amounted to a total of $268,678,000.

The vast bulk of this money had been spent, of course, since the roadway rebuilding program began in 1943. It was an expenditure on fixed-plant improvements of more than five times the rate of the 1930s. Adding the outlays on equipment, Davis calculated the company had spent by that time a total of $622,579,000 on improving its transportation property under his leadership

Dieselization

One of the most significant improvements during this period was the abandonment of steam for diesel power, the final stage of which was accomplished swiftly on the Coast Line. It was a survival move, as well as an improvement. Squeezed between slow authorizations for modest rate increases on the one hand, and rising costs on the other, railroads desperately needed the operating thrift of a diesel fuel economy, which provided lower maintenance costs and the power and speed of the diesel-electric locomotive.

The Coast Line had a relatively good start with 105 diesel units on its roster at the end of 1945, after starting with one diesel in 1939 for the first Champion train. Only a few more were added before Davis and the Board decided, in 1949, they wanted to complete the changeover. Financing such an ambitious purchase was a real challenge. They were contemplating an outlay approaching $60 million, and the company simply did not have enough cash to put down the 20% that was standard on conditional sale agreements or equipment trusts.

In October of 1949, an order was placed for 73 diesels on which the company could meet down payment requirements. Then, early in 1950, an order was placed with the Electro-Motive Division of General Motors for 200 new units; but the time for confirmation of the order approached without a financing solution in sight. Only a matter of hours remained before the 200 locomotives intended for the Coast Line would be assigned to another railroad, when Chairman Wiggins and President Davis persuaded officers of three New York banks to advance 100% of the needed money on ten-year conditional sale agreements. The Coast Line thus created a financial innovation while arranging to move into the vanguard of railroad modernization. During a period of little more than two years, 1950-52, the Coast Line received and put into service 375 diesel-electric units, most of them financed on this new basis.

The dieselization program was essentially complete by the end of 1952. The railroad had its full complement of 564 diesel-electric units, and only 11 steam locomotives remained to serve two small branch lines. The last steam locomotives on the Coast Line were retired in 1955. For many railroad buffs, the passing of the age of steam was a sad development. It made good sense, however, from a practical standpoint. The Coast Line's transportation ratio declined from 42.9% in 1948 to 36.9% in 1953, largely due to the economy of diesel motive power. Expenses were lower because diesel-electrics needed less maintenance and consumed less fuel per unit of power.

Passenger Improvements

Other additions to equipment were less dramatic but still important. Construction of passenger cars had been suspended during the war, and deliveries were slow in the postwar period. Twenty-one passenger train cars, ordered in 1941, finally became part of the *Champion* fleet between July 1946 and March 1947. At that point the Coast Line was joined by the Pennsylvania and the Florida East Coast in placing an order for 117 new passenger cars, 74 of them for the ACL. A large proportion of these streamlined lightweight cars were compartmentalized sleepers. They were put on the line beginning late in 1949, modernizing the *Florida Special* and other first class trains. Another 20 units acquired in 1950 comprised the last large purchase of new passenger equipment. Three additional units in 1955 completed the roster of lightweight cars for a total of 148. However, a very ambitious program of renovating conventional passenger cars to match the new ones, inside and out, added dozens more good quality cars.

A special addition to passenger train equipment reversed a policy set just before the turn of the century. ACL had refused way back in 1899 to haul Henry Plant's Southern Express Company refrigerator cars in its passenger trains. In the late 1940's, the Coast Line purchased 50 express-refrigerator cars, assigned them to a pool of such cars operated by the Railway Express Agency, and included them in passenger train consists, to meet the demand for top-flight perishables service. The trains could still maintain schedule speeds, thanks to the flexibility of diesel-electric power.

Adding and Innovating Freight

There was impressive expansion of the freight car fleet. The railroad made do in the immediate postwar period with its wartime equipment; but acquisition began in a big way in October of 1947, with an order for 3,960 new freight cars. Substantial orders followed, from time to time, while a few cars were built in Coast Line shops. Most of the cars were acquired under purchase plans (equipment trusts and conditional sale agreements), but many were rented from an insurance company under a new lease plan. Nearly 13,000 new freight cars were put on the line between 1948 and the point when Champ Davis retired in mid-1957. They were of various types: gondolas, coal hoppers, pulpwood flats, cement hoppers, wet phosphate hoppers, closed top hoppers for port phosphate rock, and solid box cars. No new ventilated produce cars — once a Coast Line hallmark — were acquired, however.

The freight equipment roster swelled from 23,581 at the close of 1946 to 34,744 in mid-1957. This meant improvement in quality, as well as supply. The new cars were all of large capacity (50 tons and more), and most of them incorporated improved design and construction features. The use of roller bearings on freight cars was an innovation that the Coast Line spearheaded. New passenger cars had used roller bearings in place of the old journal bearings for years, and Coast Line operating men became convinced that trouble-free service would justify the expense of mounting freight car wheels in this manner. Beginning in 1951 with 400 phosphate cars, practically all new freight cars put on the Coast Line were equipped with roller bearings. The Coast Line soon had the largest roller bearing fleet of any railroad. When all the cars on order had been delivered in the early summer of 1957, the railroad had 6,740 freight cars with roller bearings, 19.4% out of a total fleet of 34,744.

Another innovation in freight equipment literally brightened the entire railroad. Luminescent, or reflective, paint was applied to a few cars on the medallion, the identification numbers, and a dashed line along the bottom, beginning in 1948. It proved so useful as a safety and identification aid at highway crossings and in yards, that by 1951 it was being applied to all freight cars. Soon switching locomotives, and then road locomotives, were marked in this way. By the mid-1950s station signs, whistle posts, mile posts, and switch marking were "reflectorized." The excellent appearance of Champ Davis' railroad was visible even at night.

A Task Without End

Champ Davis was never fully satisfied with the condition of his railroad. There were always new technical devices to be put on the line, and some parts of the property with room for improvement. As outlay for the great improvement program peaked toward the close of 1951 he observed, "I would say that Coast Line is in splendid physical condition, though," he added in the next breath, "there yet remains much work to be done."

So the work went on. There was extensive modernization in signaling and communications. Automatic block systems were improved by replacing the old semaphore-type signals with searchlight signals, by spacing them for higher speed train movement, and by installing new coded track circuits for controls. Centralized traffic control (CTC) is a system in which train movements are governed by remotely controlled switches and signals, eliminating the need for train orders. It was introduced in the late 1940's, in high-density stretches of the main line, such as those between Dunlop and Collier, Virginia, and between South Rocky Mount and Contentnea, North Carolina. The next installations were on the single-track main line between Jacksonville and Tampa, Florida, and on the entire length of the rehabilitated Western Division. There were 167 track-miles of CTC in service at the end of 1951. The system proved so useful in permitting higher density and smoother train movements that installations were extended as fast as possible, so that the Coast Line had 703 track-miles (on 610 miles of road) in centralized traffic control at the close of 1956.

Telephone facilities were modernized and extended to new points, including the entirety of the Western Division. As the old AB&C, it had still been relying completely on telegraph for dispatching and interstation messages. Then, beginning in 1952, Morse telegraph circuits between many strategic Coast Line locations were converted to teletype operation. The earliest of these connected the headquarters in Wilmington with company offices in New York City and Washington, D. C.; but by the mid-1950s such points as Jacksonville and Montgomery, Waycross and Atlanta, and Sanford and Tampa could exchange information in this convenient way. An even more significant innovation was installation in freight yards of IBM equipment which used teletype circuits to transmit advance print-outs of train consists to yard superintendents and supervisors. This greatly expedited movement of freight cars through yards, and provided customers with up-to-the-minute information on their shipments. With five mainline freight terminals from Jacksonville northward so equipped by the end of 1956, the Coast Line was getting very modern indeed!

Introduction of radio communication also added to operating efficiency. Inaugurated at the South Rocky Mount terminal in the late '40s, radio equipment giving yard office-to-engine, and engine-to-engine, contact clearly demonstrated its value in switching operations. It was soon being introduced in yards all over the system. At the close of 1956, the Coast Line had 32 yards and terminals equipped with radio facilities, including sets in 118 diesel switching locomotives and 19 automobiles used by supervisors.

It was less certain that "line-of-road" radio installations would justify their expense. President Davis and the Transportation Department decided in 1953 to experiment with a complete line-of-road radio system on the Western Division. By early 1955, there were portable "walkie-talkie" units for end-to-end communication on both freight and passenger trains on the Western Division, and fixed installations gave contact between trains and 20 wayside stations. Radio communications between locomotives and cabooses on long trains proved to be especially useful. Soon all trains moving between Richmond and Jacksonville on the main line had end-to-end radio equipment, and the program expanded next to include through freights everywhere on the railroad. At the close of 1956, line-of-road radio facilities included fixed equipment at 27 wayside base stations, in 167 road diesel locomotives, and in 116 cabooses, plus 284 portable sets. It seemed there were infinite possibilities for refinements in communication.

Improvements of a more prosaic nature also continued. A practical technique for welding rail sections together, thus eliminating the standard joints, became available. During the early 1950s, the Coast Line roadway department began installing welded rail in hard-to-service spots, such as bridges and grade crossings.

Charleston Union Station had burned in 1947, and the Coast Line built a new one on its own main line. The new installation was finished late in 1956, freeing passenger trains from a time-consuming back-up move into downtown Charleston. A similar improvement was made at Savannah in 1962.

A difficult decision to move the general offices from Wilmington, which was off the main line, to a more convenient spot on the railroad resulted in months of studying alternative locations. The announcement was made to the board of directors on December 15, 1955, but the move did not take place until July 1960. December 15 became known as "Black Thursday" in Wilmington. A site was later selected at Jacksonville, and plans were made for a building there. Clearly, there was no end to the things that needed to be done.

Finances in the Fifties

Operating expenses remained high during the mid-1950's, largely because President Davis was so intent on achieving and maintaining the best possible railroad. Another contributing factor was sharply higher costs of labor. Average compensation per employee rose about 20% between 1950 and 1956. Settlements won by the brotherhoods in 1955 and 1956 brought particularly large increases, presenting management with a staggering cost problem. While the number of employees was increased only modestly to nearly 19,000, in response to prosperous levels of business, the total payroll rocketed from $84.6 million in 1955 to $91.4 million in 1956. As a result, net earnings actually declined in a year that saw a substantial rise in revenues, and at a time when the company had expected to begin reaping the benefits of the great improvement program. The problem showed up awkwardly in the railroad's operating ratio, which had been running high throughout the postwar period. Having registered a peak of 90.19% in 1946, and as low as 80.09% in 1950, it moved up again in 1956 to 85.27%. The fact that this index was consistently higher than the Seaboard Air Line's was due partly, as Davis pointed out, to the higher proportion of Coast Line branch mileage. Nearly 300 miles of unprofitable branch lines had been abandoned since the war. Presumably, it made little sense to discard any of the remaining lines that were adding marginally to profits, just to achieve a lower operating ratio. Even so, the high level of operating expenses reflected the constant striving for quality. Acknowledging that some were questioning why the Coast Line's maintenance ratio was still running about five percentage points higher than the average for Class I railroads, Davis stated firmly, "I should not be content to see the Coast Line revert to being an 'average railroad'."

The Rewards of Excellence

On the positive side, the investment in improvements began to pay off in better transportation service by the mid-1950s. Higher train speeds, and more efficient handling of cars in yards, shortened some freight schedules by as much as 24 hours. In the spring of 1954, a new fast freight service southbound from Potomac Yard began giving third-morning delivery at Florida points, such as Tampa, of cars originating in the Northeast. This fast-freight was cleared for speeds up to 65 miles per hour, and designated a first class train with rights equal to passenger trains. Picking up additional cars from Midwest origins at Richmond, fast freights made the 640-mile run from Acca Yard (Richmond) to Jacksonville in 16 hours and 15 minutes. A year later, this schedule was shortened by an hour, and a companion northbound train was put on the line, providing third-day service from Tampa to Philadelphia and New York City — nearly a full day faster than the previous best schedule. On numerous other freight runs all over the system, there were advancements of delivery time ranging from 12 to 24 hours.

Generally, faster train movement meant that the Coast Line's traditionally good perishables service could be made even more expeditious. In the 1955-56 season, third-morning delivery of Florida citrus and vegetables to Chicago, Detroit, and other points in Western territory, was offered for the first time. Then, closing hours at South Florida loading stations were set an hour later in May of 1956. Capping all this, the general maximum speed limit for mainline freights was raised to 65 miles per hour during 1956. These improvements in service were crucial in helping to meet growing competition from highway trucks, which were taking over a growing proportion of the nation's high-tariff commodity and merchandise traffic.

Coast Line freight trains were longer, as well as faster, thus making more efficient use of fixed-plant and labor. Trains of 100 cars and more became common on mainline runs. Reflecting this change, gross ton miles per train hour rose from 27,428 in 1947 to 44,434 in 1956. In very significant ways, all the physical improvements were contributing to a more effective railroad operation.

Coast Line passenger service gained in quality during this period, even though it was a declining facet of the business. Highway and air travel made steady and substantial inroads into the railroad's passenger traffic. Except for a brief resurgence of military travel during the Korean War, passenger miles declined steadily, from 1,449 million miles in 1946 to only 647 million in 1956, while passenger revenues dropped from $28.5 million to $17.4 million. Many local passenger trains were discontinued in 1947-48, and again in 1953-54. Reflecting this, passenger train mileage declined from 9.1 million in 1946 to 6.1 million in 1956, while the distance the average passenger was carried rose from 251 to 382 miles.

Still, passenger business remained comparatively important on the Coast Line, and in most years was actually a source of some profit, when calculated against out-of-pocket costs. In contrast to many American railroads, the Coast Line still went to great lengths to make passengers feel wanted. The physical improvements described above helped in many ways. With the first postwar deliveries of new lightweight cars in 1946-47, the *Champion* (*West Coast*) was inaugurated as regular streamliner service between New York City and Tampa and St. Petersburg. Beginning in 1952, *Champion* service was extended all the way south to Naples. The *Florida Special* revived as a winter luxury train after the war, became a modern streamliner for the 1949-50 season. The other seasonal train, the *Vacationer*, got new streamlined coaches. In 1949-50, the frequency of some Midwest-to-Florida trains, such as the *City of Miami*, were doubled. Of course, these attractive trains could move with increasing smoothness, safety, and speed over a constantly improving railroad. The Passenger Traffic Department was probably justified in claiming, "There is no more comfortable train ride than over the rails of the Atlantic Coast Line Railroad." On October 30, 1955, the speed limit for passenger trains was raised to 100 miles per hour (lowered to 90 mph shortly thereafter) on the long mainline stretches under Centralized Traffic Control. This contributed to some substantially shorter schedules, some by as much as 55 minutes, for through trains between the East and Florida points. For the 1955-56 season, the *Champion* (*East Coast*) offered a 24-hour schedule, New York to Miami, which the *Florida Special* had offered in 1941. The superior quality of the railroad no doubt helped to keep many travelers going Coast Line.

The Interminable Florida East Coast Affair

The tug-of-war over the Florida East Coast Railway went on year after year, with first one side and then the other gaining temporary advantage. The Interstate Commerce Commission having decided in favor of their company's plan to acquire and merge the FEC, Coast Line stockholders voted, on May 14, 1948, almost unanimously to approve the plan. Court decisions soon rendered their action an empty formality. United States District Court Judge Samuel H. Sibley found in favor of the St. Joe Paper Company's contention that the ICC had no authority to hand over the railway to the ACL. He concluded that "the plan is not fair and just and does not afford due recognition to the rights of the refunding bondholders." The United States Court of Appeals for the Fifth Circuit agreed with him, in a decision rendered a year later on an appeal filed by the ACL. The majority opinion held that the case was that of one railroad company "coveting and pressing to possess" a competing debtor railroad company against the wishes of 98% of the equitable owners of the debtor, and over their violent objections that consummation would deprive them of their property without just compensation. The United States Supreme Court refused the Coast Line's petition to review the case.

The entire matter was back in the lap of the Interstate Commerce Commission. New hearings were held in July and August of 1950, with both the St. Joe Paper Company and the Coast Line submitting modified plans that provided for more generous payments to FEC securities holders. The minority creditors were letting the two main competitors bid for their support. Also, the ICC was under court direction to provide for "fair and equitable" compensation for the bondholders. There were other reorganization plans presented to the commission. One of them, from the 3,000 employees of the railroad, provided for an independent company under their control. There were also two separate plans submitted by minority groups of bondholders. The Florida Railroad and Public Utilities Commission remained officially neutral, but applied some pressure by insisting that any plan should provide for a new passenger station at Miami.

The ICC took long months to deliberate. On July 13, 1951, it decided once again that the Florida East Coast Railway should be merged into the Coast Line. Its stated reason was essentially the same. The majority of the commissioners saw control of the FEC by the St. Joe Paper Company as contrary to the public interest, for the duPont empire "would be in a position, particularly because of its large banking interests, to influence shippers or receivers to route their shipments over any connecting carrier which it might wish to favor." The plan was modified, though, to give a higher return to the bondholders. The valuation of the FEC was raised to $45,000,000. Various objections to the decision — including one from Coast Line officials that the price was too high — were rejected by the commission in October. Once again the case went to the courts.

The Federal District Court for the Southern District of Florida still held responsibility for the bankrupt railroad. Judge Louis Strum, after holding hearings in Jacksonville, announced his decision to reject the plan on March 11, 1952. The Coast Line officers then appealed again to the United States Circuit Court, which reversed the District Court in a five-to-two decision delivered on January 19, 1953. It directed the District Court to approve the plan certified to it by the ICC and to take steps to put it into effect.

Now all was in readiness for the Coast Line merger of the Florida East Coast Railway. Reorganization managers were to be appointed by the District Court and they would begin the complicated steps of transferring the physical properties and cash and securities in various accounts, calculated from January 1, 1950, as the effective date. The Atlantic Coast Line Railroad Company's stockholders had already voted, on January 15, 1952, to approve the plan as it had finally emerged from the ICC. It looked now as though President Davis' railroad would soon reach from Richmond to Miami.

Edward Ball had not yet given up. His attorneys obtained a stay of the Circuit Court order, pending a petition for review by the U. S. Supreme Court. The high court agreed to review the case and heard arguments in October of 1953. It deliberated until the following April before giving its ruling. By a four-to-three vote (with two justices not participating) the court decided that the ICC had exceeded its authority in attempting to force an involuntary merger. As Justice Frankfurter put it, in stating the majority opinion, "One carrier cannot be railroaded by the commission into an undesired merger with another carrier." The court subsequently refused an ACL request for a rehearing to consider other points of law. President Davis and the ICC were once again thwarted.

After 10 years of struggle, the whole matter was at the starting point. Some Coast Line effort was needed even to get the stage set for another round. Ed Ball and his associates apparently concluded that they had little chance for a favorable decision from the ICC; they elected to pull back and bide their time. They got a decision from the District Court to abandon the reorganization proceedings under the Bankruptcy Act, and to place the Florida East Coast under a dormant equity receivership. In this way the St. Joe Paper Company, and other holders of the first and refunding bonds, would continue to receive a generous yield on their investment, including interest on accrued delinquent interest, while the carrier remained in the limbo of receivership safely out of the Coast Line's reach. After more than a year of litigation, an ACL appeal to the Circuit Court in New Orleans succeeded in getting the bankruptcy reorganization proceedings continued and remanded to the Interstate Commerce Commission. The ICC then reopened the proceedings and set dates for a new round of hearings.

In an attempt to satisfy the Supreme Court's prohibition against an involuntary or forced merger, ACL executives now took the approach of submitting a plan jointly with the Florida East Coast Railway Company. Perhaps the courts would now acknowledge that some ownership rights still resided with the sole stockholder of the old company. Thus far they had ruled otherwise, but the railroad was returning higher revenues almost every year and meeting all its current fixed charges. The plan submitted was practically the same as the one certified by the ICC in 1951; even the payments from ACL were to be the same, except that the market price of its stock had risen substantially, and enhanced the value of the securities to be paid to FEC bondholders.

Ed Ball and the duPont group, for their part, used the strengthening performance of the FEC as a basis for a higher evaluation and, thereby, a more attractive payoff for the minority creditors. The new St. Joe Paper Company plan would give 40 shares of stock, a $1,000 bond and a *pro rata* share in a substantial fund of unappropriated cash, for each $1,000 first and refunding bond in the old company surrendered. Most of the minority creditors were won over to Ed Ball's position. So was the Florida Railroad Commission. On May 7, 1956, that body filed a statement with the ICC supporting the St. Joe Paper Company plan, explaining that this plan earmarked over $4,000,000 to relocate the Miami passenger terminal and to construct a new station. The ACL plan, it observed, allocated only $1,500,000 for a new structure on the present site; moreover, the merger with the ACL would result in a reduction of employment for railroad workers.

The state regulatory agency's shift in support of the opposition was a serious blow; but President Davis still pressed on with the struggle. The ICC examiner held hearings in Washington in June and July of 1956, then again for long weeks during the autumn in West Palm Beach. The case was still in the hands of the ICC in the late spring of 1957. The Coast Line had expended 13 years of executive effort, and millions of dollars, in the fight; but President Davis was apparently undaunted. He asserted that "the case is in better shape now than ever before from the standpoint of the Coast Line." That wasn't good enough, however.

The Work Is Finished

Still energetic and capable as he reached his middle seventies, President Davis showed no inclination to relinquish his command. The board dropped a gracious hint in the form of a testimonial, on the approach of his 75th birthday, July 1, 1954, describing this as "a worthy opportunity for his colleagues and associates to register their recognition and to express their appreciation . . ."

In subsequent years the issue of Champ Davis' retirement, linked to growing doubts about the continuing high levels of operating expenditures (and probably also about the relentless pursuit of the FEC folly), clouded his relationship with the more influential members of the board. Finally, on May 29, 1957 (about a month short of his 78th birthday), Davis announced his resignation, to become effective on the appointment of his successor. He also decided not to continue as a director.

It was a painful wrench to all concerned to have Champ Davis withdraw from Coast Line affairs. His identification with the railroad had been so complete, it is doubtful that any enterprise has ever received more devoted and unstinting service from an executive. Chairman of the Board A. Lee M. Wiggins later said of President Davis: "Without question, he accomplished with relatively meager resources more rebuilding and modernizing . . . in a shorter period of time than has been accomplished on any other large railroad in the country . . . Out of a long, intimate association with him, I rate him among the half-dozen top industrial leaders in the United States." It seems unlikely that any railroad president has ever turned over to his successor a property in better physical condition than did Champion McDowell Davis.

Chapter XIX

Rice Opens the Harmony Throttle

New Kid on the Block

When W. Thomas Rice entered the presidency of the Coast Line Railroad Company on August 1, 1957, a long standing Coast Line tradition was broken. This man had not risen through management ranks on the property; Rice was an outsider. This was, however, a welcome choice by critics of railroad management who felt that top personnel in a railroad company could become too ingrown, too locked into accustomed patterns of thought and action. Clearly, from the outset, President Rice enjoyed the full confidence and firm backing of T. B. Butler, chairman of the executive committee, and the rest of the board of directors. Apparent also was the great extent to which Thomas Rice's leadership brought positive changes in management policies for the company.

Even before this, Mr. Rice had distinguished himself as a leader during and immediately following World War II. After nearly eight years with the Pennsylvania Railroad, Rice was called to active duty in the Army in April 1942, shortly after the United States entered the war. During more that three years in the European and Pacific Theaters, he received decorations that included the Legion of Merit with two oak leaf clusters. He eventually rose to the rank of major general in the U.S. Army Reserve.

Actually, Thomas Rice was not altogether a stranger to the Coast Line. He had been the president of the Richmond, Fredricksburg & Potomac Railroad Company for two years previous. Rice had joined the management of that road in 1946, and had served as its general superintendent since 1949. From the vantage point of the RF&P office in Richmond, Rice had learned much about the two big roads from the South — the Seaboard Air Line and the Atlantic Coast Line. Both were dependent on the RF&P as their only connection for through-business to the North. Both interchanged vast amounts of traffic with his road. The ACL and its leaders were familiar to Thomas Rice. Moreover, he had an operating railroader's respect for the level of excellence to which "Champ" Davis had brought the Coast Line properties.

Rice's view of railroading was undoubtedly affected by the peculiar situation of the RF&P. As explained in an earlier chapter, the RF&P was operated under the control of the Richmond-Washington Company, a proprietary corporation in which ownership was shared by six larger railroad companies — the Southern, the Coast Line, the Seaboard, the Chesapeake & Ohio, the Baltimore & Ohio, and the Pennsylvania. This situation had placed Rice in contact with many top railroad leaders, and he had interacted well enough to find them "demanding but not unreasonable bosses."

The RF&P was an unusual railroad operation. With only 109 miles of main line in 1956, it carried 915,024,000 ton-miles of freight and produced $27,130,292 in operating revenues. Small wonder that Rice asserted, at the time of his election to the ACL presidency, that most American railroads could handle much greater levels of traffic than they currently did. Moreover, he felt that these greater levels of business could be achieved by offering good service, pricing it attractively, and getting the good news to potential customers.

Unusual, still, was the fact that the vast majority of the RF&P's dense traffic both originated and terminated on other lines. Thus a conspicuous amount of this railroad's operations involved interchange of business, particularly freight business. One of the biggest challenges was the classification and dispatching of freight cars in the huge Potomac Yard. Not surprising is another opinion expressed by Rice in the summer of 1957, that freight cars spent far too much time in yards — speedier, more efficient means should be found to get them through the yards and rolling in new train consists.

A Team Player

Along with these convictions, Thomas Rice brought with him to the Coast Line a penchant for the direct communication and clear lines of authority that characterize a small railroad. At his initial executive session in Wilmington, President Rice gathered all department heads and other key management personnel — some 50 strong — for a "pep talk." He both reassured and challenged them. He was not bringing with him a new management team, nor was he contemplating any shakeups. They knew their railroad much better than he; so he would depend extensively on their effectiveness, especially during these early months. Moreover, they undoubtedly had ideas about improving operations, and he wanted to hear their suggestions. Their leadership initiative would not only be welcomed, it would be expected, unlike that of the more authoritarian style of his predecessor.

This first session was a sample of things to come for department heads and specialists at Atlantic Coast Line Railroad. Under President Rice, they would have to take more initiative and more responsibility. The seven-day work week for top management and office personnel was done away with, but executives would still be expected to be on top of events in their respective bailiwicks. The very size of the initial session was indicative of a Rice innovation. His executive conferences extended beyond department heads to include assistant vice presidents and various specialists, in a group that often numbered 25 to 30 people. These conferences were called frequently, enabling presidential leadership to reach directly to the men in charge of all facets of the business. Problems were viewed and attacked from many vantage points at once, with an unprecedented number of good heads engaged in the process. Interdepartmental communication and understanding were greatly improved. Rice had not brought his own men with him to the Coast Line, yet the positive response evolved by his approach soon provided him with a loyal management team.

W. Thomas Rice brought an imposing presence to the top position of the Coast Line. He not only knew railroading, he believed intensely in its importance, and pursued his duties with apparently limitless energy. He was direct and forceful, yet warm in his communications with associates and subordinates. Yet it was also understood that a Coast Line executive who failed to meet a responsibility would need a very good explanation. He demonstrated a willingness to talk to anyone about railroad matters — not only associates in the company, but also patrons, community representatives and leaders of service organizations. After years of Champ Davis virtually running the railroad from an office car, the Atlantic Coast Line finally had a "front office" with President Rice.

Dale Carnegie — Where Are You?

Along with many other contemporary railroad leaders, Tom Rice saw many of the problems besetting American railroads as stemming from outdated and often unjustified public hostility. Reflecting conditions half-a-century in the past, federal, state, and local governments were taxing and regulating railroads into impotency, if not bankruptcy. The public's view of railroads needed revising through greater understanding, and the Atlantic Coast Line shared in this need.

Viewed objectively in 1957, the Atlantic Coast Line had room for improvement in its public image. Certainly there were obvious factors. For many towns on the main or branch lines, ACL had been the transportation life-line for decades, and dependable at that. There were local legends about the railroad which made it part of the folklore, and relations between numerous Coast Line agents and their fellow townspeople had all the warmth of easy familiarity. Within the company itself employees observed traditions a century or more old. From top management down to the extra gangs, there was an element of pride in working for this railroad. Along extensive parts of its territory, however, traditions on the Coast Line were relatively shy of qualities to inspire loyalty in its patrons or to stir the sentiments of the general public.

We have seen some of the reasons for this in tracing ACL history. In many a southern community, formation of the Coast Line had been perceived as "Yankee capitalists" buying a home-owned railroad, or as a big impersonal corporation seizing and absorbing a familiar local organization. Due partly to the personality of Henry Walters, the Atlantic Coast Line Railroad Company had indeed been a rather reticent corporation from its inception. At a time when many captains of industry and finance swaggered their way across the national scene, evoking public reactions of adulation and imitation, but also of resentment and envy, Henry Walters had assembled his railroad system very quietly. So successful had been his efforts to shun publicity, he had practically remained invisible. People told wild stories about Henry Plant, but not about Henry Walters. An indignant public believed, if somewhat inaccurately, that Vanderbilt had roared, "The public be damned"; but few even knew of the existence of Henry Walters.

Henry Walters had passed on this determined avoidance of the limelight to his nephew, Lyman Delano, along with another characteristic — a very firmly-held view of the sanctity of private property rights and rights to privacy. The Atlantic Coast Line Railroad was private property, so it was not incumbent on its owners and managers to explain their actions to the public. This position may have been correct enough on the theoretical and legal level, but when applied relentlessly in practice if often led to poor community relations.

Many inhabitants of Southeastern states had known the Atlantic Coast Line Railroad through the years as a well run business enterprise, operating physically in their midst, but often unyielding in its policies and remote in its leadership. One famous son of the Carolina tidewater country, author Robert Rouark, gave rather symbolic testimony. In his novel, *Poor No More*, he includes in his hero's youthful impressions of objects, in a world beyond his reach, the big black automobile that carried the president of the Atlantic Coast Line Railroad Company.

For a more specific example, consider the flavor of some editorial remarks in the *Richmond Times-Dispatch*, way back in the late summer of 1906:

> Again the Atlantic Coast Line Railroad has shown its utter disregard for this community by refusing to accord the Virginia State Fair and the Horse Show the same excursion rate that was allowed by every other railroad in this State . . . . If that railroad has ever turned aside from its absorbing pursuit of dividends to assist the development or consider the welfare of the people of Richmond, we do not recall that instance. Perhaps more than any other railroad in the South the Atlantic Coast Line has prospered . . . . It has made many of its fortunate stockholders millionaires, and it has been administered with honesty and intelligence; but its sole aim has been to make money. This object has been fully achieved, but in its attainment the Atlantic Coast Line Railroad has never regarded the shippers or passengers as anything more than a necessary evil, whose sole right to exist depended upon paying top-notch rates for every service rendered.

Indeed a forthright expression of sentiment, it was significant that such a strong statement was provoked, not by a Coast Line policy decision, but by a careless oversight — someone in the passenger traffic department had forgotten to post the special excursion rate in question. Another instance dates from a few years later when a prominent citizen of Wilmington, North Carolina, made some observations at a Chamber of Commerce dinner to the effect that Wilmington & Weldon Railroad stock had grown to the value of $1,500 per share after takeover by the Atlantic Coast Line, and that all of this increase had come out of the people of North Carolina and of Wilmington in particular. Gross exaggeration, of course, but not an unusual expression of opinion. Those who felt such resentment tended to ignore important considerations, such as the facts that growth in a railroad's value was largely due to the general economic development of its territory, that the railroad itself contributed greatly to such development, and that the residents of the area shared in the benefits.

In the headquarters city of Wilmington, where ACL was the chief employer, there was some public perception that railroad officials held down wages by discouraging the arrival of new companies. President Davis was viewed as the most powerful figure in the community, yet as one focused primarily on the railroad and its welfare.

Frequently a sore point between the railroad and local communities was the location of yards and/or terminal facilities. By the middle of the 20th century, several cities in Coast Line territory, which began as a huddle of frame buildings around newly arrived 19th century railroad installations, had grown quite large. The railroad facilities, which were in many instances still in their original locations, presented frustrating obstacles to traffic flow and urban development in modern city centers.

Tampa, Florida, was such a city, and resentment had grown there over the years because of the Coast Line's refusal to consider moving its freight terminal and other facilities from a downtown site on the banks of the Hillsborough River. The city wanted the Coast Line's extensive acreage for development as a civic center, and, despairing of an agreement with the company, had instituted condemnation of property proceedings under Florida law. Also, citizens would soon vote on the issue in a special referendum.

Winning Friends and Influencing Patrons

An interesting story survives of Thomas Rice's first visit to Tampa, only a few days after assuming the Coast Line presidency. He was attending a meeting of a group of business leaders. In the milling about before the organized session began, one of the local men greeted the stranger and pleasantly inquired what firm he was with.

"The Coast Line," Rice answered.

"Well, you have a hell of a nerve coming here," the man said. "I'll bet your president wouldn't show up here. By the way, what do you do at the Coast Line?"

"I'm president," Rice replied.

In his following talk with this group, and with many other Tampans, including the mayor, the Coast Line president emphasized his willingness to consider their mutual problem and to work toward its solution. The impact of this "get-acquainted visit" was so favorable that the city government put off the referendum and suspended the condemnation proceedings. Subsequent studies and negotiations led to the Coast Line's sale, in 1959, of several acres of riverfront property to the city. The proceeds were used to relocate its freight facilities. Then, in August 1960, ACL sold the remainder of this downtown acreage to the city, and began construction of a new freight depot farther out, which went into use the following year. Tampans were revising their opinions of the Coast Line.

Actually, the Tampa episode was only one instance in a campaign to improve community relations launched by Rice immediately upon taking office. *The Wilmington*

Morning Star responded appreciatively to his inaugural press conference, which itself was an almost unprecedented event in the headquarters city of Wilmington:

> The arrival of W. Thomas Rice marks the beginning of a new era . . . It goes without saying that there have been times in the past when the people of Wilmington have not understood some of the policies and dictums emanating from the ACL's office. In fact there have been times when the people were shocked and hurt. (This is propbably a reference to the abrupt and poorly handled headquarters relocation announced two years before.)

> If Thursday's press conference is any indication of things to come, the situation will not arise again, because Mr. Rice has shown a keen insight and deep understanding of the value of good public relations. . .

After this portentous beginning, Rice set off on a series of visits to many communities served by his railroad. On August 12, at St. Petersburg, Florida, scene of some three decades of hassling between the city and the railroad company over station locations, he made another very favorable impression. Said the *St. Petersburg Times*:

> The new ACL president simply played the role of a reasonable man trying to get at the facts. Perhaps this reasonableness is the quality we liked most about Mr. Rice, and the one thing that encouraged us to feel he will put an end soon to the costly, sometimes silly, fight . . . We think Mr. Rice cares what the public thinks about ACL, that he is aware of the business value of a good name, that he knows his railroad must compete with other transportation in the field of good public relations.

By September 24, 1957, the new spirit of cooperation began to take effect, as city officials and railroad executives agreed to start work on relocation sites. Less than six years later the same newspaper gave full and appreciative coverage to the departures of the last trains from downtown St. Petersburg under the headline, "RICE OPENED HARMONY THROTTLE."

Everyone's P.R. Department

Clearly, under Tom Rice's leadership the Coast Line was turning a new face to the world. Viewing his impact on the communities served, one could easily get the impression that he had invented the idea of promoting good will for a railroad. Of course this was not the case. The idea of making a positive effort to develop friendlier relations with patrons and better public understanding of railroad problems had been accepted for many years by railroad leaders in general and on the Coast Line, too. Formal public relations offices for railroads date back to the 1920s. One of the best early examples was the program inaugurated in 1920 by Charles H. Markham, president of the Illinois Central, with the insistent theme that his company should be "taking the public into its confidence." In May of 1923, a Department of Public Relations was established for the Atlantic Coast Line. For a number of years this office served well, but in the later stages of the Davis epoch no director was hired and the office had shrunk in functions to publishing the company news magazine and performing some other internal service tasks.

Thomas Rice needed more assistance in his task of selling the Coast Line as a cooperative neighbor and an efficient transportation service. He secured the services of a fellow Virginian, Donald T. Martin, as director of public relations and advertising. Leaving Richmond, where he had run his independent business in this field, Donald Martin arrived in Wilmington in July of 1958, gathered under him some bright young men from other company offices, and set out to help President Rice win friends and patrons for the Atlantic Coast Line.

One of the main objectives in the initial sales and public relations efforts was to enlist the aid of all Coast Line employees, to get them involved. During a six-week period in November and December of 1958 a "traffic round-up" saw most of the 14,000 Coast Line employees making over 76,000 telephone calls to friends, telling of the advantages of traveling or shipping via ACL.

A system-wide courtesy campaign was initiated in the summer of 1959 by President Rice, who assured gathered employees that each person's efforts in courteous treatment of patrons would contribute to increases in business. The theme selected for the campaign was *"Thanks for Using Coast Line,"* a slogan that caught on. President Rice liked it so much that he had it printed on schedules, posted in depots and in other passenger facilities, and even painted on box cars. One imagines that many an old-timer along the line blinked in amazement the first time he saw such a sentiment roll by on a Coast Line freight.

In addition to repeated campaigns to promote courteous treatment of patrons, the company now put additional effort into advertising. By 1960, the ACL advertising program was winning top awards from national organizations. Management was also kept alert to respond graciously to events important to local communities, and especially to local emergencies. In November of 1959, for example, when a church located near the Coast Line road in Charleston burned to the ground, the road's executives responded quickly to a request for aid. They directed construction of a short track extension up to the church area and lent the congregation an 88-passenger coach for use as a Sunday School building.

As each new station opened, as each new or improved type of equipment was added, and with each innovation in service, press releases went out to interested newspapers and magazines, and paid advertisements appeared at good impact spots. The Coast Line was now being a more cooperative neighbor. It was providing better service, and President Rice wanted the public to know.

It's ironic. Champ Davis had risen through the traffic (sales) department, but as president he had concentrated almost soley on operating aspects and on bringing the property to a peak of physical excellence. Now, in Thomas Rice, ACL had a president who had come up through the operating side of railroading, but was proving to be the best salesman in its history. As Rice himself expressed it, "A railroad company is in the business of selling transportation."

Beyond Public Relations

At the time that the new president took office, the Coast Line needed more than better public relations and a more effective sales approach. It needed to improve the quality of its service and to reduce operating costs. The two other major lines in the region, the Southern and the Seaboard, had been showing more aggressiveness in adopting innovations such as specialized rolling stock, centralized traffic control, electronic devices for freight yards, and computers for various accounting functions. This was reflected in lower operating ratios than those of ACL and L&N. A comparison of the operating ratios for southern railroads during the mid-1950's showed increases over a five year period, but ACL and L&N had ratios 10% higher than the others.

Some of this was to be expected. One reason for the relatively poor showing of the Coast Line's cost level was the expensive nature of fresh produce hauling, which comprised a larger portion of its traffic than of the Southern's or the Seaboard's. Another reason was the great emphasis President Davis had placed on maintaining the road and equipment in top-notch condition. Now, however, the railroad's splendid condition would be a great asset in greater efficiency.

Reorganizing to Reduce Expenses

The need for operating thrift became urgent in the fall of 1957, when a rather sharp recession in the nation's economy caused a substantial decline in railroad business. To make matters worse, a succession of unusually hard freezes damaged Florida citrus and vegetable crops in the winter of 1957-58, cutting revenues from that traffic category. Total operating revenues slumped from $166.6 million in 1956 to $149.6 million in 1958. As usual in times of decreased traffic, reductions were made in the operating forces. This time, however, the cutbacks in numbers of operating employees were especially large, and they were not restored as business turned upward in 1959-60. The average number of employees on the Coast Line declined from nearly 19,000 in 1956, to about 14,000 in 1958, and 13,000 in 1960. With the aid of Lawrence S. Jeffords, vice president for operations, and other operating executives, President Rice was able to find enough areas of slack in the work force. Under Rice they actually accomplished lower operating ratios during two years of declining revenues, and then improved the record sharply as business improved.

One change made early under Rice's leadership was a basic reorganization of the operating structure. When he took over, there were three general superintendents and twelve operating districts, each under a district superintendent. During 1958 and 1959, these twelve districts were consolidated into six operating divisions, with each divisional superintendent reporting directly to the general manager at the central office. This clarified structure greatly improved communications, led to greater efficiency in many ways, and saved on executive costs.

Another early push for economy and greater efficiency was directed in an area of special interest for Thomas Rice — freight yards. Along with installations of the latest communication equipment, he insisted upon personnel organizations and assignments, like those that had brought efficiency on the RF&P. He accomplished some real savings and streamlining by sharing facilities. He and William H. Kendall, newly-elected president of the Louisville & Nashville, agreed upon plans for combining yard facilities of the two railroads at Montgomery, Alabama, and Atlanta, Georgia. The consolidations were approved by the ICC, and joint operations commenced at those cities on December 1, 1959. Not only did the two railroads realize annual savings in the neighborhood of $500,000, they also expedited interchange of their freight business, reducing the scheduled time for some Southeast-to-Midwest freight movement by 24 hours. This sort of combination of economy and enhanced efficiency was most gratifying. There would be many more instances of such accomplishments as President Rice and his management team searched for ways to increase operating efficiency.

Moving the Headquarters to Jacksonville

One important change for the Coast Line was already in its early stages when Thomas Rice assumed command. The general offices were to be moved from Wilmington (its location since 1902 as the Wilmington & Weldon) to Jacksonville, Florida. The need for change had been felt for some years. Wilmington's location, about 100 road miles from the main line in either direction, had been growing increasingly awkward since 1893, when the Fayetteville Cutoff was completed. In its relocation announcement, the board called Wilmington "geographically illogical," and said it lacked "ready accessibility" and added time for mail deliveries. Executive time loss, unnecessary movements of material and personnel, extra train movements, and other expenses and inefficiencies resulted from running the railroad from headquarters off the main line. The four separate office buildings in Wilmington, in their varying stages of antiquity, were becoming overcrowded. It was time to make a change.

A number of possible locations had been considered before the selection was made. In addition to being on the main line, the site should be in a favorable climate of state and local laws and in a community large enough to absorb with reasonable ease the thousand Coast Line families who would leave Wilmington. Jacksonville afforded these advantages along with one of immediate practicality — the ACL already owned some suitable land there. The site would require much preparation, including rather expensive land fill, but the cost would be justified. As part of a general waterfront renewal program, the Coast Line building would rise from a splendid location beside the St. Johns River, commanding a view at the hub of transportation movement through the "gateway" city.

In a sense, moving the headquarters to Jacksonville capped the Coast Line's evolution as a transportation line to Florida. Through the decades since 1902, the proportions of Coast Line traffic originating or terminating in Florida had grown. To have the Atlantic Coast Line building thrusting its imposing stance into the skyline of the "Gateway to Florida" seemed appropriate symbolism. It was also good advertising. One might even wonder if the prospect of acquiring the Florida East Coast Railway might have added to the appeal of the Jacksonville location for Champ Davis and his associates. After all, with its northern terminus in that city, the FEC might be seen, especially to the ICC, as a more natural part of a Coast Line that also had its headquarters in Jacksonville.

Board approval for the building project was secured in 1957. By the end of the year construction financing had been arranged, and the site clearing and filling was under way. The architectural firm of Kemp Bunch & Jackson of Jacksonville created an admirable plan for the site. The building would rise 15 stories, plus two additional stories for storage and equipment, above ground. Its longitudinal axis would be broken at the center into an obtuse angle, opening banks of windows on every floor with a view of the river and the opposite south shore. The groundbreaking ceremony took place on October 16, 1958, and the steel skeleton pushed three tiers skyward by the end of January 1959. Construction was completed early in 1960.

Moving Day with the Rice Touch

The actual move from Wilmington to Jacksonville began with the office of the chief engineer on July 5, proceeded with a sequence of all other departments, and ended with President Rice's office on August 1, 1960, almost five years after the initial announcement of the move in Wilmington. The whole process was achieved with remarkable smoothness, considering the dimensions of the task. Roughly two million pounds of office equipment and records, three million pounds of household goods, and 950 Coast Line families were transported almost 500 miles down the line with a minimum of lost time and personal grief. It was the largest volume move for one comany up to that date.

Much of the credit for this accomplishment was due to a special moving committee headed by P. R. Director Donald T. Martin. The committee circulated a moving manual with many items of information about getting settled successfully in Jacksonville.

Beginning early in the year, the railroad provided special cars for weekend family house-hunting jaunts to the new locale. The actual move included some 275 trailer-loads of household goods, most of which went via piggyback flat cars. In some cases families left Wilmington on the same train as the trailers carrying their belongings. The trailers were loaded professionally and driven onto flat cars coupled to a passenger train departing Wilmington at 5 p.m. At Florence, S.C., the piggyback flats were switched to the head of ACL's fast freight No. 109. The furniture vans thus arrived in Jacksonville soon after the families detrained, and were unloaded the same day. Certainly the uprooting of so many North Carolinians from their familiar and congenial community of Wilmington, as well as from their relatives, entailed a great deal of personal anxiety. Some chose not to go, while others took early retirement. The devotion of so much care to minimizing the individual difficulties was a clear expression of concerned and responsible management.

The One that Got Away

Not many months after President Rice had come onto the property, the long struggle to gain control of the Florida East Coast Railway came to its finale, on April 18, 1958. The hearing examiner of the Interstate Commerce Commission issued his report recommending that the plan of reorganization proposed by the trustees of the Alfred I. duPont estate, the St. Joe Paper Company, and others should be approved (with certain modifications) by the commission. In brief, Ed Ball's plan was accepted and the Coast Line plan for merging the FEC into the ACL was rejected.

Rice and the board of directors, along with Vice President and General Counsel Prime F. Osborn III, took a long and careful look at continuing to pursue the FEC case. On the one hand, there were nearly 20 years of effort and many thousands of dollars invested in the attempt to secure the FEC, which from every railroad angle would have been a valuable and natural extension of the Coast Line. On the other hand, there was the determined and powerful opposition of Ed Ball, the examiner's rejection of the Coast Line plan, the previous Supreme Court decision and the likelihood that the ACL could spend many more thousands of dollars in an ultimately fruitless attempt to get the Florida East Coast Railway.

It must have been a painful decision for T. B. Butler and other members of the board who had been party to the long struggle, but they decided to give it up. On June 26, 1958, a stipulation was filed with the ICC in which the Atlantic Coast Line Railroad Company joined with other major interests in the case in accepting the FEC plan as modified. The Florida East Coast Railway went on to be organized as an independent railroad, under the stipulated requirements that it (1) serve all its shippers, impartially, (2) continue existing joint routes and interchange of traffic with other carriers, and (3) maintain complete neutrality in handling business with other carriers.

Bigger Fish in the Sea(board)

It was not many weeks later that Coast Line leaders were considering a merger of such dimensions as to dwarf the Florida East Coast quest. In Washington, D. C., on Monday, September 29, 1958, presidents W. Thomas Rice of the Atlantic Coast Line and John W. Smith of the Seaboard Air Line issued a joint statement to the effect that "preliminary consideration of a merger of the properties of Seaboard and Coast Line indicates that tangible economies and greater efficiency may be achieved, with resulting benefits to the public."

They had intended to release the statement the following day in New York City, but they had learned that talk of the merger proposal was already circulating in Wall Street. One business commentator remarked, "Few mergers would come as more of a surprise, if not a downright shock, to the railroad industry and to Wall Street . . . . The two railroads have long been fierce competitors."

The news did indeed create something of a stir in the industry, although it was a time when many railroad executives were being affected by "merger fever." The session of Congress just ended had heard many days of testimony on the desirability of tightening the nation's rail network through mergers. Railroad men shared a widespread sentiment that continued competition among and between their lines was crippling the industry's efforts to meet challenges from highway transports and water carriers. By eliminating senseless competition and effecting significant economies, mergers might strengthen many individual railroads, and the industry in general.

Several companies had already undertaken merger actions or were studying the possibility. The Gulf, Mobile & Ohio merger of the Alton Railroad had gone into effect in June, 1957, and the Norfolk & Western had applied for permission to merge the Virginian Railway into its company. The Chicago & Northwestern and the Milwaukee Road had begun a merger study, then dropped it; but the Great Northern, the Northern Pacific, and the Burlington were readying a plan for submission to the ICC. Moreover, the Erie merger of the Lackawanna and, biggest of all, the Pennsylvania-New York Central combination were under study in the summer of 1958.

All the same, the Coast Line - Seaboard merger proposal drew attention, even beyond their long-time rivalry. There were unusual circumstances in this case. This would not be an end-to-end merger of complementary railroads, with one or both seeking a cure for acute financial distress. Here, instead, were two healthy railroad companies, both paying regular dividends and showing solid cash positions, proposing to mesh their basically parallel systems. The Atlantic Coast Line and the Seaboard Air Line served the same general territory from Richmond, Virginia, down into southern Florida, providing service and owning facilities at 121 common points. This was a strong bid by aggressive management to apply the conviction being voiced by railroad leaders — railroads must explore every possible means of increasing their efficiency. It would also be a test of the Interstate Commerce Commission's willingness to cooperate in the strengthening of railroads.

The independent consulting firms of Wyer, Dick & Company and Coverdale-Colpits, both of New York City, were retained to make studies of the merger. They submitted very favorable reports in April of 1960, including the estimate that yearly savings resulting from the merger would amount to $38,732,624 after five years. The more substantial amounts of these savings would come from consolidations of stations, yards, and terminals at 67 of the common cities, abandonment of 1,139 miles of parallel lines, common use of retained and often shortened lines, and a sharp reduction in the total number of employees. Heavy expenditures would, however, be required in joining the operations of the two railroads — some $14.5 million just for improving old facilities for joint use, building new yards and connecting lines, and providing severance payments to displaced employees.

Engaged to be Married

The boards of directors of the two companies announced their approval of a merger plan to submit to their respective stockholders on Thursday, May 2, 1960. The Seaboard Air Line Railroad Company would be the surviving corporation — a decision based on technical considerations, such as possible savings realized on securities in and, most important, the Seaboard's relatively new, "clean" charter — dating only from 1944. The name of the corporation would be changed to *Seaboard Coast Line Railroad Company*. Seaboard stockholders would retain their present shares, while Coast Line owners would receive 1.42 shares in the merged company for each Coast Line share surrendered. Stockholders in both companies met in Richmond on August 18, 1960, and voted overwhelmingly in favor of the merger.

Now the difficult part began. The two companies had filed their merger application with the Interstate Commerce Commission on July 22, 1960, but it would be over three years before ICC approval was secured and a total of seven years before the merger would go into effect on July 1, 1967. Challenges before the ICC and in the courts from labor interests, from other railroads (especially the Southern Railway and the Florida East Coast) and from the United States Department of Justice were to pose repeated delays and complications. Coast Line and Seaboard officers, however, had entered into the merger plan with the firm expectation that they could get it approved, and they proceeded on that assumption. The managements began immediately to cooperate in some limited areas such as joint use of stations, coordinated procurement of new equipment, and experimental installations on their roadways. From 1958 to 1967 President Rice worked to modernize the Coast Line, keeping in mind the possible needs of a combined Seaboard - Coast Line operation.

Tying Up Loose Ends

There was another corporate merger project initiated about the same time as the one with Seaboard, but it involved a much smaller railroad and much less delay. The Charleston & Western Carolina Railroad Company would be merged into ACL, it was announced in mid-September of 1958, if studies underway confirmed the advisability of the move. The C&WC had been effectively part of the Coast Line system since Henry Walters got control of 50% of its stock in 1898. Further, the holding company for the system, the Atlantic Coast Line Company of Connecticut, had owned all C&WC capital stock since 1907, when outright purchase of the second half of its common shares became possible. The C&WC had, however, been left as a separate company all these years, due to unacceptable conditions which the ICC intended to attach to a lease of the Charleston & Western Carolina, applied for by the Atlantic Coast Line.

Now, in the fall of 1958, merging the C&WC seemed to be sensible financial housecleaning in preparation for the Seaboard merger. Absorbed first into the Atlantic Coast Line Railroad Company, the C&WC could then pass neatly into the Seaboard Coast Line. Moreover, since the holding company would receive 130,200 ACL Railroad Company shares in exchange for its C&WC shares, it would later participate more fully in the exchange for stock in the Seaboard Coast Line Railroad Company.

The Interstate Commerce Commission approved the plan late in 1959, and the 342-mile C&WC became the Western Carolina Division of the Coast Line on December 31 of that year. This change was very much in line with Thomas Rice's campaign for streamlining operations and cutting expenditures. It was estimated that $300,000 per year might be saved once the C&WC became fully integrated into the Coast Line.

Thomas Rice's philosophy of harmony was having a positive effect in all aspects of Coast Line affairs. The public was developing a friendly attitude toward the railroad; employees were buying into the programs; cooperative efforts along the line were improving operations; and other railroads wanted to become part of the system. Under Rice's new style of leadership, Atlantic Coast Line was poised for growth and change in the next decade.

No. 13: *Chairman Tom Rice steps aboard an office car in Jacksonville,*
shortly after ACL and SAL consolidated to create Seaboard Coast Line Railroad.

No. 14: *ACL President Tom Rice, left, and L&N President John Tilford, right, meet with A.L. Wiggins, chairman of both ACL and L&N, in Jacksonville.*

No. 15: *Retiring ACL President Champ Davis, left, and incoming President Tom Rice congratulate each other.*

A Fine Railroad Prepares for a Finer Future

Setting New Goals

During his first three years at the head of the Coast Line, President Rice was doing more than meeting the public, making recession-imposed economic measures, and arranging mergers; he was also developing new policies for Coast Line operations.

As he saw it, the Southeast was a fast-growing section of the country and the tidewater and Florida areas showed the greatest promise for development in that area. The Coast Line should be doing everything possible to promote and share in this growth. There were three definite ways in which the railroad would meet this challenge:

1. Passenger service would be maintained at the Coast Line's traditional level of excellence, both as good advertising for the road and as a worthwhile source of revenue.

2. Location of new industries in the territory would be promoted more intensely by purchase and development of good acreage for industrial parks.

3. Shippers would be offered good transportation: fast schedules, attractive rates, and service tailored to fit particular needs. In many instances this would mean specially-designed rolling stock; in others, more flexible arrangements such as afforded by trailers on flat cars ("piggyback") and containers on flat cars.

In order to achieve the high level of service desired, to make it available at low rates, and still to show a good profit, operations had to be made as efficient as possible.

Good Plan — Bad Luck

The Atlantic Coast Line owed its beginning as a railroad system in large part to a conviction held by Robert R. Bridgers, president of the Wilmington & Weldon Railroad Company from 1865 to 1888. Robert R. Bridgers was certain in the late 1860s that a coastal route linking the upper east coast with Charleston, S.C., and even Florida, would be highly successful.

No better testimony to the correctness of his vision could be found than the fact that the Atlantic Coast Line still had a profitable passenger business in the early 1960s. It was a declining aspect of the industry but, thanks largely to the New York-to-Miami run, the Coast Line kept passengers longer than did most railroads.

Credit for this accomplishment must also go to Coast Line management, for their continuing provisions for a high level of "varnish" service. In a mid-1960s book that was sharply critical of American railroads in this regard, Peter Lyon found Coast Line passenger service, New York-to-Florida, one of the few pleasant spots in a generally bleak picture of railroads' policies toward passengers. Champ Davis had brought ACL passenger service to a level of excellence in equipment and schedules by the mid-1950s. Rice at first simply continued the existing policy, with some added emphasis on sales.

As the economy turned upward in 1960, passenger traffic showed a modest improvement. Then Coast Line management launched an aggressive campaign to lure travelers back to their trains. Under the direction of Philip J. Lee, who was elected vice president of traffic in August of 1961, a number of programs were initiated. Some of the changes were made possible by the transportation and maintenance departments. Schedules were improved wherever possible, and a stepped-up program for renovating passenger cars began in October. A number of sleeping cars were converted from roomette spaces to roomier bedroom and drawing room accommodations. Streamlined coaches were placed in some local trains. Many new passenger stations were under construction, and new ticket offices were opened in six major cities by spring of 1962. A central reservation bureau, in the Jacksonville general offices, added speed and accuracy to space booking in first-class accommodations. New package tours for Florida vacations were added, as were tours to Williamsburg, Washington, and cities in the Northeast. One-day excursions on interesting branch lines, called "railroad rambles," afforded attractive outings for families and railroad buffs.

All the improvements that had been accomplished, and those that were in progress, were described in a two-day sales and service meeting, for which one hundred ACL passenger representatives from fourteen states gathered in Jacksonville in November, 1961. Also announced was an incentive program with attractive prizes for agents with the greatest sales increases. President Rice told them, "Your railroad is not going out of the passenger business. Your railroad is trying to build it up."

Relocation of passenger facilities was a major project. Beyond getting rid of the "mausoleum look," there were many practical reasons for abandoning old stations and constructing new ones. In Savannah and Charleston, for examples, the old stations required expensive and time-consuming trips off the main line. At Petersburg, Virginia, and Lakeland, Florida, new passenger space was provided because new freight depots were required. In other cases, like Winter Park and Fort Myers, Florida, municipalities wanted old station sites for other uses; while at St. Petersburg trains created serious congestion problems by blocking downtown streets. There were dozens of passenger station relocations accomplished by 1963, satisfying a myriad of community and railroad objectives. In every instance, one of the benefits was a pleasant new accommodation for Coast Line passengers.

Innovations in service were tried in attempts to attract passengers. In 1962 ACL offered a special rate — $140, Washington to Miami — to customers who wished to travel by train but also have their automobiles when they arrived, brought piggyback by fast freight. By the spring of 1967, a more exciting U.S. Department of Transportation plan, with the Coast Line as principal cooperating railroad, was ready to move beyond the drawing board stage. The idea was to permit passengers to ride inside their automobiles aboard a specially-equipped train from Alexandria, Virginia, to Jacksonville, Florida. Eighty-five-foot, air-conditioned cars would carry automobiles on two levels, anchored beside large tinted windows. Although service cars would provide dining and lounge spaces, passengers could use their own autos as private compartments for riding and sleeping. This project would wait for federal appropriations. Pride of the ACL passenger fleet was still the *Florida Special.* For its 75th season, beginning in December 14, 1962, the extra-fare *Special* was made more attractive than ever before. Its scheduled time, New York-to-Miami, was again reduced to 24 hours; and hostesses presided over card and bingo games, and conducted fashion shows. Also available were television, movies, and telephone service. In the 1965 season, music and dining by candlelight were added.

With all these efforts, the Coast Line managed to keep passenger revenues fairly stable through 1966, but the number of passengers carried declined just the same. Schedules of the *Florida Special* and the *Champion (East Coast)* were slowed, and operating expenses were increased by the strike which began on the Florida East Coast Railway on January 23, 1963. The Coast Line began to operate its trains to the lower east coast via its own line to Auburndale, in south-central Florida, and from there over Seaboard tracks to Palm Beach and Miami. This arrangement persisted as the Florida East Coast failed to restore passenger train operations. Then came widespread introduction of jet airplanes. Here was competition in speed and comfort that really hurt the long haul passenger business for the railroads that still were trying.

Although the worst was to occur in the late 1960's, the decline in ACL passenger business was substantial during the Rice decade. The statistics tell a clear story. Between 1956 and 1966, revenue passengers decreased steadily from 1,693,970 to 1,117,024, with passenger miles dropping from 647,236,705 to 487,465,379. Passenger car mileage and passenger train mileage decreased in similar proportions.

The loss was even greater than the figures show. The mileage data after 1961 included the Seaboard's mileage from Auburndale to Miami. Also, an airline strike in 1966 boosted passenger numbers.

It was the United States Postal Service that delivered the coup de grace to many local passenger runs. On July 1, 1965, the Post Office Department completed its establishment of the sectional center system for distributing and routing mail. Under this arrangement, mail was handled in bulk to central locations from which it was distributed to local post offices in trucks. Most of the mail cars on passenger trains, in which mail had always been sorted en-route, were no longer needed. Railroad revenues from this source disappeared. Cancellation of local passenger train runs now became urgent. ACL filed applications with the ICC for permission to discontinue a number of trains, in the fall of 1965. Local runs between Lakeland and Fort Myers, Florida, Florence, S.C., and Wilmington, N.C., and between Jacksonville and St. Petersburg, Florida, were among those discontinued in 1966-67. Still others were pending at the time of the ACL - Seaboard merger.

Expanding Freight through Innovation

Fortunately the freight traffic picture over the decade from 1957 to 1966 was a much brighter one. Revenue from all categories of freight grew from $133,659,601 in 1957 to $187,365,668 in 1966. The figures reflect an equally substantial increase in volume of business because, although there were rate increases in 1958 and 1960, rate adjustments during the 1960s actually reduced per-unit return in some product categories. From 1961, the traffic organization under Vice President Phillip J. Lee, and with R. C. McLemore in charge of freight traffic, did an especially effective job of expanding business.

Top revenue sources for the period, with some year-to-year variation, were:
1. fertilizer and fertilizer material
2. paper mill products
3. phosphate rock
4. pulpwood
5. sand, rock, and gravel
6. coal and coke
7. canned goods
8. manufactured iron and steel
9. lumber and plywood
10. manufactures and miscellaneous

For some categories of bulk products, the main job of the traffic department was to keep rates as competitive as possible and to take advantage of industrial growth in the region. In many product areas, however, assistance of the operating departments in improving schedules and developing better equipment made all the difference.

Constant study went into ways of improving cars for specialized uses, and many new or modified forms of rolling stock were introduced. For instance, during 1959, the Waycross shops constructed some 200 jumbo-sized, high-top hopper cars, designed in cooperation with paper mills to permit large volume handling of wood chips. Somewhat later, standard pulpwood cars were modified with higher end bulkheads and transverse chains so that lumber could be fork-lift loaded and held with the chains, thus saving mills expense in loading and strapping. Twenty new flatcars went into use in 1961, as part of a total group of 50. Ordered in cooperation with the Seaboard Air Line and the Central of Georgia, they were designed specifically to permit easy loading of huge coils of tin plate by steel mills. Then in 1963, new covered hopper cars of 100-ton capacity with special interior linings for handling bulk food products were purchased.

These were some of the many ways in which rolling stock was constantly being tailored to fit particular traffic needs. An example of Coast Line's willingness to experiment along this line was the "Whopper-Hopper," a 135-ton, 5,006-cubic foot capacity, stainless steel beauty ordered from Pullman-Standard in 1963. One of its features was an automatic interior washing system, to prepare the steel hoppers for whatever the next load would be. It performed well after delivery in September 1964, but its per-unit cost apparently proved too high to justify a fleet order. Every improvement in rolling stock design advanced by the mechanical department and every shortening of freight train schedules by the transportation department made the traffic man's job of selling easier.

"Landing" New Business

Help came from still another direction, pushed by President Rice — industrial promotion and development. The Atlantic Land and Improvement Company was used effectively to acquire industrial development sites. Approximately $8 million was spent from 1961 to 1966 for thousands of choice acres near Southeastern towns like Greenville and Spartanburg, S. C., Tampa and Jacksonville, Florida,and Augusta and Atlanta, Georgia. ACL's Fulco Industrial District at Atlanta was a model of such development late in 1963, with streets, electricity, water, and a railroad spur already there for use by new plants. The Coast Line's industrial department kept a staff of experts to aid potential "settlers" in choosing and developing sites to fit their needs, whether on ACL parks or their own land. By 1966, executives of interested corporations were being taken to see good locations along the road in Coast Line's DC-3 airplane.

Revenue was up. New carloadings were high, with many of the new industries in fields like merchandise fabrication, metalworking, chemicals, and other fields were bringing in relatively high-return lading for the railroad. Moreover, new freight cars carried larger loads and handled the contents more gently. By the early 1960s most of the new box cars were 50-foot, 70-ton cars, equipped with "damage-free" loading equipment and cushioned underframes. New sources for high quality freight traffic were being effectively tapped.

Reviving Lost Traffic

There was one category of freight traffic which the Atlantic Coast Line had pioneered but had largely lost to motor carriers by the 1950s — the fresh fruit and vegetable business. In some areas highway trucks were carrying up to 75% of the produce movement.

The Coast Line mounted a successful campaign in the 1960s to retrieve a good proportion of the perishables traffic. For one thing, fast freight schedules were improved somewhat. Also, the Fruit Growers Express began to use "reefer" cars with mechanical refrigeration, which afforded lower cost and speedier movement than the old icing techniques. It was "piggyback" service, however, that really put Coast Line back into the perishables business in a large way.

A Fine Railroad Prepares for a Finer Future... 289

Piggybacks — Giving Truckers a Run for their Money

The most revolutionary innovation in railroad freight handling in the mid-20th century was the hauling of highway trailers. Designated as "TOFC" (trailer on flat car) or more commonly called "piggyback," this system recaptured categories of traffic lost to truckers. It added flexibility of pick-up and delivery to the long-haul economy offered throughout by railroads. In addition, piggyback saved the time and expense of loading and unloading, reducing the need for warehouses; plus it eliminated many loss and damage claims.

The Coast Line began offering this service in June of 1959, with a small shipment from Alexandria, Virginia, to Jacksonville, Florida. TOFC handling by a few lines had begun in the early 1950's and gathered momentum after 1954, when the ICC gave railroads permission to carry trailers without having to be certified as highway carriers, and set up five different plans under which the service could be offered. Between 1955 and 1960 piggyback service in the nation grew from 168,000 to 550,000 carloadings annually.

One reason for the Coast Line's late entry into the piggyback service was the failure of connecting roads to the North to alter overhead structures and tunnels for the necessary vertical clearance. One of the first railroads to use TOFC extensively, the Pennsylvania Railroad, did not get its Baltimore tunnel cleared for such traffic from the South until November 1, 1959. This became "D-day" for Coast Line's full-scale entry into piggyback service. There was an advantage in having waited this long — many of the basic problems in piggyback operations had been ironed out.

A specially strengthened, 85-foot flat car with tie devices to hold two highway trailers had become standard equipment. To provide a pool of these rather expensive cars, and to facilitate interchange, a number of railroads had invested in a car supplying corporation — the Trailer Train Company. ACL began on an ambitious scale, purchasing 500 shares in this company for $84,970, thus acquiring the use of about 300 cars. Under joint jurisdiction of the traffic and operating departments, Coast Line's Trailer Train Service was established, with J. W. Plant as manager.

A supply of highway trailers was purchased, and loading/unloading facilities were set up at Tampa, Orlando, Jacksonville, Savannah and Atlanta. The Coast Line began moving piggyback loads in its fast freights from south Florida centers through Jacksonville to the Richmond and Atlanta gateways, with a corresponding movement southbound.

Piggyback service caught on and expanded very quickly for Coast Line. It was an ideal way for moving high-value merchandise from industrial centers to Florida. It proved extremely valuable in transporting perishables (both in refrigerated and ventilated trailers) from Florida and tidewater areas for fast delivery to metropolitan centers. Over 1,300 trailers were being carried each month by the end of 1960. In January of 1961, ACL inaugurated the first regularly scheduled all-piggyback train between the South and the Northeast. It departed Lakeland, Florida, at 5 p.m. each Saturday and arrived in New York City early Monday, for second-morning delivery. There were intermediate pick-up points at Orlando, Palatka and Jacksonville, and cut-out points at Baltimore and Philadelphia. A second such regular run (leaving Tampa on Tuesdays) was begun in November, and a third in June of 1962. These trains ran at passenger train speeds, bypassing freight yards and local stops on their runs from Jacksonville to Richmond, and made the entire Tampa or Lakeland-to-New York runs in 33 hours. The first such train from Tampa to the Midwest, the *Dixie Piggyback Flyer*, was instituted late in the summer of 1962 on a schedule that offered second-morning delivery in Chicago. By the spring of 1965, the Coast Line had these special piggyback trains between New York and Florida six days a week, and between Chicago and Tampa every day, with the schedule time for most reduced to just 31 hours. There were loading ramp facilities at 20 Coast Line points in 1960, and at 70 points in 1965. The business was booming — and it was profitable.

Piggyback and More

There were related services established. Railroads had lost most of the new automobile transporting business to highway carriers, but now they were able to recapture this traffic. By placing double and tri-level racks on their heavy duty piggyback flat cars, they could carry large numbers of automobiles at very low per-unit cost. Coast Line went after this business at the outset of its piggyback operations, placing orders for 17 bi-level and 31 tri-level automobile racks in 1960 and more in subsequent years. Revenues from this source soon constituted a substantial portion of receipts from piggyback operations.

By March of 1963, the Seacoast Transportation Company was operating a trucking auxiliary service for Coast Line's piggyback operations, and also offering fast merchandise delivery to some 100 Florida and 50 Georgia towns. Chartered in Florida in 1960 and organized as a wholly-owned subsidiary in 1962, this trucking operation became instrumental in an all-out campaign to recapture less-than-carload (LCL) traffic. Most railroads had given up on LCL, but as P. J. Lee, vice president of traffic stated: "President Rice is a firm believer in the theory that our railroad can handle profitably anything within reason that it ever handled profitably." Piggyback and a trucking auxiliary certainly helped. A shipment of merchandise large enough to fill a trailer, but not a box car, could now be handled by Coast Line at reasonable operating expense, affording the shipper the flexibility of highway transport plus the economy of rail rates.

The growth of the entire piggyback service was spectacular. Starting from scratch in 1959, and grossing less than $1,000,000 in 1960, it produced revenues of $6,676,900 in 1963 and expanded to $14,379,500 in 1966. A service that was especially useful to Coast Line territory, piggyback had been organized and marketed effectively, producing substantial volume gains in total freight.

Rice's Rules Boost Efficiency

Paralleling the successes in expanding traffic was a marked improvement in efficiency. From 1954 to 1966 the Coast Line made solid, and sometimes spectacular, advances in technology. One measure of the accomplishment is the fact that the work force actually declined during a period when such enormous increases in business occurred. The Coast Line was producing more transportation with fewer employees. The company averaged over 16,000 employees in 1957, about 13,000 in 1960, and little more than 12,000 in 1961.

Particularly significant were the large reductions in numbers of workers needed for transportation, maintenance of equipment, and maintenance of way. In the latter two categories the actual dollar figures for payrolls declined 8% and 10% over the ten years, in spite of repeated and substantial wage increases. Of course, some cut-backs in employees were caused by cancellations of passenger trains. Others were permitted by changes in outmoded operating work rules that went into effect from 1963 to 1965. But most of the work force reductions and other operating savings were made possible by technological innovations. A trend throughout the railroad industry during the 1950s and 1960s, it moved with unusual speed on Rice's Coast Line.

Thomas Rice established strict rules: "Don't build — buy; buy carefully; maintain economically; increase track capacity; modernize railway maintenance; join the computer revolution."

Don't Build — Buy

Improvements in design and maintenance of rolling stock and motive power were important facets of the modernization picture. At the top policy level, President Rice insisted that car procurement be placed on a carefully planned basis, to take into account shippers' anticipated needs as well as operating utility. A committee comprised of executives from the traffic, accounting, transportation, and mechanical departments studied car needs for coming years and made recommendations for car purchases. By the early 1960's a new approach to car design and procurement had evolved, aimed at reducing maintenance costs and the percentage of bad-order cars. The idea was to purchase high-quality, long-lasting cars that required light maintenance and could be scrapped when worn out.

Accordingly, the Coast Line built fewer cars, itself, and sharply reduced its rebuilding of rolling stock. As early as 1958, a spot repair shed was installed at Rocky Mount to speed up light repairs, and to keep cars out of the shops. Heavy repair shops for freight equipment were removed from all points on the line except Waycross, where procedures incorporated mass production techniques as much as possible. For example, in 1963 an assembly line operation for overhauling brake valves was initiated, reducing the number of shopmen needed for this work and greatly increasing output.

Although car procurement was uneven over the period — practically none were acquired in 1958-59 — the nine-year record reflected sharp upgrading of rolling stock. On December 31, 1957, Coast Line had 6,986 freight cars equipped with roller bearings, representing 21.9% of its total supply. By the end of 1966, the cars with roller bearings numbered 20,885, comprising 67.4% of a fleet of 30,987 revenue freight cars. During the years 1962 through 1966 nearly 11,500 new units of new freight equipment were acquired and some 9,000 old cars retired from service. The higher proportion of roller-bearing equipment reduced the incidence of hotboxes, thereby avoiding delays in train schedules and freight shipments.

The new cars also carried more. Although the 50-ton box car remained a common size, a growing number of 70-ton capacity cars were purchased in the later years. Covered hopper cars that were acquired for carrying cement and phosphate grew from a capacity of 70 tons, to one of 90 tons in 1960, and then to 100 tons beginning in 1964. Pulpwood cars were now built at 70-ton capacity, and flat cars changed from 50-ton to as large as 90-ton size by 1965. A train of these larger cars obviously hauled more freight tonnage, so unit costs of transportation went down.

Buy Carefully

Advances in motive power were even more striking. Recalling the 1890's, the Atlantic Coast Line under Rice's leadership again set the pace in locomotive procurement. Facing a growing need for more motive power in the early 1960's (practically none had been bought since 1952), President Rice and his operating officers decided to reap the greatest possible benefit from the investment. They would wait for manufacturers to get larger, more powerful models out of the planning stage and into production before buying a new locomotive. Instead, they repaired the road's aging freight locomotives of 1,350 and 1,500 horsepower as necessary; and made do with them until late in 1962, when absolute necessity impelled a stop-gap order for nine standard 2,250 horsepower units.

Then the Coast Line began to score a succession of first deliveries of new model, high-powered locomotives. General Motor's first GP-35 (2,500 hp) was placed in service on November 7, 1963, and closely following in December were the first Century 628s (2,750 hp) produced by Alco Products. Also delivered at this time were four of General Electric's U-25Cs (2,500 hp), the first to be used by a common carrier. The U-25Cs and C-628s represented an innovation beyond the higher horsepower. They had six traction motors driving six axles instead of the conventional four. Six-axle General Motors and Alco units arrived a little later in 1964. Known through its history as a flat railroad, the Coast Line was now taking first deliveries on locomotives designed especially for hilly terrain, reflecting expansion of its territory by acquisition of the AB&C and the C&WC. President Rice reported at the end of 1964 that the locomotive consists for many Coast Line freight trains had been reduced from six to three as the new units were placed in service. Capping the pioneering trend to higher motive power was a mammoth Alco Century 630 (six axles, 3,000 hp) delivered in July of 1965, the first of three. In four years, 1963-1966, the Coast Line extensively reconstituted its locomotive fleet by acquiring a total of 108 of the new high-power units. Retirements of old units kept the entire roster at the 630 level. ACL would take into the merger with Seaboard one of the most modern locomotive complements among American railroads. Best of all, its fast freights were hauling more tonnage, on closer schedules, with fewer locomotives, for greater revenues.

Maintain Economically

In keeping with the obvious economy of the new units were savings effected in maintenance and servicing. It was a sentimental loss, but the traditional, and quick-fading, purple finish of ACL locomotives had been changed to black, beginning in late 1959 for the surprisingly large annual savings of about $100,000. Heavy diesel repairs were consolidated at Waycross, and the facilities at Jacksonville and Tampa were discontinued. Several main line fueling stations were closed, leaving only two (Sanford, Florida, and Florence, South Carolina) besides those at major servicing points. In 1965 a huge gantry sander began operation at Waycross. It sanded up to six coupled locomotives while they were spotted for fueling, thus eliminating the previous need to move a train several times in order to fill the sand boxes of each locomotive.

On quite a different level, a 1964 pooling agreement with the Richmond, Fredricksburg & Potomac enabled that road to run ACL locomotives all the way to Washington, D.C., and the Atlantic Coast Line to run RF&P units all the way to Jacksonville and Tampa. The savings for both companies were substantial.

Increase Track Capacity

There were other improvements in operating technology which speeded up train schedules and enhanced utilization of rolling stock and roadway. The areas of signaling, electronic control, and communications saw much development. By 1957, American railroads, Coast Line included, had made great progress in centralized traffic control (CTC). With CTC installations on nearly 30,000 miles of line, railroads were demonstrating a resulting large increase in train movement capacity. Some roads had even discovered that they could now remove stretches of double track and still accommodate high-speed, two-directional traffic of reasonable density. In 1959, the Atlantic Coast Line began such a program on a 368-mile stretch between Rocky Mount, North Carolina, and Savannah, Georgia. Sections of double track varying from 2 to 20 miles in length were left as sidings or passing tracks for high speed train meets, and the rest of the second main track was taken up. This program was extended to other segments of the main line and was accomplished in stages through 1965. The reduction of second track was extensive — from 722 miles operated in 1957 down to 557 miles in 1961 and then to only 320 miles in 1966. Removal of so much second track brought substantial savings in capital outlay, maintenance, and taxes. Also, thanks to the effectiveness of CTC, the Coast Line was still left with plenty of surplus road capacity.

In fact, train handling capacity on many segments of the line and over the total system was greatly expanded through extension of CTC installations from 798 track-miles in 1957 to 1,433 track-miles in 1966. Increasing numbers of Coast Line train miles were run under dispatcher control rather than on pre-set schedules or train orders. From a traffic control center, such as the important main line ones at Rocky Mount and Waycross, an operator-dispatcher sitting at an information and control console could direct train movements by setting blocks of switches and light signals for a hundred miles or more in each direction. Information given him electronically included not only locations and speeds of trains, but also their lengths and the presence of any hotbox or dragging equipment. Devices for detecting such conditions were installed at dozens of strategic points on the lines in 1959-60. Now train crews could be notified of problems and given directions by radio.

Extending the program begun earlier, all switching locomotives and most road units, as well as 95% of cabooses, were radio-equipped by 1967. Additional wayside stations were scheduled to make the line-of-road radio system more effective. These technical improvements resulted in better roadway utilization, faster and smoother train movements, and significant accident and damage reduction.

Modernize Roadway Maintenance

Some of the longest strides toward modernization were made in the area of roadway construction and maintenance. The first change occurred early under Rice's leadership. In 1957, section gangs were equipped with highway motor trucks — 193 of them —thereby extending the length of roadway sections and reducing the number of section hands needed. This step had been long resisted as a treasonous surrender to the rubber-tired, off-track vehicle, almost on a level with railroad executives making business trips in airplanes. Yet the trucks did increase productivity of section gangs.

New roadway machines such as spike pullers and tie cutters and ejectors were soon introduced and a number of special timbering and surfacing gangs were formed to use them. Additional machines for ballasting, tamping, and track alignment were purchased between 1962 and 1964, as equipment for six mechanized gangs employed in surfacing. Due largely to such new equipment and techniques, Chief Engineer L. E. Bates reduced the number of track sections under his command from 358 in 1957 to only 118 when he retired in 1965. Under his successor, M. M. Clark, the drive for greater efficiency continued. The autumn of 1966 saw a test of three new machines, including a spectacular tie-inserting apparatus, which, when added to the equipment of one of the regular timbering crews, enabled the 16 men to install replacement ties at the rate of 130 per hour (a 30% increase in productivity). The number of workers in maintenance of way declined from 3,186 in 1957 to 1,709 in 1966. Of course, an investment of some $6 millions in track and roadway machines had to be balanced off against the savings; but the cost of maintenance of way and structures relative to the trend in operating revenues was still impressively low.

An innovation which contributed both to economy and to better track was continuous welded rail. Coast Line began to install 132 lb. welded or "ribbon" rail on its main line in 1958. As part of the same program, the regular lengths of 131-lb. rail taken up were cropped, welded together, and installed as relay rail on branch lines. By 1966, the rail was being welded in a plant at Rocky Mount into ribbons 1,400 feet in length. These were hauled, 40 at a time, on a special 29-car rail train to installation areas, and laid in pairs as they were pulled from the train. The joints between the long ribbons were then welded in place, largely eliminating the special fastening requirements and rail wear at joints, associated with the old system. There were 441 miles of this continuous welded rail in the line at the end of 1966.

Even more revolutionary was an experiment with concrete ties undertaken in 1960, in cooperation with the Research Center of the Association of American Railroads and the Seaboard Air Line Railroad. Test sections of pre-stressed concrete ties were laid in the ACL main line at Four Oaks, N. C., about 50 miles south of Rocky Mount, and in the SAL line about seven miles east of Tampa. Performance of the concrete ties was very satisfactory, especially after some modification to correct surface cracking and rail fastening problems. They proved to be competitive with timber in installation costs, and promised big savings through longer life. A drawback was that they could not be used for random replacement as wooden ties wore out; and the cost of tearing up and rebuilding whole stretches of existing roadway with concrete would be prohibitive. For the foreseeable future, concrete ties in main lines would be limited to reroute or rebuilt segments; but they would be used increasingly for new industrial and other spur tracks by the end of the 1960s. If it made for better track and maintenance economy, Coast Line would use it.

Join the Computer Revolution

On the subject of up-dating operations there remains one final word — computerization. ACL installed the first "on-line - real time" data processing system in the railroad industry in 1964-66. Railroads had always been concerned with gathering and compiling staggering amounts of information — not only data on the nature, weight, movement, and billing of each freight shipment carried, but also comparable details of all other aspects of operations. Small wonder that several railroads in the 1950s began to use computers when they were developed for business applications.

Coast Line waited until the early 1960s, spent three years on planning and development, and achieved a real breakthrough. A sophisticated multiple-computer system, organized initially around two IBM 1460s, was located in a center at the Jacksonville offices. Under direction of L. H. Scott, manager of special studies, data processing commenced on a modest scale late in 1964 and grew in volume as successive components were installed. A company-wide talent hunt located the 200 specialists needed to man the electronic information network. These Coast Line people were trained and assigned as the system expanded.

When all was completed, computer terminals (IBM 1950s) at 34 different stations on the railroad received information from within their territories. Such things as waybills on freight shipments, train consists and movements, arrival and departure of every unit of rolling stock at every yard, spur, sidetrack, and repair facility and more was transmitted from the individual terminals to the Jacksonville computer center, and stored on magnetic tape for instant item retrieval or for statistical compilation.

By 1966, with newer computers already being substituted, the system was giving prodigious service. ACL yards were notified of train consists in advance of arrival. A Central Car Tracing Bureau was able to notify shippers of the exact location of their cars at the moment of inquiry. A central agency had taken over billing of customers from local freight agents in addition to all freight accounting and settling of waybill balances with other railroads. Also in progress was a computer-based study of car and locomotive utilization that promised to point the way to more efficient use of transportation equipment. The potential pay-off from the entry into computer technology was incalculable, especially since the system had been designed with adequate capacity for the larger railroad to be formed by the anticipated merger with Seaboard.

Hard Work Pays Off

Aptly enough, the theme of an ACL advertising campaign in 1966 was "We've been working on the railroad." Indeed they had, and it showed. The Coast Line was in the vanguard of practically all aspects of railroad technology, and demonstrating that it paid off in efficiency and profits.

Quite a different picture than the earlier one given for the mid-1950's was presented by a comparative listings of operating ratios through 1966. It showed a steady drop in the operating ratio of 84.1% in 1957, to 76.7% in 1966.

Of course the reduction of expenses relative to revenues showed up in improved income reports. Net railway operating income in 1957 was $9,206,332, in 1962 it was $16,144,178, and in 1966, $21,421,190. The rates of return on the depreciated book value of the property for the same years were 2.12%, then 3.52%, and finally 3.81%. Earnings per share of common stock were $4.20 in 1957, $5.40 in 1962, and $8.20 in 1966. The Atlantic Coast Line would go into the merger with Seaboard as one of the healthiest and most profitable railroad systems in the country.

The Impossible Take A Little Longer

Any survey of overall accomplishment tends to miss the flavor of countless everyday, individual struggles to get the job done. A freight agent trying to pacify one customer who is sure that he has been overcharged and another whose shipment seems to be lost, a car accounting clerk discovering that a foreign road has paid only one-third the mileage due on a freight car, a yard superintendent somehow making do with four or five too few classification tracks in a rush week, an electrician who finally discovers an elusive shorted circuit in a radio control panel of a locomotive — such trials along with all the scheduled actions proceeding according to routine, made up the total picture of day-to-day operations. Then there were the unexpected mishaps, the extraordinary challenges.

Consider the Cuban missile crisis in October of 1962, when the Coast Line was called upon to marshall all its resources to help move the more than 100,000 Army troops, and tremendous amounts of military hardware that were sent to staging areas in Florida. Fortunately, the need for a contemplated invasion of Cuba was removed when the Russians agreed to dismantle entire missile installations; but once more the railroads had demonstrated their importance to national defense.

Sometimes it was nature that hurled the challenge. Hurricane Dora hit north Florida and south Georgia in September of 1964, tearing up trees and power lines with 100 mph winds over large areas of Coast Line territory, and dumping quantities of rain — up to 20 inches at some points. Not a single scheduled ACL train failed to make its run, in contrast to suspensions of service up to 48 hours by bus and air lines. With ditches and streams filled to overflowing, constant checks had to be made against the possibility of weakened bridges or roadway washouts. Crews armed with power saws rode the trains and cleared fallen trees and other debris from the tracks. All operating hands joined in the effort, with President Rice and the other general officers remaining on duty constantly, except for an occasional nap, for the three-day period. The trains were kept running, sometimes with urgently needed lading like the carload of dry ice delivered at the height of the storm in Jacksonville, a city largely without electricity and therefore suffering some critical refrigeration problems.

An Ending . . . and Another Beginning

A railroad operation necessarily contains an element of drama. It involves hundreds of people engaged in moving heavy pieces of equipment at impressive speeds over long distances. Moreover, the equipment carries people and goods — a service that we take for granted until a transportation stoppage reminds us of how vital it is to our everyday lives. Jet airplanes and spacecraft have carried us past the days when the latest speed record set by a new locomotive was a matter of high excitement; yet even today the job of keeping the trains running occasionally takes on heroic proportions.

Every railroad displays an individual style, both in meeting unusual challenges and in carrying on everyday operations. Over its history — including the life of its parent Wilmington & Weldon Railroad— the Atlantic Coast Line was characterized by an emphasis on quality and dependability. Typically the demands of unusual circumstances, as well as those of normal business, were met with quiet competence and little fanfare. Its long-term image as "The Standard Railroad of the South" was being revised in these last years in the direction of a more dynamic style, but the stress on quality still remained. On its final day Atlantic Coast Line officers could point to the fact that the company had never defaulted on an obligation.

All through the 1960s, the merger with Seaboard Air Line had been hanging fire. The first hurdle after stockholder approval in the summer of 1960 was the Interstate Commerce Commission. Application was filed on July 22. The ICC assigned to the case examiner Hyman Blond, and 35 days of hearings took place in several cities, including Richmond and Miami, between November 1960 and July 1961. Examiner Blond released a favorable report on August 24, 1962, recommending the case for the consideration of the entire ICC

Determined opposition to the merger had already been expressed by other railroads, labor organizations, and the U.S. Department of Justice. The Southern Railway voiced vehement objections from the beginning, stating certain conditions as absolutely essential to allowing the merger. The Southern's main objection, along with the GM&O and the Illinois Central, was that the merger would profoundly alter existing competitive relationships in the South by creating a 17,000-mile system through the ACL's control of the Louisville & Nashville. At first both the Southern and the Illinois Central petitioned the ICC for permission to buy the ACL's block of L&N shares. Later, the Southern subsided to the position that the ACL be required to divest itself of its L&N interest. Examiner Blond reacted to the position of the Southern and the other intervening railroads with this observation:

> The ownership of L&N stock by Coast Line has continued for about 60 years, and represents an important asset which has been given consideration in evaluating Coast Line's contribution to the merged company, and in supporting the ratio of exchange of stock. While the stock owned by Coast Line is equivalent to approximately 33% of voting power of L&N, and Coast Line has owned as much as 51% thereof in years past. Coast Line never exercised control of the operations or traffic policies of L&N. The same voluntary restraint would be the policy of the merged company.

Also rejected by Examiner Blond and the commission were Southern demands for 999-year trackage rights from Hardeeville to Savannah, and demands for either ACL's or SAL's line from Savannah to Jacksonville, a "suitable line" from Jacksonville to central Florida and Tampa, and a "suitable connecting line" from such Florida road to the Southern's line in south Georgia.

The Florida East Coast leadership naturally opposed the merger as destructive of their traditional competitive alignment with ACL against the Seaboard Air Line route to Miami. Strike-disrupted and financially distressed, the Florida East Coast petitioned the ICC to reopen hearings in July of 1963. They charged that the ACL and SAL had, by joining in a "ruthless drive" to crush the Florida East Coast, demonstrated why the merger should not be permitted.

The ICC did not reopen the hearings, but some of the FEC and the Southern objections were met. They ruled that Jacksonville was to be continued as a gateway, with special open-route and competitive joint rate requirements applying, so that connecting roads such as the FEC would be guaranteed full interchange of business with the merged company. Also, Southern Railway could keep its existing trackage rights over ACL lines into Jacksonville and Norfolk. On December 2, 1963, the ICC issued a favorable order on the merger.

More than five years had passed from the beginning of the merger studies until approval was secured from the ICC Another 3½ years would be consumed by legal proceedings brought by the opponents. After their petitions for reconsideration were denied by the ICC, the Southern Railway, the Florida East Coast Railway, the Justice Department, and the Railway Labor Executives' Association appealed to a three-judge federal court in Jacksonville on March 18, 1964. The court enjoined Seaboard and Coast Line from proceeding with an April merger date. It heard arguments July 17 and 18, 1964, and took until May 13, 1965, to render a decision setting aside the commission's order. The ICC, the court found, had failed to satisfy certain requirements under the Clayton Antitrust Act. The Interstate Commerce Commission joined the ACL and the SAL in an appeal to the U.S. Supreme Court. On November 22, 1965, the case was remanded to a lower court with instructions that it make a full review of the commission's action on the basis of its being consistent with the public interest, and without the requirement of specific findings on elimination of competition under the Clayton Act. The three-judge court in Jacksonville delivered a unanimous opinion on June 8, 1966, in support of the ICC order for the merger. A subsequent appeal by the opponents was denied by the U.S. Supreme Court on April 10, 1967. The long battle was over.

All the labor involved in actually merging the operations of the two companies now began. The task had its human as well as material challenges, for many employees had viewed the merger with misgivings all along. As one Coast Liner expressed it, "What the hell! We've been fighting them all these years, and now all of a sudden they tell us we're supposed to love them!" The long wait to get the merger cleared had permitted time to dispel many doubts. Personnel dislocations, for one, would be kept to a minimum.

But others saw the merger as "the greatest opportunity that has confronted me in 30 years of railroading. I am thrilled and enthusiastic." An operating man in the merged company exclaimed, "We're turning handsprings. We've got a route now that nobody can beat. And let me tell you, we're going to give truckers a fit!"

On July 1, 1967, the Atlantic Coast Line Railroad passed into the combined entity that would be the Seaboard Coast Line Railroad Company. Each of the constituents brought a rich history and strong organizational character to the combination. The new company would be a composite of both; neither was swallowing the other. Henry Walter's and Samuel Spencer had tried to bring about this union somewhat differently back in the

1890's. Apparently time had proved the essential truth of their convictions — the Atlantic Coast Line and the Seaboard Air Line should be joined. Now it was done. It would be more accurate to say that, on the practical level, it was just beginning. There was a very large new railroad to organize. Some 9,600 miles of line had to be unscrambled into shorter routes. Rosters of 1,000 locomotives and some 60,000 freight cars had to be consolidated. Employees had to settle into new positions. A myriad of other jobs had to be done. The Seaboard Coast Line Railroad would do it all; do it well; and make a history of its own.

Presidents of Atlantic Coast Line Railroad Company
1900-1967

Warren G. Elliott .... 1900 - 1902
Robert G. Erwin .... 1902 - 1906
Thomas M. Emerson .... 1906 - 1913
John R. Kenly .... 1913 - 1928
Lyman Delano .... 1917 - 1920
(federal manager during WWI)
George B. Elliott .... 1928 - 1942
Champion McD. Davis .... 1942 - 1957
Thomas W. Rice .... 1957 - 1967

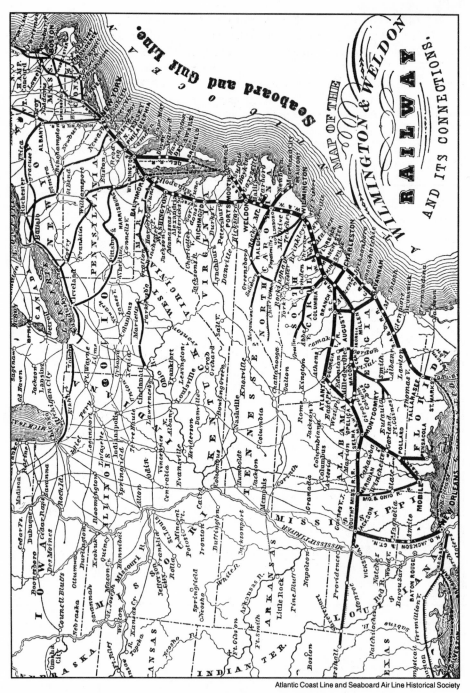

No. 16: *Wilmington & Weldon Railway, with its connections, served customers from New Orleans to Portland, Maine.*

ℰpilogue

The Atlantic Coast Line Railroad and the Seaboard Air Line Railroad merged to form Seaboard Coast Line Railroad Company on July 1, 1967. Some of the more important events, which took place after the date of that merger, are recorded here.

Seaboard Coast Line Industries Inc. was formed as the holding company of Seaboard Coast Line Railroad. The Atlantic Coast Line Company of Connecticut, which had been created in 1891 to bring together the components of the Atlantic Coast Line Railroad, was dissolved.

Other railroads became part of Seaboard Coast Line in 1967: Tampa Southern Railroad Co., Fort Myers Southern Railroad Co., Virginia & Carolina Southern Railroad Co., Rockingham Railroad Co. and Columbia, Newberry & Laurens Railroad Co.The Piedmont & Northern was merged into SCL in 1969.

Seaboard Coast Line Industries Inc. merged with the Chessie System Inc. on Nov. 1, 1980, to form CSX Corporation. The two rail systems consolidated their operations in 1985.

On December 29, 1982, Seaboard Coast Line consolidated with the Louisville & Nashville, the Clinchfield, the Atlanta & West Point Route and the Georgia Railroads to create the Seaboard System Railroad.

Effective July 1, 1986, the Seaboard System Railroad, the Baltimore & Ohio Railroad, the Chesapeake & Ohio Railroad (Chessie) and the Western Maryland Railroad became CSX Transportation, the operating component of CSX Corporation. High Point, Thomasville & Denton Railroad, Winston-Salem Southbound Railway and Western Railway of Alabama remained separate companies.

CSX's ventures included ownership of more than railroads. Prior to their merger, Atlantic Coast Line and Seaboard Air Line each owned one-third of Florida Publishing Company, publisher of Jacksonville's daily newspapers, the Jacksonville Journal and the Florida Times-Union. After the merger, in July 1967, Seaboard Coast Line obtained the remaining stock, giving it 100 percent ownership. In 1983, CSX sold the newspapers, and the Journal was merged into the Times-Union by the new owners.

It also should be mentioned that The Atlantic Land and Improvement Company (AL&I), a wholly owned subsidiary of the Coast Line, held about 250,000 acres of non-railroad properties located primarily in South Florida. To facilitate agreement for its merger with Seaboard Air Line, Coast Line formed Alico Land Development Company (Alico), to which was transferred the stock of AL&I. Alico stock was then spun off to Coast Line shareholders on a share-for-share basis.

The railroad properties owned or controlled by the former Coast Line became part of CSX Transportation Inc., a subsidiary of CSX Corporation.

Beginning with the relocation of Atlantic Coast Line headquarters to Jacksonville from Wilmington in the summer of 1960, and including all the mergers and consolidations with other railroads throughout the east, Jacksonville remained the headquarters city of the railroad. This continued with the acquisition by CSX Transportation of one half of Consolidated Rail Corporation (Conrail) of Philadelphia, in 1998.

— Editor

*No. 17: Atlantic Coast Line Railroad celebrated its centennial in 1930.
It had experienced extraordinary growth in the Florida Boom, and would continue
to do well even during the Depression.*

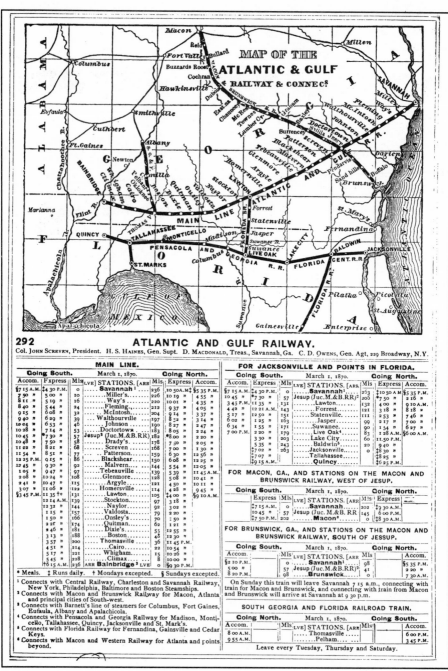

292

ATLANTIC AND GULF RAILWAY.

Col. JOHN SCREVEN, President. H. S. HAINES, Gen. Supt. D. MACDONALD, Treas., Savannah, Ga. C. D. OWENS, Gen. Agt, 229 Broadway, N.Y.

MAIN LINE.

Going South.				Going North.	
Accom.	Express	Mls	LVE] STATIONS. [ARR	Mls	Express	Accom.

Accom.	Express	Mls	LVE] STATIONS. [ARR	Mls	Express	Accom.
†7 15 A.M.	‡4 30 P.M.	0	......Savannah¹......	236	10 50A.M|	§5 35 P.M.
7 50 "	5 00 "	10	......Miller's......	226	10 19 "	4 55 "
8 11 "	5 19 "	16	......Way's......	220	10 01 "	4 35 "
8 40 "	5 44 "	24	......Fleming......	212	9 37 "	4 05 "
9 15 "	6 08 "	32	......McIntosh......	204	9 14 "	3 37 "
9 40 "	6 29 "	39	......Walthourville......	197	8 52 "	3 14 "
10 04 "	6 53 "	46	......Johnson......	190	8 27 "	2 47 "
10 28 "	7 14 "	53	......Doctortown......	183	8 05 "	2 24 "
10 45 "	‡7 30 "	57	......Jesup³ (Juc.M.&B.RR)	182	*8 00 "	2 20 "
10 48 "	7 50 "	58	......Drady's......	178	7 50 "	2 05 "
11 22 "	8 21 "	68	......Screven......	168	7 00 "	1 30 "
11 54 "	8 51 "	77	......Patterson......	159	6 30 "	12 56 "
12 25 P.M.	9 15 "	86	......Blackshear......	150	6 08 "	12 25 "
12 45 "	9 30 "	92	......Malvern......	144	5 54 "	12 05 "
1 05 "	9 47 "	97	......Tebeauville......	139	5 39 "	11 45 A.M.
2 08 "	10 24 "	108	......Glenmore......	128	5 08 "	10 41 "
2 41 "	10 47 "	115	......Argyle......	121	4 50 "	10 11 "
3 07 "	11 06 "	122	......Homersville......	114	4 28 "	9 45 "
‡3 45 P.M.	11 35 †"	131	......Lawton......	105	‡4 00 "	§9 10 A.M.
	12 14 A.M.	139	......Stockton......	97	3 18 "	
	12 32 "	144	......Naylor......	92	3 02 "	
	1 15 "	157	......Valdosta......	79	2 20 "	
	1 50 "	166	......Onsley's......	70	: 50 "	
	2 2["	174	......Quitman......	62	1 2["	
	‡46 "	181	......Dixie's......	55	12 55 "	
	3 13 "	188	......Boston......	48	12 30 "	
	3 57 "	200	......Thomasville......	36	11 45 P.M.	
	4 51 "	214	......Cairo......	22	10 54 "	
	5 17 "	221	......Whigham......	15	10 26 "	
	5 45 "	228	......Climax......	8	10 00 "	
	†6 15 A.M.	236	ARR Bainbridge³ LVE	0	§9 30 P.M.	

* Meals. ‡ Runs daily. † Mondays excepted. § Sundays excepted.

¹ Connects with Central Railway, Charleston and Savannah Railway, New York, Philadelphia, Baltimore and Boston Steamships.
² Connects with Macon and Brunswick Railway for Macon, Atlanta and principal cities of South-west.
³ Connects with Barnett's line of steamers for Columbus, Fort Gaines, Eufaula, Albany and Apalachicola.
⁴ Connects with Pensacola and Georgia Railway for Madison, Monticello, Tallahassee, Quincy, Jacksonville and St. Mark's.
⁵ Connects with Florida Railway for Fernandina, Gainsville and Cedar Keys.
⁶ Connects with Macon and Western Railway for Atlanta and points beyond.

FOR JACKSONVILLE AND POINTS IN FLORIDA.

Going South.			March 1, 1870.		Going North.	
Accom.	Express	Mls	LVE] STATIONS. [ARR	Mls	Express	Accom.
§7 15 A.M.	‡4 30 P.M.	0	......Savannah¹......	263	‡10 50 A M	§5 35 P.M.
10 45 "	*7 30 "	57	Jesup (Juc.M.&B.RR)²	205	*7 50 "	2 16 "
3 45 P.M.	11 35 "	131	......Lawton......	132	4 00 "	9 10 A.M.
4 42 "	12 21 A.M.	143	......Forrest......	121	3 18 "	8 18 "
5 17 "	12 50 "	151	......Statenville......	111	2 53 "	7 46 "
6 02 "	1 25 "	163	......Jasper......	99	2 17 "	7 00 "
6 34 "	1 55 "	171	......Suwanee......	90	1 54 "	6 27 "
7 00 P.M.	2 20 "	179	......Live Oak⁴......	83	1 28 A.M.	§6 00 A.M.
	3 30 "	203	......Lake City......	60	11.50 P.M.	
	5 35 "	243	......Baldwin⁵......	20	9 40 "	
	‡7 02 "	263	......Jacksonville......	0	‡8 30 "	
	‡7 07 "		......Tallahassee......		‡8 25 "	
	‡9 15 A.M.		......Quincy......		‡6 25 P.M.	

FOR MACON, GA., AND STATIONS ON THE MACON AND BRUNSWICK RAILWAY, WEST OF JESUP.

Going South.		March 1, 1870.		Going North.	
Express	Mls	LVE] STATIONS. [ARR	Mls	Express	
‡7 15 A.M.	0	......Savannah¹......	202	‡7 30 A.M.	
10 45 "	57	Jesup (Juc. M.&B. RR	145	6 00 P.M.	
‡7 50 P.M.	202	......Macon⁶......	0	‡8 30 A.M.	

FOR BRUNSWICK, GA., AND STATIONS ON THE MACON AND BRUNSWICK RAILWAY, SOUTH OF JESUP.

Going South.		March 1, 1870.		Going North.	
Accom.	Mls	LVE] STATIONS. [ARR	Mls	Express	
§2 10 P.M.	0	......Savannah¹......	98	§5 35 P.M.	
	57	Jesup (Juc.M.&B.RR)²	41	2 20 "	
8 20 P.M.	98	......Brunswick......	0	7 30 A.M.	

On Sunday this train will leave Savannah 7 15 a.m., connecting with train for Macon and Brunswick, and connecting with train from Macon and Brunswick will arrive at Savannah at 9 30 p.m.

SOUTH GEORGIA AND FLORIDA RAILROAD TRAIN.

Going North.		March 1, 1870.		Going South.	
Accom.		Mls	LVE] STATIONS. [ARR	Mls		Accom.
8 00 A.M.			......Thomasville......			6 00 P.M.
9 55 A.M.			......Pelham......			3 45 P.M.

Leave every Tuesday, Thursday and Saturday.

No. 18: *Map and schedule of Atlantic & Gulf Railway in Georgia and Florida in 1870.*

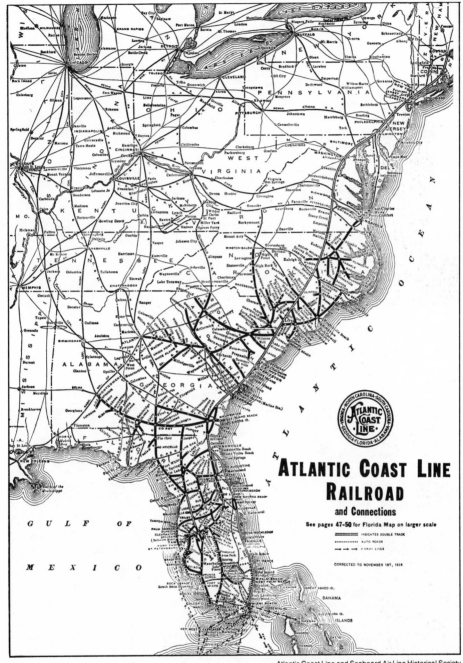

No. 19: *Railroads in the East, including Atlantic Coast Line predecessors, as they were drawn in 1870.*

No. 20: *Distinctive ACL Headquarters Building in Wilmington of the 1920s*

No. 21: *Aerial view shows ACL presence in 1950s Wilmington.*

Some of the Locomotives that Served the ACL So Well

No. 23: *This locomotive, built by M.W. Baldwin & Co. in Philadelphia, joined the Wilmington & Weldon fleet in October 1859.*

No. 24: *This locomotive No. 59, also built by Baldwin, joined the fleet in 1891. It was sold to the Virginia & Carolina Southern in June 1934, and closed out its long career as No. 32.*

No. 25: *This engine, powering a Knight of Pythias train, set a speed record of 95.7 miles in 95 minutes, on August 26, 1994 on the Atlantic Coast Line Northeastern Railroad.*

No. 26: *The "Old Woodburner," shown here in about 1900 at Rooks, N.C., served the area between Wilmington and Fayetteville.*

312

No. 27: *Waycross, Georgia, an important locomotive maintenance center for ACL, underwent major expansion and entered the technological age in the 1950s, as a modern classification yard.*

313

No. 28: ACL Railroad had a major presence in downtown Tampa (show here during a Gasparilla Parade in the 1920s), but would eventually yield to public pressure and move to the suburbs, selling the downtown property to the city.

No. 29: Coast Line passenger station and division office building in Rocky Mount, N.C., in the 1920s. This building would become the centerpiece of downtown redevelopment and house the ACL/SAL Historical Society Museum at the end of the 20th century.

No. 30: *Champ Davis is cheered by fellow ACL employees in Wilmington,
as he retired in July 1957.*

No. 31: *ACL became the nation's leading hauler of phosphate in Florida's Bone Valley, and (above) was the only railroad to operate its own deepwater port at Rockport, near Tampa.*

No. 32: *Locomotive No. 250, shown here in Kerr, N.C., in about 1946, was built by Baldwin in 1910. Today, No. 250 is on display at the Wilmington Railroad Museum.*

No. 33: *Directors, other railroad officers and public officials gather for the groundbreaking of new ACL General Office Building in 1958.*

No. 34: *New headquarters building takes shape in Jacksonville skyline.*

No. 35: *The new Atlantic Coast Line building when it opened in 1960. In 1967, the building would become headquarters for the Seaboard Coast Line Railroad;in 1983, the Seaboard System Railroad; and in 1986, CSX Transportation.*

Glossary of Railroad Abbreviations

The following is a list of railroad companies, with their abbreviations, that became part of, or played an important role in the growth and development of, the Atlantic Coast Line Railroad Company.

AS	Abbeyville Southern Railway
AM	Alabama Midland Railway
ATR	Alabama Terminal Railroad
A&F	Alexandria & Fredericksburg Railroad
A&R	The Abbemarle & Raleigh Railroad
AR	Ashley River Railroad
AB&A	Atlanta, Birmingham & Atlantic Railroad
AB&AR	Atlanta Birmingham & Atlamtic Railway
A&WPR	Atlanta & West Point Route
A&B	Atlantic & Birmingham Railroad
AB&C	Atlantic, Birmingham & Coast Railroad
ACD	Atlantic Coast Despatch (Dispatch)
ACL	Atlantic Coast Line Railroad Co.
AC,St.J&IR	Atlantic Coast, St. Johns & Indian River Railway
A&G	Atlantic & Gulf Railroad
AM&O	Atlantic, Mississippi & Ohio
A&Y	Atlantic & Yadkins Railway
B&O	Baltimore & Ohio Railroad
BLR	Belt Line Railway
B&A	Brunswick & Albany Railroad
B&F	Brunswick & Florida Railroad
B&B	Brunswick & Birmingham Railroad
B&W	Brunswick & Western (Ga.)
CF&YV	Cape Fear & Yadkin Valley Railroad
CC&O	Carolina, Clinchfield & Ohio (Clinchfield)
C&EP	Chattahoochee & East Passs Railroad
CR of SC	Central Railroad Company of South Carolina
C of G	Central of Georgia Railroad
C&SRR	Charleston & Savannah Railroad
C&S	Charleston & Savannah Railway
CRG	Central Railroad of Georgia
CR of SC	Central Railroad of South Carolina
CS&N	Charleston, Sumter & Northern Railroad

C&WC	Charleston & Western Carolina Railway
CC&A	Charloftee, Columbia & Augusta
C&CF	Cheraw & Coal Fields Railroad
C&D	Cheraw& Darlington Railroad
C&S	Cheraw & Salisbury Railroad
C&S	Chowan & Southern Railroad
C&F C&W	Clinton & Warsaw Railroad
C&F	Clinton & Faison Railroad
CN&L	Columbia, Newberry & Larens
C&S	Columbia & Sumter Railroad
CRR (Conrail)	Consolidated Rail Corportion
C&S	Conway & Seashore Railroad
CC&W	Conway Coast & Western Railroad
DL	Deep Lake Railroad
D&ST.J	DeLand & St. Johns Railway
DL&W	Delaware, Lackawanna & Western
EFR	The East Florida Railway
ERA	Eastern Railway of Alabama
F&F	Fayetteville & Florence Railroad
FRR	Florence Railroad Co.
FCR	Florida Central Railroad
FC&P	Florida Central & Peninsular Railroad
FEC	Florida East Coast Railway
FECL	Florida East Coast Limited
FM	Florida Midland Railway
FSR	The Florida Southern Railway
FS	The Florida Southern Railroad
FWCL	Florida West Coast Limited
FMS	Fort Myers Southern Railroad
F&C	Franklin & Carolina Railroad
GO&CH	Gainesville, Ocala & Charlotte Harbor Railroad
GR	Georgia Railroad
GT	Georgia Terminal Co.
G&R	Greenville & Roanoke Railroad
GN&O	Gulf, Mobile & Ohio Railroad
GW&B	Greenpond, Waterboro & Branchville Railroad
HR	Hartsville Railroad Co.

JG&G Jacksonville, Gainesville & Gulf Railroad

J&ST.JR Jacksonville & St. Johns River Railway

J&SW Jacksonville & Southwestern Railroad

JT&KW Jacksonville, Tampa & Key West Railway

LOP&G Live Oak, Perry & Gulf Railroad

LO&RB Live Oak & Rowland's Bluff Railroad

LOT&CH Live Oak, Tampa & Charlotte Harbor Railroad

L&N Louisville & Nashville Railroad

M&A Manchester & Augusta Railroad

M&C Moorehaven& Clewiston Railway

M&C Memphis & Charleston Railroad

MNC Midland North Carolina Railway

M&F Montgomery & Florida Railroad

MS Montgomery Southern Railway

M&C Moorehave & Clewiston Railway

NF Northwestern Florida Railroad

NCR Northern Central Railway

NER Northeastern Railroad (also spelled North Eastern)

N&C Norfolk and Carolina Railroad

N&W Norfolk & Western Railroad

NAR Northwestern Alabama Railway

N&F Northwestern & Florida Railroad

O&I Ocilla & lrwinville Railroad

O&W Offerman & Western Railroad

OBR Orange Belt Railway

ORD&A Orange Ridge, DeLand & Atlantic Railroad

P&IR Palatka & Indian River Railway

PR Pennsylvania Railroad

P&A Pensacola & Atlantic Railroad

P&G Pensacola & Georgia Railroad

P&A Petersburg & Asylum Railroad

P&W Petersburg & Western Railroad

PAL Piedmont Air Line Railroad

P&C Pittsburgh & Connellsville Railroad

R&D Richmond & Danville Railroad

RF&P Richmond, Fredericksburg & Potomac Railroad

R&P Richmond & Petersburg Railroad

S&E Sanford & Everglades Railroad

S&LE Sanford & Lake Eustis Railroad

S&IR Sanford & Indian River Railroad

S&SP Sanford & St. Petersburg Railway

SJ&LE St. Johns & Lake Eustis Railway

SJ&LER St. Johns & Lake Eustis Railroad

S&A Savannah & Albany Railroad

SA&G Savannah, Albany & Gulf Railroad

SF&W Savannah, Florida & Western

S&C Savannah & Charleston Railroad

SC&SB St. Cloud & Sugar Belt Railway

S&R Seaboard & Raleigh Railroad

S&R Seaboard & Roanoke Railroad

SP,O&G Silver Springs, Ocala & Gulf Railroad

Southern Express

SG&F South Georgia & Florida Railroad

SCP South Carolina Pacific Railway

SF South Florida Railroad

SE Southeastern Railroad

SRC Southern Railway Company

TS Tampa Southern

TPC&ST.J Tampa, Peace Creek & St. Johns River Railway

T&T Tampa, Thonotosassa Railroad

T&NE Tifton & Northeastern Railroad

TT&G Tifton, Thomasville & Gulf Railway

UP Union Pacific Railroad

W&V Washington & Vandermere Railroad

W&W Waterboro & Western Railroad

WAL Waycross Air Line Railroad

W&F Waycross & Florida Railroad

WSL Waycross Short Line

WR Western Railroad

WofA Western of Atlanta Railroad

W&A Western & Atlantic Railway

WBR Western Branch Railway

WR Williamsburg Railroad

WC&R Wilmington, Charlotte & Rutherford Railroad

WC&C Wilmington, Chadbourn and Conway Railroad

WC&C Wilmington, Chadbourn & Conwayboro Railroad

WC Wilmington, Conway Railroad

WC&A Wilmington, Columbia & Augusta

W&M Wilmington & Manchester Railroad

W&N Wilmington & Newbern Railroad

WO&EC Wilmington, Onslow & East Carolina Railroad

Wilmington Railway Bridge Co.

W&R Wilmington & Raleigh RailroadW&T

W&T Wilmington & Tarboro Railroad

WN&N Wilmington, Newbern & Norfolk Railroad

W&W Wilmington & Weldon Railroad

W&BV Winston & Bone Valley Railroad

Y&W Yalana & Western Railroad

Photo Catalogue

Photo Catalogue

Index

Green Cove 36
Green Cove Springs 36
Greensboro 44

ATLANTIC COAST LINE
NEWS

WILMINGTON, N. C.   JUNE, 1945   VOL. XXVI—No. 6

TO THE AMERICAN PEOPLE:

Your sons, husbands and brothers who are standing today upon the battlefronts are fighting
for more than victory in war. They are fighting for a new world of freedom and peace.

We, upon whom has been placed the responsibility of leading the American forces, appeal to
you with all possible earnestness to invest in
War Bonds to the fullest extent of your
capacity.

Give us not only the needed implements of war,
but the assurance and backing of a united
people so necessary to hasten the victory and
speed the return of your fighting men.

No. 36: *Atlantic Coast Line supported the war effort among employees
during World War II.*